Putting
Ideas to Work

Putting Ideas to Work

A Practical Introduction to Political Thought

MARK MATTERN

ROWMAN & LITTLEFIELD PUBLISHERS, INC.

Lanham • Boulder • New York • Toronto • Oxford

ROWMAN & LITTLEFIELD PUBLISHERS, INC.

Published in the United States of America
by Rowman & Littlefield Publishers, Inc.
A wholly owned subsidiary of The Rowman & Littlefield Publishing Group, Inc.
4501 Forbes Boulevard, Suite 200, Lanham, Maryland 20706
www.rowmanlittlefield.com

PO Box 317
Oxford
OX2 9RU, UK

British Library Cataloguing in Publication Information Available

Library of Congress Cataloging-in-Publication Data

Mattern, Mark, 1954–
  Putting ideas to work : a practical introduction to political thought / Mark Mattern.
    p. cm.
  Includes bibliographical references and index.
  ISBN-13: 978-0-7425-4889-3 (cloth : alk. paper)
  ISBN-10: 0-7425-4889-9 (cloth : alk. paper)
  ISBN-13: 978-0-7425-4890-9 (pbk. : alk. paper)
  ISBN-10: 0-7425-4890-2 (pbk. : alk. paper)
  1. Political science—Philosophy. 2. Political ethics. 3. Political planning. 4. United
States—Politics and government. I. Title.
JA71.M125 2006

                                    320.01—dc22 2005037439

Printed in the United States of America

♾™ The paper used in this publication meets the minimum requirements of American
National Standard for Information Sciences—Permanence of Paper for Printed Library
Materials, ANSI/NISO Z39.48-1992.

Contents

List of Figures

Acknowledgments

Much of my appreciation for the political values expressed in this book emerged initially and primarily from personal experience. Working during the 1970s and 1980s in the Minnesota new wave cooperative movement, I experienced firsthand the value of participatory democracy, community, and political activism. The co-ops served as focal points for political organizing around issues ranging from feminism to foreign policy to food politics. They offered daily evidence of themes emphasized, as I later learned, by democratic theorists: the personal and political value of community, the importance of civic virtue, the benefits of workplace democracy, the value of political and economic equality, and the developmental impact on character of political participation. The many remarkable individuals who worked in the co-ops offered living proof that widespread civic virtue is possible. For their friendship and commitment to a more humane political economy, I especially thank Alan Beck, Johanna den Boer, Craig Cox, Alice de la Cova, Joe de la Cova, Patrice Doub, David Druker, Jamie Fagrelius, Charlene Grant, Barbara Jensen, JoAnn Johnson, Omar Johnson, Jane Johnston, Rhonda Korol, Terri LaPlante, Chris Olson, and Michael Redmond.

Similarly, my appreciation for traits of respect, compassion, generosity, fairness, and concern for others came initially and primarily from a lifetime of exposure to their expression in others. Few I know embody them more deeply and consistently than my parents, Bill and Marilyn Mattern. Their integrity and goodness is (was, in the case of my father, now deceased) exceeded only by their unwillingness to draw attention to themselves for it. I hope some of it wore off on me; I know it did on my seven siblings. I thank Pat Mattern, Kate Derickson, Ben Mattern, Mary Gonderinger, Matt Mattern, Elizabeth Rhodes, and Bill Mattern Jr., their spouses Patty Mattern, Craig Derickson, Maureen Mattern, Bob Gonderinger, Janice Bially Mattern, Rod Rhodes, and Jean Mattern, and honorary siblings Karen Morin and Dan Olivetti for exemplifying those traits and for so carefully covering my back, and my wife's and son's.

I thank my in-laws on my wife's side, Larry Garifo, Sandy Garifo, Drake Hokanson, Amy Kratz, Carol Kratz, John Kratz, Mark Kratz, Mary Kratz, Peter Kratz, Sally Ann Kratz, Tom Klink, Lynn Miller, and Kate Molitor, for their inexhaustible goodwill, generosity, and lively camaraderie. Veni, vidi, vehemi indeed. They, too, deserve heartfelt thanks for taking such good care of my immediate family. I especially thank my mother-in-law Sally Kratz, whose righteous indignation at the often-shabby treatment of marginalized people and unflagging, passionate commitment to justice could and should fill every statehouse.

My professional communities have lent support, friendship, and inspiration. Various professors and fellow students helped me refine and extend whatever understanding of politics I brought to graduate school. I thank Terry Ball, Susan Bickford, Harry Boyte, Dana Chabot, Liz Conway, Barbara Cruikshank, Mary Dietz, Lisa Disch, Raymond Duvall, James Farr, Tom Fiutak, Edwin Fogelman, Donald Geesaman, Steven Gerenscer, James Jernberg, Matt Kane, Robert Kudrle, David Schultz, Kathryn Sikkink, Ron Steiner, and Mark Watts for helping me understand that political practice is sometimes best served by careful analysis of ideas past and present.

At Chapman University, where I first taught the course this book is based upon, I thank Paul Apodaca, Earl Babbie, Art Blaser, Bill Cumiford, Lee Estes, Mike Fahy, Joe Kertes, Nick Larson, Roberta Lessor, Michael Phelan, Pat See, Fred Smoller, Ron Steiner, Don Will, and Karen Young for their friendship and for modeling engaged scholarship and teaching.

At Baldwin Wallace College, I thank my colleagues in political science Charlie Burke, Haesook Chae, Robert Drake, Judy Krutky, Tom Sutton, and Donald Vance for their support, friendship, and dedicated service to Baldwin Wallace College and its students. I also thank Craig Heinicke and Sandy Peart for their friendship and intellectual comradeship, and for tolerating my annoying dissension from economic orthodoxy. Thanks are due as well to Laura

Canis and David Krueger for support in grant-hunting, and to Baldwin Wallace College for various grants in support of this project. I thank Donna "Radar" McKeon, the best imaginable secretary and office manager, for her assistance and support in writing this book. Her unflappable good humor in the face of the many daily torments inflicted on her by political science faculty defies emulation or comparison. More than any other single person, she helps make personal and professional life in the political science department satisfying and rewarding.

I thank members of the New Political Science Section of the American Political Science Association for offering an alternative to the sterile work that too often characterizes the discipline. NPS members are united by a commitment to justice, to activism, and to linking theory and practice in their teaching and scholarship. They offer concrete evidence that passion and intellectual rigor are not mutually exclusive.

I thank Steve Hollender and Kelly Coble for bringing so much soulful music and friendship to my "front porch." Both are excellent musicians, and even better friends. A special thanks is also due to Mike Telin, who combines the best in professional colleague and friend. Thanks also to Erika Coble, David Connor, Paula Maeder Connor, Heather Dove, Matt Gregg, Peggy Gregg, Daniel Hathaway, Eve Hollender, Sharareh Shirvani, Lidja Smoller, Colleen Sutton, and Sabina Thomas for helping me feel rich in friends.

I thank Ryan LaFountain, Mark Lammon, David Leone, Doug Nelson, Heather Ramsey, Sarah Serfass, Liesel Stevens, Kristin Tarajack, and Chris Ventura for their research assistance. I thank the students at Chapman University and Baldwin Wallace College upon whom I've inflicted this problem-solving approach to political theory. Their enthusiasm for the approach increased my confidence that the book was worth writing.

Special thanks go to Dana Chabot, Kelly Coble, Elizabeth Kelly, and Matt Mattern for their careful readings of a preliminary draft. Their criticisms and suggestions helped overcome some of the manuscript's shortcomings. If I didn't follow all their advice, it surely isn't their fault.

I thank my spirited, creative, talented son Leon Kratz for teaching me patience and humility, and for adding joyful dimensions to my life that I could never imagine in their absence. Finally, I thank Katherine Kratz, my best friend, my intellectual companion, my soul mate, my true love for enriching my life beyond measure. To her I dedicate this book.

Introduction

Political philosophy can be studied for its own sake, as an interesting and fascinating record of our political and conceptual history. But political philosophy can also be put to immediate practical and imaginative use. In this book, political ideas drawn from historical and analytical political philosophy are enlisted to help rethink and potentially solve current political problems. Of course, rarely if ever does a political idea emerge from purely intellectual sources. Most ideas in political philosophy emerge as attempts to address specific historical issues and problems. Some political philosophers simply make the practical dimension more pronounced, while others' ideas bear little if any *apparent* connection to the mundane world of practical politics.

Asking the question "what is political philosophy?" is a bit like asking "what is art?" Answers will vary widely. In the world of art, if it hangs on a museum wall, it probably is art. If it has been spray-painted on a freeway underpass or a railroad car, at least some will argue that it is not art. Similarly, if someone's musings on politics are included in a typical textbook that presents a historical canon of political philosophy, it probably counts as political philosophy. If others' political ideas are expressed through rap lyrics or poetry, at least some will argue that it is not political philosophy. Some purists will insist that political philosophy be defined in a way that ensures inclusion only of the thinkers already deemed "great" or their subsequent imitators, while guaranteeing exclusion of alternatives. Alternative definitions that seek greater inclusiveness will make those purists shudder.

In this book, political philosophy will be understood in terms appropriate for the task of putting ideas to work. This means that the question more important than what form it takes is whether it helps us solve our political problems. Political philosophy in this sense can be defined as any attempt to think about the ends and means of political life. It is an ongoing attempt to imagine and develop political goals and ideals and to create viable means of attaining them. It encompasses attempts to understand why people behave politically as they do. Political philosophy is a continuing conversation among past and present political thinkers. Most political thinkers are engaged, explicitly or implicitly, in a debate with others. Their ideas presume a previous history of political thought and practice, and build upon it. Political philosophy is thus a continuous, interactive process.

Unlike political science, which some attempt to purge of value considerations, political philosophy forthrightly embraces these value considerations. What do we *care* about? What *should* we care about? Why? Should freedom take precedence over equality, as it often does in the United States? Should citizens get more involved in politics? Should access to food and medical care be considered fundamental human rights? Should there be more or less curbs on the flow of money through the U.S. electoral system? When, if at all, should the needs of national security take precedence over the rights of citizens? Should violent men be excused because of their "testosterone poisoning"? These kinds of questions form the core of political philosophy.

The form that political philosophy takes can vary considerably. The established Western political philosophy canon itself draws from sources that are only marginally diverse. The list of "great thinkers" generally includes, in chronological order, Plato, Aristotle, Cicero, St. Augustine, Niccolò Machiavelli, Martin Luther, Thomas Hobbes, John Locke, Jean-Jacques Rousseau, G. W. F. Hegel, Karl Marx, John Stuart Mill, John Dewey, Hannah Arendt, Jürgen Habermas, and John Rawls. Although it would surprise few to see Machiavelli's name on that list, many would likely be surprised that Augustine and Luther are both included, because they are mostly remembered as theologians. Other lists might include Max Weber, who is primarily read today as a sociologist. Some professors assign Sigmund Freud's *Civilization and Its Discontents* in courses on the history of political philosophy as a challenge to the rationalist strain that dominates the discipline. Other professors include Thucydides, St. Thomas More, St. Thomas Aquinas, David Hume, Mary Wollstonecraft, Immanuel Kant, James Mill, Jeremy Bentham, and Friedrich Nietzsche.

The history of political philosophy includes treatises on topics that most people recognize as political such as justice, freedom, democracy, equality, and political obligation. But it also includes works drawn from linguistic philosophers such as Ludwig Wittgenstein, and political economists such as Joseph Schumpeter or Milton Friedman. The standard Western historical canon also tends to emphasize relatively formal, systematic efforts in political philosophy. From Plato's *Republic* to Machiavelli's *The Prince* to J. S. Mill's *On Liberty*, the central canonical texts tend to be formal treatises on politics and political philosophy. On the other hand, the canon of American political thought draws from a more diverse array of sources including sermons, letters, speeches, autobiographies, and brief essays.

Although the Western political philosophy canon contains disparate thinkers, with few exceptions it is composed primarily of contributions by white, European or Euro-American men. The canon thus contains many blind spots. It has little to offer feminists, for example, other than a field ripe for criticism given the overwhelming silence on gender issues or, worse, the sexist treatment of them. Aristotle (384–322 B.C.), for example, wrote bluntly that "the relation of male to female is naturally that of the superior to the inferior" and agreed with Sophocles that "a modest silence is a woman's crown." According to Jean-Jacques Rousseau (1712–1778), "the law of nature bids the woman obey the man," and "the indispositions peculiar to the woman" disqualify her from positions of authority within the family.[1] Even when attitudes toward women were more positive than these, women have historically been discouraged from writing, from participating in public life, and from securing an education. These historical conventions undermined potential contributions to the canon of political philosophy by women. This does not mean that women have not contributed to the history of political philosophy, only that their contributions have seldom been included in the canon of "great" thinkers. Some examples of women political philosophers who have been included have already been mentioned. Mary Wollstonecraft's *A Vindication of the Rights of Woman* (1792) is sometimes referred to as the first feminist publication in English. Hannah Arendt's work has received considerable attention in the last several decades, and many now include her in the historical canon. The history of American political thought includes contributions from many women, though those contributions arrived relatively late and generally have not taken the form of extensive, systematic, formal treatises on politics. Generally, contributions from men continue to dominate the historical canon of political philosophy.

Similarly, people of color will find little to read in the Western canon of political philosophy that either directly addresses their unique concerns or is written by a person of color. This problem is tied to the history of slavery and
colonialism. Most slaves were denied literacy by their masters, out of the conviction that an ignorant slave was a more submissive slave. Whatever political
thoughts they had were seldom put into writing. If not enslaved outright, many
people of color were nevertheless viewed during earlier centuries as uncivilized
or even subhuman. Any political philosophy emerging from colonial Africa or
South America would have been automatically discounted as inferior to the
work of Europeans. Again, exceptions can be found in the history of American
political thought in short essays, autobiographies, speeches, and occasionally
extended works of political philosophy by men and women of color.

Whatever the silences of previous centuries and decades, women and people of color have themselves begun to fill in the silences. Feminists have contributed extensively to the development of political philosophy since the
1960s, as have women and men of color. Also, many academic political
philosophers have responded by either rejecting the canon outright or seeking
to fill in some of its blind spots. In the last thirty or forty years, they have integrated readings by women, minorities, and non-Western thinkers into their
course syllabi. When the historical canon is taught more or less intact in its
white, male European mold, accompanying texts are sometimes included to
offer critical perspectives.

Much of the political philosophy that has endured and that is still read today *as* political philosophy was produced by thinkers intent on making an explicit contribution to political thinking about an issue or set of issues. They
self-consciously saw themselves as political philosophers. They wrote systematically, developing their ideas around a coherent idea or set of ideas. However,
some of the most potent political philosophy can be found in unsystematic
form. Thomas Jefferson's letters, for example, are rich with political ideas,
some of them profound and original. They constitute the prime source of his
political philosophy. He wrote them to friends and acquaintances while pon-
dering some of the issues of his day and while participating in the creation of
the United States. Martin Luther King Jr.'s "Letter from a Birmingham Jail" is
another example of a relatively informal attempt to make sense of concrete
circumstances and to convince others of the soundness of a particular activist
strategy. It stands today as an eloquent defense of civil disobedience.

In determining what counts as political philosophy, sooner or later one must also determine what counts as political. This turns out to be a complicated question. Politics, like some of the other concepts that will be addressed in this book, is an essentially contested concept: its meaning is internally complex and subject to recurring debate.[2] Some people define politics so broadly that it encompasses all of human experience. Many theorists consider this a mistake since it makes any meaningful distinction between our public and private lives difficult to maintain. This distinction between public and private helps protect individual rights, including the right to privacy, and helps maintain the importance and usefulness of a distinct public sphere where political participation occurs. Others define politics as synonymous with power. However, since power is normally present in all human relationships regardless of whether, or how, it is exercised, this too makes politics ubiquitous and therefore suspect for many political theorists.

One text in political philosophy defines politics as "the processes by which public decisions are made."[3] This has the advantage of being broad enough to include at least some nongovernmental instances of politics. Yet, it excludes other processes that some might want to count as political such as conflict between a married couple over parental and housekeeping responsibilities. Also, it would appear to exclude the *results* of political processes—the policy decisions themselves—since it defines politics entirely in terms of process.

No attempt will be made in this book to resolve the dispute over the nature of politics. Politics will be understood in sufficiently broad terms to encompass gender, race, class, disability, and other forms of politics as well as governmental politics, but not so broad as to encompass all aspects of human life. A working definition that captures this sense of politics is *any intentional attempt to define, change, or reinforce the rules of human association.* This definition leaves as apolitical all those aspects of people's lives that entail routine, habitual behavior. To use the example from above, if a married couple are satisfied with their division of responsibilities within the family, they carry them out on a day-to-day basis apolitically; they politicize their relationship in this area, however, when one decides to challenge the division of responsibilities.

Potential problems with this definition include the fact that it excludes unconscious and unintentional behaviors and processes that often have profound influences on people's lives. Take, for example, a marriage in which the husband firmly and explicitly dominates and the wife willingly submits and obeys, viewing her submission and obedience as rightful. The definition above would exclude this as an example of politics. Yet, at least some contemporary feminists might want to challenge this exclusion from politics, perhaps calling the wife's attitude an example of "false consciousness" in which she profoundly misunderstands the character of her own life and her choices. Of course, unconscious and unintentional behaviors and processes can be politicized simply by challenging them, as the hypothetical feminist does in this example.

Academic political philosophers sometimes distinguish between the history of political philosophy and analytical political philosophy. The history of political philosophy, as the name implies, addresses the historical development of political philosophy, often focusing on specific canonical thinkers who have had the most impact on political thinking. Analytical political philosophy addresses particular issues more directly and systematically. Examples include conceptual political analysis, democratic theory, feminist political theory, and contemporary debates over the nature of justice. This book integrates both kinds of political philosophy. Analytical political philosophy will sometimes be used to develop issues and themes, while selected thinkers in the history of political philosophy will be drawn upon to shed light on particular issues.

GOOD VERSUS BAD POLITICAL PHILOSOPHY

Having defined political philosophy broadly, can any musing on politics be considered political philosophy? Since answering this question is likely to lead into a morass of contention, a more useful question to ask is, how do we tell the difference between good and bad political philosophy? One way to begin distinguishing between the good and the bad is to first examine some examples of everyday thought and expression that a political philosopher might reject as being inconsistent with good political philosophy. Consider the following statements:

1. People with blond hair are stupid.
2. The reason for all the pedophilia in the Catholic Church is that so many priests are gay.
3. The United States is the greatest country on Earth.
4. Abortion is wrong because my religious leaders say so.
5. Nuclear weapons are peacemakers.

The first statement, "People with blond hair are stupid," is an opinion based on prejudice. Prejudice means that the holder of the opinion has prejudged others based on their real or imagined ethnic, religious, gender, class, or other characteristics. Prejudice remains very alive and well in the twenty-first century, despite increasing attention to it and some progress in certain areas. Although political philosophers are not immune to the problem of prejudice, and sometimes incorporate it into their work, in general they attempt to avoid it. The statement is also a sweeping generalization that would be difficult to prove empirically. Good political philosophy requires that assertions be consistent with available evidence, and no amount of evidence is likely to support such a sweeping conclusion. The political philosopher avoids such sweeping generalizations in the interests of greater rigor of thought.

The second statement about pedophilia is based on three unexamined assumptions and beliefs: that the pedophilia in the Catholic Church exceeds the pedophilia in the general society, that many priests are gay, and that gay men are more likely than others to commit pedophilia. Many opinions rest on unexamined assumptions such as these. Each assumption begs critical analysis, argument, and evidence. A political philosopher would take each assumption and, as the American pragmatist John Dewey (1859–1952) once put it, subject it to "the purifying light of consciousness." One of the tasks of a political philosopher is to identify hidden assumptions and expose them to critical reflection. This may be a difficult task since many are deeply embedded and difficult to discern.

The third statement, that "the United States is the greatest country," is a bald assertion sometimes heard in the United States. Standing alone as it does, it cannot persuade a rigorous thinker. Most political philosophers would minimally require a set of criteria for determining greatness. This set of criteria would itself be subject to debate and disagreement. Does military power make a country great? Economic power? Cultural richness? The degree to which it meets the basic human needs of all its citizens? Each of these criteria is likely to yield a different ordering of greatness.

The fourth opinion relies for its plausibility upon an authoritative mandate that some would accept but others reject. An authoritative mandate is a decree or order issued by an authoritative individual or institution, ranging from a parent to a religious leader to a political party. Some people deem an opinion sound if a respected authority figure articulates it. Many people believe that

Jesus Christ rose from the dead, because the Bible says so and their religious leaders today insist on the point. Many Catholics oppose abortion and birth control because their religious leader, the pope, makes that opposition doctrinal. Some people believe that stripes should not be worn with plaid because their mothers said so. Today, most political philosophers are reluctant to deem an idea sound simply because it originates with an authoritative figure or text. This has not always been the case. In earlier, less secular times, many political philosophers relied heavily on Scripture. Some still do, but their work is perceived as less credible today than previously.

The fifth statement illustrates the corruption of political speech. In one of his best-known works, the futuristic novel *1984*, George Orwell (1903–1950) painted a picture of life in the future in which language had grown so corrupted that war was portrayed as peace, slavery as freedom, and ignorance as strength. He called this corruption of language "newspeak." Orwell's pessimistic portrayal proved prescient. In modern times, public discourse often resembles "newspeak" as politicians and other public figures make claims and counterclaims that stretch the truth or ignore it completely. For a political philosopher, this corruption of political speech represents one of the most troubling developments of modern times. If war can be called peace and oppression can be called justice, speech loses its meaning. Once words lose their meaning, meaningful political distinctions dissolve, rendering political judgment exceptionally difficult. The distinction between fact and fiction itself erodes. As Orwell's main character, Winston Smith, mused, "How could you establish even the most obvious fact when there existed no record outside your own memory?"[4] Both analytical and historical political philosophers strive to maintain important conceptual distinctions that make sound political judgment possible.

At least some holders of each opinion above might respond that the assertion "is obvious," "my intuition leads me" to that conclusion, or "common sense tells me" that the opinion is sound. However, nothing is, or should be, obvious to a political philosopher. Jefferson's "We hold these truths to be self-evident" may be good rhetoric, but by itself it should not satisfy a political philosopher. Careful thinkers will reject the temptation to rest their case on intuition or common sense, though both may be useful starting points. Intuition and common sense often turn out to be nothing more than familiarity with a particular culture and its predominant beliefs and values, which may in turn be based on myth rather than fact. Precisely the value of good political philosophy is that it helps us become critically aware of the difference between myth and reality.

Political philosophers are not, of course, immune to problems of prejudice, unexamined assumption, assertion, authoritative mandate, and corruption of political thought and speech. However, at least in principle, political philosophers adopt values of thought and communication that increase, rather than decrease, rigor and accuracy. These values include:

- convincing evidence, including both empirical facts and reasoned argument
- clarity of thought and expression
- honesty in recognizing and acknowledging assumptions and shortcomings
- coherency and consistency of ideas
- willingness to engage in discussion and debate

Taking each of these points in turn, political philosophers value good evidence that includes empirical facts, critical reflection, and a good argument. Although political philosophy often addresses normative concerns, the validity of particular ideas can sometimes be empirically verified. Evidence can include empirical facts taken both from current conditions and the historical record. For example, the argument that "the Earth is flat" will convince few of its validity, no matter how skillfully or enthusiastically articulated, since the evidence convincingly refutes the claim. Many political ideas, though, cannot be subjected to empirical verification. Especially when thinking about the normative dimensions of our lives, a definitive answer based on empirical evidence is often impossible. Is freedom more important than equality? How would one begin to answer that kind of question? What are the criteria? Sometimes empirical evidence is unavailable or mixed. In a context of mixed or missing empirical evidence, a political philosopher must rely more heavily on other forms of evidence, including the results of critical reflection, and making a good argument. Critical reflection requires careful and rigorous thought. It involves probing beyond obvious answers, challenging received assumptions, and thinking outside current conventions. A good argument means that a position on an issue is carefully and thoroughly articulated and then defended against actual or potential critics.

Second, political philosophers value clarity. Are ideas expressed clearly in a way that minimizes misunderstanding and confusion? It is sometimes tempting to avoid difficult conceptual knots by simply ignoring them or writing around them, but the result is more, rather than less, confusion. Compared to everyday thought and expression, political philosophy excuses relatively little of this conceptual confusion. Sometimes a tension exists between this value of clarity and the need to stretch the boundaries of language in order to articulate new ideas. We saw above how George Orwell invented the term *newspeak* to name a problem that he saw developing. Taken out of the context of his book, though, the term may have confused, rather than enlightened, his contemporaries. More recently, some thinkers such as Michel Foucault (1926–1984) and Jacques Derrida (1930–2004) are renowned for the opaque quality of their writing, making understanding difficult. Their supporters claim, in defense, that the pioneering nature of their ideas requires a new language.

Third, political philosophers value honesty. Are biases and assumptions hidden, or are they honestly acknowledged? For example, does an argument based on natural law that concludes that homosexuality is wrong actually rest on a hidden and unacknowledged prejudice against gay people? Does a person's support for capitalism rest on the unaddressed presumption that humans are inherently selfish, competitive, and acquisitive, making other, potentially more cooperative, systems of political economy impossible? A political philosopher insists that these hidden foundations be revealed and treated directly and openly. Honest political philosophers also acknowledge limitations and problems with their ideas. Few political theories are perfect. Most of the "great thinkers" in the historical canon left contradictions and silences in their philosophy. Defenders and critics alike should openly acknowledge them. An honest political philosopher also recognizes and addresses the arguments of critics. An argument is not complete until real or potential critics have been addressed. Otherwise, it is tempting to conclude that the political thinker does not fully understand the implications of his or her ideas. Some political activists and thinkers are more interested in winning a political argument than in engaging in an honest debate. Such persons are prone to using whatever tools are available, including deception, obfuscation, exaggeration, and selective use of facts in order to best the opposition. While these may be useful tools for winning mundane political arguments, they cannot withstand the critical scrutiny of a careful political philosopher.

Political philosophers also value coherency. Do ideas hang together? Are they logically related? Some apparent contradictions in a person's thinking may turn out to be superficial, and further explanation and reflection may reveal that the contradiction disappears. For example, Rousseau famously argued in *The Social Contract* (1762) that citizens in his ideal state would be "forced to be free." Some have taken this to suggest a totalitarian regime far out of character with the democratic state Rousseau claimed to envision. However, since Rousseau defined freedom as "obedience to the law that one has prescribed for oneself," he was simply arguing that citizens would be required to obey the laws that they had a hand in creating.[5] On the other hand, some ideas simply cannot be reconciled with other ideas. For example, support for the idea of rule by one all-powerful individual or by a wealthy elite cannot be reconciled with the idea of democracy, which rests on a commitment to rule by the people.

Fifth, political philosophers value a willingness to engage in discussion and debate, a willingness to keep the conversation going. They recognize that this conversation itself constitutes a democratic politics in which diverse people with different perspectives negotiate their differences. This conversation may be more systematic and formal than the average political discussion, but the aims are the same—presenting and evaluating ideas and deciding the best course of action.

The distinctions between these values of political philosophy and everyday thought and speech are matters of degree rather than absolute. Many people practice these values in their everyday speech and expression, and at least some political philosophy resembles everyday thought and speech. Also, this sketch of the values of political philosophy presents an idealized picture. In practice, most political philosophers fall short of the ideal.

THE NATURE OF TRUTH AND THE FOUNDATIONS OF POLITICAL PHILOSOPHY

Implicit or explicit assumptions about the nature of truth and the foundations of political philosophy underlie all political philosophy. Some political philosophers believe in absolute truth, which they see as singular, timeless, and universal. These political philosophers seek bedrock principles and laws about humans that apply to all people at all times, and these form the foundations for political philosophy. Once they have established these principles and laws, political philosophy can be built upon them. They judge the validity of any work in political philosophy according to how closely it corresponds to those truths.

One example of this kind of approach is natural law philosophy. Political philosophers working within a natural law tradition seek to discover, using reason and empirical facts if available, basic laws underlying human behavior and to build their theories upon them. They seek to discover timeless, universal truths of human nature and behavior and then to create theory and practice that corresponds to them. One familiar example is Jefferson's Declaration of Independence which asserts, "We hold these truths to be self-evident, that all men are created equal, that they are endowed by their Creator with certain unalienable Rights." Jefferson claims here that humans have inherent natural rights, by virtue of their humanity. These precede society. They are "self-evident" because they are "Laws of Nature and of Nature's God." Natural law philosophy has exerted considerable influence on the history of political philosophy and remains influential, though less so than in earlier times.

Political philosophy anchored to religious principles also tends to build upon absolutist foundations. Most political philosophers working explicitly within a religious tradition argue that there are underlying principles and laws that originate with God. The task for humans is to discover these principles and laws, build their theories upon them, and live in accordance with them. Many Christians, for example, take the Bible as an indisputable source of truth originating in God's will. Political thinkers who build upon biblical foundations look to the Bible for insight and understanding about absolute, immutable truths of human existence. The same is true for many Muslims, who look to the Koran for guidance. Like natural law philosophy, religious absolutism has played a central role in the history of political philosophy and, also like natural law philosophy, its influence in political philosophy has waned in modern times.

On the other extreme, some political philosophers reject the notion of absolute truth. They believe that truth is historical, in that it may vary through the ages, and cultural, in that it is tied to particular circumstances. Thus, multiple truths are possible and likely. What is true for one person or group in one particular historical and cultural context may not be true for a different person or group in a different historical and cultural context. Rather than seeking foundational principles and laws that apply to all people at all times, these political philosophers typically evaluate political philosophy by considering its consequences. Does it increase our understanding? Does it help us achieve our goals?

Three examples of traditions that rely wholly or partially on nonabsolute conceptions of truth are postmodernism, utilitarianism, and pragmatism. Postmodern political thinkers, increasingly influential in the last two decades of the twentieth century, are defined in part by their rejection of absolutes of any sort, including absolute truth and absolute foundations. They also reject universalisms of any kind, insisting instead that the world is a collection of particulars. The influence of postmodernism has reverberated throughout political philosophy, leading generally to increased attention to the diverse particularities of the world, to specific cultural differences, and to historical contingency. Postmodern insights have also helped us understand how some central concepts that we take for granted as natural are actually a result of historical contingency and, sometimes, struggle. Michel Foucault's *The History of Sexuality* (1978), for example, describes the varied understanding through the ages of gender and sexuality. What we take today as stable and inherent categories of sexual orientation and experience are actually historically and culturally contingent. Richard Rorty's (1931–) *Philosophy and the Mirror of Nature* (1979) shows how even our concept of the mind was an invention traceable in particular to the work of the French philosopher René Descartes (1596–1650) during the seventeenth century. Edward Said's (1935–2003) *Orientalism* (1978) demonstrates that the notion of an "oriental" culture is a fiction, a lumping together of many diverse cultures into one in a way that fundamentally misleads and distorts.[6]

Utilitarianism is a political philosophy developed during the nineteenth century by the British thinkers Jeremy Bentham (1748–1832), James Mill (1773–1836), and John Stuart Mill (1806–1873). It sought "the greatest good for the greatest number," and political theory and action were evaluated according to whether or not they advanced this goal. Utilitarians defined *good* in terms of the concept of utility. If a particular idea or action increased a person's utility, it could be deemed good. Given the vague character of the concept of utility, in practice it tended to be equated with happiness or pleasure. Most utilitarians rejected the notion of an absolute standard of good for everyone. Instead, different individuals decided for themselves what made them happy. Utilitarianism remains influential, especially within the fields of public policy studies and the dominant neoclassical strain of contemporary economic theory.

Although most pragmatists reject absolute foundations, most prefer simply to evade the question, arguing that it needlessly distracts us from our main interest in action toward goals. According to pragmatists, we do not need absolute truth or certainty in order to act practically and intelligently. A more modest understanding of truth, characterized by Hilary Putnam (1926–) as "warranted assertibility,"[7] adequately serves the goal of action. This means that, based on what we know now, we are warranted in asserting that one idea or plan of action is better than another. As conditions change, says the pragmatist, we may be warranted in changing our minds and asserting a different truth whose consequences we like better.

This unwillingness to adopt absolute standards of truth makes some people uneasy. Do standards of right and wrong, good and bad, disappear along with any notion of absolute truth? For pragmatists, the answer is no. Adhering to more modest notions of truth need not set us completely adrift in relativity. We can still adopt high standards for thought and action. Some pragmatists, including and especially John Dewey, measure consequences against a standard of strong, participatory democracy. This gives them a critical foothold that utilitarians lack. By insisting that no critical judgment is possible about people's choice of what gives them happiness, utilitarians reject the possibility of distinguishing between good and bad choices, except insofar as one may give more happiness, or pleasure, than another. To a utilitarian, the choice of not voting is morally and politically equivalent to voting so long as both bring equal happiness and pleasure to the chooser, and so long as neither impinges on the rights of others. The pragmatist is in a stronger position to say that some choices are better than others, apart from whether or not they give pleasure, because some move us closer to an ideal of democracy and others do not.

Nonabsolutist thinkers may embrace some of the ideas and principles used by absolutist thinkers. However, they justify the ideas and principles differently. While the absolutist may adopt the idea of human rights based on an argument of their inherent value and because they accord with a timeless, universal human nature, the nonabsolutist might embrace the notion of rights because they serve us well. They would ask, "What might we gain by adopting the principle of a right?" If the consequences of human rights are positive, then we are justified in adopting them. If they help individuals and groups protect and extend their autonomy, without undermining the autonomy of others, then they are good and useful.

Consequentialists cannot always escape absolutist foundations. Evaluating an idea or practice according to its consequences presumes a standard against which those consequences will be measured, and that standard often represents intrinsically held values that resemble absolutist principles. Dewey's embrace of a standard of participatory democracy, for example, rested in part on his belief in the developmental effect of participatory democracy on individuals. But this presumes a deeper standard: the inherent worth of every individual. Similarly, the consequentialist defense of rights presumes the value of individual autonomy.

There is more at stake in settling competing claims over truth than simply who gets to be right. First, especially in politics, being "right," justifiably or not, often means being a winner, while being "wrong" means being a loser. Winning a political debate often translates into policy decisions that create winners and losers. Winners enjoy extensive social benefits and sanctions while losers may have to shoulder a variety of costs. Second, how we answer each question of truth determines to a great extent our political horizons. If we adopt an absolutist position on human nature, it limits our options for theory and practice to those consistent with that absolutist understanding. On the other hand, if we view human nature as partly or wholly malleable, then we can legitimately attempt to redesign institutions that determine human identity and behavior in alternative directions from the status quo. If we view inequality as natural or divinely ordained, then logically we should abandon efforts to overcome it. If we view inequality as a product of specific social and cultural circumstances, then we can legitimately attempt to transform those social and cultural circumstances in order to move closer to equality.

TENSIONS IN THEORY AND PRACTICE

The five parts of this book each address a central tension in political theory and practice. Many of our contemporary political problems can be understood in terms of these tensions in theory and practice. While the tensions probably cannot fully be resolved, the relative emphasis in each case can be reexamined and adjusted so that public problems can be more adequately addressed. Each part contains two chapters. The first chapter in each part includes a description and analysis of some of the contemporary public problems that emerge from the tension, and a discussion of some underlying intellectual causes. In the second chapter of each part, different political thinkers from past and present are called upon to help think about the issues and offer alternative ways of addressing the problems.

Part 1 is organized around the tension between the individual and community. In contemporary America, the individual is emphasized to such an extent that the theory and practice of a common, public good is overwhelmed. Many contemporary public problems can be understood as a consequence of radical individualism, with too little concern for the impact of individual behavior on others. Different political theorists will be called upon to help think about alternatives to radical individualism that might better enable citizens to recognize and address problems arising from it.

Part 2 addresses the twin ideals of freedom and equality. Since most Americans embrace both ideals, many naturally assume that they are compatible goals. However, they actually may conflict with each other in fundamental ways. In the United States, equality has generally yielded to freedom rather than vice versa, and the result is radical inequality. To understand the roots of radical inequality and help imagine alternatives, different political thinkers and their ideas are critically reviewed.

Part 3 addresses the tension between justice and political order. The contemporary world offers many examples of political order taking precedence over justice. Achieving greater justice may entail precisely upsetting the prevailing political order. Various thinkers are enlisted to help challenge current formulations and to imagine alternatives more consistent with both justice and political order.

Like freedom and equality, most Americans are committed to both democracy and capitalism. And like freedom and equality, the twin commitments actually coexist in uneasy tension. Part 4 explores this tension. According to many democratic theorists, the two have been uneasily reconciled by redefining democracy as a "thin" version of its historical self. Problems associated with this redefinition are first explored, and then different political thinkers are used to imagine alternatives.

Finally, part 5 examines the tension between power and citizenship. Undemocratic uses of power can be cited as a prominent reason for the decline of citizenship in contemporary times. On the other hand, democratic forms and uses of power are necessary to revitalize citizenship. Different thinkers and concepts are considered that might help challenge undemocratic forms of power and support active, effective citizenship.

None of these parts comprehensively addresses the political ideas, practices, and problems raised in them. A comprehensive treatment would require

a multivolume effort. Instead, each part raises key ideas and issues and introduces readers to some of the dominant and alternative ways political philosophers think about them.

PUTTING IDEAS TO WORK . . . FOR DEMOCRACY

Political philosophers are sometimes roughly divided into two kinds: those
who pursue their task as relatively disinterested observers and those who use
ideas to engage critically with the world in order to change it. The former
adopt a stance of neutrality. They attempt to set aside whatever political values they personally hold in favor of disinterested analysis. Political philosophers of the second type, characterized as "connected critics" by
contemporary political philosopher Michael Walzer (1935–),[8] reject neutrality in favor of practical commitment. They evaluate political ideas according
to how well they advance a particular political agenda. The difference between
the two cannot be neatly characterized as one of objectivity versus subjectiv-
ity, nor one of value-free versus value-driven political philosophy. The neutral
stance of the one theorist sometimes disguises values and standards adopted
without acknowledgment. Moreover, neutrality itself is a value. Finally, the
committed stance does not disallow objective, rigorous analysis of information and ideas, albeit in terms of their relationship to a particular standard or
set of values.

This book is defined in part by its practical commitments. Throughout, it
presumes a political standard against which political ideas and practices are
measured. An ideal of democracy in its strong, participatory form shapes both
the analysis of public problems and the types of solutions considered to address them. For example, part 1 makes the case that many contemporary public problems can be understood in terms of the consequences of radical
individualism, and solutions emphasize public-spiritedness, informed, responsible public opinion, and common citizens' action rather than elite-
driven technocratic alternatives. Part 2 makes the case for upgrading equality
in the hierarchy of political values, part 3 emphasizes the satisfaction of basic
human needs and self-determination as key elements of distributive justice,
part 4 addresses arguments for reversing the current domination of democracy by capitalism, and part 5 emphasizes the importance of political participation by common citizens, in each case because these are central ingredients
in a vital democracy. The rationale for this standard of democracy will appear

in various forms throughout the book, but it can be summarized in Deweyan terms: democracy best ensures the growth and development of every person.

Readers seeking a book that offers equal consideration and credibility to all sides of an issue or debate should thus continue looking. This is not the book for them. The ideal of participatory democracy rules out some ideas for serious consideration while favoring others.

Readers should beware of attempting to locate all of the ideas presented in this book along a simple left–right political continuum. Many ideas and sets of ideas cannot be so easily located, and participatory democracy is one of them. For example, participatory democrats share conservatives' suspicion of concentrated political power (while adding a suspicion of concentrated economic power, absent from most conservatives' considerations), and thus share conservatives' dismay over big government and its impact on human freedom, albeit for somewhat different reasons. Humanist economics, discussed in part 4, would be difficult to locate on a simple left–right continuum, as would contemporary communitarianism, discussed in part 1. They employ ideas taken from both sides of the traditional left–right continuum, while adding others found in a third dimension.

Solving contemporary public problems frequently requires that this book adopt a critical stance on contemporary politics and the ideas that legitimize them. Some readers may mistakenly equate this critical stance with "liberalism" or "leftism," but careful readers will note sustained criticism of both liberal and conservative ideas and practices. The criticisms are united by a conviction, first of all, that many contemporary public problems are rooted in dominant conservative and liberal ideas. Throughout *Putting Ideas to Work*, these dominant ideas are subjected to critical scrutiny. The criticisms are united, secondly, by the conviction that, if offered truly democratic alternatives, most Americans would prefer to move closer to a strong democratic ideal. Hopefully, most liberals and conservatives can agree that more democracy is better than less. The criticisms are united, finally, by the conviction that greater democracy is possible. As part 4 addresses at length, the version of democracy currently practiced in the United States represents a narrowing of the democratic ideal. The stronger ideal may be impossible to fully achieve in practice; some may argue as well that it is inadvisable. However, there is no question that we can do better. Doing better presumes that we have a sense of what "better" would look like. Emphasizing a strong ideal of democracy enables us to clarify and maintain that vision.

QUESTIONS, PROBLEMS, AND ACTIVITIES

1. Compare and contrast absolutist and nonabsolutist approaches to the question of the family. To sexual orientation.
2. Brainstorm a list of opinions about politics. Which of them do you think can be empirically proved or disproved? What kind of empirical evidence is, or might be, available? How might you supplement it with a good argument? Develop an argument to support or oppose at least one opinion that cannot be proved or disproved solely with empirical evidence.
3. Identify a particular nonempirical political idea that you believe is true. How would you justify this idea? Because it is absolutely true? Because it is useful to believe it? Because you like its consequences?
4. Select one political opinion that might be defended on consequentialist grounds. Select another that might be defended on the basis of religion or natural rights. Defend them against critics.
5. Based on what you know thus far, would you identify yourself more as an absolutist or nonabsolutist thinker? Why?

NOTES

1. Aristotle, *Politics* 1:1254b, 1:1260a; Jean-Jacques Rousseau, *Émile*, trans. Barbara Foxley (1762; London: Everyman, 1911), p. 370; Rousseau, *Discourse on Political Economy* [1755], in *Rousseau's Political Writings*, ed. Alan Ritter and Julia Conaway Bondanella (New York: W. W. Norton, 1988), p. 59.

2. On essentially contested concepts, see especially William Connolly, *The Terms of Political Discourse*, 2nd ed. (Princeton: Princeton University Press, 1983).

3. Robert Booth Fowler and Jeffrey Orenstein, *An Introduction to Political Theory* (New York: HarperCollins, 1993), p. 3.

4. George Orwell, *1984* (New York: Penguin Books, 1949), pp. 7, 33.

5. Jean-Jacques Rousseau, *The Social Contract* [1762], in Ritter and Bondanella, *Rousseau's Political Writings*, p. 96.

6. Michel Foucault, *The History of Sexuality*, vol. 1, *An Introduction* (New York: Vintage Books, 1978); Richard Rorty, *Philosophy and the Mirror of Nature* (Princeton: Princeton University Press, 1979); Edward Said, *Orientalism* (New York: Vintage Books, 1978).

7. Putnam, quoted in Richard Rorty, *The Consequences of Pragmatism* (Minneapolis: University of Minnesota Press, 1982), p. xxv.

8. Michael Walzer, *The Company of Critics: Social Criticism and Political Commitment in the Twentieth Century* (New York: Basic Books, 1988).

I

THE INDIVIDUAL AND THE COMMUNITY

1

Radical Individualism and the Tragedy of the Commons

Americans emphasize the primary importance of the individual. This may seem both self-evident and inherently appropriate, but it actually represents the culmination of centuries of thought and action. Although there have always been alternative thinkers in Western culture who emphasize a social grouping, the dominant strain has been individualistic for centuries. Within this dominant strain, individuals form or join groups as a rational calculation of individual self-interest. Groups are thus conceptually and practically secondary to individuals.

What would we emphasize if not the individual? Alternatives include socioeconomic class, the state, society, social structures, and community. China, which like the United States has an "extraordinary imbalance" between individual and society, represents a good example of emphasis on the social group rather than the individual. In China, we find a "general hostility toward individualism. . . . No people have ever outdone the Chinese in ascribing moral virtues to the state or in deprecating the worth of the individual, . . . [or] in extolling the importance of rulers and society and in minimizing the rights of individuals."[1] Of course, China's relative emphasis on the social group over the individual may change as it increasingly comes into contact with Western culture through economic and cultural exchanges.

Other countries blend the two extremes. Israel's constitution expressly imposes individual responsibilities to society as well as individual rights. The former include compulsory military service, the obligation to pay taxes and lend money to the state, the obligation of parents and guardians to take care of the educational and other needs of their minor children, and the obligation to support immediate and extended family members. The Japanese constitution cites the responsibility of all citizens to help prevent environmental pollution. In Morocco, the constitution states explicitly that every right implies a duty, and article 29 reminds individuals that their duties to the community include abiding by the laws, respecting the religion of others, and respecting the homes of others. Pakistan's constitution obligates its citizens to assist in the detection of crimes. Many countries' constitutions list duties and responsibilities that complement rights. Most frequently, these include the obligation to work, to pay taxes, to support the country, and to serve in the armed forces.[2]

An emphasis on the individual helps ensure that each of us can lead a life that best suits our own unique interests and talents. Increasing individual choices expands our freedom and enables each of us to pursue our own conception of our best interests. It makes possible an expansive degree of self-actualization and the development of individual talents. Giving relatively free rein to individual initiative, expression, and creativity sometimes also produces social benefits. Individual economic initiative sometimes creates new jobs. Intellectual freedom granted to individuals sometimes results in new knowledge and inventions that improve our lives. Individual expression often gives us new art forms that enrich our lives.

However, the emphasis on the individual in Western culture has reached radical proportions, creating multiple public problems and undermining our collective ability to solve them. Biologist Garrett Hardin (1915–2003) captured this in his parable of the tragedy of the commons.[3] Hardin asked us to imagine a small, seventeenth-century English village surrounding a grassy commons. The villagers live in separate familial homes, but they drive their livestock each day to the commons to graze. The finite pasture can sustain only so many head of livestock. If radical individualism defines the norms for behavior, each individual and family will seek to maximize their share of the community's wealth without concerning themselves with potential harm to the community as a whole. Individuals and family members will calculate that they can increase their income by increasing the size of their herd. While the individual or the family will realize all the benefits of adding an additional animal, the community as a whole must bear the costs in the form of overgrazing and potential destruction of the common pasture. If enough families add to their herds, the commons becomes overgrazed resulting in a "tragedy of the commons" that compromises the well-being of all villagers. In effect, individually rational behavior produces collectively irrational outcomes. This parable illustrates many problems actually occurring in the world today.

[handwritten marginalia: comparing overpopulation women over cows: not enough food: not enough resources.]

PUBLIC PROBLEMS

Resource Depletion

In many ways, the self-interested behavior of countless individuals adds up to problems of resource depletion. The commons in each case is the resource itself. While it is often rational for individuals and individual groups to maximize their own use of the resource, in many cases the collective outcome is irrational in the sense that the resource's management and ultimate survival are threatened. The commons experiences a "tragedy" of depletion that approaches or exceeds sustainability levels.

One example is the ocean fish stocks that are rapidly dwindling as individual fishing companies and nations increase or maintain the size of their catches, using more sophisticated technology and larger boats. Individuals seeking to maximize their own interests in profit have a rational incentive to increase, or at least maintain, the number of fish they catch. Unfortunately, these individually rational decisions produce a collective tragedy of declining and disappearing fish stocks. According to the Food and Agriculture Organization of the United Nations, the primary international organization monitoring fish stocks, "Global fish production from most marine resources and many inland waters has reached or exceeded the level of maximum sustainable yield. . . . The productive capacity of almost every sea has been reached or passed, and almost all catches today come at the expense of other fishers or of future stocks."[4] Although increasing population exacerbates this problem, the dynamic occurs as well in stable or declining populations. The nations that contribute the most to the problem are industrialized nations such as the United States, Japan, and Norway, each of which has a low birth rate. Experts agree that the ability of fish stocks to maintain and recover is at this point seriously compromised. If left unchecked, fish stocks will continue to decline and, potentially, disappear.

The most popular solutions to declining fish stocks emphasize technical and scientific, rather than political, means. Many cite fish farming as the best solution. Supporters of this approach argue that we can make up the shortfall in fish stocks found in nature by increasing our production in fish farms. Fish farming, which originated in China some 5,000 years ago in the production of carp, has increased dramatically in the last several decades. Proponents of fish farming anticipated a "Blue Revolution" akin to the "Green Revolution" in agriculture, but failed to anticipate that the Blue Revolution would duplicate many of the same problems encountered in the Green.[5] Though yields from fish farming have increased, as did edible plant production under the Green Revolution, so have associated problems, including waste, pollution, poor land-use practices, disease, and genetic inbreeding.

Even if these problems could be solved, fish farming would still represent a net loss in global protein. Most relatively affluent Westerners prefer to eat carnivorous fish, which must be fed other fish. Two of the most popular farmed species are salmon and shrimp. Both of these are fed fishmeal made of edible schooling fish such as mackerel, capelin, sardines, and anchovies. Approximately five kilograms of ocean fish, reduced to fishmeal, are necessary to produce one kilogram of farmed ocean fish or shrimp, making them net consumers rather than producers of fish protein. This represents a net loss of protein, increases the drain on ocean fish stocks, and shifts marine biological wealth from the poor to the rich who essentially outbid the poor for use of scarce resources. Often, as was the case with the Green Revolution, increasing yields from fish farming have done little or nothing to alleviate the problem of hunger. Instead, these increasing yields are typically exported to relatively wealthy consumers in industrialized countries. Bangladesh, Indonesia, India, Thailand, and China have each increased their production of shrimp for export, yet they have problems producing enough food to feed their own people.[6]

Some of these problems associated with declining fish stocks are surmountable. Yet, they require either voluntary changes in consumers' behavior—such as shifting from carnivorous fish and shrimp to catfish, carp, and other more efficient fish—or government intervention in order to guide and mandate shifts in production and consumption. In a culture that emphasizes radical individualism, average consumers resist voluntarily changing their consumption habits. In the same culture, which tends to view government as an impediment to individual autonomy, increased government regulation rarely proves politically palatable and may exacerbate citizens' cynicism and antagonism toward their government. Either way we face the problem of convincing individuals through persuasion or enforced compliance to think and act with the common interest, as well as their individual interest, in mind. Alternatively, we could ask or force fishing companies to reduce their catches. This too, however, would require reliance either on voluntary compliance or unwanted government intrusion into the marketplace.

Many other examples of resource depletion can be cited to illustrate the basic logic of the tragedy of the commons. Rain forests are being harvested at a rate that threatens to deplete them, for instance. Their depletion would be catastrophic given the role of rain forests as planetary "lungs" that turn carbon dioxide into oxygen. In the short term, though, it is rational for peasants to slash and burn rain forest in order to grow food, and it is rational for developers to harvest and even clear-cut the forest for profit.

Fresh water is another example of a resource that faces pressures from many directions. It may be individually rational for people living in the southwestern United States to water their lawns, but doing so contributes to the need to divert water from the Colorado River and elsewhere. Similarly, it is economically rational for farmers in the Midwest to draw water via wells from the underground Oglala aquifer, but the collective result in the form of a receding aquifer may produce catastrophic consequences for agriculture in the region. While these problems may be exacerbated by population growth, they also emerge in stable or declining populations as per capita usage exceeds sustainable levels.

Environmental Degradation

The same dynamic posed in Hardin's tragedy of the commons fuels environmental problems such as global warming and acid rain caused by the burning of fossil fuels, ozone depletion caused by the use of fluorocarbons, and water and air pollution caused by toxic discharges and emissions. These problems result in part from countless individual choices with too little attention to the aggregate effects. Individuals in industrialized countries contribute the most to these environmental problems. In 1997, the wealthy industrialized countries together consumed 66 percent more energy than all countries combined of Asia, Africa, the Middle East, and Central and South America. Industrialized countries (excluding Russia), with approximately 13 percent of the world's population, consume approximately 47 percent of its fossil fuels. Residents of the United States consume far more energy per capita than in any other country. With less than 5 percent of the world's population, it consumes approximately a quarter of the world's energy in a given year.[7]

Global warming, or the gradual rise in average global temperatures, represents a global tragedy of the commons. The Earth's atmosphere and climate systems together comprise the commons in this instance. The cumulative result of countless individual actions, especially since the onset of the Industrial Revolution in the mid-nineteenth century, has been a gradual global warming trend that threatens massive disruptions worldwide. Most scientists now agree that global warming is a reality, that human activity causes or exacerbates global warming, that it is already too late to avert at least some global warming and its consequences, and that the only meaningful choices at this point are how to slow and hopefully reverse within the next fifty to one hundred years the inertia of global warming before its effects become cataclysmic.

Global warming is caused by a gradual thickening of a layer of "greenhouse gases," primarily carbon dioxide, that trap heat in the Earth's atmosphere. This carbon dioxide, once released into the atmosphere, remains there for a century or more. The human contribution to this comes mostly from the burning of fossil fuels such as coal, oil, and natural gas in power plants and automobiles, numbers one and two, respectively, in their contribution to the problem.[8] Fossil fuel use is currently increasing at a rate of approximately 1 percent per year, which means that the problem is likely to get worse rather than better without drastic changes and meaningful coordinated action.[9] Deforestation exacerbates the problem by eliminating a major means of absorbing the excess carbon dioxide.

Consequences of global warming include, most obviously, warmer temperatures.[10] Average temperatures are rising, along with the frequency of heat waves, and scientists project a 2–10°F (1–5°C) rise in global temperatures due to global warming. The warmer temperatures produce faster evaporation, increasing the intensity of droughts and the risk of wildfires. Warmer temperatures also increase the energy of climate systems, causing more intense rainstorms at some times in some areas, and more frequent and intense hurricanes, which gain their force from water evaporation. The higher temperatures cause the melting of glaciers and ice caps and thaw river and lake ice earlier in the season. As the Arctic thaws, it reflects less sun, and therefore heat, back into space. Also, the large amounts of carbon dioxide stored in frozen peat in the Arctic will be released as it thaws. The melting glaciers and ice caps, plus thermal expansion of existing oceans and seas, will cause sea levels to rise, resulting in the inundation of some low-lying areas such as the Florida Everglades, coastal wetlands, and the banks of estuaries such as Chesapeake Bay. Rising temperatures will also cause ecosystem shifts and species extinctions. Some species will prove unable to adapt to rising temperatures and the climatic changes they produce. Rising temperatures will also produce human health declines in some areas, caused by increased heat waves and diseases that thrive in heat and are spread by heat-loving insects.

But isn't global warming a myth, as some argue? And even if the Earth is warming, is human activity really a contributing factor? Won't global warming produce benefits that outweigh costs? Isn't the science of climatology too crude and imprecise to accurately predict anything like global warming? According to Eileen Claussen, president of the Pew Center on Global Climate Change, "There is overwhelming scientific consensus that the earth is warming, that this warming trend will worsen, and that human activity is largely to blame."[11] This was also the conclusion of the United Nations' Intergovernmental Panel on Climate Change, which draws on the expertise of hundreds of climate scientists around the world. U.S. President George W. Bush, who doubted the science, commissioned a review by the U.S. National Academy of Sciences. The academy returned the same verdict: the climate is warming, and humans are causing it.[12]

In the short term, global warming will produce both winners and losers. Farmers in colder latitudes will benefit from longer growing seasons while farmers in warmer latitudes will likely see their crops diminish by increased heat and drought. In the long term, however, "any possible benefits from global warming will be far outweighed by the costs."[13] As for the reservation concerning the imprecision of science and the resulting uncertainty, it is worth noting again that an overwhelming majority of scientists agree that the science is accurate enough to warrant taking immediate steps to stabilize carbon dioxide concentrations in the range of two to three times the preindustrial level.

A problem of this magnitude and scope will require aggressive government action both domestically and globally. Domestically, governments can adopt policies that combine positive incentives with punitive regulations. Among the positive incentives are policies aimed at stimulating investment in research and development of alternative energy technologies and public transportation systems. Disincentives include fines levied on energy polluters and large-scale producers of carbon dioxide emissions, as well as increased gasoline taxes aimed at pushing people out of their cars and into mass transit options. Globally, the U.S. government will need to work with other nations to craft policies aimed at reducing greenhouse gas emissions.

None of these measures are likely, though, without widespread support among individual Americans. Absent that broad-based support, many people in power will seek to deny the realities, hiding behind myths and avoiding the difficult issues. The United States currently relies on voluntary programs such as the Energy Star program, which rates appliances for energy use and offers rebates to consumers who purchase the best energy savers. This represents, at best, an extremely weak response. U.S. noncommitment was starkly revealed by the refusal of the George W. Bush administration to sign the Kyoto Protocol, the result of a plan drafted in 1997 by 160 nations. It called for the 38 industrialized countries now releasing the most greenhouse gases to cut emissions to 5 percent below 1990 levels, by a target date of 2012.

Politicians fear punishment in the next election if they pass legislation aggressive enough to address the problem of global warming. The problem lies partly in individual reluctance to support changes in their lives that are likely to produce inconvenience and sacrifice. Claussen, who agrees that government will act decisively only when "the force of public opinion" is brought to bear on the problem, explicitly articulates the problem of global warming in the framework of a tragedy of the commons, and she rightly concludes that the same economic forces that created the problem cannot alone solve it:

> The market, of course, helped create global warming. . . . The climate, as they say, is the quintessential "commons," the public good that is free to everyone, and therefore valued by no one. But even now that we understand its value, and the risks of continuing to overburden it, the market cannot possibly fix the problem of its own accord. It is simply incapable of factoring in the very long-term costs and benefits, of giving them sufficient weight, to drive the investments that are needed in the short-term. That is why government must give it direction.[14]

Although government action is essential to adequately address the problem of global warming, individuals need not wait for government action. The same kinds of choices that reduce other kinds of pollution will help reduce emissions contributing to global warming. Examples include recycling, using energy-efficient appliances, turning down the thermostat in the winter, using fans rather than air conditioners during the summer, adding insulation to the house, and, especially, reducing reliance on automobiles. Are Americans likely to support aggressive government action and make individual choices aimed at reducing their contributions to greenhouse gases? Skeptics say no. However, Americans have not yet truly been asked to make these kinds of choices. They have not been asked, for example, to park their cars and opt into public transportation. They are bombarded with messages to consume, and in particular to consume a new automobile annually. They are invited repeatedly in myriad ways to make precisely the wrong kinds of choices. Leaders who want to win reelection promise Americans everything except sacrifice and inconvenience. This will likely continue so long as average Americans punish leaders for adopting needed policies by voting them out of office.

Transportation

Transportation offers another mundane but vivid example of the tragedy of the commons. Individuals calculate that owning and using an automobile best serves their self-interest. While each person benefits from car ownership and use, excessive use of automobiles compromises the common good, producing enormous costs to society in the form of air pollution, congestion, urban sprawl, global warming, and carnage on the roads. Each year, Americans pour billions of dollars into infrastructure supporting the automobile. This money could be used elsewhere, including in the development of public transportation. Americans tolerate concrete jungles and the steady encroachment of concrete over agricultural land, losing sight of what alternative urban landscapes could look and feel like. Automobiles create multiple environmental problems, most of which will be passed along to future generations. They require the destruction of natural habitats in order to discover and pump more oil, and they cause dependence on oil-producing countries. Americans tolerate approximately 45,000 annual traffic deaths and innumerable accidents that maim and injure millions. Their waistlines expand and blood pressures rise as they drive, rather than walk, three blocks for a loaf of bread. According to a 2003 study, people who live in the suburbs are likely to weigh six pounds more than their urban counterparts, a consequence partly of the greater need in suburbs to drive everywhere. According to the study, "Each extra degree of [suburban] sprawl meant additional weight, less walking and a little more high blood pressure."[15]

The sport utility vehicle, the ubiquitous SUV, vividly illustrates this emphasis on individualized transportation and its consequences. These vehicles pose a danger to non-SUV drivers, since a sedan–SUV crash is three times more likely to kill the sedan driver than is a crash between two sedans. SUVs careen more easily out of control if turned too abruptly, ride up over the safety features of most sedans in a collision, jump curbs that stop most sedans, block the vision of sedan drivers, and burn fuel at higher rates. Nor is the SUV the largest passenger vehicle on the road today. Hummers, commercial versions of the military Humvees that gained fame during the 1991 Desert Storm conflict in the Middle East, are seen with increasing frequency on the road. Most of these vehicles are eight feet wide, only two feet narrower than an average street lane. The stretch-limousine version of the Hummer measures up to forty-five feet in length and can seat up to twenty-five passengers. Like many large SUVs, they average 10 miles per gallon or less. Popular recreational vehicles, some the size of buses, average as little as 2 or 3 miles per gallon.

At their best, most vehicles powered by internal combustion engines consume gasoline at high rates. Model-year-2005 SUVs averaged approximately 15–16 miles per gallon overall, while 2005 pickup trucks averaged 12–13 miles per gallon. The average model-year-2000 large sedans averaged approximately 20 miles per gallon; smaller sedans averaged 25–30. Of 205 vehicles included in the April 2005 issue of *Consumer Reports*, only seven averaged more than 30 miles per gallon.[16] Relatively cheap gas prices in the United States make this high consumption of gasoline possible. The average 2005 level of approximately $2.30 per gallon was just one-half to one-third the price of gasoline in most Western European nations, where gasoline taxes are considerably higher. At relatively low rates, Americans subsidize their individualized transportation at the expense of future generations, who will have to contend with declining oil reserves, increased pollution, and global warming. Even at the post–Hurricane Katrina price of around $3.00 per gallon, the price does not fully capture the real costs of burning gasoline, which include longer-term and environmental costs difficult to capture accurately in a short-term supply-and-demand calculation.

Proposals for restricting the automobile and developing mass transit systems rarely merit serious attention. Most Americans understandably express reluctance to use public transportation, given the badly underdeveloped state of public transit systems in most areas. Why is public transportation in most areas of the United States so undeveloped? One answer is that Americans have thus far shown little interest in mass transit. Some may argue that they would show more interest if the alternatives to automobiles were convenient, safe, and affordable, but this creates a dilemma: We are unlikely to develop good mass transit until the demand for it increases sufficiently, but the demand will not increase until the mass transit systems are well developed. Others may argue that mass transit is not economically feasible in most parts of the United States because of relatively low population densities, and thus would require massive subsidies. Yet, we already extensively and expensively subsidize the automobile via uncaptured costs and billions spent annually on highways and other infrastructure.

It may be tempting to blame politicians who are assigned the responsibility for maintaining the public interest. Understandably, if unfortunately, most elected representatives only reluctantly consider measures that redirect transportation priorities. Their political fortunes are on the line, and they know it. The politician who supports measures to decrease automobile use and increase mass transit options faces defeat in the next election. Imagine the electoral fate of the politician who campaigns on a platform that includes doubling gasoline taxes. In short, the problem lies ultimately with individual voters reluctant to consider other transportation options.

Like many problems arising from the tragedy of the commons, technical solutions to transportation problems tempt us away from political solutions. Rather than encourage or even force people out of cars, we seek instead to solve the problems associated with the automobile by redesigning the automobile and developing alternative systems of individualized transportation. Automobile manufacturers, in response to some prodding by government, are attempting to increase the gas mileage of their vehicles and to lower emissions. Some futurists anticipate "individualized rail transit" systems in which individual commuters would drive their vehicles to a rail entry station where they would link up with others. From that point, these vehicles would work like a train, with computers guiding each pod to its destination. This futuristic scenario may, indeed, contribute to solving some of our transportation problems. However, these partial solutions simply postpone a full reckoning. Even if alternative fuels such as hydrogen someday fully replace fossil fuels, the problems of overcrowding, urban sprawl, carnage, and the paving of America that occur as a result of individualized transportation will remain.

Trash

Americans generate mountains of trash every year, more than any other nation. On average, Americans produce 4.4 pounds of garbage per capita per day, for a total of 217 million tons in 1997 alone. Despite increasing emphasis on recycling, the problem is actually getting worse: the annual production of municipal solid waste in the United States has more than doubled since 1960. As of 2000, New York City alone was generating 12,000 tons of garbage daily, more than it could dump in its one landfill, the 3,000-acre Fresh Kills Landfill. The city responded by exporting its trash to surrounding states for dumping. Ohio alone in 1998 buried 553,000 tons of New York City garbage, and the figures for importers of New York City garbage rose even higher when Fresh Kills closed in 2001. New York City is not alone in generating more trash than it can dispose of locally. In 1989 Ohio buried 3.7 million tons of trash generated in other states.[17]

Beginning with radical individualistic assumptions about human nature as rational egoists, each individual has an incentive to minimize the effort expended on dealing with trash or avoiding generating trash in the first place. It is easiest to simply throw something away. Doing so has no direct impact on our pocketbook or on our individual lives. By contrast, recycling the trash or avoiding generating trash in the first place requires additional effort. In an individualistic culture, despite increasing exhortations to recycle, the momentum of daily life takes most people willingly or unwillingly along with the trash stream, rather than toward efforts to avoid it or reduce it. The dominant motivation inclines most to throw things away and let others deal with the resulting mountains of trash.

Countless individual decisions in millions of households produce a large and growing waste stream, most of it dumped in landfills where it sits for hundreds and perhaps thousands of years. Some of the trash is toxic, and this can leach down into the groundwater. Making matters worse, as illustrated above with the New York example, landfills are filling up. Burning the trash offers one alternative, but this too produces unpleasant side effects, including toxic ash and pollutants. The NIMBY (Not In My Back Yard) problem compounds this problem of trash. Though most individuals help create the problem, most are understandably reluctant to allow waste dumps or waste burners in their "backyard." Instead, they strive to displace the costs of their individual consumption choices into someone else's backyard. Typically, this cleaves along class lines: burners and dumps too often end up in the backyards of working-class and minority neighborhoods.

Production and distribution systems further compound the problem by overpackaging. Well-intentioned consumers face few options for decreasing their contribution to the waste stream. Many grocery stores no longer offer paper sacks. They in effect force the consumer to use plastic, which takes longer to biodegrade and requires more energy to recycle. Although many communities nationwide now offer recycling programs, most items bought in grocery stores come packaged in materials that cannot be recycled.

Like the problems of overfishing and transportation, it is tempting to await a scientific or technological solution to the problem of trash. We await development of a "microbug" that can be released into landfills to eat up the waste, leaving environmentally clean, rich composted soil. We hope that scientists invent biodegradable packaging, rather than pressure grocers to offer more unpackaged food. Perhaps soon we will begin launching our trash into space.

Housing

Housing strongly reflects our emphasis on the individual over the community. In this case, the commons is both the physical neighborhood itself and the civic community that once grew out of neighborly interactions. Many older homes built in the early twentieth century or earlier were designed to facilitate at least minimal private–public interactions. Many included a large front porch on which residents could sit, watch, and interact with neighbors as they walked past. Many also included large picture windows, or a series of smaller windows, that allowed residents to see outside and passersby to see in. The garage, if the home included one at all, generally sat behind the house. Most residential neighborhoods also included sidewalks, enabling pedestrians to circulate afoot in the neighborhood, where interactions with others could occur. Of course, many of these homes remain standing in urban neighborhoods, and they continue to contribute to the possibility of urban community.

Most newer suburban homes, built within the last fifty or sixty years, stand in marked contrast to that image. Most lead with a two- or even three-car garage, leaving a blank, windowless wall facing the street. A small stoop with a door offers entrance into the house, and relatively small front windows allow some light and visibility. Many suburban communities omit sidewalks, as the culture of cars replaces the pedestrian culture of interactive neighborhoods. The absence of sidewalks makes personal encounters with neighbors relatively difficult and rare. These suburban homes orient family and limited social interaction toward the backyard, a private cloistered space frequently secured by a privacy fence. These homes intentionally restrict residents' public interactions and separate the individual from the rest of the community.

Some attempts have emerged in recent times to reorient housing toward public space. In some pockets of new development, builders are attempting to respond to a growing niche market for community-oriented housing by developing enclaves that integrate features enabling more interaction among neighbors. This "traditional neighborhood development" (TND) movement includes design features such as placing garages in the rear of the lot, sidewalks, narrower streets, smaller but more numerous parks, and an emphasis on more traditional styles of American homes that feature front porches and large windows. Nevertheless, the overall trend in American residential architecture continues to move away from TND and toward greater privacy and isolation in the model of suburban development.

MORE GOVERNMENT COERCION?

Many other issues can be cited which illustrate the effects of radical individualism. While it may be individually rational to use a cell phone while driving, doing so produces an irrational collective outcome. According to one study published in the *New England Journal of Medicine*, drivers are four times as likely to have an accident while talking on a cell phone.[18] This matches the ratio for driving while drinking. Even without the accidents, inevitably people talking on their cell phones pay less attention to driving. They may forget to use a turn signal, run through a red light, or wait at a green light until the driver behind honks. The cell phone user follows the logic of the tragedy of the commons in emphasizing individual interests while passing the costs on to society. Of course, the same can be said for applying makeup or eating while driving.

Capital flight also illustrates the tragedy of the commons. An individual corporation finds it rational to move its operations offshore in order to take advantage of cheaper labor and relaxed environmental and safety regulations. Collectively, however, the move devastates American workers.

Multiple problems in the electoral political realm also illustrate the inability to locate and protect a commons that outweighs or at least balances individual and group interest. The huge national debt—predictable when individuals and groups seek to maximize their shares of government resources while minimizing their contributions in the form of taxes—offers one prominent example. The same dynamic operates in other public policy areas such as health care reform and banking deregulation. Private interest groups representing medical insurers and doctors looking out for their own interests—arguably at the expense of average citizens and a more general, common good—derail significant health care reform. Similarly, private, parochial interests in profit succeeded in deregulating the savings-and-loan industry in the early 1980s, resulting in costs to the public treasury and taxpayers of more than a quarter of a trillion dollars. Individuals and groups aspire to rig the system in a way that benefits them, even if their favored policies do not benefit the majority of U.S. residents, frequently resulting in private gain at public expense.

Finally, endless mundane examples can be drawn from everyday life. Dog owners who fail to clean up after their dogs, and men who urinate without picking up the toilet seat, choose individually convenient behavior that adds up to a collective problem. Every person who wears strong perfume into a movie theater may be increasing their own individual sense of well-being, but at a cost to others. Loud music may feel good to the individual playing it in a public park, but others must pay the costs. These problems, endemic to American culture, reflect the logic of the tragedy of the commons, in which individuals seek their private self-interests with too little consideration of the collective consequences. Each can be traced to a one-sided emphasis on the rights, privileges, and freedoms of the individual, along with a corresponding failure to balance them with a consideration of the common good.

Government, the vehicle through which democratic majorities exercise their will, offers one kind of solution to these public problems. If private fishing companies cannot find appropriate solutions on their own to the problem of declining fish stocks, government regulation can force the issue through limits on catches, limits on the types of technologies that can be used to catch fish, or limits on the areas where fishing is allowed. If individual commuters decline to limit their use of automobiles, government can step in, doubling or tripling the price of gasoline to discourage consumption, limiting the scope of street and freeway systems, or even rationing the use of automobiles. The rationing option is less far-fetched than many realize. The cities of Toronto and Portland, Oregon, both limit the use of automobiles in their respective downtowns. As the mayor of Toronto once put it, "Sure, everyone has the right to come downtown, but he doesn't necessarily have the right to bring a ton of metal with him."[19] Legislators can pass new laws requiring higher-efficiency gasoline engines, making cell phone use illegal while driving, and imposing fines on dog owners who fail to clean up their pets' mess. Proponents of government intervention emphasize the ability of government to assemble needed leadership, expertise, and resources, to back policy options with appropriate incentives and punitive measures, and to act forcefully to create change.

This solution of more government intervention and regulation, though sometimes essential and at least partly effective, brings its own set of problems. Among them are the antigovernment attitudes that it fuels as government encroaches ever more deeply into our private lives. Government gets bigger and bigger as we ask it to do more and more for us. Every law that we pass inevitably restricts someone's choice and freedom. This induces resentment against government and increases cynicism about politics and public life. Also, this solution will never fully solve many problems. If we attempt to reduce trash production by charging by the pound, many consumers will pitch theirs into abandoned lots, alleyways, roadside ditches, and neighbors' backyards. This, of course, adds the necessity for increased government oversight and enforcement. The same can be said for regulating the use of cell phones while driving. Enforcing such a law will require adding punitive measures for offenders and increasing the number of police officers to catch the offenders. This punitive response would have to be carried to a bizarre extent in order to address every tragedy of the commons. Imagine, for example, a police force dedicated to apprehending criminal dog owners who did not clean up after their pets. Rather than protecting members of the community against serious crime, they would spend their time busting people for leaving poop on the parkway.

An additional problem with relying on government to solve these problems is that legislators will pass legislation aimed at balancing individual and communal interests only when public opinion favors it or when the problems reach crisis proportions—when it may be too late. Thus far, it appears that public opinion opposes this kind of legislation. Most policy makers are reluctant to impose sacrifice and inconvenience on their constituents. Such action requires exceptional political courage, since the representative who does this runs the risk of getting thrown out of office at the next election. Finally, the propensity in Western culture for turning responsibility for public problems over to government further empowers the state at citizens' expense and undermines citizenship by depriving average citizens of opportunities for political participation. Increasingly, politics emphasizes what government can do for the people and not what citizens can do for themselves.

In order to overcome the multiple public problems captured in the parable of the tragedy of the commons without relying on government coercion, the relation between the individual and the community must be reconsidered in Western culture. There are at least three options when thinking about this relationship between individuals and the community.

First, we can continue to favor the individual while ignoring the community. We can continue to focus on individual rights, privileges, entitlements, and freedoms and live with the consequences. This option may simply postpone a reckoning on issues such as global warming and urban sprawl until the situation gets so bad that we cannot hide any longer. Worse, by that time it may be too late to reverse. A variant of this option is to hope for solutions from science. It is easy to appreciate the allure of technical solutions to political problems. They promise to circumvent stubborn obstacles to agreement and collaboration. They make sacrifice and inconvenience unnecessary. Technical solutions also make debate, negotiation, and compromise—in a word, politics—unnecessary. In the meantime, the problems increase in number and scope.

The second general option for handling the tension between the individual and the community is to reverse the current emphasis. Instead of emphasizing the individual, we could emphasize the community. This would be a mistake. Despite the problems noted above, individual autonomy and freedom represent impressive accomplishments that we should tamper with carefully, if at all. Extreme individualists might respond that no individual choice and freedom should be compromised, ever. This position is unrealistic and dangerous. Freedom and safety are impossible without *some* checks on individual behavior.

Third, we can seek greater balance between the individual and the community. This requires a conception and practice of civic responsibility. Civic responsibilities are what the individual owes to others, to the community, and to government. These include such things as community service, participation in solving shared political problems, local involvement in civic associations, mutual respect, and taking responsibility for future generations. If many of our contemporary problems lie in our overemphasis on the rights and entitlements of individuals, the solution need not entail a complete reversal where the well-being of others and the social whole overrides the rights and entitlements of individuals. Rather, solutions may lie in finding ways to balance the needs and interests of the individual against the needs and interests of others. This option relies on individual political will, not government coercion, nor science and technology. It preserves autonomy and choice while helping overcome the multiple public problems that emerge as tragedies of the commons. Chapter 2 will address various options for pursuing this third strategy of seeking greater balance between the individual and the community. Understanding the historically contingent nature of radical individualism may increase the palatibility of those options.

ROOTS OF RADICAL INDIVIDUALISM

Writing in 1973, sociologist Steven Lukes (1941–) identified two predominant sources of individualism in Western culture: the Judeo-Christian tradition and liberalism.[20] According to Lukes, the New Testament of the Bible clearly sets out the fundamental importance of each person in God's eyes. In Matthew 25:40 we read that, at the time of judgment, God will say, "Truly I tell you, just as you did it to one of the least of these who are members of my family, you did it to me."[21] And in Colossians 3:11, at the coming of Christ, "there is no longer Greek and Jew, circumcised and uncircumcised, barbarian, Scythian, slave and free; but Christ is all and in all!"

Various Judeo-Christian thinkers added impetus to the development of individualism. Lukes mentions two in particular. In disagreeing with the medieval doctrine that all directives from superiors must be obeyed, theologian Thomas Aquinas (1224–1274) pried open a space for individual conscience and choice. According to Aquinas, "Everyone is bound to examine his own actions in the light of the knowledge which he has from God."[22] This gave permission to individuals to follow the "light" of individual conscience, even when it diverged from official and sanctioned rules. Individualism was largely submerged during the Middle Ages, when individuals possessed relatively little autonomy in relation to the dominant authorities of the times. Monarchs were thought to derive their authority directly from God and consequently could not legitimately be challenged. The Catholic Church held dominant power over the lives of all who came under its wide jurisdiction.

Some thinkers nevertheless challenged the dominance of the monarch and the Church, thus helping create space for the individual in Western theory and practice. One such figure was Martin Luther (1482–1546), the German theologian and philosopher who in 1517 set in motion the Protestant Reformation by posting his ninety-five "theses" on a church door, challenging the authority of the Catholic Church. Prior to the Reformation, the Catholic Church exercised near-absolute authority over the spiritual and, sometimes, secular lives of people under its jurisdiction. The Church claimed to offer the only gateway to salvation, in that believers could only gain salvation through good works sanctioned by the Church and through the sacraments administered by the Church. Luther rejected these Catholic teachings, arguing instead that each person can earn salvation on his or her own, simply through faith. According to Luther, our innermost thoughts, feelings, and intentions mattered more to God than our outward actions. A mountain of good deeds and sacraments gained the doer nothing if done reluctantly or motivated by fear of punishment or hope of reward. How do believers gain assurance that they are properly motivated? According to Luther, they gain it in one way only, through "faith in Jesus Christ."[23] And faith depends on the fortitude of each believer, not on performance of the sacraments nor on good works. Consequently, every Christian "should be fully assured that all of us alike are priests, and that we all have the same authority in regard to the word and the sacraments."[24] Naturally, Luther's "priesthood of all believers" shook the foundations of the Catholic Church, undermining its stranglehold by giving to individuals the ability to decide their own spiritual fate. Anyone who believed strongly enough in the Christian God would be guaranteed salvation without going through the Church. This awarded individual believers an independent, autonomous status that they previously lacked.

Radical individualism traces its secular origins primarily to the history of liberalism and central liberal thinkers beginning with Thomas Hobbes (1588–1679) and John Locke (1632–1704). *Liberalism* refers to the dominant political and economic tradition extending from the seventeenth century to the present, marked by an emphasis on the individual, individual rights, freedom as a primary value, and limited, constitutional government. Although in recent times the term has come to be associated solely with left-leaning Democrats, as used by political theorists it encompasses both Democrats and Republicans who generally agree on its major tenets. Two dominant strands of liberalism can be identified today: a neoclassical or neoliberal strand indebted to early thinkers such as Hobbes, Locke, and Adam Smith (1723–1790), and a welfare or "egalitarian" strand indebted to nineteenth-century thinkers such as T. H. Green (1836–1882), L. T. Hobhouse (1864–1929), and John Stuart Mill (1806–1873), whose work straddles the two strands. The two strands diverge primarily over the issues of human nature, the value of equality, and the appropriate size and role for government. While neoclassical thinkers emphasize inherent human characteristics of self-interest, greed, competitiveness, and acquisitiveness, welfare liberals argue that human nature is both perfectible and malleable in response to social environments. Neoclassical liberals value freedom highly and equality relatively lowly. Though they too value freedom highly, welfare liberals also seek greater equality. Some neoclassical liberals such as libertarians continue to emphasize a strictly limited size and role for government, while others seek to use government extensively to promote "conservative" values and programs. Welfare liberals remain relatively more willing to use government to provide social welfare programs aimed at increasing equality and guaranteeing everyone's basic well-being.

British thinker John Locke figured prominently in this liberal tradition, and his name will surface frequently throughout this book. Locke wrote his *First Treatise of Government* (1690) in response to Sir Robert Filmer's (1588–1653) *Patriarcha; or, The Natural Power of Kings* (1680). Filmer defended the divine right of monarchs and the subjects' duty of passive obedience to the monarch. Basing his argument on natural law in general, and specifically the natural authority of parents, he argued that the biblical Adam was the first king, and that the present kings were descended from Adam. Locke's response emphasized the distinction between paternal and political power, the nonabsolute character of paternal power and authority rightfully exercised over children, and the practical impossibility of exactly tracing the lineage from Adam to contemporary rulers. By countering this long-held belief in the divine right of monarchs, Locke followed Luther in helping pry open a space for individual autonomy.

Locke's more famous *Second Treatise of Government* (1690) began from the presumption that individuals, whose inherent characteristics include rational egoism, acquisitiveness, and aggressiveness, exist independently in a state of nature preceding society where they enjoy certain fundamental rights, including and especially the rights of self-preservation, liberty, and private property. These individual rights take precedence over any obligations one might have to others. However, since in this state of nature there exist no civil institutions to protect individuals from others' aggression, individual rights are insecure. He argued that rational, self-interested individuals would conclude from this insecurity of life, liberty, and possession that their individual interests would best be served by crafting a social contract that forms a limited government and brings them out of a state of nature. This limited government exists solely to protect property, defined by Locke to include individuals' "life, liberty and estate."

Liberal political economists such as Adam Smith and David Ricardo (1772–1823) also contributed ideas that fueled the trajectory of individualism. Smith, an eighteenth-century Scottish political economist and the author of *The Wealth of Nations* (1776), argued that the common good results from the unregulated self-interested behavior of individuals. According to Smith, by pursuing our individual interest we "frequently promote . . . that of the society." In words that have become famous, he argued that, as if by an "invisible hand" at work in our lives, an aggregate common good results from individual, self-seeking behavior.[25] Smith's "invisible hand" argument has stood for centuries as a powerful justification for individual self-interest, limited government, and lack of direct concern for public life. His ideas live on most prominently in the ideas of contemporary libertarian economists such as Ludwig von Mises, Milton Friedman, and F. A. Hayek.

Later thinkers, some of them nonliberal, added impetus to the development of individualism. Emphasizing the dignity of each person, Jean-Jacques Rousseau (1712–1778) wrote in the eighteenth century that "man is too noble a being to serve simply as the instrument for others," and Immanuel Kant (1724–1804) wrote that "man, and in general every rational being, exists as an end in himself, not merely as a means for arbitrary use by this or that will."[26] This idea of the dignity of each human found powerful expression in Thomas Jefferson's Declaration of Independence (1776), in Thomas Paine's "Declaration of the Rights of Man" (1791), and in the United Nations' 1948 Universal Declaration of Human Rights, which opens with a "recognition of the inherent dignity and of the equal and inalienable rights of all members of the human family."

Though he concentrated most of his attention on socioeconomic class, Karl Marx (1818–1883) also wrote eloquently about individuals and their development. Marx believed that humans possess a creative potential largely thwarted under capitalism. A person's "own self-realization," he wrote, "exists as an inner necessity, a *need*." Communism, he argued, would enable "a new manifestation of *human* powers and a new enrichment of the human being," when "man appropriates his manifold being in an all-inclusive way, and thus is a whole man." The alienation experienced under capitalism would be replaced by "the wealth of subjective *human* sensibility (a musical ear, an eye which is sensitive to the beauty of form, in short, senses which are capable of human satisfaction and which confirm themselves as human faculties)."[27] Communism would replace the exploited worker who is "reduced to the mere fragment of a man" under capitalism with "the fully-developed individual" for whom "the different social functions he performs are but so many modes of giving free scope to his own natural and acquired powers."[28] These words reveal a thinker passionately committed to the inherent dignity and development of each person.

John Stuart Mill (1806–1873), a nineteenth-century liberal, wrote one of the most powerful defenses of individualism, articulated as a defense of individual freedom. It would not be entirely accurate to portray Mill solely as a radical individualist, since he sometimes advocated ideas and practices inconsistent with radical individualism. Nevertheless, his *On Liberty* (1859) stands as one of the most powerful defenses of the individual and the individual's freedom. In it, Mill addressed the question of whether, and to what degree, we are justified in impinging on the freedom of individuals. Mill's larger aim was to secure the best possible social environment for the full development of each person. He first distinguished between two types of illegitimate use of power over the individual under a system of popular government: majority tyranny and social tyranny. Majority tyranny occurs when the people collectively op-press a smaller part of their number. Social tyranny occurs when "society collectively" oppresses "the separate individuals who compose it." Mill called this latter kind "more formidable than many kinds of political oppressions" since "it leaves fewer means of escape, penetrating much more deeply into the details of life, and enslaving the soul itself."[29] Mill concluded from this that protection against the government alone is insufficient to guarantee individual liberty. Individuals also need protection

> against the tyranny of the prevailing opinion and feeling; against the tendency of society to impose, by other means than civil penalties, its own ideas and practices as rules of conduct on those who dissent from them; to fetter the development, and, if possible, prevent the formation, of any individuality not in harmony with its ways, and compels all characters to fashion themselves upon the model of its own.[30]

Mill admitted the necessity of some restraint of individual action and argued that the key question was "where to place the limit—how to make the fitting adjustment between individual independence and social control."[31] During his time, according to Mill, those limits were derived primarily from social custom and from religious belief rather than from rational principle. He set for himself the task of determining that rational principle and defending it. According to Mill:

> That principle is, that the sole end for which mankind are warranted, individually or collectively, in interfering with the liberty of action of any of their number, is self-protection. That the only purpose for which power can be rightfully exercised over any member of a civilized community, against his will, is to prevent harm to others.[32]

Mill dismissed the idea that interfering with individuals' freedom for their own good was legitimate. He justified the limitation of individual freedom only when the individual's actions affect others. In all other cases, Mill argued, the individual alone is sovereign. This individual sovereignty finds expression, first of all, in "the inward domain of consciousness," in which Mill included "the liberty of expressing and publishing opinions" since, in his view, the holding of an opinion and expressing it are "practically inseparable"; second, the "liberty of tastes and pursuits," which he also called "doing as we like, subject to such consequences as may follow"; and third, the freedom of "combination among individuals . . . for any purpose not involving harm to others."[33]

Having earlier noted his special concern for "social tyranny," Mill addressed himself extensively to the question of liberty of thought and discussion. Under what conditions, if any, are we collectively justified in silencing the opinions of an individual? Mill answered that under no conditions can this be justified. "If all mankind minus one were of one opinion," he wrote, "and only one person were of the contrary opinion, mankind would be no more justified in silencing that one person, than he, if he had the power, would be justified in silencing mankind." As he did throughout On Liberty, Mill offered consequentialist reasons to justify this claim. Silencing an opinion, he argued, "rob[s] the human race. . . . If the opinion is right, they are deprived of the opportunity of exchanging error for truth: if wrong, they lose, what is almost as great a benefit, the clearer perception and livelier impression of truth, produced by its collision with error." Mill then asked if the same level of toleration should be applied to actions. He answered that "no one pretends that actions should be as free as opinions." Even the expression of opinions cannot absolutely be tolerated if they create an "instigation to some mischievous act." Any actions that "do harm to others, may be, and in the more important cases absolutely require to be, controlled by the unfavorable sentiments, and, when needful, by the active interference of mankind."[34]

Mill conceded limited social obligations in return for the protection offered by society. Individuals first of all owe it to others not to injure them or their interests. This is both implied and explicit throughout On Liberty. Noting that inaction can sometimes harm others, Mill also conceded that the individual can be coerced in special cases where inaction might be prejudicial to others. Examples include giving evidence in a court of law, contributing to the common defense, and intervening to save someone's life. These social obligations form a limited conception of duty and obligation to others. Hinting at some of his other, less radically individualist work, Mill denied that On Liberty presented a doctrine of selfishness. His doctrine of individuality required not a diminution but "a great increase of disinterested exertion to promote the good of others."[35] The central point was that this "disinterested exertion" must be voluntary and private rather than coerced through the public power of the state. In explicitly rejecting selfishness as a great motivating force, Mill put a great distance between himself and those contemporaries who today would deny any responsibility for others' welfare.

At the heart of Mill's *On Liberty* is the distinction he made between actions that affect only the individual who performs them and actions that affect others, a distinction he called self- versus other-regarding acts. Mill's conception of individual freedom—what the individual can and cannot do without social restraint—hinges on the validity of this distinction. Unfortunately, the distinction often muddies in practice. For example, it would seem that a person who smokes a cigarette while standing alone in an open field is performing a self-regarding act. However, there are hidden social costs to this act that make it partially other-regarding, including the financial and emotional loss to family members should this person die from lung cancer, the cost to society of addressing the problem of cancer, and the individual's medical costs borne in part socially. Similarly, one could argue that the person who downloads child pornography while alone in a private bedroom performs a self-regarding act. Again, however, the act is also other-regarding in that it helps enable child pornographers' profits, helps perpetuate the exploitation of children by making it profitable, and perhaps contributes to violence against children by objectifying them in the viewer's psyche. Capital flight, the movement of investment capital from one location to another, offers a third example. On the one hand, it may appear that moving capital that one owns is purely self-regarding. However, the social costs are sometimes devastating as aggregate capital flight destroys jobs and destabilizes entire communities.

Mill was not blind to this problem. "No person is an entirely isolated being," he wrote, and therefore "it is impossible for a person to do anything seriously or permanently hurtful to himself, without mischief reaching at least to his near connections, and often far beyond them." Though he acknowledged the difficulty of completely separating self- from other-regarding acts, Mill opted for individual freedom over social obligation. The most he would admit was that individuals whose actions harmed others indirectly became "amenable to moral disapprobation." For Mill the cause of individual freedom took precedence over any real or perceived need for society to control these "merely contingent" injuries. Moreover, if the public were to intervene in these indirectly other-regarding acts, "the odds are that it interferes wrongly."[36]

In contemporary times, libertarians have positioned themselves as the heirs to J. S. Mill and his defense of individual liberty. Their ideas have grown increasingly influential. Contemporary libertarians embrace Mill's *On Liberty* because it "sounds important libertarian themes: that individuals should be free to live as they choose so long as they don't harm others and that the power of government should be strictly limited."[37]

Contemporary libertarian David Boaz (1953–) lists nine "key concepts of libertarianism." Each is related directly or indirectly to the libertarians' advocacy of radical individualism. The first, individualism, means that "libertarians see the individual as the basic unit of social analysis. Only individuals make choices and are responsible for their actions."[38] Libertarians believe, second, in individual rights. These are inherent in human nature; they are not granted by the government nor are they socially created. This concept of individual rights constitutes the limits of the libertarian conception of justice. If an individual's rights to life, liberty, and property are protected, justice is served. Echoing Adam Smith, libertarians believe third that if individuals are left alone, their choices and behavior will ultimately result in a spontaneous social order. Fourth, since libertarians "have a great antipathy to concentrated power," and since "government is a dangerous institution," libertarians follow Mill and other early liberals in advocating a limited government and deny the validity of using government to construct a more just social order. They fear that a "state's attempt to impose order or alter the results of spontaneous processes is likely to produce discoordination, poverty, and social conflict."[39] Noting that each new task taken on by government means less responsibility and purpose for the neighborhood, the community, and the church, libertarians seek to limit the size of government in order to protect the viability of civil society. Fifth, libertarians believe in the rule of law, as long as the law is based primarily on a foundation of individual freedom and rights. Sixth, drawing from classical liberal political economists such as Smith and Ricardo, libertarians embrace free markets as the only economic system consistent with free individuals. While recognizing that free markets will naturally produce inequality, libertarians deny both that free markets are unjust and that government should intervene on behalf of those who fare badly. Seventh, the libertarian principle of the virtue of production means that those who produce wealth should get to keep it. They distinguish crudely between "those who produced wealth and those who took it by force from others." Primarily, it is the government that seizes others' wealth through taxes. Eighth, libertarians believe in a "natural harmony of interests among peaceful, productive people in a just society" that are worked out by free markets and sabotaged by government intervention. Finally, libertarians believe in peace and point out that war "puts more power in the hands of the ruling class."[40]

Critics of libertarianism respond that a sole focus on individuals as the basic unit of analysis overlooks structures of class, race, ethnicity, and gender that harden into structural barriers facing many. While acknowledging the usefulness of individual rights, critics argue that the libertarian absolutist position on property rights sometimes undermines other rights such as the right to food, housing, and health care. Also, in assuming the equal guarantee of rights, libertarians fail to see that some people are systematically deprived of rights on account of factors such as race, gender, and class. Any given social order, spontaneously arisen or not, represents the result of power relations that favor the relatively powerful over the relatively powerless. This, they argue, is precisely why government must intervene, if a just social order is to be achieved, not just a social order.

Many critics share the libertarian antipathy toward concentrated power but insist that the libertarian one-sided emphasis on concentrated political power in the government overlooks the threats posed by concentrated economic power. Libertarians do to the law and to markets what they do to social order and economic relations: they empty them of power and the consequences of power. The law often favors those who possess sufficient power to develop laws and enforce them in their private interests. When combined with the libertarian emphasis on the centrality of property rights, the legal status quo often protects the interests of the wealthy and powerful against the interests of others. Similarly, markets are social institutions saturated with power that coerce as well as enable, ensuring that some market outcomes will be unjust. This coercion calls into question the notion of "free" markets.

Critics fault on several counts the libertarian simplistic distinction between those who produce wealth and those who take it. Libertarians ignore the fact that more than 40 percent of the wealthiest Americans did not produce their wealth, they inherited it; that average Americans produce most of the wealth in America and watch as it is transferred upward, not downward as libertarians think; that Thomas Jefferson, claimed by libertarians as one of their own, specifically endorsed a progressive, redistributive income tax; and that Jefferson and Thomas Paine, also adopted by libertarians as a one of their own, both favored an egalitarian society in general and rough economic equality in particular, goals ruled out by libertarian absolutist commitments to free markets, private property rights, and anti-taxism.

Critics argue that the libertarian claim of a natural harmony of interests can be sustained only by ignoring profound, persistent class structures and conflicts that arise precisely from the operation of so-called free markets, and by ignoring deep-seated class, racial, and gender inequalities and injustices. This claim, and the attribution of blame to government as the source of the problem rather than its solution, represents an ideological commitment rather than actual empirical reality. Finally, critics charge libertarians with failing to note that war and aggression more generally originate from a competition for profit, the motor driving a capitalist political economy.

Mill and the libertarians both emphasize social constraints on individual self-development and argue that leaving the individual alone best ensures self-development. In the following chapter, an alternative proposition will be considered: that any social context *both hampers and supports* individual development. Though in some instances the goal of individual development is best met by leaving the individual alone, in many cases that goal is best met by intervening to provide social support, as Mill himself eventually acknowledged.

Of course, there are other sources and causes of radical individualism in addition to political and economic philosophy. The capitalist political economy that emerged alongside and intertwined with liberalism provides a powerful impetus to radical individualism. The competitive framework of capitalism presumes that individuals compete against each other for profit and gain. The incessant drive to sell products encourages the embrace of private, individualistic consumption. Capitalism also often undermines stable communities representing deep, rich ties among individuals, as thinkers as diverse as Karl Marx and Joseph Schumpeter (1883–1950) argued. According to Marx:

> Constant revolutionizing of production, uninterrupted disturbance of all social conditions, everlasting uncertainty and agitation distinguish the bourgeois epoch from all earlier ones. All fixed, fast-frozen relations, with their train of ancient and venerable prejudices and opinions, are swept away, all new-formed ones become antiquated before they can ossify. All that is solid melts into air, all that is holy is profaned.[41]

According to Schumpeter, a mainstream economist of the early twentieth century and unapologetic defender of capitalism, the dynamic character of capitalism produces constant change that unsettles established traditions and destroys communities. Capitalism, he argued, is "by nature a form or method of economic change and not only never is but never can be stationary." It causes "creative destruction,"[42] meaning that capitalism constantly creates new social forms while destroying traditions, settled communities, and established ties among individuals.

Western cultural forms strongly emphasize and celebrate the individual. Cultural icons such as the Lone Ranger represent the solitary, heroic individual who rides in and saves the day. Individual sports heroes such as Michael Jordan garner celebrity status, even when they play a team sport. Hollywood projects and celebrates this individualistic ethic by portraying the Rambo and Rocky ideals of individuals who triumph over adversity. Popular culture celebrates the "rags-to-riches" success of individuals who start with nothing and, through sheer determination and pluck, achieve great wealth. Their success, according to popular narratives, results from their plainly heroic individual qualities such as independence, talent, and resolve.

Some forms of technology both reflect and promote an emphasis on individualism. Cars represent the promise of individual freedom and mobility. People commute alone, or in small families. Automobiles make suburbs— which are relatively isolating compared to denser urban environments— possible. They make ownership and use of individualized transportation practically essential by undermining commitments to public transportation. One of the latest technological innovations, the Internet, can link disparate people but can also drive them into solitary work and leisure situations. These various material and cultural forms help create and sustain the Western emphasis on the individual.

What options are available for overcoming the problems of radical individualism without undermining individual autonomy? The next chapter attempts to answer this question.

QUESTIONS, PROBLEMS, AND ACTIVITIES

1. Apply the tragedy of the commons to two contemporary issues not covered in this chapter.

2. In what ways do you contribute to global warming? In theory, what changes could you make in your life to decrease your contribution to global warming? What changes would you be willing to make? Answer the same questions in regard to the problem of trash.

3. Design an urban landscape as if there were no cars, only highly developed public transportation systems. What would be the same? Different? Is this situation better or worse, in your opinion?

4. Does our right to personal freedom include a right to bring a ton or more of metal with us wherever we go? Do you think there ought to be limits to the size and character of vehicles on the road? At what point should individual freedom yield to public safety and environmental concerns?

5. Create a survey that gathers information about people's driving preferences and habits. Ask respondents about the general type of vehicle they drive, the mileage per gallon their vehicle gets, their willingness to pay higher gasoline taxes, their likelihood of obeying traffic laws, their use of cell phones while driving, and other questions that interest you. Administer the survey to friends and family and report the results back to the class.

6. Describe and analyze your family home in terms of its private and public features. To what degree does it facilitate private–public interactions?

7. Brainstorm a list of self-regarding acts, and another of other-regarding acts. How well, in your opinion, does J. S. Mill's distinction hold up? Do you think society (or government) can justifiably intervene in the other-regarding acts on your list, but not in the self-regarding acts?

NOTES

1. Lucian W. Pye, "The State and the Individual: An Overview Interpretation," in *The Individual and the State in China*, ed. Brian Hook, 16–42 (Oxford: Clarendon Press, 1996), p. 16.

2. Erica-Irene A. Daes, *Freedom of the Individual under Law* (New York: United Nations, 1990), pp. 25–38.

3. Garrett Hardin, "The Tragedy of the Commons," *Science* 162 (1968): 1243–48.

4. Hal Kane, "Growing Fish in Fields," *World Watch* (September/October 1993): p. 21.

5. Anne Platt McGinn, "Blue Revolution: The Promises and Pitfalls of Fish Farming," *World Watch* (March/April 1998): p. 13.

6. See especially McGinn, "Blue Revolution," on this point.

7. See James Heintz and Nancy Folbre, *The Ultimate Field Guide to the U.S. Economy* (New York: New Press, 2000), p. 151; and the U.S. Energy Information Administration report "Regional Indicators: European Union (EU)," August 1999, available at http://www.eia.doe.gov/emeu/cabs/euro.html.

8. Natural Resources Defense Council, "Global Warming: In Brief: Fact Sheet," http://www.nrdc.org/globalWarming/fcons.asp.

9. John Hart, "Global Warming," *Microsoft Encarta Online Encyclopedia 2005*, http://encarta.msn.com/encyclopedia_761567022/Global_Warming.html.

10. Natural Resources Defense Council, "Global Warming." See also Hart, "Global Warming."

11. Eileen Claussen, "Climate Change: Myths and Realities," presented at the conference "Emission Reductions: Main Street to Wall Street," New York, July 17, 2002, available at http://www.pewclimate.org/press_room/speech_transcripts/transcript_swiss_re.cfm.

12. According to the U.S. Environmental Protection Agency: "Scientists know for certain that human activities are changing the composition of Earth's atmosphere. Increasing levels of greenhouse gases, like carbon dioxide (CO_2), in the atmosphere since pre-industrial times have been well documented. There is no doubt this atmospheric buildup of carbon dioxide and other greenhouse gases is largely the result of human activities. It's well accepted by scientists that greenhouse gases trap heat in the Earth's atmosphere and tend to warm the planet. By increasing the levels of greenhouse gases in the atmosphere, human activities are strengthening Earth's natural greenhouse effect." ("Global Warming—Climate: Uncertainties," http://yosemite.epa.gov/oar/globalwarming.nsf/content/climateuncertainties.html.)

13. Claussen, "Climate Change."

14. Ibid.

15. "Suburban Sprawl Adds Health Concerns, Studies Say," *New York Times*, August 31, 2003.

16. *Consumer Reports*, April 2005, pp. 32–38.

17. T. C. Brown, "New York May Dump Extra Trash on Ohio," *Cleveland Plain Dealer*, July 17, 2000.

18. Donald Redelmeier and Robert Tibshirani, "Association between Cellular-Telephone Calls and Motor Vehicle Collisions," *New England Journal of Medicine* (1997): 453–58.

19. Quoted in Barbara Ward, *The Home of Man* (New York: W. W. Norton, 1976), p. 149.

20. Steven Lukes, *Individualism* (Oxford: Basil Blackwell, 1973), pp. 45–122.

21. Biblical quotations use the New Revised Standard Version.

22. Lukes, *Individualism*, p. 52.

23. Martin Luther, "Preface to the Epistle of St. Paul to the Romans" [1522], in *Martin Luther: Selections from His Writings*, ed. John Dillenberger (Garden City, NY: Anchor Books, 1961), p. 21.

24. Martin Luther, "The Pagan Servitude of the Church" [1520], in Dillenberger, *Martin Luther*, p. 349.

25. Adam Smith, *The Wealth of Nations* (1776; New York: Random House, 1937), p. 423.

26. Jean-Jacques Rousseau, *Julie, ou la Nouvelle Héloise*, V, letter 2, ed. D. Mornet (1761; Paris: Hachette, 1925), vol. 4, p. 22; Immanuel Kant, *The Moral Law*, trans. and ed. H. J. Paton, 3rd ed. (1785; London: Hutchinson, 1956), pp. 95–96.

27. Karl Marx, *Economic and Philosophical Manuscripts of 1844* [1844], in *Karl Marx: Early Writings*, trans. and ed. T. B. Bottomore (New York: McGraw-Hill, 1963), pp. 165, 168, 159, 161; emphasis in original.

28. Karl Marx, *Capital*, vol. 1 (1867; Moscow: Progress Publishers, 1954), chap. 15, sec. 9, p. 488.

29. J. S. Mill, *On Liberty* [1859], in *Mill: A Norton Critical Edition*, ed. Alan Ryan (New York: W. W. Norton, 1997), p. 44.

30. Ibid.

31. Ibid.

32. Ibid., p. 48.

33. Ibid., p. 50.

34. Ibid., pp. 53, 84.

35. Ibid., p. 100.

36. Ibid., pp. 103–6.

37. David Boaz, ed., *The Libertarian Reader: Classic and Contemporary Readings from Lao-Tzu to Milton Friedman* (New York: Free Press, 1997), p. 25.

38. David Boaz, *Libertarianism: A Primer* (New York: Free Press, 1997), p. 16.

39. Boaz, *Libertarian Reader*, pp. 17, 205.

40. Boaz, *Libertarianism*, p. 18.

41. Karl Marx, *The Communist Manifesto*, ed. Frederic L. Bender (1848; New York: W. W. Norton, 1988), p. 58.

42. Joseph Schumpeter, *Capitalism, Socialism, and Democracy* (1942; repr., New York: Harper & Row, 1950), pp. 68, 81.

2

Democratic Community

Addressing the tragedies of the commons without resorting to extensive government coercion requires that people be willing and able to consider common, public interests as well as their own private interests. Is this asking too much of average citizens? The answer depends very much on one's view of human nature. How we think about human nature determines the range of options that we can consider politically. Ideally, theory and practice will be built on a foundation compatible with human nature, however conceived. This topic of human nature has two central dimensions. First, what are the specific characteristics that comprise human nature? Second, are these characteristics inherent, or are they the result of social learning?

The dominant strain of thinking in America about human nature emerged within the same two traditions of Judeo-Christianity and liberalism from which the tradition of radical individualism emerged. As we saw above, the Judeo-Christian tradition emphasized the fundamental importance of each individual. However, it emphasized a profoundly imperfect individual. Beginning with the biblical story of the fall of Adam and Eve, Judeo-Christianity has emphasized human imperfection and proneness to sin. Yet, the Judeo-Christian tradition has also emphasized the ability of most individuals to choose and act in accordance with godly principles.

The dominant early liberal thinkers, epitomized by Thomas Hobbes (1588–1679) and John Locke (1632–1704), emphasized a view of human nature that persists into the present among neoclassical liberals. Writing at a time of great instability and uncertainty in British history during and at the end of the Thirty Years' War, Hobbes described human nature in profoundly unflattering terms. Calling self-preservation the fundamental "right of nature," he concluded that humans act solely on the basis of self-interest in order to preserve their life and possessions. "Of the voluntary acts of every man," he argued, "the object is some *Good to himselfe*." Inevitably, he believed, the interests of one person will collide with the interests of another. When this happens, they "become enemies . . . [and] endeavour to destroy, or subdue one another." Power—the more the better in order to stay ahead of adversaries—offers the means to prevail in these conflicts. This results in "a perpetuall and restlesse desire of Power after power, that ceaseth onely in Death." Putting these together, Hobbes asserted that humans are primarily driven by self-interest, fear, competitiveness, and hunger for power.

Approximately forty years later, Locke adopted slightly less pessimistic assumptions about human nature, but nevertheless retained the emphasis on characteristics such as self-interest, aggressiveness, competitiveness, and acquisitiveness. However, he denied Hobbes's assertion that these traits led to a "Warre of every one against every one" in which life for humans would be "solitary, poore, nasty, brutish, and short."[1]

Hobbes and Locke illustrate the importance of assumptions about human nature in political philosophy. Having emphasized such unsavory, aggressive, and violent human traits, and fearful of a return to a dangerous and unsettled state of nature made likely by such humans, Hobbes notoriously awarded the *Leviathan* ruler nearly absolute power. Having adopted a less pessimistic view of human nature, Locke feared a return to the state of nature less than Hobbes and so created a limited government that could be changed.

The nineteenth-century utilitarian liberals Jeremy Bentham (1748–1832) and James Mill (1773–1836) proposed a variation on the liberal theme of rational egoism. According to Bentham and Mill, individuals choose and act in accordance with their perception of potential gains to their own "utility." Given the vagueness of this concept of utility, it quickly became synonymous with pleasure and later with wealth as the surest—or, anyway, the most easily quantified and measured—route to pleasure. Utilitarian liberalism thus reaffirmed the early liberals' emphasis on the self-interested pursuit of individual gain, adding wealth as the primary motivation for individual striving.

John Stuart Mill (1806–1873), son of James Mill, distanced himself from this aspect of utilitarian liberalism. He denied his predecessors' belief in the universal selfishness of individuals and viewed humans instead as strivers and developers. Whatever their biological legacy, humans are capable of exerting themselves toward socially desirable ends and of developing their characters progressively. Unlike his father and Bentham, he also refused to equate happiness with material wealth. He believed that individuals could critically distinguish between different kinds of pleasures, and he thought that precedence should be given to those pleasures that progressively develop human character both intellectually and morally.

Many thinkers in the history of political philosophy leaned more toward J. S. Mill's view than toward the static, pessimistic views of Hobbes, Locke, and the early utilitarians. Participatory democrats such as Jean-Jacques Rousseau (1712–1778) and Thomas Jefferson (1743–1826), for example, argued that, if humans are sometimes inclined toward self-interest, they are also capable of considering the interests of others and the common good.

Today, if the world offers extensive evidence of selfishness, competitiveness, greed, and materialism, it also offers testimony of selflessness, cooperation, generosity, and sacrifice. If people are only selfish, how do we make sense of Mother Teresa, blood bank donations, and volunteerism? If people are only greedy, how do we explain widespread philanthropy and charitable giving? If people are only competitive, how do you explain a community's successful creation, out of the cooperative efforts of hundreds of community members, of a children's park? Some may respond that selfishness underlies acts of apparent selflessness in that they make the person doing them feel good; that generosity masks less noble interests such as tax write-offs and currying favorable public relations; and that apparent cooperation originates in a competitive instinct to keep up with the neighbors. If this is true, we should strike words such as *love* and *altruism* from our lexicon. *Love*, in the sense of loving one's child, entails a level of other-regarding sentiment that does not exist if all human motivation can be reduced to self-interest. Similarly, the word *altruism* must go since it denotes behavior that does not entail a calculation of self-interest. The insistence by some on a one-sided view of human nature emphasizing selfishness, greed, competitiveness, and acquisitiveness reflects an ideological stance more than an empirical reality. Their insistence serves to justify and legitimize selfish, greedy, competitive, and acquisitive behavior.

So far, this discussion of human nature has presumed that attributes apply equally to men and women. In theory and practice, they do not. Americans have always held different expectations and assumptions about the attributes of girls and boys, women and men. During the mid-nineteenth century, for example, opponents of female suffrage argued that women were inferior to men in a variety of ways, that women were too frail for the aggressive world of male politics, that women were less interested in politics than men, and that women's place was in the home. Contemporary Americans continue to hold quite different expectations of men and women, based partly on different presumptions about their different natures. A Gallup poll taken in December 2000 showed that most Americans believe that men are more aggressive, courageous, and easygoing than women, and that women are more emotional, talkative, intelligent, patient, creative, and affectionate than men.[2]

Men and women who defy traditional expectations of masculinity and femininity, respectively, may face ridicule and contempt. In recent decades some of these gender codes have been challenged and changed. Compared to thirty years ago, many more girls and women today participate in athletics. Today women find it more acceptable to develop their bodies as athletes, to compete with the same level of effort and commitment as men, and to pursue careers that once admitted only men. Similarly, more men today choose the role of househusband and feel comfortable adopting traits such as sensitivity and nurturing that once applied exclusively to women. Nevertheless, gender codes remain powerful determinants of identity and behavior, limiting the choices of both women and men.

Are human characteristics biologically determined, or are they learned in response to a particular environment? If we use the empirical record as our guide, it appears that humans are capable of both profound evil and saintly good. History offers many examples of both boundless greed and profound generosity, of cutthroat competition and public-spirited cooperation, of insatiable acquisitiveness and selfless asceticism. The variations in traits across history and culture suggest that human nature is at least partly a result of social learning. If this is true, we should exercise caution in asserting that humans are hard-wired for any particular kind of behavior. While humans may be born with a set of innate potentialities, how those potentialities develop will depend substantially on the social and cultural environment. Human nature is both diverse and malleable. It represents a project, a challenge to be won.

RECOGNIZING INTERDEPENDENCE, CHOOSING SOLIDARITY

If individuals are to address their common interests, they must begin from an understanding of how their fates are intertwined with others'. Efforts to isolate oneself from others are doomed to failure when some of our most pressing public problems, such as global warming, public health crises, and overcrowded freeways, cannot be avoided. Individuals must recognize that their behavior affects others, just as the choices and actions of others affect them.

An early Euro-American political thinker, the Puritan John Winthrop (1588–1649), offered one model for understanding the interdependent relations among individuals. In his essay "A Modell of Christian Charity," written as a sermon in 1630, he envisioned a tightly knit community in the New World in which individuals were related to each other and to the community in the same way that different body parts are related to each other and the human body as a whole. According to Winthrop:

> There is noe body but consistes of partes and that which knitts these partes together giues the body its perfeccion, because it makes each parte soe contiguous to other as thereby they doe mutually participate with eache other, both in strengthe and infirmity in pleasure and paine.

Winthrop used this analogy to justify Christian charity. Different individuals, like the different parts of the body, are linked in a system of mutual interdependence. What happens to one part will affect the other parts. One part's suffering diminishes other parts and the community as a whole. In Winthrop's words:

> All the partes of this body being thus vnited are made soe contiguous in a speciall relacion as they must needes partake of each others strength and infirmity, joy, and sorrowe, weale and woe. . . . If one member suffers all suffer with it, if one be in honour, all reioyce with it.

In the same way that an athlete cannot perform at peak form if one leg is ailing, a people cannot achieve their full potential if even one individual is allowed to suffer.

Furthermore, each individual prospers best when situated within a supportive community. The different individuals in a community can be separated only artificially, according to Winthrop. We must think of each part in relation to each other and to the whole. Winthrop argued that recognition of this mutual interdependency would knit different individuals together in common commitment to each other and to the community as a whole. Winthrop's ideal community was bound together by the "ligaments" of Christian love that, he believed, perfects the community. "When Christ comes," he wrote, "and by his spirit and loue knitts all these partes to himselfe and each to other, it become the most perfect and best proportioned body in the world."

Beginning with this model of the relation between individuals and the community positioned Winthrop to argue persuasively for Christian charity. If our well-being is intertwined with others', then the rich ignore a responsibility to the poor at their own peril. Christian charity helps maintain order and peace since, without it, "the poore, and dispised rise vpp against theire superiours, and shake off theire yoake."[3] If individuals thought of themselves as mutually interdependent, they would be more likely to respond to the needs of others, especially the less fortunate. Similarly, if individuals saw their lives connected to others' by common interests, outcomes, and fates, it is more likely that they would weigh them when making individual choices.

On the other hand, Winthrop sacrificed much individual freedom to this vision. He and most other members of the Puritan communities made little effort to accommodate significant differences of identity, belief, and behavior. Their religious convictions and the sectarian Christian code to which they adhered made accommodation impossible. Members of the community were required to adhere to this code, and dissenters such as Roger Williams were either persecuted or simply expelled from the community. Although Winthrop's vision provides a useful starting point, we should be cautious about adopting it in its entirety in the context of a diverse, heterogeneous culture where individual freedom ranks highly in value. Winthrop's failure to preserve extensive individual freedom while recognizing and acting upon mutual interdependence does not mean that it cannot be done.

In contemporary times, Pope John Paul II (1920–2005) echoed Winthrop's theme of interdependence and used a combination of practical and moral arguments similar to Winthrop's to advocate steps to care for the poor and marginalized. For practical reasons, according to the pope, we must recognize the fact of our "radical interdependence," one that now extends across nation-state boundaries. The recognition of interdependence, while essential, must be augmented by an active choice and "a concrete commitment." John Paul II characterized this active concrete commitment as solidarity. While interdependence simply reflects an empirical reality and requires no act of will, solidarity requires precisely an act of will. While we simply recognize interdependence, we choose or reject solidarity. Choosing solidarity means that we intentionally and willfully commit to a "common destiny which is to be constructed together."[4] We stand with others, affirming our common humanity and voluntarily linking our fates. We accept reciprocal responsibility for our common welfare.

Solidarity has a moral as well as practical basis, according to the pope, tied to the basic moral sameness of all humans. We ought to stand together simply because we are fellow humans made equally in God's image. The pope particularly advocated solidarity with those who are most in need. As he put it, "The church feels called to take her stand beside the poor." John Paul II saw redistribution from rich to poor as the practical embodiment of solidarity. Solidarity, he argued, requires active choice and an "effective political will." He chided affluent individuals and countries for showing too little political will for redistribution. "Solidarity," according to the pope, "demands a readiness to accept the sacrifices necessary for the good of the whole world community" and making inconvenient lifestyle changes if necessary.[5]

The French political philosopher and activist Albert Camus (1913–1960) made similar, but wholly secular, arguments about interdependence and solidarity in his novel *The Plague* (1947), a story about a pestilence that occurred unexpectedly in the city of Oran, Algeria. The pestilence appeared with no apparent cause, ran a course that defied control, and disappeared just as mysteriously. The plague affected everyone, without regard to status. It honored no special classes and no elites. It gave no special dispensations and no privileges. The plague "was no respecter of persons and under its despotic rule everyone, from the warden down to the humblest delinquent, was under sentence." In responding to the plague, city officials placed the entire city of Oran under quarantine, exiling the townspeople from friends, lovers, and family members outside the city.

How we respond to the plague was of crucial importance for Camus. We can try to escape our shared fate, to ignore it, to seek refuge in God, or to seek distractions in play and romantic love—or we can each commit to doing what we can to ease the suffering. While refusing to condemn any of these options,

Camus embraced the last option, the option of solidarity. His main characters all chose this option of solidarity and joined in attempts to address the plague collectively. Dr. Rieux, the narrator, chose solidarity by focusing quietly on his duty. "The thing was to do your job as it should be done," he said simply. "There are sick people and they need curing. . . . What's wanted now is to make them well. I defend them as best I can, that's all." His friend Tarrou chose solidarity by helping organize sanitary squads to dispose of the corpses. The quiet, humble Grand volunteered to help with the accounting of the plague's victims. Even Rambert, an outsider exiled in Oran by the plague, eventually opted for solidarity over escape. In the early and middle stages of the plague, Rambert felt a desperate desire to escape in order to reunite with his lover. Though he eventually found a means of escape, he decided not to take it, saying that "he'd thought it over very carefully. . . . If he went away, he would feel ashamed of himself. . . . It may be shameful to be happy by oneself." He initially felt like an outsider with no stake in the plague other than escaping it, but changed his mind. "Until now," he said, "I always felt a stranger in this town, and that I'd no concern with you people. But now that I've seen what I have seen, I know that I belong here whether I want it or not. This business is everybody's business."

Though he did not condemn those who attempted to escape, Camus believed that escape was impossible. Speaking through Dr. Rieux, he argued that the plague is "the concern of all. . . . No one on earth is free from it" and no one can escape it. In experiencing the plague and attempting to grapple with it, the townspeople of Oran came to the realization that their fates were interlinked. As one character, Tarrou, said in attempting to console the manager of a luxury hotel: "But, you know, everybody's in the same boat." Government could not by itself solve the problem of pestilence. Nor could turning to God solve the plague, though doing so might offer meaning and hope to believers. Having ruled out government and God, Camus embraced human commitment to each other and to collective struggle against pestilence, with no guarantees of success or even of relief.[6]

On the one hand, Camus presents a bleak story of pestilence, exile, random injustice, suffering, and eventual death. On the other hand, his positive act of choosing solidarity affirms a life of commitment. With no final answers to the problems of everyday existence and to the mystery of life itself, Camus believed that we could at least work together with others to root out suffering. It is in the end a deeply life-affirming choice: to throw your lot in with others and to commit to working against plague wherever we find it. Like the quietly and humbly courageous Grand, according to Camus, we can each do our part. We can recognize and acknowledge that our fate is intertwined with others and commit to working toward our common good, which is inseparable from our individual well-being.

SELF-INTEREST RIGHTLY UNDERSTOOD

It may appear that attention to the common good requires altruism and the rejection of self-interests. However, altruism is unnecessary and self-interest legitimate. The challenge is to find ways of addressing shared, public interests without ignoring or rejecting private self-interests. Alexis de Tocqueville (1805–1859) described one such way. Tocqueville, a Frenchman traveling in the United States during the 1830s and 1840s, recorded his observations about American politics and culture. He observed that Americans recognized their interdependence and reacted pragmatically to it by balancing and trading self-interests against the interests of others. He called this "self-interest rightly understood." Tocqueville, like many other political thinkers of his time, feared that the equality and individualism entailed in a democracy would eventually lead to ruin as individuals pursued private goals irrespective of public needs. In attempting to explain why this was not happening in mid-nineteenth-century America, Tocqueville argued that U.S. citizens found it convenient to "sacrifice some . . . private interests to save the rest" and this muted the negative consequences of individualism. If we refuse to sacrifice some of our interests, he argued, we may fail to achieve any of them. As Tocqueville put it, "We want to save everything, and often we lose it all."

According to Tocqueville, this sacrifice had less to do with virtue than with recognition of the need to balance some individual claims against the claims of others. The result in practice was the same: Americans, he believed, found it prudent to be good in that being good—considering the needs and interests of others as well as the self—ensured that their own interests would be addressed. Americans, wrote Tocqueville,

> do not deny that every man may follow his own interest, but they endeavor to
> prove that it is the interest of every man to be virtuous. . . . American moralists
> do not profess that men ought to sacrifice themselves for their fellow creatures

because it is noble to make such sacrifices, but they boldly aver that such sacrifices are as necessary to him who imposes them upon himself as to him for whose sake they are made.

Self-interest rightly understood, or what Tocqueville also called enlightened self-love, "constantly prompts them to assist one another and inclines them willingly to sacrifice a portion of their time and property to the welfare of the state."[7] Americans whom he observed were motivated not by altruism, but by a form of political prudence in which they recognized the legitimacy of others' claims and were willing to balance their own claims against the claims of others in order to achieve their ends.

The American pragmatic philosopher John Dewey (1859–1952) echoed Tocqueville's words nearly a century later. In a diverse democracy, he argued, citizens must learn to "adjust" their diverse interests and claims. They must each "refer [their] own action to that of others, and to consider the action of others to give point and direction to [their] own." Dewey here emphasized Tocqueville's point that the claims of others must be acknowledged and taken into consideration when choosing and acting. Each citizen must view "the consequences of his own acts as having a bearing upon what others are doing and take into account the consequences of their behavior upon himself."[8] Dewey believed that participating in democratic life requires that citizens think and act in terms not only of the self but also in terms of the needs, interests, and aims of others. Like Tocqueville's "self-interest rightly understood," this required not altruism but a pragmatic recognition of interdependency and of the legitimacy of competing and contradictory claims.

CIVIC VIRTUE

The ancient Greeks—and many subsequent political theorists, including some members of the American founding generation—believed that a healthy public life requires civic virtue. *Civic virtue* means attention and commitment to the common good, as well as to individual, private ends. Like John Winthrop's understanding of interdependence, civic virtue presumes that individual and collective well-being are linked. Virtuous citizens heed the common good under the assumption that their well-being is inseparable from the well-being of others.

Proponents of civic virtue do not, like Adam Smith (1723–1790) and his "invisible hand," assume that the common good will automatically emerge as the aggregation of individual self-interests. Such an idea would have been nonsensical to the ancient Greeks, who believed to the contrary that the common good would not emerge at all if citizens failed to create it and sustain it through acts of political will. Unlike self-interest "rightly understood," civic virtue entails no calculation of prudence aimed at satisfying individual interests by trading or weighing them against others' needs and interests. It involves doing the right thing just because it is the right thing, for the collective and individual good. Virtuous citizens vote, not simply in order to protect private interests but because voting helps sustain necessary public life in a representative democracy. Virtuous citizens recycle, even though they derive no immediate personal gain from the effort, to maintain the long-term viability of our physical and social environments. A virtuous citizen might also accept a higher tax burden in order to pay down the national debt and avoid passing along the burden to future generations. And a virtuous citizen might use public transportation because it benefits the community, even if the choice brings less comfort and convenience than private transportation.

Civic virtue played a central role in the history of civic republicanism, a political tradition with roots in ancient Greece and the Roman republic that has influenced political theorists and practitioners up to the present. Niccolò Machiavelli (1469–1527), a fifteenth- and early sixteenth-century Florentine public servant and political theorist, was among them. Most people today associate Machiavelli with a cold, prudent, and cynical use of power to achieve political ends. This was the Machiavelli of *The Prince* (1513), a short book analyzing power politics of his time. However, Machiavelli also wrote *The Discourses* (1513–17), a wide-ranging analysis of the rise and decline of the Roman empire. In it, he theorized the requirements of republican politics, in which he prominently included civic virtue.

According to Machiavelli, "Good habits of the people require good laws to support them," but so too do laws "need good habits on the part of the people.... To give life and vigor to those laws requires a virtuous citizen, who will courageously aid in their execution against the power of those who transgress them." Republican self-government can be maintained, Machiavelli argued, only so long as the citizens are uncorrupted by private and parochial aims that detract from the public good. Of the Roman "mode of making the laws," he wrote:

> At first a Tribune or any other citizen had the right to propose any law, and every citizen could speak in favor or against it before its final adoption. This system was very good so long as the citizens were uncorrupted, for it is always well in a state that every one may propose what he deems for the public good; and it was equally well that every one should be allowed to express his opinion in relation to it, so that the people, having heard both sides, may decide in favor of the best. But *when the citizens had become corrupt, this system became the worst possible, for then only the powerful proposed laws, not for the common good and the liberty of all, but for the increase of their own power.*[9]

When citizens pass laws promoting private rather than public interests, according to Machiavelli, civic virtue has been lost, and this threatens republican government. Machiavelli argued that the erosion of civic virtue partly explains the fall of the Roman republic.

This republican tradition continued in the political thought of the Englishman James Harrington (1611–1677) and the Frenchman Jean-Jacques Rousseau. Harrington and Rousseau agreed with Machiavelli that good institutions and laws are important but alone are insufficient for the survival of republican self-government. A republican character in each citizen is also essential, and paramount in this character is civic virtue. In *The Commonwealth of Oceana* (1656), Harrington argued that, in a sound republic, citizens should "shake off that inclination" toward self-interest and instead "take up that which regards the common good or interest." This, he says, is "to no more end, than to persuade every man in a popular government not to carve himself of that which he desires most, but to be mannerly at the public table, and give the best from himself to decency and the common interest."[10] This echoes Machiavelli's insistence on the necessity of public spiritedness in a healthy republic.

Rousseau, too, believed in the necessity of civic virtue and a republican character. He argued that "every man is virtuous when his particular will is wholly in conformity with the general will." The general will represents the common good enacted into law. In his *Discourse on Political Economy* (1755), Rousseau argued that "the mainstay of public authority lies in the hearts of the citizens, and . . . nothing can take the place of moral habits in the maintenance of the government." These moral habits form a republican character necessary for making good laws, which by definition are laws in accordance with the general will. Like Machiavelli, Rousseau pointed out that good laws are necessary but not sufficient. Civic virtue entails duty, specifically the duty to obey the laws that advance the common good. Rousseau added that good leaders can sometimes overcome the deficit of virtue; however, like good laws, good leaders are second best because "the longer virtue reigns, the less need there is for [leaders'] talents."

Citizens who think primarily or entirely in terms of their individual interests will frequently have an incentive to bend or break the laws. To the degree that citizens seek to evade the law, or obey the law only insofar as they must in order to avoid punishment, the state must grow in size and scope in order to enforce compliance. Machiavelli, Harrington, and Rousseau each recognized this and pointed out that virtuous citizens will obey just laws because they see the value of the laws and their necessity in promoting a common good. In a republic where civic virtue is widespread, citizens thus enjoy more freedom in that they require less government coercion. Rousseau drew this connection between virtue and freedom explicitly. If you sacrifice virtue, he argued, "the voice of duty no longer speaks in men's hearts, and leaders are forced to substitute the cry of terror. . . . The homeland cannot subsist without liberty, nor liberty without virtue."[11] Virtuous citizens align their particular wills with the general will and embrace the laws that embody the general will. This maintains their liberty because they simply obey laws that they helped create and because a coercive state is unnecessary when citizens voluntarily obey the laws. Rousseau, Machiavelli, and Harrington all added the caveat that the laws must be just if average citizens are to heed them. And for all three, a just law is one that promotes the common good rather than the parochial good of privileged elites.

The American Founders inherited this republican tradition, with its emphasis on civic virtue. However, they also were immersed in the emerging tradition of liberalism, with its emphasis on self-interest. Most of the Founders considered themselves republicans and insisted that they were creating a republican form of government. However, they disagreed over the meaning of republicanism, resulting in a rough split between Federalists such as Alexander Hamilton (1755–1804), James Madison (1751–1836), John Jay (1745–1829), and John Adams (1735–1826) and Anti-Federalists such as Patrick Henry (1736–1799), Samuel Bryan (1756–1837), James Winthrop (1752–1821), and Robert Yates (1738–1801). Federalists, who abandoned the earlier commitment to civic virtue and attempted to rely entirely on institutions and laws, ultimately won this debate. While the Anti-Federalists insisted that republican government required civic virtue, the Federalists assumed the worst about human nature and opted instead to design institutions that would "supply in some degree the defect" of human character.[12]

Both sides agreed on the desirability of civic virtue, but the Federalists doubted that average citizens were capable of it. Hamilton, for example, charged that the "turbulent and changing" masses "seldom judge or determine right." Gouverneur Morris (1752–1816), a wealthy Federalist from Pennsylvania, went beyond Hamilton in expressing disdain for average people, saying that "the mob begin to think and reason. Poor reptiles! . . . They bask in the sun, and ere noon they will bite, depend upon it." From Jeremy Belknap (1744–1798), a New England clergyman, we read, "Let it stand as a principle that government originates from the people; but let the people be taught . . . that they are not able to govern themselves."[13] Madison shared his Federalist colleagues' suspicion of human nature and their desire to design institutional remedies for it. "If men were angels," he argued, "no government would be necessary."[14] Properly designed institutions, he believed, would counter the weight of self-interest.

The Federalists' formula of relying on institutional mechanisms still defines the nature of American politics. Their presumption of competitive self-interest without virtue found institutional permanence in the U.S. Constitution in the two design principles of separation of powers and checks and balances. The Federalists hoped that the separation of powers into three branches of government, as well as between the state and national governments, would prevent the centralization of power. They intended the numerous checks and balances they wrote into the Constitution to discourage irresponsible exercises of power within the different institutions of government by erecting rival institutional obstacles. Madison and the other Federalists hoped that these institutional mechanisms would make it difficult for ambitious individuals to distort policy on behalf of private and parochial interests.

Madison did not completely give up on the idea of virtue, however. He believed that elections would allow average citizens—while not necessarily virtuous themselves—to elect virtuous leaders, and to keep them virtuous. "The aim of every political constitution," he argued, "is, or ought to be, first to obtain for rulers men who possess most wisdom to discern, and most virtue to pursue, the common good of the society; and in the next place, to take the most effectual precautions for keeping them virtuous whilst they continue to hold their public trust."[15] According to Madison, elections accomplish this by making leaders accountable at regular intervals to voters.

Unlike the Federalists, the Anti-Federalists remained faithful to the republican emphasis on civic virtue. Anti-Federalist Samuel Bryan argued that "a republican, or free government, can only exist where the body of the people are virtuous."[16] Though in some ways Jefferson straddled both sides of the Federalist–Anti-Federalist split, on the issue of civic virtue he firmly supported the Anti-Federalist position. Jefferson acknowledged the importance of good institutions, but insisted also on the importance of virtue. He believed that we could rely on common citizens to participate responsibly in self-government only "as long as [they] remain virtuous." Jefferson did not share the Federalists' distrust of common people and human nature. "I am not among those who fear the people," he wrote. According to Jefferson, we should "educate and inform the whole mass of the people. Enable them to see that it is their interest to preserve peace and order, and they will preserve them. . . . They are the only sure reliance for the preservation of our liberty. . . . This reliance cannot deceive us, as long as we remain virtuous."[17]

Are average citizens capable of civic virtue? A fair appraisal of contemporary citizenship could easily lead one to conclude that the Federalists were right about human nature and to condone their abandonment of civic virtue. Recent events and trends in American politics provide ample evidence to suggest that average citizens are not capable of responsible self-government. Many citizens do not vote and, when they do, they cast their votes based on single issues or superficial factors such as the telegenic quality of candidates. Most voters appear inclined to punish politicians who support necessary but politically unpopular policies by voting them out of office.

Yet, in times of national emergencies Americans at least temporarily show themselves willing and able to set aside some of their personal needs and interests in order to maintain the common good. Americans' enthusiastic response to the call for blood donations after the September 11, 2001, terrorist attacks on the World Trade Center and Pentagon suggested a capacity for civic virtue. More mundanely, millions of average citizens routinely recycle, even though they gain no direct benefits from it. Apart from specific emergencies, millions of Americans routinely donate blood. Almost all American drivers pull to the side of the road when an ambulance approaches. Neighbors often help each other out with child care and household projects and offer food and comfort to families grieving a death. These mundane examples suggest an ability and willingness to engage in actions that benefit the common good, even when they return few if any direct benefits to the doer. In short, the Federalist Founders may have given up too quickly on average Americans.

DEMOCRATIC COMMUNITY

In recent decades, the theory and practice of democratic community has emerged as a prominent theme in political philosophy. Community defines our shared life. It refers to the things we have in common as individuals in society. The specific character of commonalities of interest, awareness, memory, history, identity, and commitment defines the nature of the community. Members of a specifically political community share political interests. These can be either procedural or substantive, or both. For example, a shared interest in compromise and discussion characterizes members of a democratic community. Similarly, members of a democratic community share an interest in maximizing freedom and equality for themselves.

Proponents of democratic community believe that it offers a foundation for public problem solving and a social milieu conducive to democratic character development. Both of these ways of conceptualizing community can be found in the work of John Dewey. Dewey's *The Public and Its Problems* (1927) presented his analysis of community as a foundation for public problem solving. Although Dewey did not use the language of the tragedy of the commons, his analysis of the genesis of public problems closely resembled it. He viewed public problems in terms of the consequences of individual behavior and the failure to account for those consequences. Dewey attributed responsibility for addressing public problems not solely to government officials but to all citizens working in democratic communities that provide the necessary conceptual and practical framework.

Dewey began by noting that human behavior has consequences, some of them experienced directly in intimate associations and some experienced indirectly. He defined a public as "all those who are affected by the indirect consequences of transactions to such an extent that it is deemed necessary to have those consequences systematically cared for." This public requires some form of organization in order to systematically address that common interest. In contemporary times, members accomplish this end through the formation of a state. Dewey argued that this process of state formation had been undermined by a "machine age" that had so enormously complicated and expanded indirect consequences that the public could not find itself, leaving a host of unidentified and uncontrolled indirect consequences. A new form of organization was required to account for them. In the absence of this new form of organization, the public remained scattered, fractured, and bewildered, unable to recognize and form itself and unable to act collectively to address common concerns and solve its problems.

Dewey posed community as a solution to this problem of a disorganized, bewildered public. He argued that society must be transformed into a "great community" that would enable citizens to recognize themselves as members of a collective body with mutual interests and would provide a social basis supporting collective political action to address those mutual interests.

What are the distinguishing commonalities of this great community? First, Dewey presumed that even in an extended republic citizens share certain interests generated by the indirect consequences of human behavior. However, the presence of common interests by themselves only marks the fact of interdependence. To act on them, citizens must, second, be aware of their common interests and understand them. To achieve mutual awareness and understanding of each other and of shared interests, Dewey argued, the indirect consequences of social experience must be disseminated via various forms of communication. He advocated democratization of the major means of communication to ensure their conformity to public, rather than private, ends and goals. Dewey advocated more open and democratic media, oriented more to public-interested dissemination of knowledge and information and less to the bottom line.

Third, Dewey argued that a common commitment is required to form and sustain a great community. This commitment has two dimensions. On the one hand, he believed that commitment to the community itself is required in the form of "an energetic desire and effort to sustain it in being just because it is a good shared by all." Community is a "good shared by all" because it enables public problem solving and because it represented for Dewey an ideal form of social life in which "fraternity, liberty and equality" come to full fruition.[18] On the other hand, a specifically democratic community also requires commitment to democratic principles, values, and methods. Dewey's list emphasized democratic methods of discussion, debate, and inquiry; democratic principles such as freedom and equality; and the democratic value of the growth and development of every person.

Finally, Dewey's great community integrated common goals associated with common interests and pressing public problems. Before citizens could hope to act collectively on their interests, they must be translated into common aims and purposes. Mutual concerns and interests would be forged into plans for action. Although Dewey focused most of his discussion of the problems of public life on developing a great community, he also viewed local, neighborly communities as important for revitalizing the public life of problem solving that he envisioned. In local communities, average citizens actually participate in problem solving and also learn the arts of democratic citizenship.

Dewey's second major justification for democratic community emphasized its impact on individual character. Democratic community represented for Dewey the most promising social milieu for individual development and growth, including development and growth specifically as democratic citizens willing and able to participate in public problem solving. Rather than an impediment to individuality, as conceived by early liberals and contemporary libertarians, a social environment in the form of democratic community makes individuality possible. Dewey's view of community as a positive support for individuality presupposed that human identity is a project rather than a fully formed set of traits and capacities. "Individuality," he wrote, "is at first spontaneous and unshaped; it is a potentiality, a capacity of development."[19] It is "something to be wrought out. It means initiative, inventiveness, varied resourcefulness, assumption of responsibility in choice of belief and conduct. These are not gifts, but achievements."[20] Desirable individuality is thus an accomplishment, not a given; a project, not something to take for granted; something to be won from social institutions that both constrain and enable human thought and action. As this suggests, Dewey's view of the individual rested on a social psychology that emphasized social learning and presupposed a view of human nature as changeable and malleable. He believed that humans grow and develop according both to innate characteristics and in response to their environment.

Dewey viewed democratic community as a special kind of association, one defined in part precisely by the commitment of its members to the growth and development of every individual. This commitment went well beyond simply leaving people alone. He advocated government action to provide for basic material needs, and transformation of the existing political economy from one that produced insecurity and economic determinism into one that provided equal opportunities to all for personal development. How, he asked, could people be expected to develop their unique talents and capacities while struggling daily simply to survive?

While libertarians and others extol the virtues of individuality in the abstract, Dewey argued that individuality is a project to be won. Simply assuming individual capacities and then turning individuals loose to succeed, or not, assumes what does not exist for millions of Americans: requisite social supports and access to resources enabling the attainment of a full individuality that amounts to something more worthwhile than mere survival. The libertarian goals of protecting the individual from undue coercion, from enforced conformity, and from subtle indoctrination are worthy. But the way there, according to Dewey, cannot be along a path defined asocially. Individuality, in the sense of the growth and development of each person, is a social product, not something defined apart from others, from social institutions, from associations, from communities. By defining society as hostile to individuality, the libertarian both distorts the empirical reality and sets up an impossible dilemma in which the needs and interests of individuals are at permanent odds with each other and their social environment. By defining the social environment as potentially supportive of individuality rather than in opposition to it, Dewey opened the possibility of reconciling the individual and the community. If social conditions support individual growth and development, then the tension between the individual and the community at least partly dissolves.

COMMUNITARIANISM

These themes of interdependence, solidarity, self-interest rightly understood, civic virtue, and democratic community converge in the contemporary communitarian movement. Since the early 1990s, this loose collection of scholars and activists has organized around the theory and practice of community. While the communitarians are a diverse set of thinkers, they endorsed a common set of themes published in the 1992 "Communitarian Platform." First, unlike classical liberal political thinkers who focused myopically on asocial human traits such as self-interest and painted a picture of humans as naturally isolated and independent of social ties, communitarians emphasize human sociability. As they point out, this is simply an empirical fact. Individuals cannot isolate themselves from others even if they wanted to, except under exceptional circumstances. A second theme of interdependence follows from sociability. Communitarians ask that we recognize and acknowledge the effects that our actions have on others and vice versa within our communities. What each of us does affects others in the present and in the future. "No one of us is an island unaffected by the fate of others," according to the communitarians.

A third communitarian theme—commitment to the common good—emerges from this presumption of human sociability and interdependence. According to the communitarian platform, self-interest alone cannot create and maintain healthy communities. No community can survive "unless its members dedicate some of their attention, energy, and resources to shared projects. The exclusive pursuit of private interest erodes the network of social environments on which we all depend, and is destructive to our shared experiment in democratic self-government." Citizens must acknowledge the legitimacy of common interests as well as individual, private interests—and act accordingly.

Fourth, communitarians argue that we need to recover a set of common moral values, because we live in a society "that increasingly threatens to become normless, self-centered, and driven by greed, special interests, and an unabashed quest for power." While this raises cautionary flags for anyone who fears the imposition of values contrary to their own, the communitarians insist that their list of moral values includes those that Americans already share, including respect for the dignity of all persons, tolerance, peaceful rather than violent resolution of conflicts, truth-telling in most circumstances, democracy, hard work, and saving for one's own and one's country's future. Anticipating the critics' arguments, the communitarians insist that moral voices in a democracy employ education and persuasion rather than coercion. According to the platform's signers, "We say to those who would impose civic or moral virtues by suppressing dissent (in the name of religion, patriotism, or any other cause), or censoring books, that their cure is ineffective, harmful, and morally untenable." The moral values must meet certain criteria:

They must be nondiscriminatory and applied equally to all members; they must be generalizable, justified in terms that are accessible and understandable: e.g., instead of claims based upon individual or group desires, citizens would draw on a common definition of justice; and, they must incorporate the full range of legitimate needs and values rather than focusing on any one category, be it individualism, autonomy, interpersonal caring, or social justice.

These common moral values would be taught in schools as well as in the home.

Fifth, the communitarians argue that freedom requires civic engagement. This cuts against the grain of dominant understandings of freedom as being left alone to pursue individual interests and goals. Communitarians echo Machiavelli, Harrington, and Rousseau in arguing that liberty erodes under an extreme emphasis on self-interest and failure to recognize and act upon common interests. Liberty, they argue,

depends on the active maintenance of the institutions of civil society where citizens learn respect for others as well as self-respect; where we acquire a lively sense of our personal and civic responsibilities, along with an appreciation of our own rights and the rights of others; where we develop the skills of self-government as well as the habit of governing ourselves, and learn to serve others—not just self.

Engagement in communities is thus "essential if we are not all to fall back on an ever more expansive government, bureaucratized welfare agencies, and swollen regulations, police, courts, and jails."[21]

Sixth, communitarians seek balances between individuals and groups. They take pains to avoid simply reversing the emphasis on the individual over the community. While seeking to cultivate attention to common interests and the common good in general, communitarians insist that individual interests and our private ends are equally important and should not be sacrificed. While each citizen has an obligation to others and to the polity, each also has the freedom to formulate and pursue individual goals. Their call for increased social responsibilities is therefore "not a call for curbing rights. . . . The pursuit of self-interest can be balanced by a commitment to the community, without requiring us to lead a life of austerity, altruism, or self-sacrifice."[22]

Seventh, in a closely related point, communitarians also seek balances between rights and responsibilities. The language of rights is incomplete, according to the communitarians. It needs to be completed with "a richer moral vocabulary" that includes "principles of decency, duty, responsibility, and the common good."[23] Communitarians note that the U.S. Declaration of Independence and Constitution notoriously exclude statements found in the Universal Declaration of Human Rights endorsing the position that "everyone has duties to the community" and that our rights and freedoms are subject to limitations "for the purposes of securing due recognition and respect for the rights and freedoms of others and of meeting the just requirements of morality, public order and the general welfare in a democratic society."[24] The obligations are reciprocal: "Each member of the community owes something to all the rest" and "the community owes something to each of its members." They suggest drafting a Bill of Responsibilities to balance the U.S. Constitution's Bill of Rights. It would include responsibilities such as voting, serving on juries, being informed, paying one's taxes, materially supporting our offspring, and participating in a national social movement to revitalize public life.

Finally, communitarians advocate strong democracy. To the communitarians, this means that

> We seek to make government more representative, more participatory, and more responsive to all members of the community. We seek to find ways to accord citizens more information, and more say, more often. We seek to curb the role of private money, special interests, and corruption in government. Similarly, we ask how "private governments," whether corporations, labor unions, or voluntary associations, can become more responsive to their members and to the needs of the community.

In a strong democracy, everyone's needs and interests are addressed, not just the needs and interests of wealthy and powerful elites. If needs and interests "compete with one another, the community's standards reflect the relative priority accorded by members to some needs over others." Echoing John Winthrop, the communitarians believe that the wealthy should take care of the less fortunate and that "vulnerable communities should be able to draw on the more endowed communities" when necessary.[25] Though it may appear that the communitarians seek a more powerful state to bring about the changes they recommend, they advocate instead a decentralization of power and reliance upon individual choice and voluntarism rather than state coercion.

Like John Dewey, the communitarians argue that community involvement increases the moral and civic development of individuals. It nurtures civic-oriented attitudes, skills, and dispositions, including, for example, commitment to a common good, speaking and listening skills, the ability to recognize and respond to the interests of others, and the ability to balance individual private and public lives. Through participation in politics, we learn to be better democratic citizens. We learn about others and their needs and interests. We develop civic virtue. We practice balancing rights and responsibilities, private and public interests.

COMMUNITY AND DIVERSITY

The communitarians' insistence that we take responsibility for the well-being of others, and their advocacy of a set of common moral values, raises concerns for many about the potential incursion into people's private lives and restrictions on their freedom. Some feminist scholars have highlighted these concerns, offering potent criticisms of the idea of community and its potential hostility to diversity. The common in community, they argue, requires that differences be set aside, ignored, or squelched.

Iris Marion Young (1949–), for example, charged that the ideal of community "privileges unity over difference," "generates borders, dichotomies, and exclusions," and "denies difference by positing fusion rather than separation as the social ideal." Pursuing an ideal of community, she argued, will result in the suppression of differences and the exclusion of dissenters. According to Young, any attempt to "define an identity, a closed totality, always depends on excluding some elements, separating the pure from the impure." Any definition or category "creates an inside/outside distinction." Applied to community, this means that any attempt to define the contours of a social grouping called "community" entails including some while excluding others. In their zeal to achieve community despite irreducible differences, community advocates are easily tempted to simply deny or suppress differences. Ultimately, she concluded, the desire for unity in community is "the same desire for social wholeness and identification that underlies racism and ethnic chauvinism on the one hand and political sectarianism on the other." Young posed—as an alternative to community—an ideal of "the unoppressive city," marked by inexhaustible differences, a "great diversity of people and groups, with a multitude of subcultures and differentiated activities and functions," and "openness to unassimilated otherness." Her opposition to community, however, is really opposition to a specific kind of community: an organic, face-to-face community based on affective ties and privileging unity over diversity. She admitted as much, saying that the model of community she attacks is one of "small, face-to-face, decentralized units" in which community members "can understand one another as they understand themselves."[26]

A second, related concern of feminist critics of community is that the commonalities that define it are specifically male, which ensures biases against women. Given male domination historically in public arenas, men largely defined the history of thought and action in public arenas, constructing the world along male lines. As Jane Mansbridge (1939–) wrote, "Men's unequal power has made male practices and traits the norm for 'mankind.' . . . The labor, traits, and even philosophical terms that are coded as male are usually more highly valued" in Western culture. The net effect may be that specifically and uniquely female dimensions of human experience are typically excluded as defining characteristics of community, and gender diversity is sacrificed to the call for community.

This gender domination may show up in decision-making processes. In any community, decisions must be made that define its identity and commitments. If these decisions are made coercively, it is easy to see the domination. However, even when the decisions are made via persuasion rather than coercion, male domination may be present. Women have typically been trained for "listening and supportive speech" that disempowers in relation to more aggressive, assertive modes of speech. As a result, men tend to dominate in discussions. The effect, writ large in community, is that the interests of men (or other powerful groups) take precedence over the interests of women (or other less powerful groups).

Even more fundamentally, according to Mansbridge, language itself incorporates gender domination of men over women. This is a problem given that, as John Dewey noted, it is through communication that the commonalities of community are developed and sustained. Community requires some means of communication, most typically language, and a common vocabulary. According to Mansbridge, this common vocabulary "is not neutral among those who use it" since many words imply both a dominant and subdominant category and this "exclud[es] by implication the less powerful or the minority." She points as an obvious example to the still-lingering use of "men" to refer to human beings more broadly. To the degree that this problem of gender domination in language holds true, it undermines gender diversity in community by privileging male identities, norms, and interests.

Though she raises several points of concern about domination and autonomy in community, Mansbridge remains hopeful about the possibility of community:

> Although American society has established an equilibrium of sorts between the competing claims of individualism and community, thought and experimentation should allow us to create a better equilibrium strengthening the community ties that must advance the ends we desire while at the same time creating and strengthening institutions that guard against community domination. . . . A polity can strengthen community ties and respect for the individual at the same time.[27]

These concerns suggest caution in uncritically adopting the ideal of community. Any conception of community adopted for use in a democracy must be compatible with diversity and with individual freedom and autonomy. Without dismissing the validity of organic, face-to-face communities that privilege homogeneity, it is important to acknowledge and address the concerns of community's critics and develop an understanding of community that can better accommodate difference and diversity. Yet, it is also important to recognize that difference and diversity do not preclude the presence of some commonalities. Difference is not absolute. Common and different exist in most social environments. People from very different backgrounds and living in disparate circumstances nevertheless experience similar, if not identical, challenges and problems, and respond to them in similar ways. Some level of commonality marks even Iris Young's ideal diverse city. Residents of New York City share common political interests in ensuring timely trash pickup, the presence in the city of decent jobs, maintaining effective police and fire protection, and overall public health. Residents of most cities also share some level of common identification with the city and its unique history and characteristics. The presence of these basic commonalities is simply an empirical fact, one around which residents, activists, and leaders can organize their efforts to solve shared problems.

The tension between individual and social that appears in the tragedy of the commons partly dissolves if and when people realize their interdependence with others and begin to build upon it rather than reject it as an impediment to individuality. If the well-being of the individual cannot be separated from the community, and vice versa, it expands attention beyond immediate private concerns and makes it reasonable for individuals to consider the needs and interests of others as well as the self. Self-interest rightly understood and civic virtue both build on a recognition of interdependence and a willingness to choose solidarity with others to encourage attitudes and behaviors that take into account both individual and public goods. Democratic community provides a context for nurturing these attitudes and behaviors and serves as a social basis for citizen participation in public problem solving. None of these is a fail-safe solution to tragedies of the commons, and none eliminates all tension between individuals and their social surroundings. However, each provides possible directions for thought and action that potentially alleviates the frequency and severity of various tragedies of the commons.

In each of the examples of tragedies of the commons that were discussed earlier, interdependence is simply a fact of social life. Withdrawal into private spaces may delay or circumvent the repercussions on some of the issues, but on others such as global warming there can be no escape. Members of democratic communities recognize their interdependence with others and with future generations. They choose solidarity with members of their own, and others', communities, including and especially those members who are most adversely affected by public problems. In general, that means those members who are most politically and economically marginalized. Members of democratic communities understand their individual self-interest rightly, in the context of interdependence and the need to yield some private interests in order to "save the rest." They internalize civic virtue and routinely practice it in their everyday lives by considering the needs and interests of others as well as the self, even if it involves some sacrifice and inconvenience. Members of democratic communities assume responsibility for the consequences of their individual choices and actions. They recognize and acknowledge the repercussions of their actions for others, including future generations. They make appropriate choices and take appropriate actions that build on their interdependence. Without denying the legitimacy of their private and self-interests, they consider the needs and interests of others. They recognize a common good and commit to its realization.

Some public problems will undoubtedly persist despite the best efforts by citizens to solve them. At least some individuals will ignore their responsibilities to others and continue to focus exclusively on their own needs and interests. Given these factors, individuals will often have to work through various levels of government to foster the collective action needed to address shared concerns and problems. Ideally, every member of a democratic community contributes to the common good and to the resolution of specific public problems. And ideally those with exceptional resources and power contribute more than others. However, in a democratic community that is diverse by definition, members will disagree over causes of problems and how to resolve them. Democratic community offers no magic palliatives, no guarantees, no utopias. But members of democratic communities commit to trying anyway.

QUESTIONS, PROBLEMS, AND ACTIVITIES

1. Draw how John Winthrop envisioned the relation between individuals and the community. Draw how you see this relation in actual fact today and how you see it ideally.
2. Brainstorm a list of contemporary examples of self-interest rightly understood. Make a similar list for civic virtue.
3. Draft a Bill of Responsibilities to complement the Bill of Rights. Keep in mind that, like the Bill of Rights, the Bill of Responsibilities would be codified as law and backed up by government sanctions and the coercive power of the state.
4. Do you agree with the communitarians that "individuals have a responsibility for the material and moral well-being of others"? Yes / No
5. List the personality traits of a man, and then of a woman. Compare and contrast the two lists. Are there significant similarities and differences? If there are differences, are these biologically determined or socially learned? Do the same for the ideal moral characteristics of a man and a woman.
6. Are common people capable of civic virtue? Gather empirical evidence to help answer the question by creating and administering a survey in which you ask if, and why (or why not), people recycle, donate blood, volunteer, and consider others' needs when making decisions.
7. Identify a public problem in your neighborhood, city, or region. Consider ways to address the problem while minimizing or eliminating the need for government involvement.

NOTES

1. Thomas Hobbes, *Leviathan* (1651; New York: Penguin Books, 1985), part 1, chaps. 11–14, pp. 192, 184, 161, 185, 186; emphasis in original.

2. "Gallup Poll: He Said, She Said," *Cleveland Plain Dealer*, February 24, 2001.

3. John Winthrop, "A Modell of Christian Charity" [1630], in *Political Thought in America*, ed. Michael Levy, 2nd ed. (Prospect Heights, IL: Waveland Press, 1988), p. 9.

4. John Paul II, *Sollicitudo Rei Socialis* (Encyclical on social concerns), in *Origins* 17, no. 38 (March 3, 1988): p. 649; John Paul II, *Centesimus Annus* (On the 100th anniversary [of Pope Leo XIII's *Rerum Novarum*]), in *Origins* 21, no. 1 (May 16, 1991): p. 19; John Paul II, *Sollicitudo Rei Socialis*, p. 649.

5. John Paul II, *Sollicitudo Rei Socialis*, pp. 654, 653, 657.

6. Albert Camus, *The Plague*, trans. Stuart Gilbert (New York: Modern Library, 1948), pp. 153, 38, 117, 188, 121, 229, 27.

7. Alexis de Tocqueville, *Democracy in America* (1840; New York: Random House, 1981), pp. 417, 415, 416; emphasis in original.

8. John Dewey, *Democracy and Education* [1916], in *John Dewey: The Middle Works, 1899–1924*, vol. 9, ed. Jo Ann Boydston (Carbondale: Southern Illinois University Press, 1985), pp. 93, 35.

9. Niccolò Machiavelli, *The Prince and The Discourses* (1513–17; New York: Random House, 1950), pp. 168, 399, 169–70; emphasis added.

10. James Harrington, *The Commonwealth of Oceana* [1656], in *The Political Works of James Harrington*, ed. J. G. A. Pocock (Cambridge: Cambridge University Press, 1977), p. 172.

11. Jean-Jacques Rousseau, *Discourse on Political Economy* [1755], in *Rousseau's Political Writings*, ed. Alan Ritter and Julia Conaway Bondanella (New York: W. W. Norton, 1988), pp. 69, 67, 68, 72.

12. John Adams, "Letter to Samuel Adams [1790]," in *The Political Writings of John Adams*, ed. George W. Carey (Washington, DC: Regnery, 2000), p. 665.

13. Quoted in Richard Hofstadter, *The American Political Tradition and the Men Who Made It* (1948; repr., New York: Vintage Books, 1989), pp. 6, 7, 9.

14. James Madison, "Federalist No. 51" [1788], in Alexander Hamilton, James Madison, and John Jay, *The Federalist Papers* (Toronto: Bantam Books, 1982), p. 262.

15. James Madison, "Federalist No. 57" [1788], in Hamilton, Madison, and Jay, *Federalist Papers*, p. 289.

16. Samuel Bryan, "Letter of Centinel, No. 1" [1787], in *The Anti-Federalist*, ed. Herbert Storing (Chicago: University of Chicago Press, 1981), p. 16.

17. Thomas Jefferson, "Letter to James Madison [1787]," in *The Life and Selected Writings of Thomas Jefferson*, ed. Adrienne Koch and William Peden (New York: Random House, 1944), p. 407; Thomas Jefferson, "Letter to Samuel Kercheval [1816]," in Koch and Peden, *Selected Writings of Thomas Jefferson* (1944), p. 161; Jefferson, "Letter to James Madison [1787]," p. 407.

18. John Dewey, *The Public and Its Problems* [1927], in *John Dewey: The Later Works, 1925–1953*, vol. 2, ed. Jo Ann Boydston (Carbondale: Southern Illinois University Press, 1988), pp. 245–246, 328, 392.

19. John Dewey, *Individualism, Old and New* [1929–30], in Boydston, *John Dewey: The Later Works*, vol. 5 (1988), p. 121.

20. John Dewey, *Reconstruction in Philosophy* [1920], in Boydston, *John Dewey: The Middle Works*, vol. 12 (1985), p. 194.

21. Rodolfo Alvarez et al., "The Responsive Communitarian Platform: Rights and Responsibilities," *Responsive Community* 2, no. 1 (Winter 1991/92): pp. 14, 4–7, 10.

22. Amitai Etzioni, *The Spirit of Community: Rights, Responsibilities, and the Communitarian Agenda* (New York: Crown Publishers, 1993), pp. 1–2.

23. Alvarez et al., "Responsive Communitarian Platform," p. 14.

24. Etzioni, *The Spirit of Community*, p. 10.

25. Alvarez et al., "Responsive Communitarian Platform," pp. 14, 6, 11.

26. Iris Marion Young, "The Ideal of Community and the Politics of Difference," in *Feminism/Postmodernism*, ed. Linda Nicholson (London: Routledge, 1990), pp. 300, 301, 307, 303, 302, 317, 319, 300, 302.

27. Jane Mansbridge, "Feminism and Democratic Community," in *Democratic Community*, ed. John Chapman and Ian Shapiro (New York: New York University Press, 1993), pp. 345, 363, 366–67, 374–75.

II

FREEDOM AND EQUALITY

3

Radical Inequality and Its Roots

Freedom lies at the heart of "our way of life" as understood by most Americans. In its national anthem, the United States proclaims itself "the land of the free," and the First Amendment to its Constitution guarantees freedom of religion, press, and speech. Popular musicians, pundits, and patriots all celebrate it. Although freedom is a complex concept, in Western culture it has one dominant meaning: being left alone to choose and act as you please. Political theorists call this kind of freedom "negative freedom," not because it is a bad kind of freedom, but to indicate that it is a kind of freedom that entails the absence or removal of obstacles and other restraints on human volition and behavior.

Equality, too, ranks highly on most Americans' list of top political values, at least in rhetorical terms. The Declaration of Independence states, "We hold these truths to be self-evident, that all men are created equal, that they are endowed by their Creator with certain unalienable Rights, that among these are Life, Liberty and the pursuit of Happiness." But unlike freedom, which has one dominant meaning in Western culture that overrides other meanings, several meanings of equality appear in common use among Americans. Political equality means that each citizen has an equal say in politics. We attempt to guarantee minimal political equality in the principle of one-person-one-vote. Each of us can vote once, and once only, for the candidates of our choice. Political equality also means that the law applies equally to everyone and we each enjoy equal political rights such as the right to assemble, the right to competent legal representation, the right to free speech, and the right to run for office.

Equal opportunity is another dominant form of equality. This means that each of us faces no more and no fewer obstacles to success than others, and that each of us begins with the same set of advantages and disadvantages as others. To use some often-employed sports metaphors, equal opportunity means that the playing field is level, that we all begin at the starting line, and that nobody gets a head start. For example, in principle, each of us enjoys equal access to a quality education, which guarantees each person an equal chance of achieving success in a chosen career.

Economic equality means that each of us possesses and controls the same economic resources as others. Generally, this principle has been applied weakly, if at all, in Western culture. Most Western industrialized nations seek to guarantee a minimal level of economic equality through social programs that provide a welfare floor. These include a minimum wage, social security, unemployment compensation, and food stamps. Medicare and Medicaid in the United States are intended to guarantee minimal health care access for the elderly and indigent, respectively. Food stamps are intended to provide minimal nutrition for all families in the United States. The Servicemen's Readjustment Act of 1944, popularly known as the GI Bill, helped guarantee greater equality of access to a college education for millions of returning war veterans after World War II. Economic equality supports other forms of equality. For example, guaranteeing everyone a minimal level of education and health care helps boost equal opportunity by providing more chances, and the physical well-being to take advantage of them, to everyone.

This section will focus on these first three types of equality: political equality, equal opportunity, and economic equality. However, other kinds of equality can be identified, and they are worth mentioning.

Some people today are rethinking the dominant presumption of human superiority over nature and are calling for greater equality between humans and nature. They note that human misuse of nature often begins from a presumption of human superiority over other animate and inanimate forms. This presumption is rooted deeply in Western history and the Western psyche. The Book of Genesis, for example, awards dominion over nature to humans, who are exhorted to "be fruitful and multiply, and fill the earth and subdue it; and have dominion over the fish of the sea and over the birds of the air and over every living thing" (1:28). Pope John Paul II (1920–2005) more recently asserted that "Man is made to be in the visible universe an im-

Pope John Paul II

age and likeness of God himself, and he is placed in it in order to subdue the earth." Human work, he argued, "presupposes a specific dominion by man over 'the earth.'"[1]

This language clearly poses humans as masters of the Earth, with the theologically sanctioned right and responsibility to "dominate" and "subdue" it. Those who seek greater protection of the Earth sometimes argue that we must dispense with our presumption of superiority and adopt instead a framework of equality within nature of all things. They point to alternative traditions, such as those of American Indians, that generally emphasize a unity of humans and their natural environment. This view presupposes equality among all living and inanimate creatures and objects on the Earth. According to some, adopting this view would increase humans' respect for nature and decrease humans' destruction of nature and the environment.[2]

Equality can also mean equal respect and dignity. Each person is unique, yet is imbued with fundamental value simply by virtue of our common humanity. Each person merits respectful, humane treatment. This principle found expression in the Universal Declaration of Human Rights, adopted by the General Assembly of the United Nations in 1948, which proclaims "the inherent dignity and . . . equal and inalienable rights of all members of the human family." As expressed by the U.S. Catholic bishops, "Each person possesses a basic dignity that comes from God, not from any human quality or accomplishment, not from race or gender, age or economic status." This principle of equal respect and dignity often underlies other calls for programs aimed at providing minimal treatment and living standards for all citizens. For example, Article 23, Section 3, of the Universal Declaration of Human Rights states that "everyone who works has the right to just and favorable remuneration ensuring for himself and his family an existence worthy of human dignity, and supplemented, if necessary, by other means of social protection." Article 25, Section 1, of the declaration states that "everyone has the right to a standard of living adequate for the health and well-being of himself and of his family, including food, clothing, housing and medical care." John Paul II based his call for greater social and economic justice on this principle of equal human dignity. The U.S. Catholic bishops oppose capital punishment in part because of their "belief in the unique worth and dignity of each person from the moment of conception, a creature made in the image and likeness of God."[3]

Since Americans claim to value both freedom and equality, presumably they complement each other. However, the dominant understanding of freedom—doing what we want free of restrictions and impediments—often undermines equality in each of its forms, and vice versa. This tension between equality and freedom primarily exists as a tension specifically between equality and the negative freedoms associated with private property. Generally, the tension between freedom and equality has been resolved in the United States in favor of freedom, reducing political equality to a formal principle of one-person-one-vote, equal opportunity to an equal right to strive, and economic equality to minimal and declining efforts to support those on the bottom. The commitment to equality in the United States is weak, and declining, in the early twenty-first century. The chasm between rich and poor widens steadily, with far-reaching consequences for other kinds of equality.

PUBLIC PROBLEMS

Economic Inequality

The United States can boast the world's largest economy and one of the highest per-capita incomes in the world. Unfortunately, it also has "the most unequal income distribution and one of the highest poverty rates among all the advanced economies in the world."[4] In spite of an economic boom in the 1990s, the national poverty rate in 1998 remained at 12.7 percent, down from 12.8 percent in 1989, but a full percentage point higher than in 1979 (see figure 3.1). An unexpectedly large decline in 1999 dropped the poverty rate tem-

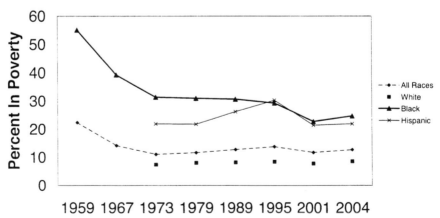

FIGURE 3.1
Poverty Rate, by Race/Ethnicity

porarily to 11.8 percent, approximately the same as 1979, but by 2003 it had returned to 12.8 percent.

In 1998, approximately one in five American children (18.9 percent) lived in poverty (see figure 3.2). In 1999, 16.9 percent of American children lived in poverty, slightly above the 1979 rate of 16.4 percent. By 2003, the percentage had risen again, to 17.6 percent (20.1 percent for children under six years of age). While these poverty measures are sobering enough, they actually understate the real rate of poverty by an average of 3.6 percent, according to the U.S. Census Bureau. In 1963, a statistician at the U.S. Social Security Administration developed the formula for setting the poverty line. Using current survey information, she determined that the average family spent approximately one-third of its income on food. She calculated modest food budgets, then multiplied them by three to arrive at the poverty line. In 1963, that method of calculating the poverty line may have been reasonably accurate. However, at the beginning of the twenty-first century, the average household now spends only one-sixth of its income on food, yet the guidelines still assume one-third. Other costs such as transportation, housing, and child care now account for relatively higher percentages of the average household budget. The result is a

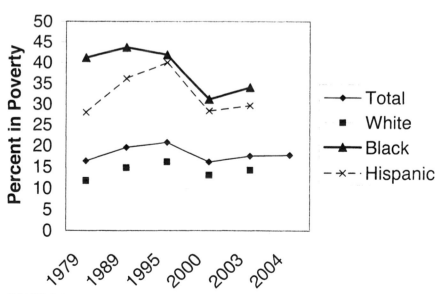

FIGURE 3.2
Poverty Rate for Children, by Race/Ethnicity

poverty line set artificially low at $14,824 for a single parent with two children and $18,660 for a family of four at 2003 levels, understating the actual poverty rate in the United States by an estimated 3–4 percent.[5]

Radical and growing economic inequality during the last two decades appears in both income and wealth data. During the 1980s and 1990s, the already wealthy saw their income and wealth surge. The number of millionaires increased dramatically, and many millionaires became billionaires. Only a small percentage of these were newly rich. During the 1990s, the share of total income received by the top 5 percent of households increased from 17.9 percent in 1989 to 20.3 percent in 1999. Owners of capital did especially well during the 1990s, a decade in which, "for the first time in the postwar period, the division of total corporate income between income paid to workers and income paid to owners of capital shifted strongly in favor of owners of capital." Owners of capital saw their share of profits increase by 2.3 percent during the 1990s, compared to 0.5 percent during the 1980s. The fortunes of the wealthy during the 1980s and 1990s can be most dramatically illustrated by looking at changes in chief executive officer (CEO) salaries, which surged dramatically. Inflation-adjusted wages of the median CEO rose rapidly during the 1990s, pushing the ratio of CEO compensation to average worker pay from 71 in 1989—and 24 in 1965—to 300, meaning that the typical CEO now earned 300 times the average worker (see figure 3.3). Comparing CEO pay to that of factory workers re-

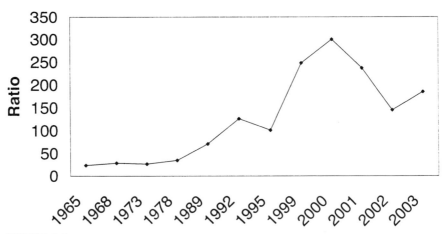

FIGURE 3.3
Ratio of CEO Pay to Average Worker Pay, 1965–2003

veals an even more dramatic difference. In 1980, the average CEO earned 42 times the average factory worker. Eighteen years later, in 1998 the average CEO earned 419 times the average factory worker, compared to average Japanese CEOs who earned 16 times the average Japanese factory worker.[6]

On the other hand, the lowest rung of wage earners saw their income stagnate or decline as real wages, adjusted for inflation, continued to decline overall from late-1970s highs. During the 1990s, the share of total income received by the bottom 20 percent of households fell by 0.3 percentage points. Income for this group grew during the late 1990s, pushed by raises in the federal minimum wage and sustained low unemployment. However, when adjusted for inflation, wages remained approximately the same as 1970s levels and the minimum wage remained 20 percent lower in 2000 than in 1979. More than one-fourth (26.8 percent) of all U.S. workers in 1999 officially earned poverty-level wages, set at $8.19 per hour in 1999. This figure understates the actual problem, for the same reasons noted above. Less than a third of these poverty-wage earners received employer-provided health benefits in 1998, and less than a fifth of them received employer-provided pension benefits.[7]

The middle class also suffered continued declines in inflation-adjusted wages through most of this period, partly offset by increasing wages during the late 1990s. Nevertheless, overall income increased slightly for the average middle-class family through most of this period. The most important factor explaining this rise in family incomes, counteracting falling wages through most of the two decades, was an increase in the number of hours worked per family (see figure 3.4). At the end of the twentieth century, the average family worked 91 person-weeks each year, compared to 80 in 1969, yet family income overall barely rose. The typical middle-income married-couple family worked 247 hours more in 1999 than it did in 1989. In other words, the average family needed to work the equivalent of an additional month and a half each year in order to increase its income slightly during the decade. Middle-class families have added 12.5 weeks to their annual workload, or approximately three months, since 1979. Upper-income households increased their work time during this period by approximately half as much as middle-class families.[8] Among industrialized economies, only Portuguese workers work longer hours than U.S. workers. This extra work stresses family life as wage earners tag-team household duties and child care. Balancing work and family has become a major challenge for most families today.

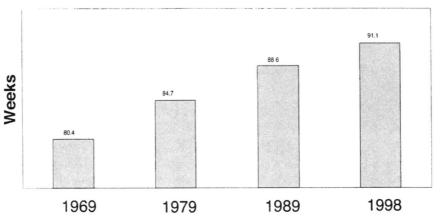

FIGURE 3.4
Average Weeks Worked per Year, Married-Couple Families with Children, 1969–1998

Economic inequality is entwined with issues of race and gender. In 2003, 24.4 percent of all African Americans and 22.5 percent of all Hispanics lived in poverty, compared to 8.2 percent of whites; 34.1 percent of African-American children and 29.7 percent of Hispanic children lived in poverty, compared to 14.3 percent of white children; and 26.2 percent of black men, 33.9 percent of black women (30.4 percent overall for blacks), 35.7 percent of Hispanic men, and 45.8 percent of Hispanic women earned poverty level wages (see figures 3.1 and 3.2). During the ten-year period 1989–1998, African-American median household income averaged 59.0 percent of white, non-Hispanic median household incomes. In other words, on average, African Americans earned approximately 59 cents for every dollar earned by whites.[10] Median family income of minorities, at 62.0 percent for African Americans and 61.8 percent for Hispanics, remains less than two-thirds that of whites. Median family income for African Americans in 1999 was $31,778 and for Hispanics it was $31,633; for whites it was $51,244.

The good news for minority families is that these income levels are higher than previous levels. The bad news, in addition to the fact that minority families continue to earn substantially less than white families, is that minority families work longer hours than white families in order to maintain incomes at less than two-thirds of the levels of white family incomes (see figure 3.5). Black middle-income families worked almost 500 more hours per year, and Hispanic middle-income families approximately 140 more hours, than white

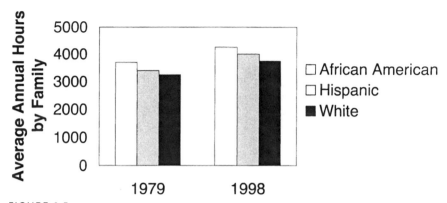

FIGURE 3.5
Average Family Work Hours, by Race/Ethnicity, Middle-Income, Married-Couple Families with Children, 1979 and 1998

middle-income families at the end of the twentieth century. High-income minority families worked more than 4,500 hours in 1998, meaning that they had more than two full-time incomes. To achieve middle or high income, minority families "have to put in extremely long hours relative to whites."[11]

During the ten-year period 1989–1998, the median earnings of year-round, full-time female workers averaged 71.8 percent of year-round, full-time male workers. By the late 1990s, women earned 76.9 cents on the male dollar, rising to 81 cents by 2003. If gender equity in pay is a goal, then this increase in women's incomes relative to men's is good news. However, this improvement in equity was achieved largely from declines in males' earnings, more than increases in female earnings.[12]

Wealth inequality surpasses income inequality. *Wealth* measures the accumulation of economic and financial resources, while *income* measures the annual stream. Wealth can be likened to a reservoir, while income is the stream flowing into it. The 1990s stock market boom gave the impression that most Americans were pumping up their wealth and that most Americans shared in the boom times. The truth, however, is that most Americans own relatively little stock and consequently did not share in the boom times—which anyway were followed by bust times in the early twenty-first century. Less than half of Americans own stock in any form, and approximately two-thirds (64 percent) of all households own stock worth less than $5,000, or none at all. The wealthiest 1 percent of Americans owns 40 percent of all net financial assets, while

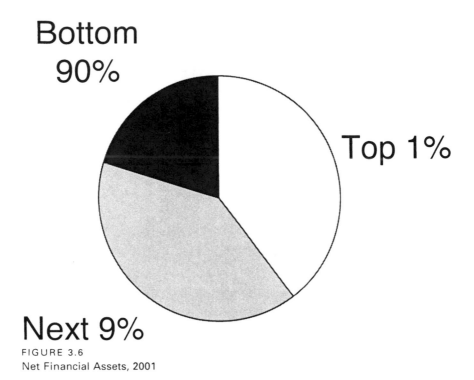

Bottom
90%

Top 1%

Next 9%

FIGURE 3.6
Net Financial Assets, 2001

the bottom 90 percent owns only 20 percent; the top 1 percent of Americans owns almost half (47.7 percent) of all stocks by value, while the bottom 80 percent owns a mere 4.1 percent. Though most middle-income families experienced a slight increase of household wealth during the 1990s, due largely to a surge in home values, these gains were offset by approximately equal gains in household debt. In short, "for the typical household, rising debt, not a rising stock market, was the big story of the 1990s."[13]

Poverty remains widespread in America for reasons that include the structural shift in America away from manufacturing toward a service economy in which wages tend to start low and stay low. According to one popular myth, the computer industry and the high-technology sector of the economy in general produces new jobs sufficiently quickly to offset losses in manufacturing. In fact, the information technology sector contributed only 7.5 percent of all new jobs during the 1990s, and many of these new jobs disappeared during the dot.com bust of the early twenty-first century. Of the 20 million new jobs created during the Reagan administration (1981–1989), most paid an average of $5.04 per hour, only slightly above minimum wage for the period. That trend continued during the 1990s, when, "despite economic boom times, most new jobs [were] low-wage, service-sector positions with few benefits." Three of the four fastest-growing jobs during the 1990s—waiting tables, cashiering, and retail sales—paid less than $16,000 per year. Other reasons for the persistence of poverty and increasing inequality include the decline of labor unions; global economic treaties that benefit capital at the expense of labor; a minimum wage that has not kept up with inflation; and big tax cuts for the wealthy with relatively little tax relief for working families.[14]

Defenders of inequality in the United States might insist that a high degree of mobility makes poverty for most people temporary. Do official and unofficial poverty measures paint an unduly harsh picture by failing to note the rate at which poor people work their way up and out of poverty? The unfortunate answer is no. The United States "offers less economic mobility than other rich countries." Low-wage workers in the United States are more likely to remain in low-wage occupations than their counterparts in other developed countries, and poor households in the United States are less likely to leave poverty than their counterparts in those countries. At 28.6 percent, the annual exit rate from poverty in America is the lowest among relatively rich countries covered in one study. Compounding the problem, 18 percent of those who exit poverty return to poverty within one year.[15] Despite the promise of social mobility, most poor Americans face a relatively inflexible economic caste system that limits their options and the likelihood of upward mobility.

Educational Inequality

Equal opportunity is undermined to the extent that different individuals have unequal access to a quality education. Increasingly, career opportunities and overall success require a good education that includes a college degree. Workers with a bachelor's degree earn 54 percent more than workers with some college education but no degree, and those with some college but no degree earn 12 percent more than those with a high school degree only (see figure 3.7).[16] The obstacles to getting a college degree from a quality school can be thought of as filters that selectively eliminate opportunities and undermine the educational achievement of some.

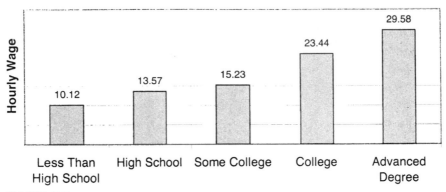

FIGURE 3.7
Real Hourly Wage, by Education Level, 2003

The first filter is the K–12 system, which varies widely in quality. In the United States, everyone is guaranteed a free public education through high school, and this is an important minimal guarantee. However, the quality of that K–12 education varies widely for different people in different circumstances. In general, the wealthier the school district, the better the public schools. Many inner-city schools face mounting problems that include too few and outdated textbooks, disintegrating infrastructure, disciplinary issues, and overworked, stressed staff. The tax base in most cities eroded steadily during decades of suburban growth and flight from inner cities by families and jobs, leaving relatively few funds to support quality K–12 education. Of course, many inner-city schools succeed in providing a quality education anyway, many excellent teachers work in inner-city school systems, and many students attending inner-city schools still do well. Nevertheless, they face more obstacles than better-funded schools, making success relatively more difficult to attain. All other things being equal, including talent and effort, many students attending these schools graduate from high school relatively underprepared for college and for performance on college entrance exams.

College entrance exams such as the ACT and SAT act as a second filter. These derail some otherwise qualified students who, due to inadequate preparation, perform poorly on the exams. Assuming the same level of talent, test scores of inner-city students often lag behind test scores of students who attend relatively strong school systems. In addition to the problem of underpreparation by poor K–12 systems, people of limited means cannot afford to

pay for relatively expensive exam-preparation courses available to people of
adequate means. The net effect of these factors is that children from higher-
income families tend to score better than children from lower-income families, independent of talent or effort. Figure 3.8 dramatically illustrates this
point. The data in this graph, covering 1,260,278 test takers in 2000, show a
perfect correlation between income and SAT score: every increase in income
is matched by an increase in SAT score.[17] This vividly indicates a tie between
economic inequality and unequal opportunity in education.

The challenge of financing a college education creates a third filter. Students from families with limited financial means face daunting cost challenges
in comparison to students from more affluent families. Although loan and
grant programs partially overcome this inequity, they do not entirely eliminate the obstacles for members of lower-income families. For many students,
the prospect of borrowing many thousands of dollars to finance higher education is discouraging at best. Many lower-income students also face a related
fourth filter: the need to hold part-time or even full-time jobs while they attend college. Students from affluent backgrounds can elect to skip the job and
concentrate on their studies. Inevitably, this increases the challenges facing
working students relative to students whose parents' support eliminates the
need to work a paid job.

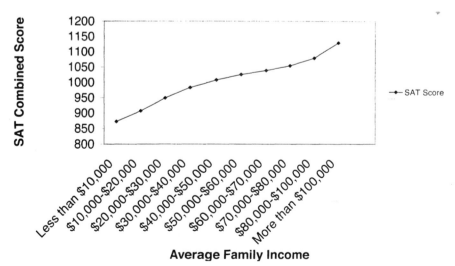

FIGURE 3.8
SAT Scores and Income

Thus far, these filters affect all students of limited means, no matter their race or ethnicity. However, access to a quality education cannot presently be separated from race and ethnicity. As noted above, black and Hispanic families overall earn less than two-thirds of white families, and minority families are more likely to live in poverty than white families. Minority students are thus more likely to face these class barriers to a quality education. Since class and race are intertwined, SAT scores among different racial groups vary along with income. In 2000, combined SAT scores of African Americans lagged nearly 200 points behind those of white students. In 1996, African Americans between the ages of 25 and 29 were as likely as whites to have graduated from high school. However, among this age group, whites were twice as likely as African Americans to have attained a college degree. Twenty-eight percent of whites and 14 percent of African Americans in this group had attained college degrees.[18]

Minorities face additional filters. The fifth filter, the curriculum itself, remains primarily Western European and Euro-American in character, despite sometimes-heroic attempts since the 1980s to diversify it. People from different backgrounds often find their concerns and interests underrepresented in the curriculum, and this can discourage attendance and retention. Similarly, faculty of color are underrepresented in proportion to their overall population at most higher-education institutions, and this may subtly discourage some students from attendance. This is a sixth filter that may discourage students from marginalized circumstances, who find relatively few role models at the college level with whom they can readily identify.

These filters act in combination. For lower-income students, their effect is cumulative and, for many, devastating in terms of inadequate preparation for attaining decent jobs. For many who do make it into college, the pressure to withdraw before graduation cannot be ignored. It should surprise no one that "students from low-income families are significantly more likely to leave a four-year institution of higher education without a baccalaureate degree than are students with higher incomes." According to one study, top traditionally white colleges graduate only 18 percent of their black students within six years. Retention is a chronic problem at traditionally black colleges and universities as well. Nationally, the average retention rate for African-American college students is 45 percent within five years, compared to 57 percent for white students.[19]

Compounding these problems, tuition and related costs have risen steadily in recent decades, in a context of flattened incomes among lower- and middle-class families. Adjusted for inflation, colleges and universities increased their costs nearly threefold since the 1970s. In 1975, the median annual household income was approximately 30 percent higher than the cost of four years at a private institution and three times more than the cost of four years at a public institution. In 1994, attending a private institution for four years cost twice the median income of an American household, and the cost of attending a public institution was almost equal to the median household income. This shift in the ratio of costs to income increases the relative burden of financing a college education.

Making the problem worse, many colleges and universities in recent years have switched from need-blind to need-sensitive admission policies, meaning that they are less likely to admit students with significant financial aid needs. One consequence is higher real costs to lower- and middle-income students and their families of attaining a college education. Finally, federal and state governments began divesting in higher education in the early 1980s, and increasingly emphasize loan rather than grant programs, further shifting the cost to students. The net result of these changes is "greater inequality for opportunity to higher education."[20]

Privilege in education, like other forms of privilege, once attained tends to perpetuate itself. High educational achievement tends to result in high economic and financial achievement, which in turn allows parents in these circumstances to purchase a high-quality education for their children. As the real cost of college for students of lower- and middle-income backgrounds increases, so too does inequality of opportunity in higher education.

Money and U.S. Electoral Politics

The issue of campaign finance provides a clear example of how the freedoms associated with money and wealth overwhelm relatively feeble commitments to political equality. At the time of the American founding, this was expressed in property requirements for voting and in blunt comments by Founders such as the wealthy planter, Charles Pinckney (1757–1824), who proposed that no one should be president who was not worth at least $100,000, and John Jay (1745–1829), one of the authors of the Federalist Papers, who stated simply that "the people who own the country ought to govern it."[21] Though property requirements for voting have subsequently been eliminated, the influence of private wealth on politics has, if anything, increased. Money awards political power and privilege to those who possess and wield it. To the degree that money buys political power, the central democratic principle of political equality is violated.

Private money influences and distorts American electoral politics in multiple ways. The cost of an effective campaign has risen exponentially in the last several decades. Candidates for president now routinely spend hundreds of millions of dollars during their campaigns, while congressional and gubernatorial candidates spend several million or more in theirs. Wealthy campaign contributors naturally figure heavily in determining who can compete effectively in elections. Political theorist William Hudson (1948–) refers to "hidden elections" in American politics that occur before Americans actually get to vote for a particular candidate. The voters in a hidden election are the wealthy campaign contributors who determine the relative viability of different candidates. The candidate who attracts sufficient contributions can remain in the race until the primary, while others inevitably must drop out or run an increasingly ineffective campaign. Major campaign contributors enjoy exceptional access to policy makers. Politicians actively court the support of financial backers, who contribute with the expectation that it will buy them access to power.

Some individuals and organizations gain exceptional access whether or not they contribute directly to campaigns, by virtue of their ability to hire lobbyists. Nearly three-fourths of the approximately 7,000 lobbying groups in Washington, DC, represent business interests. These include, for example, the U.S. Chamber of Commerce, the National Association of Manufacturers, the American Bankers' Association, and individual business corporations. Philip Morris alone employed 245 lobbyists in the late 1990s.[22] The figures are even more lopsided when measured in dollars, as figure 3.9 shows. These lobbyists command large amounts of money that, at the very least, buys the attention of policy makers, and in many cases also buys specific favored policies. Wealthy candidates need not rely on contributions from others. Unlike average Americans, these candidates can simply declare their candidacy and begin spending their own money. At least some of these wealthy politicians, especially those born into wealth, are out of touch with average Americans' lives. Even assuming the best intentions, their policy choices inevitably tend to reflect their class backgrounds and interests.

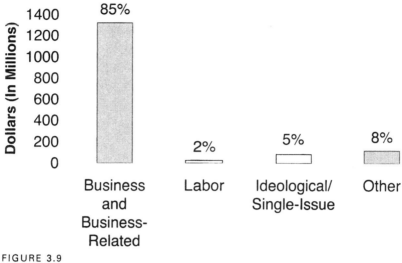

FIGURE 3.9
Lobbyist Spending, 2000

Defenders of the status quo in U.S. electoral politics sometimes respond that the influence of the wealthy is not a problem. If there is a problem, they insist, it is the nonparticipation in voting by millions of the nonwealthy. The system provides the opportunities for participation—most adults are eligible to vote, and anyone can run for office—and if millions routinely choose non-participation, the resulting political inequality is their own fault. Defenders of the status quo are partly right, in that nonvoting tends to reinforce and perpetuate political inequality. People who choose not to vote tend to fall into specific demographic categories. Since lower-income demographic categories are underrepresented in elections, the views and interests of lower-income citizens are underrepresented in policy matters. However, it is at least as true to say that existing political inequality causes nonparticipation, rather than vice versa. Many voters calculate that, in terms of the impact on their lives, the choice between a Democrat and a Republican, both beholden to major campaign contributors, is often no choice at all. One way or another, they conclude, the status quo will remain largely untouched, and the concerns and interests of relatively marginalized Americans will remain underrepresented.

Both liberal and conservative politicians have proposed options for reform, and some of these have been enacted. The major obstacles have included an indifferent or even intransigent Congress, whose incumbent members generally benefit from the status quo, and a Supreme Court that until recently interpreted campaign contributions as free speech protected under the First Amendment to the Constitution.

Most law governing campaign financing and spending at the end of the twentieth century originated in the Federal Election Campaign Act of 1974. This required disclosure of money raised and spent; placed partial limits on contributions by individuals and groups to candidates, party committees, and political action committees (PACs); and prohibited direct contributions and expenditures by corporations, labor organizations, federal government contractors, and foreign nationals. Major loopholes remained, however. An individual or group such as a PAC could make unlimited "independent expenditures" in connection with federal elections. This so-called soft money typically finds expression in issue and attack ads. Also, federal law imposes no limits on expenditures by candidates. The result is that major party candidates spend increasing amounts in election campaigns, and soft money plays a very heavy role in elections. The Bipartisan Campaign Reform Act of 2002 ended soft money contributions to national political parties and doubled the limit on direct "hard money" contributions to specific candidates from $1,000 to $2,000. However, the legislation allowed unlimited soft money contributions to state political parties. This simply redirected the flow of money without stanching it.

Although the U.S. Congress generally refuses to act effectively on the issue, some states have enacted legislation reforming their campaign finance procedures. By 2000, twenty-four states provided some form of public financing of elections. This helps the more marginal candidates who have difficulty raising sufficient money to compete effectively in an election. Usually strings are attached, especially spending limits and limits on the acceptance and use of private money. Public financing usually falls well short of the amount collected from private sources. Twelve states have also enacted some form of expenditure limitations. State reformers continue to face legal challenges from opponents who litigate on the grounds that the reforms are unconstitutional. The most popular reform option combines public financing of elections with voluntary spending limits. Candidates are under no legal obligation to abide by the voluntary spending limits, making this reform fall well short of effective. No state currently imposes mandatory spending limits, and no state limits the amount of money an independent committee can spend on behalf of a candidate.

The freedom granted to affluent Americans to purchase political power remains more important in practice than any real or potential commitments to political equality. As many conservatives and liberals agree, the choice is clear. If we value political equality, fundamental campaign finance reform is necessary. Until then, Americans continue in practice to embrace the principle not of political equality but of "those who own the country ought to govern it."

U.S. Tax Code

Though the commitment to equality via redistribution of wealth and income has always been relatively weak in the United States, since the 1980s that commitment has wavered and declined precipitously. American policy makers' faltering commitment to a progressive tax system illustrates this decline. A *progressive* tax takes a higher percentage from higher incomes than it does from lower incomes, while a *regressive* tax does the opposite, taking a higher percentage from lower incomes than it does from higher incomes. In everyday terms, a tax can be viewed as regressive if it falls more heavily on the shoulders of lower-income taxpayers than it does on the shoulders of higher-income ones and as progressive if it shifts the relative burden onto higher-income taxpayers.

The rationale for a progressive tax system can be demonstrated by comparing the effect of a flat-rate tax on two incomes, one a modest $10,000 and the other $1 million. Assuming a flat tax rate of 10 percent, the $10,000 income will be assessed $1,000 in taxes while the $1 million income will be assessed $100,000. Though the latter is considerably more money, it nevertheless affects the payer less adversely. Subtracting 10 percent from the $10,000 income leaves a relatively small amount for subsistence, drives the taxpayer more deeply into poverty, and seriously compromises the taxpayer's ability to pay for basic necessities like food and shelter. On the other hand, the individual or family with $1 million income suffers little, if any, change in lifestyle. Subtracting 10 percent from this income still leaves a small fortune to sustain both basic necessities and luxury consumption. The flat rate of 10 percent thus falls more heavily on the shoulders of the lower-income earner, making it practically, if not technically, regressive. To compensate for this relative difference in tax burden, a progressive tax attempts to partially equalize the burden by requiring higher-income earners to pay a higher rate in order to ease the burden carried by lower-income earners.

The income tax deserves special attention for what it reveals about the relation between freedom and equality in America. Americans have historically used a progressive income tax to increase equality and ensure fairness. Support for a progressive income tax in the United States can be traced back at least as far as Thomas Jefferson (1743–1826). One means of "lessening the inequality of property," he argued, is to "exempt all from taxation below a certain point, and to tax the higher portions of property in geometrical progression as they rise." Jefferson's support for a progressive income tax emerged partly from his commitment to democracy, which, as he noted, requires a minimal level of equality.

Over a century later, Franklin Delano Roosevelt (1882–1945) echoed Jefferson's support for a progressive income tax. In justifying his proposals for a graduated income tax on corporations, an increase in the top individual income tax rate from 63 to 79 percent, and an inheritance tax, Roosevelt explained to members of Congress that accumulations of wealth represent "great and undesirable concentration of control in relatively few individuals over the employment and welfare of many, many others." Also, he argued, "whether it be wealth achieved through the cooperation of the entire community or riches gained by speculation—in either case the ownership of such wealth or riches represents a great public interest and a great ability to pay." Note the three separate rationales for redistributive taxation contained in these statements. First, in noting that "the entire community" produces wealth even when it lodges in the hands of a few individuals, Roosevelt suggested that if everyone contributes to the creation of wealth, then everyone should benefit. Second, Roosevelt argued that individuals' possession of great wealth represents a responsibility to the community and to "a great public interest." A responsible wealthy citizen could and should willingly shoulder a heavier burden of taxation. Third, he noted that wealthy individuals have "a great ability to pay." Those who can, should pay a higher rate of taxation. Later that year, Roosevelt added a fourth rationale for redistribution. He argued that his purpose in raising taxes on corporations and wealthy individuals was "not to destroy wealth, but to create a broader range of opportunity" for all Americans. Redistributing wealth through taxation increases opportunity by breaking strangleholds held by wealthy and powerful individuals and groups, and by redistributing resources to those who need a boost.[23]

The Sixteenth Amendment to the Constitution, passed in 1913, established a national income tax. Its progressivity has varied widely since then. In 1918, during World War I, the top bracket reached 77 percent. This declined during the interim between the two world wars, but surged again to a high of 94 percent before World War II ended. In 1964, Congress cut tax rates to a range of 16 to 77 percent, down from a scale of 20 to 91 percent.

Since the early 1980s, some members of Congress and succeeding presidential administrations have attempted to cut taxes paid by wealthy Americans, arguing that it unfairly penalizes the rich and that it represents an unwarranted and excessive encroachment on their freedom. President Ronald Reagan and congressional Republicans succeeded in lowering the top tax bracket to 28 percent, and the fourteen tax brackets were reduced to two, 28 percent and 15 percent. In 1990 President George H. W. Bush and a Democratic Congress pushed the top bracket slightly upward to 30 percent. President Bill Clinton and Congress raised the top bracket further to 39.6 percent.

After Republicans took control of Congress in the 1994 elections, pressures increased for reducing taxes on the wealthy again. The 1997 Taxpayer Relief Act, sold as middle-class tax relief for its child credits, education tax credits, and education savings accounts, actually emphasized a capital gains tax cut, a reduction in inheritance taxes, and corporate tax breaks. These latter three components of the bill primarily addressed the interests of the wealthy who own most investment capital, bequeath large inheritances to their children, and own corporations. One study estimated that "over 45 percent of the 1997 tax cuts went to the richest 5 percent of U.S. households, with incomes over $130,000."[24]

In 2001, under President George W. Bush, the five brackets were reduced to four and the top rate was lowered to 33 percent. Of course, the effective tax rate is much lower than these figures suggest. Few people actually pay the full percentages that they are assessed. A variety of deductions and credits reduce and sometimes eliminate entirely the tax liability of individuals and corporations. The popular belief that wealthy individuals and corporations use loopholes to reduce their tax liability is not unfounded.

Supply-side economics, which came into vogue in the 1980s, provided one dominant rationale for cutting taxes on the wealthy. According to this economic philosophy, reducing taxes on the wealthy stimulates the economy by freeing up more money to invest in new and more efficient production. In theory, according to proponents, supply-side tax cuts benefit all Americans as productive investment creates new jobs. The benefits of the tax cut "trickle down" and "a rising tide lifts all boats." Critics note that during the 1980s this strategy resulted instead in a massive unproductive surge in corporate mergers and hostile takeovers. In 1981, before the adoption of supply-side economic and tax policy, Americans invested approximately 12.2 percent of their total income in new plant and machinery. In the immediate years after the supply-side tax cuts, new investment fluctuated between 11 percent (1983) and 12.6 percent (1985). Net business investment at its peak in the 1980s fell below the average for the 1950s, 1960s, and 1970s.[25] According to critics, supply-side economics has also contributed since the 1980s to a surge of overseas investment and the resulting loss of jobs in the United States paying living wages.

Some opponents of redistributive tax policies advocate a flat-rate income tax. Economists Robert Hall and Alvin Rabushka first proposed the flat tax in the mid-1980s. Republican Steve Forbes brought the issue to national attention during his presidential campaigns in the 1996 and 2000 elections. Forbes, along with Rep. Dick Armey (R-Texas) proposed the Forbes-Armey flat-tax plan as part of a Freedom and Fairness Restoration Act in June 1995. The title of their bill indicates both their emphasis on individuals' freedom to dispose of their own income and their attempt to disconnect the historical association of fairness with a progressive income tax. Their plan exempted income for individuals up to a threshold of $13,100 and for married couples up to a threshold of $26,200, with an additional $5,300 income exemption for each dependent. A family of four would begin paying a flat income tax rate of 17 percent on any income earned over $36,800. Additionally, their plan called for abolishing all deductions and credits, all inheritance taxes, and all taxes on investment income.

Proponents argue that a flat tax eliminates the problem of penalizing the rich. They also argue that eliminating all deductions and credits simplifies the tax code and closes the loopholes through which individuals and corporations evade taxes. Opponents counter that the complexity of the income tax code cannot be blamed on its progressivity. A progressive tax liability can be calculated nearly as quickly as a flat tax by simply applying different percentages on different levels of income or, better yet, simply referring to a tax table. Opponents of the flat tax also argue that the multiple deductions and credits that complicate the tax system overall help make the tax code more fair and equitable. Eliminating some of them, especially the home mortgage interest deduction, would adversely affect middle-class taxpayers who currently rely on these deductions. Also, the deduction for charitable contributions induces millions of Americans with disposable income to support worthy causes. Eliminating it would cause serious hardship to organizations that rely on charitable contributions. Opponents also point out that the various credits have a net positive impact on Americans' spending and investment habits. They note, too, that eliminating the investment income and inheritance taxes would significantly reduce taxes on the wealthy. Many wealthy Americans earn income *only* from capital gains; eliminating the capital gains tax would potentially reduce their tax liability to zero. The net impact would be to shift the burden of taxation from the wealthy to the middle and lower classes. Finally, since the proposal is not revenue neutral at 17 percent—some analysts estimate that the flat rate would have to be as high as 24 percent in order to remain revenue neutral—the proposal would hurt working-class Americans by forcing a reduction of social spending. The U.S. Treasury Department calculated that even a 20 percent flat-tax rate would fall approximately $30 billion short in revenue and, more importantly, increase taxes substantially on all income groups except those earning over $200,000 annually.[26]

The retreat from progressive tax policies reached a milestone in 2001 with the repeal by Congress and the president of the inheritance tax. Americans have historically viewed inheritance taxes as one of the key means of ensuring and maintaining economic opportunity by undermining at least some inherited privilege, in effect forcing more people at least slightly closer to the starting line at birth. Andrew Carnegie (1835–1919), the wealthy industrialist of the late nineteenth century, argued for a steep inheritance tax, saying that "of all forms of taxation, this seems the wisest." Presaging President Franklin Delano Roosevelt, he argued that wealth should be used for the public and common good: "The surplus wealth of the few will become, in the best sense, the property of the many, because administered for the common good, and this wealth, passing through the hands of the few, can be made a much more potent force for the elevation of our race."[27] A steep inheritance tax would best guarantee this result.

In recent years, Republican opponents of the inheritance tax attempted to change the terms of the debate by dubbing it a "death tax." Arguing that it forces some small business owners and small farmers to sell off their estates in order to pay the tax, they set out to eliminate it. Their opponents called their bluff by agreeing to reduce the inheritance tax on those small business owners and small farmers who suffered from it. They also pointed out that the estate tax in 2000 affected only the richest 2 percent of Americans. Nevertheless, opponents of the inheritance tax prevailed, passing legislation that will gradually repeal the inheritance tax over a period of ten years. This dramatically signals a further departure from the historic commitment in the United States to using the tax code to increase equality at least slightly.

Although they garner little attention, some tax reform proposals would increase equality, rather than decrease it. One proposal calls for an expansion of the Earned Income Credit, available only to low-income families. This reduces, and sometimes eliminates, their income tax liability. Another proposal would eliminate the distinction between wage income and income from capital gains. Both would be taxed progressively. Others propose a wealth tax of 1–2 percent imposed annually on the wealthiest Americans. Each of these proposals would increase the progressivity of the U.S. tax code and contribute to greater income equality by redistributing income from top to bottom.

Public Assistance Welfare versus Corporate Welfare

Welfare spending in the United States further illustrates a declining commitment to equality. Public assistance welfare refers to the "welfare" of everyday language, the kind most people have in mind when they use the term to refer to spending on programs and services for low-income people. Corporate welfare refers to preferential treatment awarded by local, state, or federal government to businesses, corporations, or entire industries, typically in the form of subsidies, grants, real estate, low-interest loans, special services, and tax breaks. Corporate welfare enjoys extensive and increasing support by contemporary policy makers, while public assistance welfare has been slashed in recent years. Estimates vary considerably, but point to the same conclusion: the United States spends far more on corporate welfare than it does on public assistance welfare. During the mid- to late 1990s, the federal government alone spent approximately $125–150 billion annually on corporate welfare. Total state and local government expenditures on corporate welfare far exceed that amount. One 1996 study estimated that Americans annually spent $1,186 per capita on corporate welfare and $415 on public assistance welfare. Another estimated that corporate welfare costs every American worker the equivalent of two weeks' pay, while public assistance welfare costs every American the equivalent of just an hour and a half's pay.[28]

Public assistance welfare achieved its acme during the New Deal of the 1930s. A culmination of decades of reaction to corporate excesses of the Gilded Age and the early years of the twentieth century, the New Deal established public assistance welfare policies in areas of income support, social security, and unemployment insurance. Its centerpiece, Aid to Families with Dependent Children (AFDC), distributed cash benefits directly to the poor. In its final year, 1996, AFDC cost taxpayers $17 billion, approximately 0.8 percent of total federal spending for that year. According to the nonpartisan Tax Foundation, at that level of funding the average American spent approximately 21 seconds of his or her typical workday generating taxes to pay for AFDC. The average annual payment to recipients never exceeded 70 percent of the poverty line. In 1996, the average payment fell below 40 percent of the poverty line.[29] These figures suggest that, despite the few high-profile cases of abuse and the inflamed rhetoric among its opponents, AFDC provided relatively little cash assistance at little cost to taxpayers. Why, then, dismantle it, as a Republican Congress and Democratic president did in 1996?

The increasing tendency among policy makers to remove support for public assistance welfare spending reflects an ideology that came to prominence with Ronald Reagan in 1980. It took shape in the Contract with America, a platform for change created and adopted by Republicans in Congress in 1994. Central tenets of this ideology included individual liberty, free markets, limited government, and personal responsibility. These elements culminated during the Democratic Clinton administration in a new policy on public assistance welfare spending, the 1996 Personal Responsibility and Work Opportunity Reconciliation Act. This legislation replaced AFDC with Temporary Assistance for Needy Families (TANF). The Act took a historic turn in eliminating public assistance welfare as an entitlement. TANF eliminated the role of the U.S. government in direct public assistance, replacing it with block grants to states. Most notably, TANF imposed a lifetime limit of sixty months on public assistance benefits and forced recipients into the workforce after twenty-four months of receiving benefits. If recipients' circumstances remain dire after five years, they nevertheless lose eligibility.

As expected, TANF produced a decrease in the welfare rolls and an increase in employment of welfare recipients and former recipients. However, since most current and former recipients find jobs only in low-paying service sector areas, the net effect has been an increase in the number of working poor. In other words, as one observer noted, TANF produced "less welfare, just as much poverty."[30] Child care also presents huge challenges to recipients and former recipients trying to balance work against family needs. The available poverty-level jobs pay too little to afford decent child care services. Federal policy makers simply overlooked the problem when drafting the legislation, preferring to let states address it, or not. Critics also point out that by forcing single mothers into the workforce at poverty-level wages, the legislation undermines one of the very "family values" espoused by the legislators who dismantled AFDC: having at least one parent at home with the children.

The same policy makers who slashed public assistance welfare are maintaining or increasing corporate welfare. They award millions annually to corporate farms. The Accelerated Depreciation Subsidy, which costs the federal government approximately $32 billion annually, allows companies to depreciate their equipment faster than it actually wears out. The "advertising subsidy" allows corporations to deduct the cost of their advertising. The United States lets mining and logging companies pay subsidized rates to exploit and profit from federally owned land. Five large corporations alone—AT&T, Bechtel, Boeing, General Electric, and McDonnell Douglas—received billions of dollars in subsidized loans, grants, and long-term guarantees from the federal government during the 1990s. One corporation, Lockheed Martin, received $1 billion in federal assistance to cover the costs of its merger, including more than $16 million for paying top executives. In 1989, the state of Illinois gave Sears, Roebuck & Co. $240 million as an incentive to keep its corporate headquarters in the state. Indiana gave United Airlines $451 million to build an aircraft-maintenance facility. Alabama convinced Mercedes-Benz to build an assembly plant in Alabama with a subsidy of $253 million. Pennsylvania awarded Kvaerner $307 million as an incentive to open a shipyard in Philadelphia. These examples could be multiplied many times over at local, state, and national levels.[31]

Proponents argue that corporate welfare is good for business and thus for all America because it creates and retains jobs. Every company lured with promises of tax breaks or outright subsidies in theory brings new jobs that outweigh the cost of the corporate welfare. Critics respond that corporate welfare is simply a polite name for bribes to secure or reward the cooperation of business leaders. Increasingly, businesses and corporations hold government hostage using threats of relocating or downsizing. It fuels a competitive race to the bottom as different local, regional, state, and even national governments attempt to outbid each other in order to entice a particular corporation into desirable behavior. Unlike public assistance welfare spending, which goes primarily to the poor, corporate welfare directly subsidizes owners and managers of corporations.

In practice, the jobs won through corporate welfare rarely measure up to the promise. The largest beneficiaries of corporate welfare, the Fortune 500 companies, eliminated more jobs than they created during the 1990s. The five Fortune 500 companies noted above—AT&T, Bechtel, Boeing, General Electric, and McDonnell Douglas—eliminated over a third of a million jobs during the period in which they received their corporate welfare. Lockheed Martin, also noted above, fired 50,000 of its employees. Critics also note that, even if the corporate welfare produces jobs, the cost per job makes the deal questionable. Of the state deals noted above, Illinois spent $44,000 for each of the 5,400 jobs it retained, Indiana spent $72,000 for each job, Alabama paid $169,000 per job, and Pennsylvania paid $323,000 for each job.[32] Critics note, finally, that the competition among states does not create more jobs for the nation as a whole, since each state's win is often another state's loss.

Most businesses and corporations that receive corporate welfare are owned by relatively affluent people, while public assistance recipients are, by definition, economically marginal. Though corporate welfare sometimes increases job opportunities for average Americans, frequently it does not. Policy makers' increasing preference for corporate welfare over public assistance welfare thus often contributes to radical inequality by shifting income and wealth upward. Welfare policy, like tax policy, shows a weak and declining commitment to equality in the United States.

INTELLECTUAL DEFENSES OF INEQUALITY

Perhaps, like Sisyphus pushing his boulder up the hill, efforts to increase equality are doomed to perpetual frustration. History shows no shortage of political thinkers who have adopted this view. They have defended inequality on the grounds that it is either natural or ordained by God. Either way, by implication we should not attempt to overcome it. Both of the most influential ancient Greek philosophers, Plato (427–347 B.C.) and Aristotle (384–322 B.C.), presumed a natural inequality among humans, and both favored political systems that built upon this natural inequality.

In his *Republic* (375 B.C.), Plato built a just state on a foundation of inequality, requiring that different people assume roles appropriate to their level of quality and ability. At the top in positions of leadership, Plato placed philosopher-rulers characterized by their superior intellectual and moral virtue. At the bottom, Plato placed artisans, farmers, and other laborers. At an intermediate level, Plato placed the "auxiliaries," a military caste assigned the role of supporting the philosopher-rulers in ruling the state. These three levels corresponded to the metals gold (philosopher-ruler), silver (auxiliaries), and iron and bronze (workers), in a clear hierarchical pattern of quality and ability. According to Plato:

> When god fashioned you, he added gold in the composition of those of you who are qualified to be Rulers (which is why their prestige is greatest); he put silver in the Auxiliaries, and iron and bronze in the farmers and other workers. . . . The State will be ruined when it has [Rulers] of silver or bronze.

Plato added an additional layer of gender inequality. He acknowledged that, in theory, women should be allowed to do the same things as men. In practice, however, he believed that women were inferior to men except in domestic matters that he deemed unimportant:

> Is there any human activity at which men aren't far better in all these respects than women? We need not waste time over exceptions like weaving and various cooking operations, at which women are thought to be experts. . . . In general the one sex is much better at everything than the other. A good many women, it is true, are better than a good many men at a good many things. But the general rule is as you stated it. . . . It is natural for women to take part in all occupations as well as men, though in all women will be the weaker partners.[33]

Like Plato, Aristotle presumed a natural hierarchy of talent and virtue. And like Plato, he felt that the state was best guided by an elite few with exceptional talent and virtue. He preferred an aristocracy of merit to other political forms, including democracy. Aristotle went beyond Plato, however, in dismissing outright the notion that women could compete with men. "The relation of male to female," he argued, "is naturally that of the superior to the inferior—

of the ruling to the ruled."[34] Like slaves, women existed for the sake of male citizens. They managed domestic affairs, leaving men free to pursue the superior calling of politics. Aristotle's views on equality also appeared in his conception of distributive justice, which can be summarized as giving equal amounts to equals—and unequal amounts to unequals. An injustice would be committed, he argued, if unequals received equal amounts.

With some exceptions, the Federalist Founders followed Plato and Aristotle in presuming natural inequality. Much like Plato and Aristotle, John Adams (1735–1826) believed in a "natural aristocracy" of merit constituted by the best and brightest adult white men. "The people in all nations," he wrote, "are naturally divided into two sorts, the gentleman and . . . the common people."[35] Like Plato and Aristotle, he hoped that public officials would be drawn from the natural aristocracy. The rest of the people were to be controlled and, if possible, blocked from direct access to power. The U.S. Constitution, with its separation of powers and checks and balances, reflected the Federalists' fear of democracy and the equality it represented to them.

John Calhoun (1782–1850), a U.S. Senator from South Carolina between 1810 and 1850, argued that inequality, including its most extreme form of slavery, made civilization possible. Slavery, he argued, is "instead of an evil, a good—a positive good. . . . There never has yet existed a wealthy and civilized society in which one portion of the community did not, in point of fact, live on the labor of the other."[36] Proslavery advocate George Fitzhugh (1806–1881) based his defense of slavery partly on an assertion of natural inequality between white and black races. He argued that black people lacked the talent and ambition for free subsistence. "The negro," he asserted, "has neither energy nor enterprise . . . [and so] finds, with his improvident habits, that his liberty is a curse to himself, and a greater curse to the society around him. . . . There is one strong argument in favor of negro slavery . . . : that he, being unfitted for the mechanic arts, for trade, and all skillful pursuits, leaves those pursuits to be carried on by the whites." Like Calhoun, Fitzhugh also argued that slavery benefited master and slave alike: "Our Southern slavery has become a benign and protective institution, and our negroes are confessedly better off than any free laboring population in the world."[37]

Proponents of slavery were not alone in defending inequality in America during the mid-nineteenth century. Abraham Lincoln (1809–1865) conceded only partial equality among blacks and whites. Speaking of a black woman, he wrote that "in some respects she certainly is not my equal; but in her natural right to eat the bread she earns with her own hands without asking leave of any one else, she is my equal, and the equal of all others." Like many of his contemporaries, Lincoln believed that blacks were inferior in "intellect, moral developments, [and] social capacity," but equal in "certain inalienable rights, among which are life, liberty, and the pursuit of happiness." Lincoln revealed his deep feelings about the moral status of blacks in his expressions of disgust at the possibility of "amalgamation" of black and white races. In part, these feelings reflected his apparent recognition that this "amalgamation" occurred primarily through the systematic rape of black female slaves by their white masters. However, Lincoln also felt a deep antipathy toward the idea of inter-racial romance and marriage. According to Lincoln, "There is a natural disgust in the minds of nearly all white people, to the idea of an indiscriminate amalgamation of the white and black races. . . . Judge Douglas [Lincoln's political opponent] is especially horrified at the thought of the mixing blood by the white and black races: agreed for once—a thousand times agreed. There are white men enough to marry all the white women, and black men enough to marry all the black women; and so let them be married."[38]

The defense of inequality in America attained its most aggressive character in the late nineteenth century with the Social Darwinists, such as William Graham Sumner (1840–1910) and Andrew Carnegie, who applied Charles Darwin's (1809–1882) evolutionary theory to the human species. They concluded that humans, like other species, compete for survival. Over time, the most fit survive by virtue of their superior physical and intellectual capacities. The least fit naturally and beneficially die off. The human species progresses precisely through this process of natural selection. As this brief description suggests, the Social Darwinists not only presumed natural inequality, they made it a driving force in the development and progress of the human species. In short, like Calhoun and Fitzhugh, they made a virtue of inequality, arguing that civilization founders without it. According to Carnegie:

> The contrast between the palace of the millionaire and the cottage of the laborer with us today measures the change which has come with civilization. This change, however, is not to be deplored, but welcomed as highly beneficial. It is well, nay, essential for the progress of the race. . . . We accept and welcome, therefore, as conditions to which we must accommodate ourselves, great in-

equality of environment, the concentration of business, industrial and commercial, in the hands of a few, and the law of competition between these, as being not only beneficial, but essential for the future progress of the race.

Inequality, Carnegie argued, is "beyond our power to alter. . . . It is a waste of time to criticize the inevitable."[39]

The Social Darwinists took the principle of natural selection to its logical conclusion, arguing that we should not help those on the bottom, save at a minimum level of offering them opportunities to compete. They made of this a moral principle: thou *shalt not* help the weak, the poor, the sick; the losers in the competition for survival *should* die off, for only through this process of natural selection can the species survive and progress. By prolonging their demise, we retard the development of the species. Though the Social Darwinists' ideas may sound jarring to contemporary ears, they exerted significant influence in the late nineteenth century.

The belief in the innate superiority of some racial groups continues to surface today. In 1994, two American scholars, Richard J. Herrnstein (1930–1994) and Charles Murray (1943–) of Harvard University and the American Enterprise Institute, argued that intellectual inequality among blacks and whites is innate, with whites naturally superior. They noted that "the average black and white differ in IQ at every level of socioeconomic status," with blacks having lower IQs than whites. They denied that these differences can be explained as the result of test bias, socioeconomic status, or other social cause. According to Herrnstein and Murray, different ethnic groups "differ intellectually for genetic reasons."[40]

NEGATIVE FREEDOM AND ITS LINKAGE TO PROPERTY

The tension between equality and freedom is primarily a tension between equality and the negative freedoms associated with private property. Most Americans take private property rights for granted. Most also assume that people should be able to amass as much property as they can and that people should in general be able to do whatever they want with their property. In other words, they should be free, subject to as few restrictions as possible, to acquire property and enjoy the freedoms and privileges that accompany its possession. Although these presumptions may be justifiable, in practice they exact high costs in terms of equality.

The deep conceptual and practical linkage in Western culture of negative freedom to property, and the costs to equality, can be found clearly in the writings of John Locke (1632–1704). Locke considered freedom the most fundamental political value, the "foundation of all the rest." In Locke's view, prior to the establishment of civil society, humans existed in "a state of perfect freedom" in which they "order their actions, and dispose of their possessions and persons as they think fit . . . without asking leave or depending upon the will of any other man." This classic expression of negative freedom emphasizes the right to do whatever we want without interference from others. Locke's natural freedom yielded to freedom within civil society upon establishing a government, but its essential character changed little. Upon entering civil society, individuals give up the freedom to do entirely as they please, in exchange for greater protections afforded by government. In civil society, according to Locke, freedom still meant "to be free from restraint," to which he added freedom from violence and theft made possible by the protective role of government.[41]

Equality played a much smaller role in Locke's thinking. According to Locke, individuals have, first of all, an equal right to self-protection. In the "state of nature," each person wields this himself, as well as a corresponding right to punish transgressions. Second, our natural right to self-protection yields in civil society to equal protection under the law. Once formulated, the laws apply equally to all citizens. Third, humans have an equal right to consent to government and its laws. Locke understood that this consent cannot feasibly be given explicitly by everyone. To circumvent this problem, he distinguished between express and tacit consent. Citizens explicitly offer their express consent through formal agreements. They give tacit consent by living within a civil society and enjoying the benefits of that civil society.

Though Locke may have been forced by logic and practicality to this notion of tacit consent, it dilutes his commitment to political equality. Tacit consent requires nothing of an individual, save living within the boundaries of a state. More importantly, it gives nothing of practical political value to the individual, including an effective say in the affairs of government. To say that someone tacitly consents to a government and its laws is to say only that they implicitly tolerate the government, its laws, and its actions.

Locke's inclusion of these minimal forms of political equality gives his *Second Treatise* at least a flavor of democracy. However, Locke's overriding emphasis on freedom, and the association he made of freedom with property, would prove fatal to substantial political equality and other forms of equality in his time and ours. Locke justified the unlimited acquisition of property and, in doing so, radical economic inequality. He either failed to appreciate how radical economic inequality could undermine political equality, thought it was justifiable, or simply did not care.

Locke's argument about property appears at first in egalitarian guise. He began his chapter on property by arguing that God gave the Earth "to mankind in common." If the Earth belongs to all of us, then we have an equal right to enjoy it and to make use of it. But Locke did not linger long on this assertion. To make use of the Earth's bounty, he argued, humans must appropriate it as private property. "There must of necessity," he argued, "be a means to appropriate [the Earth's fruits] some way or other before they can be of any use, or at all beneficial, to any particular men." Locke did not consider the alternative—that humans could make common, cooperative use of the Earth. He simply assumed and asserted the requirement of private property without arguing the point. How does this appropriation of our common earthly bequeathal to private property occur? According to Locke, humans acquire private property by mixing their labor with the Earth and its resources. Since each person "has a 'property' in his own 'person,'" and since the "'labor' of his body and the 'work' of his hands . . . are properly his . . . whatsoever, then, he removes out of the state that Nature hath provided and left it in, he hath mixed his labor with it, and joined to it something that is his own, and thereby makes it his property."[42] Anyone, Locke argued, can acquire private rights to acorns simply by investing labor in gathering them. A farmer makes the soil his own by adding his labor to it.

Is this right to appropriate the fruits of the Earth, and thus to acquire private property, unlimited? Initially, Locke's answer implies not, in three ways. First, Locke's labor theory of private property implies that a person's ability to mix labor with the Earth limits his or her wealth. The acorn gatherer can gather only so many acorns in a day. A farmer can appropriate only the amount of soil that he or she can till. Second, Locke argued that each person's appropriation must be limited to an amount that will not spoil. This restricts the acorn gatherer's wealth. Third, Locke limited property to an amount that leaves plenty for others. Each can acquire as much private property as possible "at least where there is enough, and as good left in common for others."[43] The implications of these three points would appear to strictly limit property acquisition and, by extension, the gap between rich and poor that results from unlimited and unchecked property rights.

Locke circumvented the first limit to private property in a short phrase buried in his argument. According to Locke, "the grass my horse has bit, *the turfs my servant has cut*, and the ore I have digged in any place, where I have a right to them in common with others, become my property without the assignation or consent of anybody." Without arguing the point, Locke simply assumed that one person can acquire property by employing others to mix their labor with the Earth on behalf of the employer. In these six words—"the turfs my servant has cut"—Locke dismissed limitations on private property initially implied by his labor theory of property.

He circumvented the second problem of spoilage by introducing the concept of money. Humans consent, Locke noted, to money as a nonspoilable store of value. The acorn gatherer can effectively avoid the problem of spoilage simply by converting acorns to coins. By consenting to money as a store of value, Locke further asserted, humans also consented to the resulting inequalities. "Since gold and silver . . . has its value only from the consent of men," he wrote, "it is plain that the consent of men have agreed to a disproportionate and unequal possession of the earth." While the first claim of human consent to money as a storage of value is plausible, the second is a bare assertion that at a minimum needs more defense than Locke bothered to give it.

Locke circumvented the third stipulation by simply assuming abundance. "In the beginning," he asserted, "all the world was America." During his time, Europeans viewed America as a vast, unsettled continent. Locke himself viewed it as "vacant."[44] Like many of his fellow Europeans, Locke apparently did not view America's native inhabitants as human. America represented the promise of unlimited land and property in general.

The implications of these three intellectual moves remain with us today. In sweeping away his own objections to unlimited property acquisition, Locke legitimized vast inequalities of wealth and income. Significantly, Locke's discussion of property appeared before the social contract, while humans still live in the state of nature. By implication, the inequalities that inevitably develop are natural rather than a consequence of one or more social conventions and institutions such as private property and a market economy.

Having legitimized unlimited property, and thus inequality, did Locke envision a means of mitigating its consequences? In modern times, many countries' governments attempt to minimize inequality via progressive taxation and social welfare spending. Locke envisioned no such role for the state. Locke set out in his *Second Treatise* to justify government, but one strictly limited in scope. He argued for a minimal state with its role limited to protecting property, defined sometimes to mean property as possessions and other times to include life, liberty, and estate.

Locke's linkage of property and freedom both justified radical inequality and made it likely. Conceptually he linked them in his definition of *property*, which included the right to life and liberty as well as to "estate," the material assets that today we associate with the term *property*. Locke also linked them by awarding a central place for private property in his discussion of the state of nature, the natural freedoms associated with it, and subsequently protecting them. He devoted more space in his discussion of the state of nature to his defense of unlimited private property than to any other topic; the rest of the book concentrates on defending property via government and the social contract. This implies that Locke viewed both natural and civil freedom primarily in terms of acquiring wealth and keeping it. Third, Locke linked freedom and property conceptually and practically in awarding to government the sole role of protecting property, understood to include life, liberty, and possessions. For Locke, individuals institute government for one overriding purpose: to protect their lives, their freedoms that pointedly and primarily include their freedom to acquire unlimited private possessions, and the possessions that they actually acquire.

We can assume that Locke well knew that, having acquired private property, a person also secured certain powers and privileges and that these would be unequally distributed in accordance with the unequal distribution of property. Acquiring property positioned a person to preserve and enlarge freedom subject to as few restrictions as possible and to use the state as an instrument to protect the powers and privileges associated with freedom. On the other extreme, those unfortunates without private property could expect deprivation of power and privilege, as well as material deprivation. The scope of their freedoms would of necessity be limited in comparison. We are the heirs to Locke's intellectual and practical linkage of private property and freedom, including the radical inequality that emerges from it.

Locke's ideas exerted extensive influence on the American Founders, and some contemporary thinkers[45] continue to use Locke to argue for limited government, nearly unlimited negative freedom, and the primary importance of property rights in this formulation. Like Locke, they place a high value on property rights and freedom and a low value on equality. And also like Locke, they focus on the potential loss to freedom represented by political power, while ignoring how economic power could achieve the same results.

Of course, there are other important reasons besides political philosophy for the relative emphasis in the United States on negative freedom, at the expense of equality. A political economy of capitalism builds upon private ownership of the means of production and the right of individual owners to control the dispensation of their property. Capitalism requires extensive negative freedom, understood to mean doing what you want with your property with as few restrictions as possible from government or other social and political institutions. Capitalism also builds upon a presumption of inequality. As a competitive system, capitalism inevitably entails winners and losers. Absent 100 percent inheritance confiscation, the winners inevitably tend to perpetuate their privilege, and one generation passes wealth and corresponding power and privilege on to succeeding generations. The result is inequality of opportunity as well as inequality of means. Other determinants of an emphasis on negative freedom include a legal system that favors property rights over basic rights to food and health care, and a culture that celebrates individual freedom.

Despite the relatively weak commitment overall to equality in the history of liberalism, much has been achieved in liberalism to increase equality, if understood to mean formal and legal protections and guarantees. Though they are enforced inequitably, the granting of legal rights to most adult Americans regardless of race, ethnicity, sex, or religion is an achievement worth celebrating. Liberalism's emphasis on legal rights may represent one of its greatest accomplishments, but it also represents one of its greatest sources of myopia. Even if they were enforced equitably, legal rights alone cannot guarantee equality because they do not eliminate stubborn institutional and structural obstacles to greater equality for all Americans. Removing formal legal barriers to inequality eliminates some, but not all, impediments to real equality. Stubborn institutional and structural barriers remain firmly in place.

PRACTICAL TRADEOFFS BETWEEN FREEDOM AND EQUALITY

Looking at specific tradeoffs between freedom and equality can highlight the tension between the two. Most proposals to increase equality require at least some sacrifice of negative freedoms associated with property rights. This can easily be shown by briefly considering some of the proposals to increase political equality, equal opportunity, and economic equality.

There are several ways to achieve greater political equality. First, campaign contribution and spending laws could be reformed in order to limit the influence of money in electoral politics. Congress attempted this in 2002 but, as noted above, fell well short of its stated goal of eliminating the dominating influence of money in U.S. electoral politics. Reform efforts such as the 2002 legislation have focused on imposing limits on campaign contributions. Alternatively, Congress could impose limits on campaign spending.

Second, public financing of elections would both equalize the amount of spending by each candidate and make it more possible for average citizens to run for office. Public financing of elections would reduce or eliminate financial barriers to seeking office.

A third way to increase political equality is to require the media to cover all candidates, including the more marginal candidates representing alternative political parties and ideologies. Currently, most mainstream media cover only Democratic and Republican candidates. Candidates from alternative political parties typically find themselves locked out of the process, unable to garner media attention. When subsequent polls show them far behind in the election race, the media sagely report that "they are not viable candidates," thus fulfilling their own predictions and justifying their role in setting the conditions for the fulfillment of their predictions. Getting more media coverage would increase these alternative candidates' chances of getting elected.

Fourth, political equality could be increased by limiting the influence of professional lobbyists. Strict limits on the number of lobbyists, or banning them outright, would eliminate the problem of overrepresentation of some interests and underrepresentation of others. Alternatively, political equality could be increased by guaranteeing equal representation by lobbyists for all interested parties, much as we guarantee legal representation for anyone accused of a crime. This would increase the likelihood that all voices would be heard in politics.

The costs associated with these proposals for increasing political equality can be described in terms of loss of negative freedom. Limiting campaign contributions reduces people's freedom to spend their own money however they want, including on the purchase of political power. Public financing of elections would require that taxpayers pay for it. Any tax can be viewed as a reduction of taxpayers' freedom to keep or spend their own money as they see fit. Requiring the media to cover candidates directly infringes on their owners' property rights. Banning lobbyists, like banning campaign contributions, reduces people's freedom to spend their own money to buy voice in the political process. Equalizing the representation of lobbyists would require limits on the freedom of the affluent to outspend others, combined with subsidies for the nonaffluent to hire lobbyists—an option that would require tax dollars.

The surest way to increase equality of opportunity would be to increase economic equality. Access to money enables access to the best educational and other resources that support wider opportunities for career choice and advancement. A second way would be to reinstate the inheritance tax. An inheritance tax increases equality of opportunity by better ensuring that every person begins from approximately the same starting line. Third, we could do a better job of guaranteeing access to a quality education. Equal access to a quality K–12 education minimally requires adequate funding of public schools. Access to a quality higher education could be boosted through increases in need-based grants and scholarships. Fourth, equality of opportunity could be increased by maintaining and increasing affirmative action programs for those who need it and eliminating it for those who do not. Affirmative action policies designed to redress historically inherited systems of inequality can help boost the level of opportunities available to people marginalized through no fault of their own.

Each of these options for increasing equality of opportunity exacts a price in terms of negative freedom. Increasing economic equality, which would require greater redistribution of income and wealth from wealthy to poor, would necessarily deprive the wealthy of more of their money. Inheritance taxes decrease people's freedom to bequeath money and estate to their children. Increasing equality of educational opportunity would require either greater redistribution of resources from wealthy to poor school districts or increased taxes to support adequate funding of poor districts. The former option decreases the negative freedom of parents and taxpayers in wealthy districts to completely control the disposition of their own money. The latter option, like all options involving increasing taxes, decreases the negative freedom of taxpayers to retain control of their money. Finally, affirmative action policies decrease the negative freedom of some individuals displaced by programs and policies designed to boost the fortunes of minorities and women.

A progressive income tax offers one of the most straightforward ways to increase economic equality, by at least marginally redistributing income from top to bottom. The intent of a progressive income tax has never included achieving complete economic equality. Rather, it has sought to bring the bottom up slightly by taxing the top income earners at higher rates in order to reduce the level of inequality, without eliminating it. The tax system as a whole could be made more progressive by increasing the spread of the graduated rates of the income tax, reinstating the inheritance tax, increasing the capital gains tax, imposing a wealth tax on the largest fortunes, and adding graduated rates to the payroll tax. A second way to increase economic equality would be to increase social welfare spending on programs that provide direct services and offer income support to those who need it. These programs provide a minimal level of access to basic human needs such as food, shelter, and medical care that low-income people cannot otherwise afford. Like a progressive income tax, these programs seek a partial narrowing of the gap between rich and poor, not total equality. The so-called living wage campaign offers a third proposal for reducing economic inequality. A living wage provides sufficient income to live above the poverty line, unlike a minimum wage that does not. Providing adequate benefits to all workers could be added to this proposal for a living wage.

Each of these proposals for increasing economic equality impinges on somebody's negative freedom as it is expressed in property rights. Redistribution, whether accomplished through the tax code, through direct payments, or through service provision requires that the wealthy yield at least some of their negative freedom to keep all of their money. The proposals thus decrease the freedom of the wealthy from government interference into their economic lives. Requiring employers to pay a living wage and provide benefits reduces their freedom to pay employees as little as they can.

If increasing equality requires decreasing freedom, then we are apparently left in a bind. By even partially sacrificing freedoms associated with property rights, even if we achieve greater equality in doing so, we nevertheless may end up with a net loss of well-being. The following chapter addresses potential ways out of this bind.

QUESTIONS, PROBLEMS, AND ACTIVITIES

1. Brainstorm the benefits and costs of freedom for the individual and for society. Of equality.

2. Based on your own personal experience, how close are we to equality of opportunity? In what ways are your opportunities foreclosed by circumstances outside of your control? How does your experience compare to others in similar, and different, demographic categories?

3. Construct a balanced budget for a two-parent family with two small children, both parents working full time (40 hours per week each) at minimum wage ($5.15/hour in 2005). Subtract payroll and sales taxes (Earned Income Credit should eliminate income tax liability), estimated at 12 percent combined, from income. Estimate all household and living expenses, then subtract them from the remainder. Don't forget child care expenses. Is there room in the budget for "extra" expenses such as health care insurance (minimum wage jobs generally do not include benefits), car insurance, saving for college and retirement, purchasing a home computer, entertainment, and Christmas presents?

4. In what ways are you politically equal to a billionaire? In what ways are you politically unequal?

5. Identify songs about freedom, and about equality. Play them and analyze the lyrics. Do you agree with the ideas and sentiments they express?

6. Share stories about your own experiences about facing, or not facing, various educational "filters." What impact, if any, have the filters had on your career aspirations and your ability to attain them?

7. Many of the American Founders believed in a natural aristocracy of intellectually and morally virtuous people and hoped that public officials would be drawn from this natural aristocracy. In your estimation, have their hopes been realized in contemporary times? Why or why not?

8. What do you think of the argument that humans must give up their presumption of superiority over nature? What are the implications of this argument for the character of human life, and for protecting the environment?

NOTES

1. John Paul II, *Laborem Exercens* (On human work), in *Origins* 11, no. 15 (September 24, 1981), pp. 225, 228.

2. For Native American views on nature and the place of humans in relation to nature, see Black Elk, *The Sacred Pipe*, ed. J. E. Brown (New York: Penguin Press, 1971); John Neihardt, ed., *Black Elk Speaks* (Lincoln: University of Nebraska Press, 1961); Edward Benton-Banai, *The Mishomis Book: The Voice of the Ojibway* (St. Paul, MN: Red School House, 1988); and Vine Deloria, *The Metaphysics of Modern Existence* (San Francisco: Harper & Row, 1979).

3. U.S. Conference of Catholic Bishops, "Statement on Political Responsibility for 1996," in *Origins* 25, no. 22 (November 16, 1995), p. 376; U.S. Conference of Catholic Bishops, "Statement on Capital Punishment," November 1980, available at http://www.usccb.org/sdwp/national/criminal/death/uscc80.htm.

4. Lawrence Mishel, Jared Bernstein, and John Schmitt, *The State of Working America, 2000–2001* (Ithaca, NY: Cornell University Press, 2001), p. 11.

5. Mishel, Bernstein, and Schmitt, *Working America, 2000–2001*, p. 9; Lawrence Mishel, Jared Bernstein, and Sylvia Allegretto, *The State of Working America, 2004–2005* (Ithaca, NY: Cornell University Press, 2005), pp. 319, 309; Marie Michael, "The 'Other America' Revisited: The War on Poverty—Gains and Losses," in *Current Economic Issues*, ed. Phineas Baxandall, Tami Friedman, Thad Williamson, and the Dollars and Sense Collective, 6th ed. (Cambridge, MA: Economic Affairs Bureau, 2001), pp. 55–56. The official poverty thresholds considered here exclude taxes, which would reduce the actual cash available for sustaining a family, but include cash transfers such as welfare benefits.

6. Mishel, Bernstein, and Allegretto, *Working America, 2004–2005*, p. 214; Chuck Collins and Felice Yeskel, *Economic Apartheid in America: A Primer on Economic Inequality and Insecurity* (New York: New Press, 2000), pp. 50–51.

7. Mishel, Bernstein, and Schmitt, *Working America, 2000–2001*, pp. 3, 5, 6.

8. Ibid., pp. 4, 24.

9. Mishel, Bernstein, and Allegretto, *Working America, 2004–2005*, pp. 316, 319, 132, 133.

10. Courtenay M. Slater and Cornelia J. Strawser, eds., *Business Statistics of the United States*, 5th ed. (Lanham, MD: Bernan Press, 1999), p. 38.

11. Mishel, Bernstein, and Schmitt, *Working America, 2000–2001*, pp. 45, 4, 25.

12. Ibid., p. 5; Marc Breslow, "The Racial Divide Widens," in Baxandall et al., *Current Economic Issues*, p. 63; Mishel, Bernstein, and Allegretto, *Working America, 2004–2005*, p. 166.

13. Mishel, Bernstein, and Schmitt, *Working America, 2000–2001*, p. 8.

14. Ibid., p. 2. See also Bill Moyers, "America: What Went Wrong?" videocassette (Princeton, NJ: Films for the Humanities and Sciences, 1994); and Stephen Gregory, "80 percent of New Jobs Don't Pay 'Livable Wage,'" *Los Angeles Times*, December 9, 1998. Union workers' total compensation is approximately 27.8 percent higher than nonunion workers; see Mishel, Bernstein, and Schmitt, *Working America, 2000–2001*, p. 6.

15. Mishel, Bernstein, and Schmitt, *Working America, 2000–2001*, pp. 12, 395.

16. Mishel, Bernstein, and Allegretto, *Working America, 2004–2005*, p. 152.

17. See "Fair Test," www.FairTest.org.

18. Ibid.; Charles Dervarics and Ronald Roach, "Fortifying the Federal Presence in Retention," *Black Issues in Higher Education* 17, no. 3 (March 30, 2000), p. 20.

19. Dervarics and Roach, "Fortifying the Federal Presence," p. 20. See also Karin Chenowith, "HBCUs [Historically Black Colleges and Universities] Tackle the Knotty Problem of Retention," *Black Issues in Higher Education* 15, no. 26 (February 18, 1999), p. 39, for a discussion of challenges facing black college students that confirms the filters identified in this section.

20. "Adding It Up: The Price–Income Squeeze in Higher Education," *Change* 29, no. 3 (May–June 1997), p. 45; Anita M. Seline, "The Shift away from Need-Blind: Colleges Have Started Their Version of 'Wallet Biopsies,'" *Black Issues in Higher Education* 13, no. 13 (August 22, 1996), p. 38.

21. Quoted in Richard Hofstadter, *The American Political Tradition and the Men Who Made It* (1948; New York: Vintage Books, 1973), pp. 6, 20.

22. William Hudson, *American Democracy in Peril: Seven Challenges to America's Future*, 3rd ed. (New York: Chatham House, 2001), pp. 133–34, 163–64; Marjorie Kelly, *The Divine Right of Capital: Dethroning the Corporate Aristocracy* (San Francisco: Berrett-Koehler, 2001), p. 161.

23. Thomas Jefferson, "Letter to James Madison [1785]," in *The Life and Selected Writings of Thomas Jefferson*, ed. Adrienne Koch and William Peden (New York: Random House, 1944), p. 362; Roosevelt, quoted in W. Elliot Brownlee, *Federal Taxation in America: A Short History* (Cambridge: Cambridge University Press, 1996), p. 74.

24. Chuck Collins and John Miller, "Tax Reform Follies," in *Current Economic Issues*, ed. Marc Breslow, John Miller, Jim Phillips, and the Dollars and Sense Collective, 5th ed. (Somerville, MA: Economic Affairs Bureau, 2000), p. 30.

25. Kevin Phillips, *The Politics of Rich and Poor* (New York: HarperCollins, 1990), p. 70.

26. See Collins and Miller, "Tax Reform Follies," p. 33.

27. Andrew Carnegie, "Wealth" [1889], in *Gospel of Wealth, and Other Timely Essays*, ed. Edward Kirkland (Cambridge, MA: Belknap Press of Harvard University Press, 1965), pp. 22, 23.

28. Donald Barlett and James Steele, "Corporate Welfare," *Time*, November 9, 1998, p. 38; Lawrence Mitchell, *Stacked Deck* (Philadelphia: Temple University Press, 1998), p. 21.

29. For a summary of AFDC, including the arguments of supporters and critics, see Edward Greenberg and Benjamin Page, *The Struggle for Democracy*, 3rd ed. (New York: Longman, 1997), pp. 706–11.

30. Randy Albelda, "What Welfare Reform Has Wrought," in Baxandall et al., *Current Economic Issues*, p. 45.

31. See Chuck Collins, "Aid to Dependent Corporations," in *Current Economic Issues*, ed. Marc Breslow, Abby Scher, and the Dollars and Sense Collective, 4th ed. (Cambridge, MA: Economic Affairs Bureau, 1999), pp. 28–30; and Mitchell, *Stacked Deck*, p. 21.

32. Barlett and Steele, "Corporate Welfare," pp. 38–39; Mitchell, *Stacked Deck*, p. 21.

33. Plato, *The Republic* 3.415a–c, 5.455c–e.

34. Aristotle, *Politics* 1.5.7.

35. Quoted in Kelly, *Divine Right of Capital*, p. 29. See also John Adams, "Letter to Samuel Adams [1790]," in *The Political Writings of John Adams*, ed. George W. Carey (Washington, DC: Regnery, 2000), p. 667, for one reference to a natural aristocracy.

36. John Calhoun, "Speech on the Reception of Abolition Petitions" [1837], in *Union and Liberty: The Political Philosophy of John C. Calhoun*, ed. Ross M. Lence (Indianapolis: Liberty Fund, 1992), p. 474.

37. George Fitzhugh, *Cannibals All! or, Slaves without Masters*, edited by C. Vann Woodward (1857; Cambridge, MA: Belknap Press of Harvard University Press, 1960), pp. 199–201.

38. Abraham Lincoln, "Speech in Springfield, Illinois, June 26, 1857," in *Abraham Lincoln: Complete Works, Comprising His Speeches, Letters, State Papers, and Miscellaneous Writings*, ed. John Nicolay and John Hay (New York: Century Co., 1902), vol. 1, pp. 232–34.

39. Carnegie, "Wealth," pp. 14–15, 15.

40. Richard J. Herrnstein and Charles Murray, *The Bell Curve* (New York: Free Press, 1994), pp. 269, 297.

41. John Locke, *The Second Treatise on Civil Government* (1690; Buffalo, NY: Prometheus Books, 1986), para. 17, para. 4, para. 57.

42. Ibid., paras. 24–26.

43. Ibid., para. 26.

44. Ibid., para. 27, emphasis added; para. 50; para. 49; para. 36.

45. See, for example, Robert Nozick, *Anarchy, State, and Utopia* (New York: Basic Books, 1974). Jefferson revealed his debt to Locke in his writing of the Declaration of Independence, which includes language taken directly from the *Second Treatise*.

4

More Freedom *and* Equality?

Are we stuck in a bind in which more equality means less freedom? Before attempting to answer that question, we should first ask ourselves if greater equality is a worthy goal. To begin examining the case for equality, we can look first at equality's "most complete and eloquent defender," Jean-Jacques Rousseau (1712–1778).[1] Rousseau defended equality on several grounds. First, he argued that equality is our natural human condition. In the previous chapter, we saw several thinkers defend inequality on the grounds that it is natural and, therefore, inevitable. Rousseau disagreed, arguing instead that humans are roughly equal in their natural state. Rousseau distinguished between two kinds of inequality: physical or natural on the one hand, moral or political on the other. Physical or natural inequality includes inequality of talent and strength. Nature itself bounds these inequalities, since nature kills off anyone unfit below a threshold needed for survival. Social institutions dramatically compound and magnify this "scarcely perceptible" natural inequality into moral or political inequality.

Rousseau identified the social institution of private property as one of the most important causes of inequality. Private property, he argued, magnifies the slight differences found in nature and hardens them into enduring inequalities. Propelled initially by the slight differences in talent and strength provided by nature, inequality increases as slight advantages accumulate into greater advantages. Combined with factors such as advances in science and art, divisions of labor, geographical differentiation, and accidents, the advantages multiply. The introduction of private property institutionalizes these advantages. They become the basis for privilege and power for those who possess property, and destitution and marginalization for those who do not.

Dismissing the claim that private property is a natural right, Rousseau argued that "the right of property is only a matter of convention and human institution," one that requires "the express and unanimous consent of the human race to appropriate anything from the common subsistence that went beyond your own" subsistence needs. This imposes strict limits on wealth and, by extension, inequality. Rousseau argued further that individual ownership of property is conditional upon the common good. Owners of property are "depositaries of the public wealth." No matter how acquired, "the right of each individual to his own piece of land is always subordinate to the community's right to everything." If necessary to achieve the common good, the community's needs take precedence over the right of private property. In practice, this could mean that "the members of society should contribute some of their assets to its upkeep,"[2] presumably in the form of taxation.

Although Rousseau's condemnation of the inequality wrought by private property might suggest that he condemned private property itself, Rousseau called the right of property "the most sacred of all the citizens' rights and more important in certain respects than liberty itself." Property, he argued, is "the true foundation of civil society" because it is "the true guarantee of the citizens' commitments." Rousseau meant that private property afforded citizens a stake in the maintenance and health of civil society. "If persons had no responsibility for their possessions," he argued, "nothing would be so easy as evading one's duties and scorning the laws."[3] Rousseau's endorsement of private property may have represented his grudging recognition that a return to the state of nature and its natural equality was impossible.

The social contract establishing government represents another social institution contributing to the enlarging and hardening of inequality, according to Rousseau. The social contract grants political power to those who already possess economic power, and they use it to protect their privilege at the expense of others. The laws they pass allegedly favor no one in particular, but in reality institutionalize and protect the status quo of inequality. The establishment of law-governed society "gave new fetters to the weak and new powers to the rich," and this "irretrievably destroyed natural liberty, established forever the law of property and inequality, made clever usurpation into an irrevocable right, and, for the benefit of a few ambitious individuals, henceforth subjected the whole human race to labor, servitude, and misery."[4] This condemnation applied to the civil society actually in place during his lifetime, not the ideal civil society that Rousseau proposed in his later work, *The Social Contract* (1762).

Rousseau defended equality, second, based on his belief in the corrupting influence of inequality on the moral character of rich and poor alike, and on the civic body. The poor are "obliged to receive or to steal their subsistence from the hand of the rich" and either to accept their "domination and servitude" or engage in "violence and pillage." The rich acquire a taste for domination and a disdain for all but their own class. They grow soft and self-indulgent and lose their martial spirit and civic virtue. Natural equality yields to "the usurpations of the rich, the brigandage of the poor, the unbridled passions of all, stifling natural compassion and the still feeble voice of justice," and making men "avaricious, ambitious, and wicked."[5] To dramatize their state of dependency and dehumanization, Rousseau placed the poor only one small step above slaves. The slave, who cannot make personal decisions, is dehumanized, degraded, and robbed of a moral personality. In the same way that a master cannot be a master without a slave, so the rich cannot be rich without their dependent wage slaves who actually produce their wealth. Wage slavery deprives humans of independence and initiative while in the employ of others. They must respond to the whim and command of their bosses and to their own desperate need for subsistence. This robs them of choice and thus of moral personality.

Third, Rousseau defended equality on the basis that "liberty cannot continue to exist without it."[6] Liberty, he argued, requires at least rough economic and political equality. Economic inequality erodes liberty by breeding dependence of some on others. Dependence diminishes a person's choices and alternatives, and thus their freedom. The dependent person must respond to the commands of others, with relatively few options for autonomous choice and action. Political inequality erodes liberty, according to Rousseau, by forcing the relatively powerless to live by rules and laws created by the relatively powerful in their own interest. We are free in civil society if we obey only laws that we helped make and that represent our common interests. We enter into agreements with others of our own will, and this preserves our freedom.

Fourth, Rousseau condemned inequality because it breeds intolerable resentment, which contributes to social instability and conflict. The poor, the marginalized, and the oppressed face cruel choices. Many find themselves having to accept charity or to steal in order to survive. They must either submit to their subservient position or turn to crime.

Fifth, Rousseau believed simply that radical inequality represents a gross injustice. His language often reveals dismay at the kind of inequality that leaves some in desperate circumstances and others in luxury. He believed that the two are related, in that luxury for some requires oppression for others. He asked, "How can a man or a people seize a vast territory and deprive the entire human race of it other than by a punishable usurpation, since such an act robs the remaining men of the dwelling place and food that nature gives them in common?" Rousseau appealed to the privileged few to examine their consciences and their sense of justice. "Are you not aware," he asked, "that vast numbers of your brothers perish or suffer from needing what you have in excess, and that you needed the express and unanimous consent of the human race to appropriate anything from the common subsistence that went beyond your own?"[8]

Finally, Rousseau argued that democracy requires both political equality and some semblance of economic equality. He sought "a democratic community of equals in whose operation each has an equal and effective share" and where "every authentic act of the general will [that is, every legitimate law] obligates or favors all citizens equally." This requires political equality, understood to mean both equal say in the making of laws and equal application of the laws once formulated. Active and equal participation among all citizens helps prevent tyranny in a democratic republic by helping ensure that laws represent the common good. As soon as you admit undue influence in policy making by a particular group such as the wealthy, you lose sight of the common good, for that group will rig the system in their particular interest rather than the general interest. By definition, according to Rousseau, this creates tyranny rather than democracy. The best way to prevent this form of tyranny, according to Rousseau, is "to prevent extreme inequality of fortunes." In short, democracy requires political equality, which in turn requires at least some semblance of economic equality.

Far more than many contemporary thinkers admit, Rousseau recognized that economic inequality quickly and readily translates into political inequality.

He argued that democracy requires "great equality of ranks and fortunes, without which equality of rights and authority could not subsist for long." Does this mean that democracy requires absolute economic equality? Not according to Rousseau, who argued that "the word should not be understood to mean that the degrees of power and wealth are absolutely the same." As a standard of minimal economic equality, he believed that "no citizen should be rich enough to be able to buy another, and none poor enough to be forced to sell himself."[9] Rousseau did not mean buying and selling literally. To "buy" a citizen meant to bribe someone or in some way to control another via wealth; to "sell" oneself meant to enter wage slavery in response to destitution and lack of options.

There are few more powerful statements of equality than that found in the U.S. Declaration of Independence, authored primarily by Thomas Jefferson (1743–1826). The Declaration boldly asserts, "We hold these truths to be self-evident, that all men are created equal, that they are endowed by their Creator with certain unalienable Rights, that among these are Life, Liberty and the pursuit of Happiness." Like Rousseau, Jefferson criticized radical economic inequality for its corrupting influence on individuals and society as a whole, and he connected the need for a minimal level of economic equality to freedom and democracy.

Jefferson's fear of the corrupting influence of inequality is found most frequently in his disparaging of European inequality and its consequences. Like Rousseau, Jefferson associated luxury with "dissipation," moral decline, and corruption. He attacked the "privileges of the European aristocrats" and compared them unfavorably, if not entirely accurately, to "the lovely equality which the poor enjoy with the rich" among Americans of his time. An American educated in Europe will, he believed, inevitably decline "in his morals, in his health, in his habits, and in his happiness" through exposure to the corrupting influence of European inequality. In words that echoed Rousseau's passion for justice, Jefferson described in scathing terms "the unequal division of property" that he saw in France, where property "is absolutely concentrated in a very few hands." Jefferson was moved to write: "I ask myself what could be the reason that so many should be permitted to beg who are willing to work, in a country where there is a very considerable proportion of uncultivated lands" kept idle for the hunting sport of the rich.[10]

Like Rousseau, to deal with the "misery" created by inequality Jefferson believed that "legislators cannot invent too many devices for subdividing property."

And like Rousseau, Jefferson did not advocate absolute equality. "I am conscious," he wrote, "that an equal division of property is impracticable." Instead, he advocated rough economic equality, proposing a progressive income tax and inheritance laws to achieve it. Jefferson also admitted a willingness to confiscate uncultivated land when necessary to ensure that "the fundamental right to labor the earth" was guaranteed to all. Jefferson wanted to ensure that "as few as possible shall be without a little portion of land."[11] Having at least some property, Jefferson believed, guaranteed a minimum of independence necessary for liberty. This principle found expression in his praise of the independent small farmers of his time. Jefferson believed that farmers represented the best of America because they were hardworking, independent, and virtuous. He contrasted them to the wretched industrial workers that he observed in Europe.

Also like Rousseau, Jefferson firmly embraced political equality. He believed that all members of a political body should have an "equal voice in the direction of its concerns." One way to increase political equality, short of equalizing property, is to ensure full and equal participation in politics so that all voices are heard and none can distort policy. To achieve this, Jefferson developed a scheme of "ward" government characterized by extensive political participation at local levels. In addition to increasing political equality, this would have the added benefit of increasing citizens' patriotism and their commitment to democratic institutions. Participation in self-government, he wrote, will "attach" citizens "to the independence of [their] country, and its republican constitution."[12]

The notion that radical inequality corrupts character and undermines social cohesion did not originate with Rousseau or Jefferson. In ancient Greece, Plato (427–347 B.C.), describing his ideal state, eliminated private property for the guardian classes—those who ruled and protected it—in order to forestall the development of private interests and ensure their commitment to the common good. For everyone else, Plato allowed private property, but not in extremes. According to Plato, "There are two things that can ruin and corrupt the rest of our workers." They are poverty and wealth, which "have a bad effect on the quality of the work and on the workman himself." The one "produces luxury and idleness and a desire for novelty," and the other "meanness and bad workmanship and the desire for revolution as well." Wealth dissuades work by undermining a motivation for it, making the wealthy "idle and careless." Poverty prevents work by keeping the worker from "providing himself with tools and the other necessities of his trade," and also undermining the quality of the work.[13]

Whatever commitments we make today to racial and gender equality are relatively recent developments. Rousseau's commitment to equality applied only to men. He believed that women were inferior to men, for both natural and practical reasons. According to Rousseau, "For several reasons derived from the nature of things, it is the father who should be in command." These "several reasons" include, first of all, the fact that women menstruate and bear children, causing "indispositions peculiar to the woman" and causing her to be "inactive for a certain period." This, he concluded, "is a sufficient reason for excluding her from . . . primacy" within the family. Second, Rousseau's preference for male domination rested on an assertion that two adults of relatively equal power cannot coexist within a family. Instead, "there must be one dominant voice which decides" matters within the family. And finally, men must dominate their women in order "to make certain that the children he is forced to acknowledge and raise belong to no one but himself."[14]

In American political thought, challenges to gender inequality began appearing with some frequency during the mid-nineteenth century. Susan B. Anthony (1820–1906) was among the most prominent of the thinkers and activists who took up this challenge. She identified two major sources of gender inequality and female oppression: women's financial dependence on men, and women's exclusion from the right of suffrage. She argued that to secure equality the first step must be "to secure to them pecuniary independence" since dependence on men undermines a woman's self-esteem and autonomy. Unlike a man, who is "free to carve out his own destiny," a woman "has no such pride." Limiting women's roles to serving men as "mere adornments" wastes their talents and leaves them undeveloped. Second, according to Anthony, to attain equality women must secure the political means to protect their particular interests. It would not suffice to expect men to do it for them. "It is a downright mockery," she wrote, "to talk to women of their enjoyment of the blessings of liberty while they are denied the use of the only means of securing them provided by this democratic-republican government—the ballot." Give women the vote, she argued, "so that woman can protect herself." The exclusion of women from full suffrage created "a hateful oligarchy of sex" that directly contradicted the U.S. Constitution, which says "we, the people," not "we, the white male citizens."[15]

Active like Anthony in both the women's suffrage and the abolitionist movements of the nineteenth century, Angelina Grimké (1805–1879) grounded her appeal for women's rights on moral and practical arguments. "Human beings have *rights*," according to Grimké, "because they are *moral* beings," and since women and men share the same moral stature, they deserve the same rights. "The *mere circumstance of sex*," she argued, "does not give to man higher rights and responsibilities, than to women. . . . Whatever it is morally right for man to do, it is morally right for women to do." Grimké believed that inequality harms both women and men, though not equally. The inequality corrupts men and demeans women. It gives men "a charter for the exercise of tyranny and selfishness, pride and arrogance, lust and brutal violence." Women's dependence on men results in their infantilization and objectification. It forces women

> to lean upon an arm of flesh, to sit as a doll arrayed in "gold, and pearls, and costly array," to be admired for her personal charms, and caressed and humored like a spoiled child, or converted into a mere drudge to suit the convenience of her lord and master.

It prevents women from developing their full moral and intellectual capacities and makes them into "pretty toys" and "pet animals" for the enjoyment of men. Echoing the language of the American revolutionaries and constitutional framers, Grimké argued, "It is woman's right to have a voice in all the laws and regulations by which she is to be *governed*." And their exclusion from this voice is "a *violation of human rights; a rank usurpation of power*, a violent seizure and confiscation of what is sacredly and inalienably hers—thus inflicting upon woman outrageous wrongs."[16]

Another writer and activist of the same period, Elizabeth Cady Stanton (1815–1902), also noted the consequences of inequality in the form of "the degraded and inferior position occupied by women all over the world." This inequality is "benumbing to her faculties." Locked into the limited private roles of housekeeper and mother and out of public roles entirely, women cannot develop their full capacities as human beings. Both physically and intellectually, "it is use that produces growth and development," and women's limited roles give them few opportunities for use of their faculties and talents. This inevitably results in their stymied and stunted growth, their "degradation and ignorance." The inequality also undermines men's moral character, according to Stanton. Man's "tyranny" over woman is "injurious to himself" and, though it has "improved woman's moral nature," the cost has been "an almost total shipwreck of his own" moral nature. It retards the species as well, since women's potential contributions are neglected or lost. Stanton believed that giving women the right to vote would force politicians to heed their interests and make needed changes to liberate women from their confinement in domestic roles. Give women the right to vote, she argued, and "might not the office-holders and seekers propose some change in her condition?"[17]

Charlotte Perkins Gilman (1860–1935), an American writer of the late nineteenth and early twentieth centuries, analyzed the inequality between women and men in her *Women and Economics* (1898) and *His Religion and Hers* (1923), reiterating some of the same themes introduced by her predecessors. According to Gilman, male domination of women results in the stunted and distorted development of girls and women. Freeing girls and women to their full development requires the removal of artificial barriers. In *Women and Economics*, Gilman portrayed the relation between women and men as one of economic dependence of women on men. Her analysis reflected the dominance during her time of Darwinist thinking applied to humans. If women lag behind men in their development, she argued, it is due not to natural inferiority but to their economic dependence and their lack of access to opportunities for development of their capacities. According to Gilman, "We are the only animal species in which the female depends on the male for food. . . . With us an entire sex lives in a relation of economic dependence upon the other sex." While men "can cook, clean, and sew as well as women," public roles such as "the making and managing of the great engines of modern industry, the threading of earth and sea in our vast systems of transportation, the handling of our elaborate machinery of trade, commerce, government" are denied to women. And the results are predictable: "the male human being is thousands of years in advance of the female in economic status."

Furthermore, Gilman noted, women are denied the respect due adults with independent status. They acquire status only through the economic efforts of their fathers, husbands, and brothers. To the argument that women are economic factors in their role of domestic management, Gilman replied, "So are horses," adding, "Whatever the economic value of the domestic industry of women . . . they do not get it." They receive no independent wage, only indirect financial support through their fathers and husbands. Gilman portrayed the net result in scathing terms that remain uncomfortably familiar over a century later. "We see," she wrote, "the human mother worked far harder than a mare, laboring her life long in the service, not of her children only, but of men; husbands, brothers, fathers, whatever male relatives she has." Women work "longer and harder than most men," since their workday begins before the man's and ends after his.[18]

Gilman dramatically added women's mental health to the costs of their subservience. In her short story "The Yellow Wall-Paper" (1890), she portrayed a woman trapped behind the bars of gender domination whose entrapment eventually drives her insane. The gender domination took the form of gender codes strictly limiting women's life choices to domestic duties and childrearing. The main character in the story remains unnamed throughout, signifying a general condition of women rather than one specific to the protagonist. These codes are maintained and reinforced in part by well-intentioned intimates such as her husband who pathologizes and infantalizes her with pet names such as "a blessed little goose" and "little girl." The female protagonist believes that "congenial work with excitement and change would do [her] good," but her husband believes otherwise, hardly letting her "stir without special direction," essentially confining her to the bedroom with its yellow wallpaper. The husband dismisses her aspirations for an active, involved life outside the home as "excited fancies" and insists that she use her "will and good sense to check the tendency." He forbids her from writing, because it particularly excites her fancies, even though she finds "it is such a relief" to her. As this physical, psychological, and emotional confinement wears her down, she gradually loses her grasp of reality and begins to imagine herself trapped in the yellow wallpaper of her bedroom. As her madness accelerates, she imagines "a great many women" behind the bars that she sees in the pattern of the wallpaper. She escapes only by yielding to insanity.[19]

Although women bear the heaviest costs of gender inequality, Gilman agreed with her predecessors that it adversely affects men as well. While continuing the theme of women's dependence on men in *His Religion and Hers*, Gilman argued that the entire human species suffers, men as well as women, from inequality. Gilman called religion "our greatest help in conscious progress." But since religion has developed "through the minds of men alone," human progress has been "opposed and retarded." Gilman blamed inequality itself, rather than men. The fault lies, she argued,

> not in any essential fault in the male of our race, but in his unnatural relation to the female. By the early and universal subjection of the female to the male, by her segregation to the lowest form of service . . . we have made ourselves a crippled race, a race whose whole development was left to be carried on by one half of it.

All humans suffer because they are deprived of the potential contributions of women. Gilman, like Rousseau, used the institution of slavery as a reference point for exposing the evils of inequality. Slavery harms both master and slave, she argued. "It acts upon the slave, with well-known weakening results. It acts upon the master, tending to produce pride, laziness, and self-indulgence, cruelty, injustice, and, from its dim beginnings to its glaring end, licentiousness."[20] So too, she argued, does inequality produce these harmful results for both men and women.

Calls for greater racial equality surfaced with increasing frequency in the United States during the mid-nineteenth century. The history of slavery in the United States represents the extreme of racial inequality, and its physical, moral, and psychological consequences the most damaging to human dignity and character. Readers interested in firsthand accounts of these costs can read the personal testimonies of former slaves such as Frederick Douglass and Harriet Jacobs.[21] Both offer wrenching testimonies of brutality, degradation, and the systematic rape of black women by their white masters.

In *The Souls of Black Folk* (1903), the African-American thinker W. E. B. Du Bois (1868–1963) portrayed the spiritual and emotional costs of slavery and its legacy. Du Bois wrote of the struggles of African Americans after abolition to attain self-respect and an authentic self while avoiding destructive tendencies toward anger, hate, and listlessness. Blacks always had to see themselves through white eyes, as though through a "veil." This does not readily yield a "true self-consciousness," only an inevitably distorted understanding filtered through the eyes of the oppressor. The challenges of breaking through that veil cannot be discounted, since "the facing of so vast a prejudice could not but bring the inevitable self-questioning, self-disparagement, and lowering of ideals which ever accompany repression." This "vast prejudice" made self-abnegation a requirement for survival among African Americans:

> The young Negro of the South who would succeed cannot be frank and out-spoken, honest and self-assertive, but rather he is daily tempted to be silent and wary, politic and sly; he must flatter and be pleasant, endure petty insults with a smile, shut his eyes to wrong; in too many cases he sees positive personal advantage in deception and lying. His real thoughts, his real aspirations, must be guarded in whispers; he must not criticize, he must not complain.

Even apart from direct contact with that prejudice, it could not be ignored in the physical features of African Americans that bespoke "the red stain of bastardy, which two centuries of systematic legal defilement of Negro women had stamped upon his race." This systematic rape of black women by white slave masters left African Americans with the "hereditary weight of a mass of corruption from white adulterers."[22] Residues of white blood in African Americans represented to Du Bois defilement by the lowliest of white men, those who could find in their characters the permission they needed to rape the women and girls they possessed as chattel slaves. They daily reminded emancipated African Americans of their enslavement and its cruelties. Additionally, according to Du Bois, the choking grip of debt and sharecropping endured by many African Americans of his time deadened the spirit, and the lack of real economic opportunity undermined zeal and thrift.

Small wonder, then, amid these daily reminders that "every tendency is to excess—radical complaint, radical remedies, bitter denunciation or angry silence." Small wonder that many African Americans embraced "a gospel of revolt and revenge" as their response to injustice; that some African Americans responded with "tasteless sycophancy," while others shrank into "silent hatred of the pale world about them and mocking distrust of everything white"; that some responded with "careless ignorance and laziness" created by hopeless economic circumstances, while others turned to "fierce hate and vindictiveness" induced by a hostile white South. Du Bois's impatience at the slow pace, or even complete absence, of progress often showed through clearly:

> What in the name of reason does this nation expect of a people, poorly trained and hard pressed in severe economic competition, without political rights, and with ludicrously inadequate common-school facilities? What can it expect but

crime and listlessness, offset here and there by the dogged struggles of the fortunate and more determined who are themselves buoyed by the hope that in due time the country will come to its senses?[23]

The challenge, he believed, lay in avoiding destructive tendencies while embracing hope, despite the steep obstacles facing African Americans. According to Du Bois, "The question of the future is how best to keep these millions [of black people] from brooding over the wrongs of the past and the difficulties of the present, so that all their energies may be bent toward a cheerful striving and co-operation with their white neighbors toward a larger, juster, and fuller future." Throughout, *The Souls of Black Folk* contained a barely concealed threat: develop the black South or face anger, unrest, and rebellion. "No secure civilization can be built in the South," he wrote, "with the Negro as an ignorant, turbulent proletariat."[24]

These thinkers help us understand the value of equality and the costs of failure to achieve it more fully. Economic inequality represents a failure in its own right to provide material security and a decent life for everyone. It also may create anger, resentment, and despair on the bottom, idleness, corruption, and indifference at the top. If left unchecked, inequality can create hate growing from humiliation and may undermine social stability as it forces people to make increasingly desperate choices. The lack of genuine equality of opportunity breeds indifference in some who correctly perceive their limited chances of success, and resentment and anger among others who feel acutely the chasm between the myth and the reality of opportunity. Political inequality results in a corrupted polity marked by stunted and distorted patterns of political participation, and public policy that inevitably favors the rich and powerful and detracts from the common good. Although those on the bottom suffer worst of all, everyone ultimately shares the costs in the forms of social instability, conflict, insecurity, a lack of social progress, and a muted experience of democracy.

The remainder of this chapter presumes that Americans mean their commitment to equality, that the language of the Declaration of Independence signifies a real, not merely rhetorical, commitment to equality, and that most Americans view equality as a legitimate ideal. We saw above that both Rousseau and Jefferson viewed equality not as an impediment to freedom, but as a requirement for freedom. We saw, too, that freeing women and African

Americans from various forms of bondage required precisely that we confront and overcome historical inequalities. This suggests that freedom and equality are not always in tension and may under some circumstances be mutually supportive.

DIFFERENT KINDS OF FREEDOM

Thus far, freedom has been treated as a concept with a singular meaning. In fact, there are different kinds and meanings of freedom. The so-called negative conception thus far considered is the dominant, but hardly the only, conception of freedom. The French writer Benjamin Constant (1767–1830) proposed a distinction between negative and positive freedom. Over a century later, political philosopher Isaiah Berlin (1909–1997) further developed this distinction, and it remains influential among political theorists today.[25] The terms *negative* and *positive* do not refer to bad and good freedom, respectively. As already noted, the term *negative* when applied to freedom describes the absence of restrictions and obstacles to human volition and action. It refers to "freedom from" interference by other people and the government. This meaning of freedom best captures our everyday understanding of freedom as being left alone to do whatever we want to do, so long as our actions do not harm others. Being left alone does not guarantee that a person can actually take advantage of the resulting absence of restrictions. Simply removing obstacles does not mean that it makes choice and action possible. For example, simply removing legal impediments to African-American voters in the 1960s did not guarantee their political participation. Hostile whites, illiteracy, lack of funds or time to travel to the polls, or basic unawareness of their rights continued to limit their freedom. Similarly, saying that "all Americans are free to attend college" may be true in the sense that no laws obstruct their matriculation in college and no individuals or groups actively oppose it. However, there may be other reasons why many Americans cannot attend college. They may lack the financial resources or hold familial responsibilities that prevent their attendance. In effect, they lack the means and resources for taking advantage of their negative freedom.

The concept of positive freedom attempts to capture this insight by considering the capacity for thought and action as well as their limiting obstacles. Positive freedom means "freedom to" be or do something: to participate in politics, to develop abilities and talents, to lead a full, rich life. It requires consideration of capacity, or power, for thought and action. It entails the "positive" addition of something that increases or guarantees capacity. Theorists working with this conception ask not simply whether obstacles have been removed but also whether the individual is capable of taking advantage of the removal of restrictions in order to think and act in the world. Making good on the promise of freedom, these theorists argue, may require the addition of supporting conditions and resources, along with the development of skills and abilities that enable thought and action. These supporting conditions can come from private sources such as philanthropic groups or from personal and family income. Government can also provide them. Unlike the negative conception of freedom in which government exists as a necessary evil, the positive conception of freedom poses government as potentially fulfilling the promise of freedom. It has a positive role of supporting individual freedom, of helping bring it to fruition, of making it real rather than simply an abstraction.

Some subsequent theorists have attempted to develop conceptual frameworks for understanding freedom that integrate a consideration of both negative and positive freedom. Gerald MacCallum (1925–1987) argued that all discussions of freedom implicitly or explicitly entail both negative and positive freedom. He developed a triadic model to show this. In his model, an agent seeks to attain a goal, but first must overcome or circumvent obstacles and limiting conditions that may or may not be apparent. Thus, Agent X has freedom from Y in order to do or become Z. For example, women would like to be free from the fear of rape in order to walk alone at night. Most of us would like to be free from poverty in order to eat and live with a roof over our head. African Americans living in Selma, Alabama, in 1959 sought freedom from Jim Crow laws in order to become equal, effective citizens. For MacCallum, a thorough understanding of freedom in any given situation thus requires that we consider both negative and positive freedom.[26]

William Connolly (1938–) developed another blend by tying freedom to an ideal of autonomy. Freedom as autonomy requires an agent whose "capacities are highly developed and articulated." Requisite capacities for freedom include critical reflection and self-understanding. An autonomous agent must be capable of independent critical thought and judgment. An autonomous person "acts upon choices formed through critical awareness of his situation and the possibilities and constraints that situation provides." In Connolly's words:

> A person is autonomous to the extent that his conduct is informed by his own reflective assessment of his situation. He realizes that he is enclosed in a system of conventions that shape much of his conduct and tend to limit his self-understanding, and he explores routes to render those habits more amenable to self-conscious scrutiny and possible revision. He seeks to translate those conventions and habits, so far as possible, from forces acting upon him into considerations he can choose to accept or modify in the light of this understanding.[27]

Connolly's formulation requires not simply the absence of restraints but the presence of viable alternatives. *Viable* means that they lie within the realm of reasonable possibility. Most obviously, a proposed action or practice must be within a person's natural capacity. It does not make sense, for example, to refer to a human's freedom to fly like a bird, since humans do not naturally enjoy that capacity. Furthermore, viability requires that we be capable of acting on our choices. To say, for example, that a homeless person is free to attend Harvard is accurate only in the sense that no person or government institution stands directly in the way of this action. Or to say that a schoolteacher is free to purchase a Malibu beachfront home ignores the simple but important fact that buying a home there is impossible on a teacher's salary.

His formulation also requires an ability to reflect on our options and understand them realistically. Connolly's emphasis on freedom as autonomy presupposes a capable agent who conceives of options and reflects critically upon them without undue vicarious influence from outside forces. This requires access to information about options. We cannot conceive of our options if we do not have access to information about them. It also requires that others who may not have our best interests at heart do not unduly influence our understanding of our options and the choices we make. For example, one might ask to what degree advertising influences our consumption choices. Finally, the agent must be capable of acting on desires without constraint. These constraints include "those limits to action imposed by impersonal social forces" and by "the unintended consequences of the actions others take," as well as obvious, explicit limits imposed deliberately by others.

As some of the above examples suggest, many of the obstacles and impediments to human volition and behavior are unobservable. In addition to the
subtle influences on human choice noted already, these include stereotypes
and myths that discourage certain individuals and groups from making certain choices and pursuing certain goals. An ethnic stereotype, for example,
might discourage a person from self-assertion in a public arena. The stigma
against recent Hispanic immigrants to Southern California effectively dis-
courages some of them who have become citizens from participating in elections. This restricts their freedom in the sense developed by Connolly even
though, once they become citizens, legally they face no more nor less obstacles than Anglos in Southern California.

Connolly summarized his conception of freedom in the following terms:

> X is free with respect to z if (or to the extent that) he is unconstrained from con-
> ceiving or choosing z and if (to the extent that), were he to choose z, he would
> not be constrained from doing or becoming z. X acts freely in doing z when (or
> to the extent that) he acts without constraint upon his unconstrained and re-
> flective choice with respect to z.[28]

Note, first of all, that Connolly poses freedom as a matter of degree, not in terms
of absolute freedom or nonfreedom. We are free, according to Connolly, to the
degree that the conditions for freedom are met. He thus poses freedom as a position on a continuum from absolute nonfreedom to absolute freedom. Note
too that, like MacCallum's triadic model, Connolly's formulation integrates
both negative and positive freedom. It entails both the removal of obstacles and
consideration of the capacity to think and act to attain certain goals.

John Dewey (1859–1952) developed a conception of freedom that includes
many of the dimensions discussed above. He sometimes referred to this as "effective" freedom.[29] Freedom, Dewey argued, allows each person to engage in
self-creation, to make the best of oneself as a social being. But this requires
"positive control of the resources necessary to carry purposes into effect, possession of the means to satisfy desires; and mental equipment with the trained
powers of initiative and reflection requisite for free preference and for cir-
cumspect and far-seeing desires." In other words, freedom requires the capacity—understood to mean both intellectual and practical skills, tools, and
resources—for exercising it in the successful pursuit of goals. Without "mental equipment" enabling "powers of initiative and reflection," and without

"positive control of resources" and "possession of the means" for pursuing goals and aims, freedom is an empty ideal. Dewey also believed that negative freedom, or the freedom from restraint, is an important ingredient in the realization of effective freedom. However, "no man and no mind was ever emancipated merely by being left alone. Removal of formal limitations is but a negative condition; positive freedom is not a state but an act which involves methods and instrumentalities for control of conditions."[30]

In later works, Dewey continued these themes that freedom entails a capacity for effective action and that this requires control of means and critical reflection. Freedom, Dewey wrote in 1946, requires "power, effective power to do specific things." It requires an attention to "what persons can do and what they cannot do." Thus, "the demand for liberty is a demand for power" and an interest in freedom requires an attention to "the distribution of effective power." Moreover, "the power of action" is inseparable from "knowledge and understanding," a knowledge and understanding that must be "critically discriminating."[31] In short, in order to be free, a person must be powerful, or capable of critically formulating goals and carrying them into action, using available and appropriate means, which produce the desired results. How does one attain the requisite power for making good on the promise of freedom? Simply leaving individuals alone, Dewey argued, will not ensure that they have the capacity to pursue and actually attain their goals. Social support may prove necessary. This support may entail active government assistance and intervention in forms ranging from regulations to social welfare spending to public ownership and control of key economic resources.

Taking our cues from Connolly and Dewey, fully assessing a person's level of freedom requires that we consider also their power. This power originates in individual capabilities and talents, such as intellectual or physical ability, and in individual initiative in identifying and amassing resources. It can be augmented socially through various means, including, for example, private philanthropy and government support programs and policies. We must also consider the obstacles and limiting conditions that an individual must circumvent. These obstacles and limiting conditions include obvious ones such as physical force or restricting laws, but also less obvious ones such as subtle norms or beliefs inhibiting critical awareness, structural and systemic impediments, and the lack of viable alternatives.

FREEDOM REQUIRES RESTRAINT

Under what conditions, if any, can one person's freedom be restricted in order to guarantee freedom and equality for others? Upon first reflection, it may appear that any restriction of human choice and action is an abridgement of freedom and therefore illegitimate. However, this position cannot be sustained in any social context in which diverse humans attempt to live peacefully together. Focusing on the relation between freedom and authority can show this. *Authority* means a legitimate capacity for directing, influencing, and leading. It is distinct from power per se, which can be wielded illegitimately. Parental authority limits the freedom of children and youth to gorge on candy and television. Police authority limits the freedom of automobile drivers to drive ninety miles an hour through crowded streets. A teacher's authority to impose assignments and grades limits the freedom of students to spend their days on leisure activities. Religious authority figures prescribe rules of behavior that restrict the freedom of adherents to choose and behave in certain ways. As these examples illustrate, people in positions of authority do limit others' freedom. Yet, paradoxically, freedom cannot exist in practice without authority.

Puritan leader John Winthrop (1588–1649) wrote "A Little Speech on Liberty" in response to grumbling among congregants about his leadership. He attempted in this short piece to justify the authority of the church and its elders, and by extension the rules and guidelines they imposed on congregants. He first distinguished between two kinds of liberty, natural and civil. Humans enjoy natural liberty, he argued, in the same way that animals do. Natural liberty means the freedom "to do what he lists [wants]; it is a liberty to evil as well as to good." Winthrop rejected this model of freedom as inappropriate for Christians, since it means an ability to do evil as well as good, and because it is "incompatible and inconsistent with authority, and cannot endure the least restraint of the most just authority." Winthrop also called this kind of freedom "licentiousness." By contrast, according to Winthrop, civil liberty—which Winthrop also called federal or moral liberty—*requires* authority. It is a form of liberty that "is maintained and exercised in a way of subjection to authority." This kind of liberty "is the proper end and object of authority and cannot subsist without it; and it is a liberty to that only which is good, just, and honest." It requires submission to authority, specifically to the authority of Christian teachings as found in Scripture and interpreted by church elders. This subjection is "for your good" since, according to Winthrop, it aids each of us in choosing good rather than evil.

What makes this authority legitimate? Scripture itself possesses an inherent legitimacy that cannot be denied, according to Winthrop. As the word of God, it needs no defense. Its authority stands apart from human volition. Winthrop also added a more practical, secular defense of church authority. Just as a wife freely and willingly submits to the authority of her husband, he argued, so too does the believer submit freely and willingly to the authority of the church. This element of free choice ensures that the submission to authority does not negate freedom—on the contrary, it makes freedom possible. According to Winthrop:

> The woman's own choice makes such a man her husband; yet being so chosen, he is her lord, and she is to be subject to him, yet in a way of liberty, not of bondage; and a true wife accounts her subjection her honor and freedom.[32]

Winthrop's insistence that legitimate freedom can only be experienced in a Christian community in which individuals submit to the authority of Scripture and the church, and his use of a patriarchal marriage relationship in which the husband dominates the wife as his model of appropriate subjection to authority, will undoubtedly offend many modern readers. The very notion that freedom cannot exist without authority may also strike modern readers as counterintuitive. As we have seen, the dominant understanding of freedom today appears to emphasize quite the opposite. The belief that freedom simply entails the removal of restrictions inevitably poses authority as an obstacle to freedom. Yet, if we look more carefully at the liberal roots of our contemporary understanding of negative freedom, we may find this posing of freedom with authority less incomprehensible than it might at first appear.

Even John Locke (1632–1704), libertarian godfather and one of the most influential early liberal thinkers, argued that freedom requires the authority of government and its laws. Recall that, according to Locke, humans enjoy near-perfect freedom in a state of nature since they can do anything they want, subject only to their own physical and mental limitations and the rights of others to do the same. However, since humans in his view naturally compete aggressively against each other to attain their self-interests, they inevitably threaten each other. He argued that individuals in this predicament would find it advantageous to initiate a social compact to depart the state of nature and form a civil society with a government instituted primarily to protect people and their possessions. Government thus guarantees and preserves liberty, by instituting laws for protection. According to Locke, "Freedom of men under government is to have a standing rule to live by, common to every one of that society."[33] Like Winthrop, Locke took it for granted that a secure and lasting freedom *requires* authority. Freedom within civil society requires the authority of law and the institutions of government. Like Winthrop, too, Locke addressed the question of legitimate authority, arriving at a parallel answer. In order for the authority of government and its laws to be legitimate, we must voluntarily enter into a social contract with others. We must offer our consent to the social compact, either expressly or tacitly, for without it freedom is sacrificed.

Rousseau took this argument a step further. While Locke argued that the laws make freedom possible and that we need to yield our natural freedom in order to guarantee civil freedom, Rousseau believed that obeying the laws expresses our freedom. In words that have confounded many readers, Rousseau wrote that "anyone who refuses to obey the general will shall be compelled to do so by the entire body; this means nothing else than that he will be forced to be free."[34] Since the general will finds expression in the laws, Rousseau meant to say simply that citizens must obey the laws that, by definition in a democratic republic, they had a hand in formulating and that serve the common interest. Recalcitrant citizens will be forced to obey them. Today we take this for granted. In Rousseau's superficially misleading formulation, obeying the law makes citizens free by protecting them from dependence on the arbitrary will of others and preserving citizens' opportunity to enjoy the freedom made possible by the rule of law. Rousseau presupposed that independent individuals acting in concert through the citizen assembly must create the laws. Only then will the law fairly represent their will. Adhering to the laws therefore concedes no limitations to their freedom, since by abiding by the law they are simply expressing their own will.

As Winthrop, Locke, and Rousseau argued, freedom requires restraint. Without authoritative guidelines that impose restraints on human behavior, freedom is insecure at best, impossible at worst. The principle that Winthrop, Locke, and Rousseau took for granted helps us understand that human freedom is impossible in a context of the total absence of restraints. All three believed that we can legitimately place restrictions on certain freedoms in order to achieve a greater good both for individuals and society.

EQUALITY INCREASES POSITIVE FREEDOM

Equality is more compatible with positive freedom than it is with negative freedom. Considering an extreme example of equality, and its impact on freedom, can show this compatibility clearly. In 1888, Edward Bellamy (1850–1898) published *Looking Backward*, a utopian novel that spawned some 165 "Bellamy Clubs" throughout the United States devoted to consideration of its ideas. Although most people in the early twenty-first century have never heard of Bellamy, his influence in his time is difficult to overstate. *Looking Backward* was one of the best-selling books at the turn of the century, third only to *Ben-Hur* and *Uncle Tom's Cabin*. It sold millions of copies and was translated into over twenty languages. Three major figures of the early twentieth century, Charles Beard, John Dewey, and Edward Weeks, working independently of each other, cited Bellamy's book as the second most influential book published since 1885, with Karl Marx's *Capital* placed first. The book deeply influenced thinkers like Dewey, William Allen White, Eugene V. Debs, Norman Thomas, and Thorstein Veblen. Its influence extended to millions of average Americans in addition to some of America's premier thinkers and activists.

Looking Backward represented Bellamy's attempt to envision a just society radically unlike the America of his time, which was characterized by huge inequality, child labor, deep poverty, labor unrest, and misery for millions. In his words, "Unequal distribution of wealth, and, still more effectually, unequal opportunities of education and culture, divided society in [the late nineteenth century] into classes which in many respects regarded each other as distinct races." Bellamy used a coach metaphor to describe the existing conditions. An elite few sit comfortably atop the coach. Below them strive the masses, toiling constantly to move the coach forward in miserable conditions of mud and filth. Hunger drives them, along with the hope of someday sitting atop the coach. The elite recognize their pain and feel it mildly in sympathy. They call out encouragement and exhortations to continue striving. Occasionally, the coach hits a bump in the road, dislodging one or two of the wealthy elite, who fall to the ground and must commence straining with the rest. Bellamy here metaphorically characterized conditions of the late nineteenth century, dubbed the "Gilded Age" by Mark Twain, to describe a society in which a thin layer of wealth, power, and privilege concealed deep poverty and misery among millions. Bellamy intended a critique of this society in which the misery of millions sustained the privileged few. For these millions toiling to push the coach, freedom amounted to a choice between starvation and continuing to strain to push the coach.

According to Bellamy, defenders of this radical inequality used two "curious fictions" to defend it. First, most people of the time period believed "that there was no other way in which Society could get along, except when the many pulled at the rope and the few rode. . . . No very radical improvement even was possible. . . . It had always been as it was, and it always would be so." The second fiction consisted of "a singular hallucination which those on the top of the coach generally shared, that they were not exactly like their brothers and sisters who pulled at the rope, but of finer clay, in some way belonging to a higher order of beings who might justly expect to be drawn."

Bellamy envisioned in his novel a world marked by dramatic increases in both equality and positive freedom, while retaining most elements of negative freedom. Bellamy's central character, Julian West, falls asleep in the late nineteenth century and awakens more than a century later, in the year 2000. Times have changed dramatically during the intervening years. A great social, political, and economic transformation has occurred through a nonviolent evolutionary process in which the government gradually assumed a larger and larger role in the management of the economy. According to Bellamy:

> The obvious fact was perceived that no business is so essentially the public business as the industry and commerce on which the people's livelihood depends, and that to entrust it to private persons to be managed for private profit is a folly similar in kind, though vastly greater in magnitude, to that of surrendering the functions of political government to kings and nobles to be conducted for their personal glorification.

In place of the huge disparities in wealth and welfare between the haves and have-nots, West observes an equality of conditions and a generalized well-being. Gone are the signs of poverty such as disease, crime, filth, and wretchedness. Gone too are the rich few, for Bellamy has eliminated both classes of rich and poor. In their place, West sees prosperity in which all share.

In this utopian society, Bellamy guarantees perfect economic equality and perfect equality of opportunity. Everyone receives the same income—regardless of the type of work they do, their talent, or their productivity—sufficient not only to cover basic human needs but also to support comfortable accommodations and amenities that offer a life of relative ease and enjoyment. This guaranteed income was made possible by eliminating the class of rich and by an "industrial army" managed by the government to which everyone must contribute between the ages of 21 and 45. What justified this equality of income? According to Bellamy, each worker's "title [to an equal share of national income] is his humanity. The basis of his claim is the fact that he is a man."[35] Despite the gender-exclusive language, in Bellamy's world, women receive the same income as men. Bellamy also insisted, however, that every person was expected to contribute the best effort they could.

Contemporary critics will likely insist that different types of work are more important than others and should be paid correspondingly more; that higher talents should be more generously rewarded; and that rewarding the level of a worker's output is essential on the grounds of fairness and because it keeps workers motivated to achieve. Bellamy responded that everyone's job was important, and all workers contribute to the social and common good; that people should strive to use their talents, whatever they may be, for the common good as well as their own; and that the nineteenth-century motivators of greed and hunger had been replaced by a generalized sense of community and commitment to the common good. Since everyone enjoyed the same income, no one was excluded from educational and career opportunities, and no one enjoyed exceptional and privileged opportunities. Bellamy made a quality education available for everyone up to age 21, and career choices available equally to everyone of appropriate interest and aptitude.

By increasing economic equality and equality of opportunity, Bellamy guaranteed extensive positive freedom for everyone. No one would be forced to choose between painful, mindless toil and starvation. The state guaranteed everyone the provision of sufficient food, shelter, and clothing, a good education, a meaningful job, and an income sufficient to enable the pursuit of more creative, satisfying, and fulfilling endeavors. This increased the range of viable choices available to average people. A combination of interest, inclination, and aptitude determined career choices. In response to the obvious question of why anyone would choose to work in unpleasant occupations such as garbage hauling or animal slaughter, Bellamy answered with an ingenious, market-driven system of calibrating the length of the workday in order to find an equilibrium between labor supply and demand. If too few opted for the job of garbage hauler, the garbage hauler's workday was reduced in duration until the labor needs of that occupation were met. And vice versa, the length of the workday in more pleasant, popular occupations increased until the supply of labor in that occupation matched the demand.

The case with negative freedom is slightly more mixed. Every person retained, within broad limits, the right to choose her or his own career. Free speech, freedom of assembly, and freedom of religion remained important components of Bellamy's society. No censorship stifled creativity or critique. Everyone could emigrate freely. Most consumption opportunities remained open, since, according to Bellamy, if there existed a demand, the item would be supplied. Having eliminated the class of the rich, Bellamy excepted the boundless consumption of that class. On the other hand, Bellamy abolished certain freedoms that contemporary Americans take for granted. These include the freedom for the few to get rich, the freedom to behave as a business entrepreneur—because the state became the sole supplier of goods and services—and the freedom to choose a life of indolence, because everyone had to contribute in some way to the society.

Looking Backward has weathered many criticisms, and some of them are worth considering here. Most obviously, the vision he presents cannot be achieved in practice, even if the vision and ideals contained in it were deemed worthy of attainment. *Looking Backward* represents the author's attempt to imagine a utopia. Of course, perfection is impossible in practice. A utopian novel such as *Looking Backward* should be evaluated by how well it helps us imagine alternatives to the status quo and how well it helps us think about a different possible mix of equality and freedom than the one we take for granted today in the United States.

Other criticisms address the undemocratic elements of Bellamy's vision. First, though Bellamy increased economic equality and equality of opportunity, he *reduced* political equality. In his utopia, the state is led by retirees who are elected not by the adult population as a whole but by members of a retirees' guild. In other words, only relatively old men and women enjoy the right of suffrage. Second, political participation in general has been rendered obsolete for most Americans. Since all political problems have been solved, there remains no need for political organizing. Citizenship has essentially been eliminated, replaced by bureaucratic decision making. Third, Bellamy's state has become an all-encompassing Big Government feared by many on both the political left and right. The potential abuse of power in such a situation of concentrated power alarms many who are concerned about democratic autonomy and self-determination.

Despite his shortcomings, Bellamy demonstrated that increasing equality can increase positive freedom, while retaining key forms of negative freedom. We need not take the principle of economic equality to the extreme that he did. Achieving greater equality need not be accomplished as he does through complete socialization of the means of production, nor through total confiscation of affluent wealth. But it does require greater checks on private wealth, more social control of private capital, and in general more incursions on the freedoms associated with private property.

The connection between positive freedom and equality can also be found in W. E. B. Du Bois's *The Souls of Black Folk*. Du Bois's book describes what happens to a people granted legal freedom and political rights but with too few resources to make them effective. The thirteenth and fourteenth amendments to the U.S. Constitution, adopted in 1865 and 1868, respectively, abolished slavery and granted citizenship status to the emancipated slaves. In principle, this ensured their freedom. However, effective freedom was blocked by obvious factors such as the hate and opposition of the Ku Klux Klan, and by Southern civil courts that "tended to become solely institutions for perpetuating the slavery of blacks." Less obvious, but equally important factors included grinding poverty and lack of education.

The millions of recently emancipated African Americans without jobs presented an immediate problem, which Du Bois called a "national crisis." As Du Bois wrote: "Here loomed a labor problem of vast dimensions. Masses of Negroes stood idle, or, if they worked spasmodically, were never sure of pay." Most found work as menial laborers or sharecroppers for white landlords. Sharecroppers could labor a lifetime "beginning with nothing, and still having nothing" fifty years later, finding themselves "hopelessly in debt, disappointed, and embittered." Most sharecroppers would "end the year even, or in debt," which meant "they work for board and clothes." The result, as Du Bois clearly recognized, lay just short of chattel slavery:

In the backwoods of the Gulf States, for miles and miles, [the ex-slave] may not leave the plantation of his birth; in well-nigh the whole rural South the black farmers are peons, bound by law and custom to an economic slavery, from which the only escape is death or the penitentiary.[36]

Ex-slaves' access to education was similarly curtailed. Poor or nonexistent schoolhouses, inadequate teaching materials, a shortage of teachers willing and able to teach black children, and the desperate need for black children to work in order to contribute to family income limited educational opportunities for ex-slaves. White opposition also undermined ex-slaves' access to education. Du Bois related one anecdote of a white community taking drastic steps to prevent ex-slaves from educating themselves: they "hitched ninety yoke of oxen to the . . . schoolhouse and dragged it into the middle of the swamp."

Du Bois concluded that "despite compromise, war, and struggle, the Negro is not free." In the rural South, African Americans remained economically enslaved in a system of peonage. In the urban South, they formed "a segregated servile caste, with restricted rights and privileges." Before the courts, they stood as second-class citizens with few, if any, rights in practice. In electoral politics, they were simply shut out, so that "taxation without representation [was] the rule of their political life." Clearly recognizing the limits to freedom these factors represented, Du Bois wrote poignantly and sarcastically:

Free! The most piteous thing amid all the black ruin of war-time, amid the broken fortunes of the masters, the blighted hopes of mothers and maidens, and the fall of an empire,—the most piteous thing amid all this was the black freedman who threw down his hoe because the world called him free. What did such a mockery of freedom mean? Not a cent of money, not an inch of land, not a mouthful of victuals,—not even ownership of the rags on his back. Free!

Congress initially promised economic support for ex-slaves in the form of "forty acres and a mule," but never followed through on that promise. It established the Freedmen's Bureau in 1865 to manage Reconstruction but, presaging decades to come, failed to appropriate funds in the initial legislation. Congress's failure to act decisively practically ensured that the racist economic, social, and cultural institutions and structures persisting beyond emancipation would frustrate African Americans' quest for effective freedom.

In the context of lynch mobs, Jim Crow laws, and economic semislavery, the formal abolition of slavery by itself could ensure neither equality or effective freedom for African Americans. Abolition was a necessary but insufficient step. In this context, Du Bois's contemporary, the African-American educator Booker T. Washington, found favor among whites for publicly endorsing a "separate but unequal" status for African Americans, counseling hard work in menial jobs and advocating an educational strategy emphasizing vocational-technical skills. Du Bois called this strategy "segregated servility," an "old attitude of adjustment and submission" that "practically accepts the alleged inferiority of the Negro races." He dismissed as "propaganda" and at best a "dangerous half-truth" the notion that an African American's "future rise depends primarily on his own efforts."[37] It was a half-truth because, while necessary, individual effort could not alone overcome the daunting barriers facing African Americans of his time.

The same gap identified by Du Bois between formal freedom and actual, effective freedom remains a gaping chasm for millions of Americans. In the late nineteenth century, economic inequality took the forms of servile service work and sharecropping where hard work improving the land resulted in increased rent and higher debt. Today, if sharecropping is largely a thing of the past, the servile service work remains, in the form of minimum-wage service-sector jobs where hard work results in promotion for some but mind-numbing, deadening, persistent poverty for others. Hard work and talent applied energetically in these jobs will occasionally pay off, but for most it will at best enable survival in body if not in spirit. While legal rights are essential, they do not guarantee freedom. As Du Bois argued, freedom requires access to means and resources—to power—to make it effective. And effective freedom requires a minimal level of equality.

At the end of the previous chapter, various options were listed for increasing political equality, equality of opportunity, and economic equality. Respectively, these included limits on campaign spending, public financing of elections, more equitable media coverage, and restrictions on lobbyists; boosting economic equality, reinstating the inheritance tax, more equitable spending on education, and affirmative action programs; and increasing the progressivity of the tax code, boosting social welfare spending, and a living-wage policy. As noted, each of these proposals for increasing equality exacts a cost in terms of negative freedom. We can now see, however, that increases in positive freedom partially offset these losses of negative freedom.

Increasing political equality increases the positive freedom of common people to participate effectively in politics, to become active citizens, and to participate effectively in the determination of the circumstances of their lives. It increases their capacity for intervention in politics by reducing or eliminating class, racial, gender, and other barriers to participation, while reducing or balancing the exceptional power now awarded the affluent. It multiplies their real options for political participation. Increasing equality of opportunity gives more options to more people, while increasing their capacity to take advantage of those options. Expanding access to quality education, to cultural and leisure activities, and to careers currently foreclosed by economic deprivation or by racial and gender discrimination boosts positive freedom by better ensuring that each of us has an array of feasible life options and alternatives. Like the proposals for increasing political equality and equality of opportunity, the proposals for increasing economic equality increase positive freedom for many Americans by expanding their options and augmenting their capacity to act on them by ensuring that they have more access to the means and resources necessary to make them real options.

The proposals considered here leave most negative freedoms for most people intact and untouched. They primarily affect the negative freedoms of an affluent minority, and slightly at that. Equality and positive freedom can be increased for those most in need by funding it from exceptional income and wealth at the very top. The well-being of middle-class and upper-middle-class Americans need not be affected, except positively as we all benefit from increased equality. The proposals call neither for the complete removal of wealthy privilege nor for the complete elimination of negative freedom of the wealthy. Americans long ago established precedents for each of the proposals. They already limit individual campaign contributions and PAC spending. They impose laws and regulations that seek to limit socially destructive uses of private property. They sometimes confiscate private land for public purposes. They levy multiple taxes at several levels of jurisdiction that each claims a portion of taxpayers' money. The principles are well established, if not yet their full effectiveness.

QUESTIONS, PROBLEMS, AND ACTIVITIES

1. What are some "ineffective" freedoms in your life? In other words, what are you formally or theoretically free—but practically unable—to do? What would it take to make them effective?

2. What are your career goals? What obstacles have you overcome so far, and what obstacles do you anticipate having to overcome? Can you imagine different obstacles faced by others? What would help you overcome the obstacles?

3. Do you support affirmative action? Why or why not? Would you rather see a class-based, as opposed to gender- or race-based, affirmative action? What, if anything, would you recommend in place of affirmative action?

4. Draw freedom. Then analyze the drawing in terms of negative and positive freedom.

5. Brainstorm additional ways of achieving greater political equality, equal opportunity, and economic equality. Analyze these options in terms of implications for (different kinds of) freedom. Which of the proposals, if any, would you support?

6. Using the distinctions between different kinds of freedom, to what degree do we have free elections in the United States? To what degree is a battered woman, with children, free to leave her spouse? To what degree is a homeless person free? To what degree is an unemployed person free? To what degree are men and women free to shave or not shave? Place a mark on a continuum between absolute freedom and absolute nonfreedom for each of these. Brainstorm ways of increasing freedom in each case.

7. Should we try to reduce the gap between rich and poor in this country? Among countries? If yes, do you favor any means in particular for doing so?

NOTES

1. Judith Shklar, "Jean-Jacques Rousseau and Equality," in *Rousseau's Political Writings*, ed. Alan Ritter and Julia Conaway Bondanella (New York: W. W. Norton, 1988), p. 261.

2. Jean-Jacques Rousseau, *Discourse on Inequality* [1755], in Ritter and Bondanella, *Rousseau's Political Writings*, pp. 49, 44; Jean-Jacques Rousseau, *The Social Contract* [1762], in Ritter and Bondanella, *Rousseau's Political Writings*, pp. 97–98; Jean-Jacques Rousseau, *Discourse on Political Economy* [1755], in Ritter and Bondanella, *Rousseau's Political Writings*, p. 75.

3. Rousseau, *Discourse on Political Economy*, p. 75.

4. Rousseau, *Discourse on Inequality*, pp. 44–45.

5. Ibid., p. 43.

6. Rousseau, *Social Contract*, p. 116.

7. Rousseau, *Discourse on Inequality*, p. 43.

8. Rousseau, *Social Contract*, p. 97; Rousseau, *Discourse on Inequality*, p. 44.

9. Ritter and Bondanella, *Rousseau's Political Writings*, p. 92, n. 4; Rousseau, *Social Contract*, p. 103; Rousseau, *Discourse on Political Economy*, p. 72; Rousseau, *Social Contract*, pp. 126, 116.

10. Thomas Jefferson, "Letter to John Bannister, Jr. [October 15, 1785]," in *Basic Writings of Thomas Jefferson*, ed. Philip Foner (New York: Willey Book Company, 1944), pp. 532–33; Thomas Jefferson, "Letter to James Madison [October 28, 1785]," in Foner, *Basic Writings of Thomas Jefferson*, p. 520.

11. Jefferson, "Letter to James Madison [October 28, 1785]," p. 520.

12. Thomas Jefferson, "Letter to Samuel Kercheval [July 12, 1816]," in Foner, *Basic Writings of Thomas Jefferson*, pp. 746, 749.

13. Plato, *The Republic* 3.416d–417b, 4.421d–422a.

14. Rousseau, *Discourse on Political Economy*, p. 59.

15. Susan B. Anthony, "Suffrage and the Working Woman" [1871], in *American Political Thinking; Readings from the Origins to the 21st Century*, comp. Robert Isaak (Fort Worth: Harcourt Brace College Publishers, 1994), pp. 351–353; Susan B. Anthony, "Speech in Defense of Equal Suffrage" [1873], in Michael Levy, *Political Thought in America: An Anthology*, 2nd ed. (Chicago: Dorsey Press, 1988), p. 257.

16. Angelina Grimké, "Human Rights Not Founded on Sex" [1837], in Levy, *Political Thought in America*, pp. 259–61; emphasis in original.

17. Elizabeth Cady Stanton, "Address Delivered at Seneca Falls" [1848], in *The Elizabeth Cady Stanton–Susan B. Anthony Reader: Correspondence, Writings, Speeches*, ed. Ellen Carol DuBois (Boston: Northeastern University Press, 1981), pp. 28, 33, 30, 32.

18. Charlotte Perkins Gilman, *Women and Economics: A Study of the Economic Relation between Men and Women as a Factor in Social Evolution* (1898; Mineola, NY: Dover Publications, 1998), pp. 3–10.

19. Charlotte Perkins Gilman, "The Yellow Wall-Paper" [1890], in *The Yellow Wall-Paper, and Selected Stories of Charlotte Perkins Gilman*, ed. Denise Knight (Newark: University of Delaware Press, 1994), pp. 42, 46, 39, 40, 45, 49.

20. Gilman, *His Religion and Hers: A Study of the Faith of Our Fathers and the Work of Our Mothers* (1923; repr., Walnut Creek, CA: Alta Mira Press, 2003), pp. 202, 203, 213. Gilman's use of the term *licentiousness* likely referred to the rape of slave women by their masters.

21. Frederick Douglass, *Narrative of the Life of Frederick Douglass* [1845], in *Early African-American Classics*, ed. Anthony Appiah (New York: Bantam Books, 1990), pp. 13–110; Harriet Jacobs, *Incidents in the Life of a Slave Girl: Written by Herself* [1845], in Appiah, *Early African-American Classics*, pp. 111–315.

22. Du Bois, *The Souls of Black Folk* (1903; repr., New York: Vintage Books, 1990), pp. 8, 13, 147–48, 12.

23. Ibid., pp. 148, 80, 8, 96, 131.

24. Ibid., pp. 80–81, 79.

25. Benjamin Constant, "The Liberty of the Ancients Compared with That of the Moderns" [1816], in David Boaz, *The Libertarian Reader: Classic and Contemporary Readings from Lao-Tzu to Milton Friedman* (New York: Free Press, 1997), pp. 65–70; Isaiah Berlin, *Two Concepts of Liberty* (Oxford: Clarendon Press, 1958).

26. Gerald MacCallum, "Negative and Positive Freedom," *Philosophical Review* 76 (1967): pp. 312–34.

27. William Connolly, *The Terms of Political Discourse*, 2nd ed. (Princeton: Princeton University Press, 1983), pp. 154, 151, 154–55.

28. Ibid., pp. 162, 163, 157. Connolly benefited from the earlier work of S. I. Benn and W. L. Weinstein, "Being Free to Act and Being a Free Man," *Mind* 80 (1971), pp. 194–211, in which they argue that freedom presupposes autonomy.

29. See, for example, John Dewey, *Liberalism and Social Action* [1935], in *John Dewey: The Later Works, 1925–1953*, vol. 11, ed. Jo Ann Boydston (Carbondale: Southern Illinois University Press, 1991), p. 27; and John Dewey, *Ethics* [1908], in *John Dewey: The Middle Works, 1899–1924*, vol. 5, ed. Jo Ann Boydston (Carbondale: Southern Illinois University Press, 1978), p. 392.

30. Dewey, *Ethics*, p. 392; John Dewey, *The Public and Its Problems* [1927], in Boydston, *John Dewey: The Later Works*, vol. 2 (1988), p. 340.

31. John Dewey, "Liberty and Social Control" [1935], in Boydston, *John Dewey: The Later Works*, vol. 11, p. 360; John Dewey, "The Social Significance of Academic Freedom" [1936], in Boydston, *John Dewey: The Later Works*, vol. 11, p. 377; John Dewey, "Democracy and Education in the World of Today" [1938], in Boydston, *John Dewey: The Later Works*, vol. 13 (1991), p. 297; John Dewey, "The Crucial Role of Intelligence" [1935], in Boydston, *John Dewey: The Later Works*, vol. 11, p. 344.

32. John Winthrop, "A Little Speech on Liberty" [1645], in Levy, *Political Thought in America*, pp. 13–14.

33. John Locke, *The Second Treatise on Civil Government* (1690; Buffalo, NY: Prometheus Books, 1986), para. 21.

34. Rousseau, *The Social Contract*, p. 95.

35. Edward Bellamy, *Looking Backward* (1888; repr., New York: New American Library, 1960), p. 113, 28, 54, 75.

36. Du Bois, *Souls of Black Folk*, pp. 30, 18–19, 96, 110, 34.

37. Ibid., pp. 157–58, 34, 107, 42, 47.

III

JUSTICE AND POLITICAL ORDER

5

Thrasymachus Was Right

Justice is one of the most fundamental issues in all public life. Around it pivot debates about human nature, freedom, equality, citizenship, democracy, obligation, and a host of other political concepts and practices. The broad scope of justice encompasses both highly abstract universal issues and specific concrete issues. Many different factors potentially enter a discussion of justice, including need, merit, fairness, equality, liberty, property, rights, and more. Debates and decisions about justice produce widespread social effects, ranging from distribution of income to the use and preservation of natural resources to policies on incarceration and punishment to education and employment. Multiple and competing conceptions of justice complicate the discussion further. Like other central political concepts addressed in this book, justice is an essentially contested concept. If we disagree over the meaning of *justice*, we also disagree over the point of justice. *Why* do we strive for a just state? To protect our persons? Our property? To advance the public good? Why do we seek justice in our criminal justice system? To exact revenge? To rehabilitate? To ensure the safety of law-abiding citizens? Contemporary debates over various public policy options often presume answers to these underlying questions.

Justice should be carefully distinguished from charity, with which it is sometimes confused. Like justice, charity is sometimes invoked as a solution for a social ill. Charity presumes a relation of inequality, where the stronger or wealthier party voluntarily gives some resource or service to the weaker or poorer party. There are good reasons to encourage charity, most notably that it can ameliorate suffering and ease distress. However, charity should be viewed as a second-best option, for several reasons. First, it leaves the relationship of inequality untouched. The stronger, wealthier donor retains the position of dominance relative to the recipient. Second, charity may degrade the recipient. It openly acknowledges the weak position of the recipient who must accept the handouts from others in order to survive. Third, it may leave the recipient in a long-term position of dependency. Charity is roughly akin to a bandage. While it temporarily stanches the flow of blood, it leaves the glass on the sidewalk that wounded in the first place. While it temporarily puts food in the stomachs of undernourished people, it leaves untouched the structural and systemic causes of hunger and malnutrition. Finally, by temporarily easing suffering, charity may distract attention from the underlying problem and its causes.

Political philosophers distinguish between procedural and distributive justice. *Procedural justice* concerns the process of determining and applying justice. Two major kinds of procedural justice are familiar to most Americans. First, justice as equal opportunity entails making sure that the "contest" is fair: Each person starts in the same place, with the same set of advantages and disadvantages. A second kind of procedural justice emphasizes questions of legal procedure such as the right to a fair trial by a jury composed of peers, protection from arbitrary arrest, access to legal counsel, access to information about rights, and rules of discovery and evidence. In this approach, if the rules and procedures of the court system have been followed, then justice has been served, regardless of the actual guilt or innocence of the accused. Although procedural justice is an important dimension of justice, it may be consistent with unjust outcomes. Even if equal opportunity could be ensured, a fair contest may result in radical inequality due to historical contingencies, talent, luck, and other factors. A procedurally just trial may convict the innocent or exonerate the guilty.

In contrast to procedural justice, *distributive justice* is concerned with outcomes. Regardless of the process, where do people end up? In what kinds of circumstances do people live? As the name suggests, distributive justice concerns the distribution of resources in a society. Many political theorists view the question of "desert" as the central element in discussions of distributive justice. According to this notion of desert, people should get what they deserve. But how do we determine what a person deserves? What are the criteria? These prove to be enormously complicated questions. Some of the most commonly applied criteria include effort, talent, skill, educational attainment, and our common humanity. Like procedural justice, justice as desert allows for the likelihood of radical inequality, as exemplified by professional athletes whose athletic talents entitle them (within the dominant contemporary framework of justice as desert) to exceptional material rewards, and by chief executive officers (CEOs) who earn millions annually while paying less than living wages to employees.

A second approach to the question of distributive justice emphasizes the priority of equality over other considerations of justice. Some proponents of this approach argue simply that equality is inherently just, because it accords with our equal moral status and equal human dignity. For example, most feminists argue that women deserve pay equal to men for equal or comparable work simply because they share the same moral status as men. African Americans should receive equal treatment as whites under the law for the same reason. Other proponents of equality value it for its positive individual and social benefits. A third, related approach applies the common humanity criterion and concludes that justice requires at least a minimal level of equality in the form of meeting basic human needs.

Given the range and complexity of the concept of justice, no attempt will be made to comprehensively address it. The public problems considered below focus primarily on distributive justice and its relation to political order. In the United States, the dominant conception of distributive justice combines elements of procedural and distributive justice, while emphasizing procedural justice. "You get what you deserve" according to how well or poorly you fare in a presumably fair competitive market economy. The rules of this competition allegedly favor no one, so that individuals succeed or fail according to their own merits, defined in terms of effort, talent, skill, educational level, and motivation. Resulting inequalities, according to this conception, are deserved and therefore just.

Unlike justice, which has many different meanings, *political order* has two predominant meanings. First, political order straightforwardly means lack of disorder. A politically ordered state is a peaceful state free of violence and mayhem. Its citizens enjoy protections that guarantee their safety from domestic and foreign aggression. Sometimes we see political order in this first sense despite obvious injustices. How can we account for this? One possibility is political order maintained by repression and force. In this case, people may be widely aware of the injustices, but either fear organizing and speaking against them because of potential reprisals or cannot do so effectively because of power disparities. Another possible explanation for the presence of political order in a context of injustice is that people are convinced of the justness of their situations even though objectively their needs and interests are not justly addressed.

A second, relatively trivial meaning of political order refers to the political and economic status quo, to the way that dominant institutions and structures together create a particular way of life. It serves as shorthand for the status quo complex of existing political economy and the institutions and structures that form it. A political order in this sense may or may not be just, depending on how well or poorly it addresses the needs and interests of different people. Even if objectively unjust, a political order may be perceived as just, leading to a peaceful social milieu.

The following problems illustrate tensions between justice and one or both senses of political order, and the relative preference today among dominant decision makers for political order over justice.

PUBLIC PROBLEMS

Asymmetrical Global Development

The language of development studies is full of value assumptions and pitfalls. The notion of development suggests a continuum along which different countries can be arrayed according to their relative level of development. In dominant development discourses, the criteria for placement on the continuum are almost entirely economic. Thus relatively affluent countries are viewed as "developed," while relatively nonaffluent countries are viewed as "undeveloped," "underdeveloped," "lesser developed," or "developing." This strongly implies a generalized ranking of better and worse, good and bad, rich and poor—with the less-affluent countries naturally falling into the "worse," "bad," and "poor" categories. These categories elevate wealthy countries to superior status while condemning others to inferior status. The same can be said for the term *Third World*, which implies inferior status. Even if these terms were strictly limited to economic considerations and not generalized to encompass entire cultures, the rankings nevertheless remain based on aggregate material wealth that suggest that more is always better than less, an assumption challenged by some development critics. A different criterion for placement on the continuum emphasizing, for example, cultural richness or impact on the environment would yield a very different ordering that would, in many cases, invert the rankings based solely on material wealth.

To partly circumvent these conceptual difficulties, this text will adopt the terms *North* and *South* to designate, respectively, the relatively affluent, mostly industrialized countries of the Northern Hemisphere and the relatively non-affluent, mostly nonindustrialized countries of the Southern Hemisphere, especially in Africa, South America, and Asia. These terms are hardly perfect—most obviously because some geographically northern countries are relatively nonaffluent while some southern ones are quite affluent, and the terms obliterate vast differences among individual countries—but they are less objectionable than other terms while serving as convenient shorthand.[1]

Asymmetrical global development leads to huge gaps between economically rich and poor, and these gaps are growing rather than shrinking. By the mid-1990s, the global gap between the rich and poor countries had roughly doubled since the 1960s. Today the top 20 percent of the world's population controls more than 80 percent of the world's wealth and the bottom 20 percent controls about 1 percent.[2] Economically rich countries include Northern industrialized countries such as the United States, Canada, and most Western European nations. Economically poor countries include many of the countries in the Southern Hemisphere, particularly in Asia, South America, and Africa. While most residents of rich countries enjoy relative security, comfort, and even luxury, billions of residents in poor countries face daily challenges to survival, including chronic and acute shortages of food, shelter, medicine, and other basic necessities. Although some Southern countries have made strides toward ameliorating these problems, in general most face persistent and even worsening conditions of hardship.

The dominant understanding of what *development* means, how it should happen, and what can go wrong is found in modernization theory.[3] Most mainstream economists and most highly placed policy makers in dominant Northern countries and development institutions support this approach to development. Not surprisingly, the affluent Northern countries serve as the models for modernization theory, and the path of development reads like a list of dominant values and traits of these countries. These include secularization, increased use of science and technology, urbanization, social mobility, entrepreneurship, merit-based advancement, social innovation, intellectual diversity, limited government, the rule of law, and an extensive division of labor. Finally and most importantly according to modernization theory, development occurs as the result of participation in a market economy in which labor and capital are allocated according to principles of comparative advantage, efficiency, and maximum gain. In other words, development occurs as a result of participation in a system of free market capitalism in which goods and services are produced and traded free of governmental intrusions in the marketplace.

One central element of this ideology of free market capitalism is participation in an export-driven economy. An *export* is the sale of a good or service abroad. Which products or services should a country produce for export? The answer given by modernization theory is: those products or services in which a country enjoys a comparative advantage. This simply means that, compared to others, a particular country has an advantage in the production of certain goods and services. For example, compared to most other countries, the United States has an advantage in the production of automobiles and computer technology; compared to most other countries, Guatemala has an advantage in the production of coffee and bananas. In theory, if the United States and Guatemala concentrated on producing autos and computers, and coffee and bananas, respectively, both would be better off in the long run—assuming a second major element in free market capitalism: trade between countries. *Trade* simply means an exchange of goods or services abroad. In theory, this benefits residents of both countries, as production occurs efficiently, enabling producers to keep prices relatively low for consumers.

If capital to fund development projects is scarce within the Southern countries, modernization theory recommends both borrowing from foreign private and public banks and inviting foreign multinational corporations to participate in the development process via foreign direct investment. Access to capital provided by these investing institutions will, in theory, provide the boost needed to drive startup businesses, to fund the infrastructure needed to support them, and to motivate the individuals who provide the entrepreneurial spirit. In theory, the advantages of this development approach include, first and foremost, that it jump-starts and fuels the development process. By integrating a nonindustrialized economy into a world market system, it stimulates export capabilities, job creation, infrastructure provision, and an increase in labor productivity. Second, this approach to development is said to be more efficient than other approaches, in that different countries are urged to specialize in production of goods and services which their comparative advantage allows them to produce at the lowest possible cost.

Critics of modernization theory identify many problems with it.[4] First, despite widespread support by dominant elites and institutions, and despite decades of development assistance based on this model, many Southern countries continue to face extreme hardships of poverty, malnutrition and starvation, low life expectancy, an AIDS epidemic, and multiple health problems. Alleged success stories often require major caveats, especially the fact that the countries often cited as success stories—the so-called newly industrialized countries (NICs) South Korea, Brazil, Hong Kong, Singapore, Taiwan, and Mexico—actually pursued a strategy that departed significantly from modernization theory. Critics add that most of the industrialized countries, including the United States, also departed substantially from the model in their own development path.

Second, the development path espoused by modernization theory leads to a host of problems associated with economic reliance on cheap labor and the production and export of primary products. These include unequal exchange between Northern and Southern countries in which Southern countries find themselves locked into the production and export of primary goods, which they have to trade for value-added goods such as automobiles and computers; dependence on cheap labor; declining terms of trade and mounting trade deficits; vulnerability to the wild fluctuations in price that characterizes primary products markets; land concentration necessary for the production of primary products; a shift away from the production of subsistence food; and wages too low to support subsistence.

Third, according to critics of modernization theory, the need for development capital, combined with the free-market, export-led orientation of modernization theory, opens Southern countries to exploitation by multinational corporations. Multinational corporations aim primarily to make a profit, not to develop the host country. They gain direct access to resources, lower labor costs, less protectionist policies, more lenient environmental regulations, and often lower taxes. Host countries gain access to capital, technology, management expertise, and marketing networks. While the costs to the multinational corporation are offset by profit, costs to the host nation may be steep. Multinationals often impose conditions upon which their investment is contingent. These include demands for relaxed environmental regulations, opposition to union formation, infrastructure subsidies, and tax abatements. Host countries often find themselves responding to the needs of the multinational rather than their own people. Other costs to the host country include expropriation of profits to the home country rather than local reinvestment, overcharges for technology transfers, discouraging of local entrepreneurship as the giant multinational squelches local initiative and drives competitors out of business, transfer pricing ("juggling the books") in which tax liability to the host country is reduced or eliminated, environmental degradation, exploitation of cheap labor, and partial loss of sovereignty as the multinational makes demands to which the host country must accede.

Private and public banks provide another source of development capital. Like multinational corporations, these banks require that certain conditions be met. And like multinational corporations, the strings exact costs that often exceed the benefits of borrowing. In particular, many of these banks require that the borrowing country adopt the basic principles and practices outlined in modernization theory. One result of borrowing money from foreign private and public banks has been the shouldering of a crushing debt load among many Southern countries. This debt load today acts as a major impediment to further development efforts, as many countries divert desperately needed funds to debt reduction.

Fourth, critics argue that rather than reducing inequality between rich and poor in the world, this development model increases it. Rich countries continue to benefit from their relatively powerful bargaining position, extracting more in profit than they return in decent jobs and other benefits. Wealthy elites within Southern countries further enrich themselves by cooperating with multinational corporations and foreign banks at the expense of their fellow citizens. Resources flow from poor to rich, rather than vice versa.

Fifth, critics charge, this development model favors large-scale, capital-intensive projects that benefit elites without touching the lives of the poor and that destroy wetlands, river systems, and fragile ecosystems.

Proponents of modernization theory typically blame the Southern countries themselves for failure to benefit from modernization theory. They charge

Southern countries with corruption, poor policy choices, backward cultures, outdated systems of patronage and kinship, and protectionist barriers against free trade. Critics respond that understanding asymmetrical development requires more of a historical, structural, and systemic analysis than modernization theory can offer. Such an analysis must begin with the enduring legacy of colonialism, which includes coups, corruption, dictatorship, instability, disenchantment, and stunted economies oriented toward the export of raw materials.

European countries established colonies in order to benefit themselves, not the inhabitants of the colonies, whatever their claims of bringing civilization and Christianity to the colonials. Colonial powers took huge fortunes from their colonies to finance European development, luxury, expansion, and war; this wealth could have been used instead to support indigenous development. In addition to direct extraction of mineral and human wealth, European powers attempted, often successfully, to deliberately sabotage their colonies' economies by forcing strict monopoly trade restrictions, passing taxes, and forbidding indigenous production of goods produced by the mother country. The colonial power typically imposed its language, religion, and other cultural expressions on indigenous populations. Some indigenous elites, convinced of the superiority of the colonizer's culture, attempted to emulate it, in effect collaborating in the destruction of their own cultures.

Politically, colonial powers arbitrarily created many of the nation-states of the Southern world by drawing political boundaries that took little or no account of existing political entities. This often resulted in fragile and explosive states composed of historical enemies. The need to repress conflict between these historical enemies required a strong military, and many former colonies remain dependent on former colonial powers to provide it. Also, the perceived need to either fight or advance Communism during the Cold War made of the South a battleground of sorts on which the two superpowers jockeyed for advantage and dominance. This typically resulted in client–state relationships between superpowers and Southern countries. Collusion of indigenous elites with dominant foreign powers often led to radical inequality, with the majority of indigenous populations living in extreme poverty. This created further instability and increased the stakes of military repression, again creating dependence on foreign powers for military assistance.

Neocolonialism eventually replaced colonialism, but patterns of domination and exploitation continue. Under neocolonialism, formal ties of dependency have given way to formal independence for the former colonies, and control is exercised indirectly, primarily through financial and economic means. The relation between the Northern industrialized countries and the Southern countries remains one of domination–dependence, primarily benefiting the dominant power.

Critics of modernization theory offer alternative development strategies. One approach emphasizes negotiating better terms for Southern countries in their relations with Northern countries. The major problem with this effort lies in the uneven bargaining power of Northern and Southern nations. The wealthier, more powerful Northern countries have little incentive, other than moral claims that carry little weight in a global system oriented toward self-interest and profit, for pursuing alternative strategies. As many have pointed out, the current rules were made by the Northern countries and primarily benefit the Northern countries.

Another alternative development strategy, one that departs significantly from the neoclassical model embedded in modernization theory, is import substitution industrialization (ISI). While modernization theorists counsel extensive integration and participation in the world economy, ISI counsels selective de-linking from the global capitalist system. In this approach, a country attempts to stimulate indigenous production of goods and services that were previously imported. This may require producing products and services in which the country has a comparative disadvantage. It also involves heavy use of tariffs and subsidies in order to protect domestic producers from cheaper imports. Moreover, ISI entails encouraging domestic consumption in order to increase markets for domestic producers. Governments attempt to achieve this by maintaining the value of the domestic currency, letting wages rise, and increasing social spending in order to stimulate the economy and put money into the hands of consumers. Supporters of ISI argue that efficiency may be worth sacrificing for greater autonomy and indigenous development.

Another development model enjoying some support is mercantilist capitalism. This differs from a free market capitalist model primarily in the degree to which it shifts away from wholesale embrace of free markets and toward selective use of markets and government intervention in general. While still based on basic capitalist principles such as private ownership of the means of production and allocation via markets, this model uses government selectively to protect and promote certain of its industries through tariffs, subsidies, co-operative research, and strategic planning. This model in fact more closely approximates the development strategy actually followed by many Northern countries, including the United States, Europe, Japan, and the NICs. These countries all relied on extensive partnerships between industry and the state. Their industrialization process involved several decades or more of government protectionism, large subsidies to domestic industry, support for public utilities and state-owned industries, tax breaks and other incentives for research and development to diversify the economy, and controls on currency and capital.

Finally, some critics of dominant approaches to development propose to substitute meeting basic human needs for the pursuit of profit as the major goal. They would substitute appropriate technology for the mainstream approach's uncritical celebration of mechanization and advanced technology. They would focus heavily on human development by, for example, increasing subsidies for education. They typically emphasize smaller-scale development projects controlled at local levels by the people who will be affected by the projects. This alternative to the dominant model of elite-driven, top-down development emphasizes greater participation by local citizens in forming development strategies and carrying them out. Two additional features are the establishment of "micro-credit" opportunities to fund local initiatives, and the empowerment of women in development. Many alternative voices today emphasize the need to invest more heavily in women, who typically handle domestic duties of producing and meeting basic human and familial needs. Some of these approaches would radically redirect Northern consumerism and materialism toward meeting basic human needs and pursuing more frugal development paths based on better husbandry of resources.[5]

In the current world order, "the great powers jointly construct and enforce the international system, at times acting as 'police,' either unilaterally or in concert with other great powers. The effect is to reinforce a status quo that embraces self-interest"[6] rather than moral claims or justice. Southern countries have little choice but to play along with the rules laid down by dominant Northern countries. The inevitable unrest, instability, anger, and resentment created by asymmetrical development is simply repressed, savagely and brutally if necessary, often with U.S. financial and military support.

Global Debt

The issue of global debt merits a closer look, since it illustrates how power and self-interest converge to the detriment of Southern countries. At the turn of the twenty-first century, Southern countries owed approximately $2.6 trillion to banks, international financial institutions, and other countries.[7] This debt retards development efforts, diverting desperately needed cash from service provision and development to servicing the debt.

Most of the current debt originated during the 1970s and 1980s in a convergence of events. In 1973, the oil-producing countries formed a cartel to more effectively control the supply and price of crude oil. This cartel, the Organization of Petroleum Exporting Countries (OPEC), raised the price of crude oil by a factor of approximately eight, resulting in a dramatic increase in energy costs to all other countries and the creation of major cash reserves within the OPEC nations. The surge in energy costs added additional burdens to the costs of countries' development efforts. Banks holding the pumped-up OPEC cash reserves aggressively sought new lending opportunities. Meanwhile, the World Bank was funding large-scale, capital-intensive development projects that required borrowing by Southern nations. And at the same time, many Southern countries saw the world market for most primary commodities collapse. The decline in export earnings caused by the collapse of commodity prices, combined with surging energy costs and expensive development efforts, led to a pressing need for cash. Southern countries borrowed heavily from domestic and foreign banks, resulting in an explosion of debt. Many Southern countries soon found themselves unable to service their debts. The net result was the so-called debt crisis of the early 1980s in which indebted Southern countries barely kept pace with interest payments, and some neared default. Today, many Southern countries continue to struggle to meet debt obligations.

Bankers, economists, and policy makers immersed in ideologies and practices guiding free market capitalism dominate discussions today about how to handle the debt. The special role of the International Monetary Fund (IMF) should be noted. This global financial institution was created in 1947, along with the World Bank, as part of the United Nations. Its founders envisioned a role of managing short-term balance-of-payments problems and coordinating international monetary policy. The IMF's mission evolved into one of salvaging debtor nations and their credit ratings. In effect, it has become the lender of last resort. Without its stamp of approval, most Southern countries now find it impossible to establish credit with private banks. It patches together the frayed debtor mess. Today, the IMF focuses heavily on debt management. IMF policies are determined through a system of voting that awards voting shares based on the amount of money invested by a contributor in the fund. The largest contributors—not surprisingly, the major Northern countries—therefore control IMF policies. The United States, with the most money in the fund, controls the most votes. This voting mechanism helps ensure that the IMF pursues policies consistent with Northern countries' interests.

The IMF lends money conditionally upon the enactment of structural adjustment programs (SAPs) designed to ensure the greatest likelihood of loan repayment. It imposes two major kinds of changes on borrowing nations. First, the country must adopt policies consistent with free market capitalism. This means that it must emphasize an export-led development model focusing on one or two major exports, eliminate trade barriers erected to protect jobs and indigenous industry, privatize governmental programs and holdings, invite foreign direct investment, lower or eliminate subsidies to domestic businesses, and devalue the national currency as a way of making exports cheaper. Second, the country must cut government spending. In practice, this usually translates into slashing welfare, education, and health services. Thus, while pushing debt repayment to the top of the list, an SAP pushes social service provision and autonomous indigenous development to the bottom.

Critics charge the IMF with sabotaging Southern countries with these SAPs. They forthrightly force debtor countries into one economic mold. Countries experimenting with alternative paths such as ISI or a "food-first" strategy find themselves locked out of IMF support. SAPs require a partial loss of national sovereignty for the debtor nation, which must yield policy initiatives to bankers and the economists at the IMF. Most of the changes dramatically hurt the poorest of the poor in the debtor nations. A currency devaluation undermines the purchasing power of everyone, but the most dramatic consequences fall upon the poor whose already-meager purchasing power declines further. The SAP requirement of cutting social services compounds the hardships suffered by the poor who rely the most on them. The shift to an export economy also often hurts the most marginalized as production shifts from meeting indigenous basic human needs to exporting to an international market. Enforced privatization requires selling off government-owned utilities and factories that provided desperately needed jobs. Reductions in trade barriers often wipe out domestic businesses unable to compete effectively with foreign multinational corporations. Forcing an emphasis on one or two export products creates vulnerability of entire Southern economies to sudden drops in commodity prices. Finally, SAPs increase the need for government repression of widespread social unrest induced by the dramatic cuts in social services and increases in the cost of basic necessities.

Critics argue that all of this might be defensible if there were convincing evidence that the mid- to long-term results included development in which all would benefit. However, little evidence of this can be found. Most troubling, the international system continues to see a net annual flow of wealth from South to North. Most Southern countries remain mired in debt, their World Bank– and IMF-inspired development efforts thwarted. Currently, debtor nations and lending institutions are simply muddling through, retreading old loans and generating new ones in order to stave off default for another day or year.

Strategies for solving the problem of debt abound, but effective ones face stiff opposition from precisely those dominant individuals, institutions, and governments that control the rules and policies. The only strategy they will seriously consider is the status quo policy pursued into the present of muddling through, squeezing payments out of debtor nations in any way possible by rolling over debt and adding to it. Alternative strategies include the formation of a debtor cartel similar to OPEC in which members would form a collective bargaining front and use it to pry more favorable terms out of banks; simple refusal by debtor nations to make their debt payments; forcing wealthy elites in debtor nations to shoulder more of the responsibility for the debt by taxing the rich and by restricting capital flight; asking residents of wealthy nations to voluntarily pay higher prices for importing primary products from debtor nations; and debt-for-equity swaps in which multinational corporations would assume responsibility for some or all of the debt repayment in exchange for shares in debtor nations' national industries and resources. Most of these proposals founder on the reluctance by dominant policy makers to seriously consider them and the policy makers' ability to sabotage the proposals if tried anyway.

The strategy most favored today by debtor nations and their advocates is partial or complete debt forgiveness. This would require that banks write off part or all of the debt or reduce interest rates. Debt forgiveness would necessitate banks' acceptance of a reduction in their profits and the dividends of their shareholders and depositors. This policy option asks the relatively wealthy to shoulder more of the burden. And why not? critics ask, since they are the ones who have profited from the debt. This strategy of debt forgiveness was partially implemented in 1996 in a Debt-Relief for Heavily Indebted Poor Countries (HIPC) initiative, which financed partial debt relief for forty-one of the world's poorest countries. However, according to critics, this initiative had too many unacceptable strings attached and provided too little relief—only a small percentage of the overall debt burden.

As this problem continues, it sabotages efforts in Southern countries to meet basic human needs of residents. Money that could be used to fund indigenous development and social programs is diverted instead to service the external debt. The relatively powerful and wealthy sustain a prevailing political-economic order that benefits them, opting for the status quo over development assistance for those who need it the most. They rely heavily on repressive military force to quell the unrest inevitably created by deprivation, by SAPs, and by ongoing diversion of scarce resources into debt service.

World Hunger

In 1984, the United Nations estimated that 15 million children died annually—the equivalent of one every two seconds—from hunger and hunger-related diseases. In the mid-1980s, the Food and Agricultural Organization (FAO) of the United Nations conservatively estimated that 10 million people died annually from hunger, not including deaths from hunger-related diseases.[8] The United Nations estimated at that time that 1.2 billion people lived in poverty, regularly experiencing hunger. Overall, the number of hungry people in the world is increasing. Today in all Southern nations combined, there are approximately 800 million chronically undernourished people. There are more people hungry today than ever before.[9]

Why do so many people starve? Dominant policy makers offer various explanations. Forces of nature such as droughts, hurricanes, climate changes, or insect plagues disrupt food production and distribution. Lack of appropriate technology such as tractors, hybrid seeds, center-pivot irrigation systems, or potent fertilizers may undermine food sufficiency. Governments make bad decisions that direct resources from agriculture to industry. Some government officials steal money earmarked for assistance. Individuals and families work too little and breed too much, and they stubbornly resist transitioning to modern mechanized farming. Entire cultures prevent needed change, as the Hindus do by superstitiously refusing to eat cattle.

Each of these explanations begins from a diagnosis of too little food production and suggests a solution of growing more food. In the 1940s, various private and public entities set out to do just that. They declared a "war on hunger" and initiated a "Green Revolution" aimed at increasing food production. The Green Revolution brought together U.S. plant breeders, the World Bank, various UN agencies, private foundations, and scientists to employ science and technology to increase global food production. The scientists developed high-yield seeds that resisted drought and insects, and promoted them throughout the world. Since these new seeds would not grow without fertilizers, they promoted those, too. Irrigation systems and pesticides soon followed, and tractors to till the increasingly large land holdings. Multinational corporations and agribusinesses provide each of these at a steep cost. Their capital-intensive nature makes them unavailable and unsuitable for most small and subsistence farmers.

Food production increased but, unfortunately, so did hunger, especially in the Southern countries most devoted to the Green Revolution. The Green Revolution revealed a fundamental mistake in thinking about hunger: the major cause of hunger is not food production, but food distribution. Millions of people starve despite a global surplus of food. Brazil, pursuing the export-led development strategy favored by dominant elites and policy makers, became the world's second largest food exporter at the same time that 90–100 million of its people were chronically experiencing hunger. India during the 1970s stored 20 million tons of "surplus" wheat and rice while 300 million experienced food deprivation. Throughout the American Midwest, silos burst with corn that "nobody wants." The planet currently yields more than enough food to meet everyone's nutritional needs.

People go hungry if they lack resources such as money to buy food or land upon which to grow it. Many of the poor once had some resources, including land, to stave off hunger. However, the Green Revolution made large-scale farming profitable. This increased the price of land to own or rent, driving out small farmers and fueling a shift from subsistence to export-driven farming, and from staples such as rice and wheat to export crops like peanuts and pineapples. Food production shifted from a focus on feeding hungry locals to a focus on export-for-profit. Driven from their land, the poor now had to buy food, rather than grow it. With decent jobs, this would not have been a problem. However, large-scale agriculture eliminates more jobs than it creates, as tractors and other forms of mechanization replace old labor patterns. Once food production shifted to an emphasis on profit and export markets, citizens of richer countries outbid poor people throughout the world for food resources. The hundreds of millions of people who go hungry as a result "cannot create a sufficient 'market demand' for the fruits of the Earth. So more and more of it flows into the mouths of livestock, which convert it into what the better-off can afford. Corn becomes filet mignon. Sardines become salmon." In short, we artificially and "actively generate scarcity from plenty."[10] By feeding so much corn to cattle, and sardines to salmon, we turn them into food disposals. Thirty years ago, one-third of all grain was fed to livestock; today livestock eat half of all grain.

Development activists increasingly agree that charity cannot solve the hunger problem. In fact, charity may make the problem worse rather than better by reinforcing the status quo conditions that produce hunger. According to the Food First Institute:

> Most U.S. aid works directly against the hungry. Foreign aid can only reinforce, not change, the status quo. Where governments answer only to elites, our aid not only fails to reach hungry people, it shores up the very forces working against them. Our aid is used to impose free trade and free market policies, to promote exports at the expense of food production, and to provide the armaments that repressive governments use to stay in power. Even emergency, or humanitarian aid, which makes up only five percent of the total, often ends up enriching American grain companies while failing to reach the hungry, and it can dangerously undercut local food production in the recipient country.[11]

Since poverty is the underlying cause of hunger, real progress requires addressing that poverty. Options include land reform in which the poor gain access to land, subsidizing subsistence food production, offering jobs, financing rural education, providing low-cost irrigation water, providing public health programs, and taxing the rich to subsidize social programs such as education. According to many hunger activists, these options would likely help, but more systemic change may be necessary. Systemic change would require a fundamental shift in thinking about food and hunger. Systemic change would require moving away from an emphasis on free markets and export-led development to an emphasis on the provision of basic human needs. Although markets may be part of the answer to food sufficiency for everyone, they should not be placed first in the order of priority, according to hunger activists. Meeting everyone's nutritional needs should assume that primary position.

How we frame the problem of hunger in part determines how we deal with it. Currently, multinational corporations that reap the financial benefits of the status quo, and development experts wedded to a free-market, export-led model, dominate the debate over hunger. Transforming the status quo may require fundamental shifts in how we think about food. Is food a commodity like any other, morally equal in status to a television or an automobile, to which we have access only if we can pay for it? Or is access to food a basic human right, which all humans should be guaranteed? If the latter, fundamental changes in the prevailing political and economic order surrounding food production and distribution will likely be required.

Racial Disparities in the United States

According to a poll conducted in 2001, biracial couples today report greater acceptance than in earlier years. An "overwhelming majority" of biracial couples now say their families accept them. On the other hand, in the same poll black–white couples say that rude waiters often ignore them in restaurants and strangers stare threateningly at them in public places. According to the poll, while 86 percent of African Americans would welcome a white person into their family, only 55 percent of white Americans would welcome a black person into theirs. When white people do marry interracially, they tend to marry Latinos rather than African Americans. According to another 2001 poll, more than half (52 percent) of all black men, one-fourth (25 percent) of black women, and one-fifth (20 percent) of Asian and Latino men report that they have been racially profiled by police. "Overwhelming majorities" of blacks, Latinos, and Asians also say that they have been the victim of racially motivated poor service in stores or restaurants, disparaging comments, and encounters with people who are frightened or suspicious of them because of their race or ethnicity. By comparison, one-third of white people report similar treatment.[12]

Although whites and blacks have long differed in their perceptions of race relations, with whites more likely to minimize or dismiss the problem of racism, the gap in perceptions has widened in recent times. There has been a "steady decline in the belief among blacks that black children have the same chance to get a good education as white children, and that blacks have the same opportunities for affordable housing, even as white faith in equal treatment remains very high." In 2001, 85 percent of whites thought that black children have the same level of opportunity as white children, compared to 52 percent of blacks. This perception gap of 33 percentage points marked an increase from only 17 percentage points in 1990. In 2001, the gap in perception of equal housing opportunity stood at 35 percentage points, up from 20 in 1989. In 2001, the gap in perception of educational opportunity was 33 percentage points, almost exactly the same as in 1962. Overall, 38 percent of whites and only 9 percent of blacks believe that blacks and whites are treated the same in the United States.[13]

Whatever the perceptions among Americans, the empirical data tell a definitive story. On just about every measure, racial inequality is an enduring characteristic of American society. Blacks and Hispanics are approximately three times as likely as whites to live in families whose income falls below poverty level. In 2003, 34.1 percent of black children under 18, and 29.7 percent of Hispanic children under 18 lived in poverty, compared to 14.3 percent of white children under 18.[14] Though the household income of black families grew slightly faster during the 1990s than that of white families, the gains were attributable to the extra hours worked by members of black families. In education, test scores show black students "years behind their white counterparts in both reading and writing skills and actual knowledge." Black adult illiteracy is approximately three times that of whites. Average black SAT scores remain approximately 100 points behind white SAT scores in both verbal and math. Black college attendance in proportion to the total population of blacks is approximately 25 percent lower than whites, and a third of all black college students are in two-year programs. In the mid-1990s, approximately 82 percent of white adults had a high school diploma, compared to 73 percent of black adults, and whites were nearly twice as likely to have a college degree.[15]

Huge racial disparities also exist in the rates of incarceration and the severity of sentencing. According to Amnesty International, "When compared to white defendants, minority groups face a greater likelihood of imprisonment and serve longer sentences than whites for identical crimes." African Americans constitute 12 percent of the U.S. population but 47 percent of sentenced

inmates in state and federal correctional institutions. At 13 percent of the total population, Hispanics constitute 16 percent of those in jail. Whites, at 70
percent of the general population, make up 35 percent of state and federal inmates. All nonwhites taken together constitute 30 percent of total U.S. population, but 66 percent of the prison population. In 1997, there were 3,209
sentenced black male inmates per 100,000 black males in the total U.S. population, 1,273 Hispanic male inmates per 100,000 Hispanic males, and 386
white male inmates per 100,000 white males in the total population. For every
white arrest, there are three African-American arrests. These disparities exist
for identical crimes. While 54 percent of blacks convicted of drug offenses do
prison time, only 34 percent of whites convicted of the same offenses go to
prison. Forty-four percent of blacks convicted for possession get prison sentences, compared to 29 percent of whites convicted of the same crime; 60 percent of black defendants get prison sentences for trafficking, compared to 37
percent for whites. Although African Americans comprise 15 percent of regular drug users and whites comprise 67 percent, 35 percent of those arrested for
drug possession, 55 percent of those convicted of drug possession or use, and
74 percent of those sentenced to prison for drug possession are African Americans. The same discrepancies can be found among detained youth. Though
minority youth comprise one-third of youth nationwide, they represent two-
thirds of the total population of youth in local detention and state correctional facilities.[16]

These disparities are even more pronounced in sentencing for the death
penalty. According to Amnesty International, "Nowhere is racial discrimination more evident, or more deadly, than in the application of the death
penalty. . . . The death penalty in the U.S. is applied disproportionately on the
basis of race, ethnicity and social status." In 1997, white-on-black homicides
resulted in 7 death sentences, while black-on-white homicides resulted in 130.
Between 1977 and 1998, 500 prisoners were executed, 81.8 percent of them for
murdering a white person, even though whites and blacks are murdered in almost equal numbers nationwide. The American Bar Association concludes
that there is an "undeniable and unacceptable role of racial bias in the application of the death penalty."[17]

Defenders of the current political order deny that these figures can be attributed to enduring racism in America. If people of color suffer relative and
absolute deprivation, and if they represent disproportionate prison popula-

tions, the fault lies with their own inadequacies and choices. What may look like injustice is actually justice: they are getting what they deserve. Critics respond that racism continues to contribute to structured inequality, that police target poor black neighborhoods, that the criminal justice system deals more harshly with black than white defendants, and that contemporary policy emphasizes law enforcement and incarceration rather than drug rehabilitation, jobs and training programs, and other social services that might alleviate some of the social stresses that can lead to crime. Critics also argue that incarceration of people of color offers a clear example of the relation between injustice and the need for a repressive political order. According to this argument, the inequities that many people of color take for granted inevitably create anger and resentment, and this may translate into antisocial behavior. To maintain political order under these pressures from marginalized people of color, the dominant strategy today emphasizes simply throwing them in jail.

Wages and Salaries

Approximately one-fourth (24.3 percent) of all U.S. workers in 2003 earned poverty-level wages, based on the wage necessary to raise a family of four headed by a full-time, full-year worker, which was set officially at $9.03 per hour in 2003. In 2003, 26.2 percent of black men, 33.9 percent of black women (30.4 percent overall for blacks), 35.7 percent of Hispanic men, and 45.8 percent of Hispanic women (39.8 percent overall for Hispanics) earned

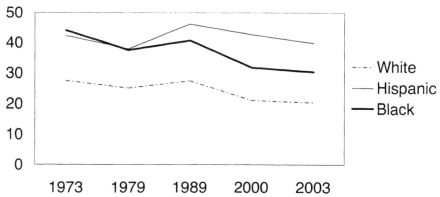

FIGURE 5.1
Share of Workers Earning Poverty-Level Wages, by Race/Ethnicity, 1973–2003

poverty-level wages. In 2003, 29.4 percent of all U.S. women and 19.6 percent of all U.S. men earned poverty-level wages (see figures 5.1 and 5.2).[18] Since, as we saw earlier, the poverty line is set arbitrarily low, even these figures understate the number of Americans earning poverty-level wages. Compounding the problem of low wages, most poverty-wage earners do not receive employer-provided health benefits.

On the other end of the wage continuum, at the beginning of the twenty-first century, American CEOs routinely received multimillion-dollar compensation packages, and many professional athletes commanded salaries in the multimillion-dollar range. Many of these athletes doubled or tripled their salaries by pitching corporate products and services. Many entertainers also reach stratospheric heights of compensation.

What justifies these huge wage and salary variations across different occupations? The common answer, like the answer to many justice questions, is that workers get what they deserve. People are rewarded, or not, more or less in just proportion to desert. In the case of wages and salaries, desert is typically seen as a function of a person's skills, talents, efforts, level of responsibility, and impact on others. Assuming for the moment that these criteria are appropriate, are current levels of wages and salaries in America more or less just?

Defenders of CEO salaries argue that each of the criteria noted above come into play. CEOs deserve huge salaries because they are talented, hardworking,

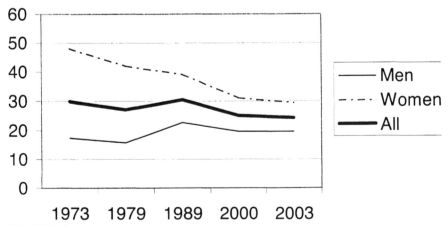

FIGURE 5.2
Share of Workers Earning Poverty-Level Wages, by Gender, 1973–2003

and well educated; hold positions of heavy responsibility; and carry the burden of affecting many others' lives. Taken together, these features of CEOs' work justify their high salaries. Fewer of these features can be cited in the case of highly paid professional athletes, who deserve their salaries because they are talented and have had to work hard to attain their level of performance. In the case of Hollywood stars, the main criteria justifying their compensation include their acting talent and, often, their physical beauty. Most Americans comfortably accept the rationale for these high salaries. Criticism of professional athletes' salaries occurs relatively infrequently, limited mostly to complaining about ticket prices.

Applying the same criteria at the other extreme, burger flippers deserve meager paychecks presumably because they are untalented and uneducated, hold little responsibility, and affect but minimally the consumers who eat their burgers. Though burger flippers work hard, the nature of their work is considered menial. They have not invested the time, energy, and money needed to acquire an education and the requisite skills that would qualify them for higher wages.

Teachers represent a more difficult case. Most earn relatively little in proportion to their level of skill, intellectual talent, hard work, educational attainment, and responsibility for educating the next generation. In 2002–03, the beginning K–12 teacher could expect to earn $27,989, and the average K–12 teacher overall earned $41,820. College professors fall even further out of proportion. At $46,330 in 2002–03, the average college professor earned very little compared to CEOs and professional athletes.

Similarly, a garbage hauler earns relatively little. Though they meet only some of the criteria of desert, so too do professional athletes, as we saw above. Though their occupation requires little education or skill, trash haulers must work hard, and the consequences of not doing their job potentially include massive public health problems as the garbage spreads disease and feeds an exploding army of hungry rats.

Finally, consider the case of airport security screeners. Until relatively recently, these workers earned even less than fast food workers. In April 2000, Cleveland airport baggage screeners earned a starting wage of $5.85 per hour, less than the starting wage of $6.00 at the Cinnabon outlet a few feet away. The airport security screeners' level of responsibility stands out among other criteria as exceptionally important. As we now know all too well, the costs of screeners not doing their job well are high indeed. Since the federal government took over these occupations as part of its response to threats of terrorism, wages have increased but, at approximately $23,600 starting and $27,100 for supervisors, remain relatively low.[19]

As these examples show, the criteria of desert apply unevenly at best. If we multiplied examples, we would find the same result. Most people get paid only partially, at best, according to rational criteria of desert. Their wages and salaries are also determined by crude market criteria of supply and demand for labor in each occupation. Professional athletes command such high salaries because few can step in to take their places at comparable talent and skill levels. College professors command relatively low salaries because the supply of Ph.D.'s exceeds the demand. A burger flipper can be replaced by any person capable of the requisite wrist action and willing to endure the punishment that job exacts.

Some may find this application of market criteria both justifiable and laudable. It establishes an impersonal equilibrium of supply and demand for each occupation without recourse to difficult criteria of justice. Yet, the departures from just wage and salary levels are sometimes extreme enough to warrant skepticism. Of the twenty richest Americans in 2002, only eleven had a college degree, and twelve of these twenty had inherited their fortunes; nationwide, more than 40 percent of America's richest four hundred residents inherited their fortunes.[20] Also, market-determined wages and salaries show a marked systematic bias in favor of some kinds of professions and against other kinds of professions, both having little or nothing to do with any rational criteria for just desert. In particular, labor markets generally reward people who work with financial capital vastly in excess of the rewards for those who work with social capital. With some exceptions such as medical doctors, careers in the "helping" professions—teachers, counselors, nurses, and nonprofit staff—earn relatively low wages compared to careers in business, wholly apart from any criteria for just deserts.

Critics also challenge the assumption that impersonal market forces determine wage and salary levels apart from human tampering. They argue that policy makers routinely and systematically manipulate labor markets in ways that favor some while hurting others. The Federal Reserve Board (the "Fed") offers one example. It attempts to manage economic growth while curbing inflation by controlling the supply and demand for money. Labor compensation will tend to increase as labor supply decreases relative to the demand for it. Especially during periods of strong economic growth, low unemployment pushes wages upward. As the pool of unemployed shrinks, employers increasingly have to pay a premium wage to entice the remaining potential employees. This is why at the end of the 1990s, a period of strong economic growth and low unemployment, even fast food workers were courted with starting wages of $7–8 per hour.

Since the Fed fears that increases in labor compensation will fuel inflation, it views a certain level of unemployment as not only acceptable but desirable. Libertarian economist Milton Friedman (1912–) pegged the ideal threshold rate of unemployment at 6 percent, calling it the "natural rate of unemployment." When confronting the possibility of strong wage growth among average workers, the Fed faces a choice. It can allow the strong period of growth and low unemployment to continue, and live with modest levels of inflation; or it can intervene to cool the economy, likely resulting in increased unemployment. In general, the Fed opts for the latter strategy, adopting policies that favor owners of capital, whose incomes from investments are more dramatically undermined by inflation than are average workers' salaries. For example, 5 percent inflation cuts in half a 10 percent return on investment, while reducing workers' wages by only the 5 percent. In effect Fed decision makers say that they are willing to live with unemployment and the relatively low wages for average working people that come with it rather than allow inflation to undermine return on capital. Fed preference for curbing inflation also benefits bankers, whose earnings are undercut by high rates of inflation as the value of loan repayments decrease over time due to inflation.

Trade policy also in recent times has favored capital over labor, at the expense of wage growth for average Americans. American policy makers increasingly favor free trade agreements such as the North American Free Trade Agreement (NAFTA), initiated in 1994 during the early years of the Clinton administration, and the Central American Free Trade Agreement (CAFTA), approved by the U.S. Congress and President George W. Bush in 2005. These policies by design increase the ability of capital, but not labor, to move freely across borders. Proponents sell the agreements as benefiting all Americans by increasing the flow of exports, creating jobs in export sectors, and ensuring cheap consumer goods. However, the increased mobility of capital increases its bargaining power relative to labor by increasing the credibility of corporations' threats to relocate abroad and offshore if labor presses too hard for increased wages and improved working conditions. Increasingly, American investors invest abroad to take advantage of lower wages and relaxed environmental regulations. This sets in motion a "race to the bottom" among different countries competing to attract investors by cutting wages and environmental protections. Average workers lose in this race to the bottom, as their ability to negotiate decent wages declines.

Finally, unions face an increasingly hostile policy environment as states pass anti-union legislation. Union membership has declined steadily since its heyday in the early twentieth century. Membership declined precipitously after the Reagan administration broke the air traffic controllers' strike of 1981. Whatever else can be said of unions, they offer workers one means of increasing their bargaining power for favorable wages, benefits, and working conditions. In 2003, union workers earned 43.6 percent more in total compensation than nonunion workers.[21] Their gradual demise inevitably undermines the ability of average workers to secure adequate wages and benefits.

As these three examples demonstrate, policy makers actively intervene in labor markets in ways that undermine wages and salaries for average working Americans. Policy makers also intervene sometimes on behalf of labor. However, interventions on behalf of labor rarely balance the equation. Minimum wage legislation offers a good example. Congress occasionally adjusts the minimum wage upward, but not enough to keep up with inflation. The 2005 minimum wage level of $5.15 per hour was only approximately 75 percent of its level in 1968, adjusted for inflation. These policy manipulations, combined with an often capricious wage and labor market, results in a wage and salary system in the United States that often diverges from just desert.

POWER AND INTEREST

Since justice is so central to political discussions, it may be tempting to conclude that considerations of justice routinely guide political decision making. Before arriving at that conclusion, we should consider the alternative: that justice is beside the point in policy considerations that really matter. In an earlier chapter we saw that Niccolò Machiavelli (1469–1527), in his relatively unknown *Discourses*, presented a republican view of politics in which civic virtue played a prominent role. The better-known Machiavelli gained infamy for his short political treatise *The Prince* (1513). In this work, Machiavelli offered advice on gaining power, wielding it, and keeping it. He set aside questions of justice in favor of prudence, expediency, and a cold, calculated focus on power in the pursuit of interests. Whatever advanced the goals of increasing power and achieving interests could be justified, no matter how shocking or offensive.

"The end justifies the means," Machiavelli famously asserted. Presuming that power enables a ruler to satisfy his interests, Machiavelli focused on power itself—getting it and keeping it—as the end. As for the means, according to Machiavelli, basically whatever works best should be employed—cruelty, butchery, deception, disloyalty, and anything else deemed prudent and expedient. Machiavelli counseled the prince to distinguish between the real and the ideal, and to live by the former. According to Machiavelli, "How we live is so far removed from how we ought to live" that the wise ruler would do well to set aside questions of justice and live by the dictates of power. This makes it necessary for "a prince, who wishes to maintain himself, to learn how not to be good."[22] Having cultivated this ability "not to be good," the prince is better able to secure power and keep it. Sometimes it may also behoove a ruler to do good things. The appropriate dictum, at any rate, is to use virtue and vice strategically, as prudence dictates.

To increase power, Machiavelli advised the ruler to simply take others' land, if possible. "The desire to acquire possessions is a very natural and ordinary thing," he wrote, "and when those men do it who can do so successfully, they are always praised and not blamed." Once the ruler has conquered another land, it is best to "despoil" it in order to ensure a secure hold on it. This is the most prudent strategy because "whoever becomes the ruler of a free city and does not destroy it, can expect to be destroyed by it." In order to consolidate newly acquired power, Machiavelli matter-of-factly counseled execution of deposed rulers and their entire families. In order to securely possess conquered states,

> it suffices that the family of the princes which formerly governed them be extinct. . . . Whoever obtains possession of [new] territories and wishes to retain them must bear in mind . . . that the blood of their old rulers be extinct.[23]

Machiavelli also counseled the ruler to plant colonies in newly acquired territory in order to better ensure dominion.

Throughout *The Prince*, Machiavelli admiringly cited historical figures renowned for their brutality. Of the murderous Cesare Borgia, son of Pope Alexander VI, Machiavelli wrote, "I know of no better precepts for a new prince to follow than may be found in his actions." As an example of Borgia's merits, Machiavelli related an account of Borgia's appointment of Remirro de Orco, "a cruel and able man," to consolidate power. Orco was "highly successful in rendering the country orderly and united." After he had thus fulfilled his mission, Borgia rewarded him by having him "cut in half and placed one morning in the public square at Cesena." This allowed Borgia to distance himself from the understandably unpopular Orco and resulted in the "satisfaction and amazement" of the people who observed it. Machiavelli concluded:

> reviewing thus all the actions of [Borgia], I find nothing to blame, on the contrary, I feel bound, as I have done, to hold him up as an example to be imitated by all who by fortune and with the arms of others have risen to power. For with his great courage and high ambition he could not have acted otherwise.[24]

If brutality and cruelty are appropriate means to gain and keep power, it nevertheless matters *how* you use brutality and cruelty. Resort to cruelty strategically rather than wantonly, Machiavelli counseled, and finish the dirty work quickly and effectively in order to diminish the need for more of it. "Well committed may be called those [cruelties]," wrote Machiavelli, "which are perpetuated once for the need of securing one's self, and which afterwards are not persisted in. . . . In taking a state the conqueror must arrange to commit all his cruelties at once." If savagery and cruelty breeds fear rather than love in one's subjects, all the better, according to Machiavelli, since "fear is maintained by a dread of punishment which never fails." Again citing Borgia as an example, Machiavelli argued that, though Borgia was considered cruel by his contemporaries, at least "his cruelty brought order to the Romagna, united it, and reduced it to peace and fealty." Machiavelli concluded that a prince "must not mind incurring the charge of cruelty for the purpose of keeping his subjects united and faithful." It is better to use cruelty and butchery than allow disorder to creep into the realm. The prince who uses some cruelty to maintain order "will be more merciful than those who, from excess of tenderness, allow disorders to arise, from whence spring bloodshed and rapine."[25]

Machiavelli also counseled dishonesty and deception if prudence dictates. "A prudent ruler," according to Machiavelli, "ought not to keep faith when by so doing it would be against his interest." He should be "a great feigner and dissembler." History showed that the greatest and most successful rulers "have had little regard for good faith, and have been able by astuteness to confuse men's brains, and who have ultimately overcome those who have made loyalty their foundation."[26]

While concentrating on the raw and often bloody exercise of power in the pursuit of interests, the ruler should if possible cultivate a favorable reputation among his subjects. "It is well," Machiavelli argued, "to seem merciful, faithful, humane, sincere, religious." How does one gain this desired reputation? One way is to prove yourself up to challenges. Rather than wait for "fortune" to present these challenges, the wise prince will pick a fight, one that he knows he can win. A prince becomes great by "rais[ing] up enemies and compel[ling] him to undertake wars against them, so that he may have cause to overcome them."[27] These wars offer the prince opportunities for demonstrating his prowess and increasing his reputation for excellence.

The argument that considerations of power and interest dislodge questions of justice can be found centuries earlier in two figures from ancient Greece: the Greek historian Thucydides, and Thrasymachus, a character in Plato's *Republic*. Thucydides (460–399 B.C.) documented the Peloponnesian War, which lasted from 431 to 404 B.C. His account highlighted the corrupting influence of empire on the Athenian participants in the war. Thucydides described a scene that occurred early in the war in which two unnamed Athenian envoys to Sparta attempted to justify Athenian power and empire while putting Spartans at ease about Athenians' aspirations. In the scene, the Athenian envoys began by establishing the validity of pursuing policies favorable to one's interests. "No one can quarrel with a people," said one envoy, "for making, in matters of tremendous risk, the best provision that it can for its interest." The envoys went on to argue that Athens's behavior was consistent with history and with the behavior of other imperial powers:

It was not a very remarkable action, or contrary to the common practice of mankind, if we accepted an empire that was offered to us, and refused to give it up under the pressure of three of the strongest motives, fear, honor, and interest. And it was not we who set the example, for it has always been the law that the weaker should be subject to the stronger. Besides, we believed ourselves to be worthy of our position, and so you thought us till now, when calculations of interest have made you take up the cry of justice—a consideration which no one ever yet brought forward to hinder his ambition when he had a chance of gaining anything by might. And praise is due to all who, if not so superior to human nature as to refuse dominion, yet respect justice more than their position compels them to do.

This speech is noteworthy for its blunt claims: that questions of self-interest predominate, that history validates the basic principle that might makes right, that justice is appealed to only in the absence of sufficient power to simply seize what you want, and that claims of justice often simply mask deeper questions of power and interest. It should be noted, however, that in this early speech the Athenians were at least willing to talk about justice.

Sixteen years later they did not want to be bothered with talk of justice. This time the envoys, who had been dispatched to the Melians to negotiate their surrender, dismissed entirely the language of justice and insisted on concentrating solely on raw power politics, which needed no justification:

> For ourselves, we shall not trouble you with specious pretenses—either of how we have a right to our empire because we overthrew the Mede, or are now attacking you because of wrong that you have done us—and make a long speech which would not be believed; and in return we hope that you, instead of thinking to influence us by saying that you did not join the Lacedaemonians [Spartans], although their colonists, or that you have done us no wrong, will aim at what is feasible, holding in view the real sentiments of us both; for you know as well as we do that right, as the world goes, is in question only between equals in power, while the strong do what they can and the weak suffer what they must.

This claim that "the strong do what they can and the weak suffer what they must" stripped away any pretence of right and wrong and validated Athenian aggression simply on the basis of power.

Unwilling to completely abandon the language of justice, the Melian representatives attempted to appeal to the Athenians' self-interest by pointing out that the language of justice may one day serve the Athenians' self-interest. They pointed out that in the event of a decline in Athenian power and empire, their fall "would be a signal for the heaviest vengeance." At that point, the Athenians might themselves want to appeal to justice. The Athenian envoys brushed aside the Melians' arguments, preferring to rest their case upon the certainty of power. According to the Athenian envoys,

> Your strongest arguments depend upon hope and the future, and your actual resources are too scanty, as compared with those arrayed against you, for you to come out victorious. You will therefore show great blindness of judgment [if you defy us].[28]

The Melians defied the Athenians anyway—and paid a heavy price: the men were all executed, the women and children sold into slavery.

Plato (427–347 B.C.) presented a similar discussion of justice in *The Republic* (375 B.C.) as a prelude to developing his own conception of justice. In his opening scene, the main character Socrates is conversing with several others at the home of Cephalus on the topic of justice. In his inimitable way, Socrates is poking holes in others' attempts to define *justice*. Throughout this conversation, a young man named Thrasymachus glares from the sidelines. Suddenly, he can restrain himself no longer. He breaks into the discussion and demands that Socrates define it himself. Socrates predictably refuses to provide an answer, pleading ignorance, and asks instead that Thrasymachus give his own definition. Knowing that he will be subjected to Socrates' uncomfortable probing if he ventures an opinion, Thrasymachus initially refuses. After some additional prodding by Socrates, though, Thrasymachus relents and offers his own answer: "I say that justice or right is simply what is in the interest of the stronger party." This surprising answer has vexed many subsequent political theorists wondering over Thrasymachus's exact meaning.

As Thrasymachus feared, Socrates began tying his answer in knots. However, Thrasymachus stopped him and attempted to explain his answer further:

> Each type of government enacts laws that are in its own interest. . . . In enacting these laws they make it quite plain that what is "right" for their subjects is what is in the interest of themselves, the rulers, and if anyone deviates from this he is punished. . . . That is what I mean when I say that "right" is the same thing in all states, namely the interest of the established government; and government is the strongest element in each state, and so if we argue correctly we see that "right" is always the same, the interest of the stronger party.

Socrates draws Thrasymachus further into conversation, in which Thrasymachus asserts:

> The just man always comes off worse than the unjust. For instance, in any business relations between them, you won't find the just man better off at the end of the deal than the unjust. . . . [There is] much more private gain . . . in wrongdoing than in right. You can see it most easily if you take the extreme of injustice and wrongdoing, which brings the highest happiness to its practitioners and

plunges its victims and their honesty in misery. . . . Injustice, given scope, has greater strength and freedom and power than justice.[29]

After more discussion, Thrasymachus withdraws.

Of course, it was Plato, the author of *The Republic*, who directed this conversation, and he painted a most unflattering portrait of Thrasymachus as noisy and impatient, in part to discredit his views. Having done this on the whole successfully, he nevertheless gave Thrasymachus's argument a second chance. Setting off on a walk with Socrates, Glaucon and Adeimantus take it up with the intention of defending it as far as possible, not necessarily because they believe in it but because they recognize that it represents a formidable challenge to anyone interested in justice. The nature and origin of justice, argues Glaucon, lies in selfish human nature and humans' basic preference for inflicting wrong or injury on others while avoiding wrong or injury to oneself. Though it is good to inflict wrong on others, it is worse to be wronged. To prevent the latter, humans make laws preventing one party from inflicting pain and hardship on another. Keep in mind, says Glaucon, that this remains a second-best option, second to having the freedom and ability to inflict wrong or injury on others and get away with it. Once laws are put in place, humans obey them reluctantly, only out of fear of punishment.

Moreover, according to Glaucon, we can see empirically that it is the unjust who prosper while the just fail miserably. The unjust man pursues

> schemes which bring him respectability and office, and which enable him to marry into any family he likes, to make desirable matches for his children, and to pick his partners in business transactions, while all the time, because he has no scruples about committing injustice, he is on the make. In all kinds of competition public or private he always comes off best and does down his rivals, and so becomes rich and can do good to his friends and harm his enemies.

In addition the rich, but unjust, man can make more splendid offerings to the gods and protect his interests in that realm. In the meantime, the perfectly just man, who pursues justice for its own sake and not for the reputation it brings, may, by failing to cultivate a favorable impression among his fellows, meet with a far worse fate. He "will be scourged, tortured, and imprisoned, his eyes will be put out, and after enduring every humiliation he will be crucified." And so, Glaucon concludes, "a better life is provided for the unjust man than for the just by both gods and men."[30]

At this point, Adeimantus took the argument another step, and concluded that the most successful and happy person is one who pursues injustice in practice but enjoys a reputation for justice. "People are unanimous," he argues

in hymning the worth of self-control or justice, but think they are difficult to practice and call for hard work, while self-indulgence and injustice are easy enough to acquire, and regarded as disgraceful only by convention; wrong on the whole pays better than right, they say, and they are ready enough to call a bad man happy and respect him both in public and private provided he is rich and powerful, while they have no respect for the poor and powerless, and despise him, even though they agree that he is the better man.

Adeimantus concluded:

It is clear from what they tell me that if I am just, it will bring me no advantage but only trouble and loss, unless I also have a reputation for justice; whereas if I am unjust, but can contrive to get a reputation for justice, I shall have a marvelous time. . . . What argument, then, remains for preferring justice to the worst injustice, when both common men and great men agree that, provided it has a veneer of respectability, injustice will enable us, in this world and the next, to do as we like with gods and men? And how can anyone, when he has heard all we have said, possibly value justice and avoid laughing when he hears it being praised?[31]

At this point, Socrates proclaims himself delighted with his friends' defense of Thrasymachus. Of course, Plato was not complimenting the ideas of Thrasymachus, only the ability of Glaucon and Adeimantus to persuasively defend them.

Did Thrasymachus really believe that justice is no more than the interest of the stronger party, that might makes right? If so, people's behavior not only is, but should be, guided by considerations of self-interest in pursuit of power and fortune. It is better to practice injustice than justice, because empirically it results in more happiness, wealth, power, and acclaim. Those, like Socrates, who want to make something more of justice are sentimental idealists. Most subsequent interpreters have adopted this view and treated Thrasymachus as a philosophical thug for offering such a patently wrongheaded definition of justice.

However, an alternative interpretation of Thrasymachus is possible. In this view, Thrasymachus simply pointed out realistically, if cynically, that the rich and powerful usually get what they want and are able to legitimize it using the rhetoric of justice. He angrily asserted an empirical point that the strong have always dominated the weak, and they have always sought to justify their relative privilege by cloaking it implicitly or explicitly in the language of justice. Thrasymachus did not endorse this; he only pointed it out as a way of injecting a note of cynical realism. Look at the facts, he said. Justice is simply a distraction that rich and powerful people use to legitimize or hide their exploitation and domination of others. Even some who dismiss Thrasymachus concede that, to the degree that justice is defined as the moral and legal right to hold onto what one has, as it partly is in the United States today, "we find ourselves faced, in neo-Thrasymachean language, with the rights of the stronger, the entitlement of the powerful and privileged to hold on to what they already have." These same thinkers ask, in terms that evoke Thrasymachus's challenge, "Are our standards of justice, ultimately, in the interests of the stronger, the more established and more powerful citizens?"[32]

YOU DESERVE WHAT YOU GET

One dominant explanation of the public problems discussed above attributes sole responsibility for them to the choices and actions of individuals or individual states. According to this view, individuals succeed or fail based on their own merits. Success stories are built upon motivation, pluck, talent, and hard work, and failures their opposite. In both cases, people and states get what they deserve. And if this is true, then no injustice has occurred and no government intervention is necessary.

This perspective of the individual as sole architect of one's fate, and the undesirability of government intervention, has appeared and reappeared in U.S. history. President Herbert Hoover (1874–1964), the thirty-first U.S. president (1929–33), clearly articulated it. In a speech delivered in the depths of the Great Depression, Hoover reaffirmed his belief in the singular importance of individual initiative and the undesirability of involving government in the economy and in social service provision. According to Hoover, government "would increase rather than decrease abuse and corruption, stifle initiative and invention, undermine development of leadership, cripple mental and spiritual energies of our people, extinguish equality of opportunity, and dry up the spirit of liberty and progress." Rather than government intervention and assistance, Hoover advocated a strict reliance on individual initiative, because "progress can be attained only as the sum of accomplishments of free individuals," and not as a result of government action. And when individuals fail to succeed, it is not the system that is at fault since "it is men who do wrong, not our institutions."[33]

The belief in the individual as the sole architect of one's fate found its most ardent twentieth-century expression in the political philosophy of Ayn Rand (1905–1982). Among her best-known works is *The Fountainhead* (1943), a fictional portrayal of the life of a brilliant architect who struggles to achieve his individual vision in the face of social pressures to conform. In this book, all good, creative, and dynamic human endeavors emerge from within the lone individual, and conversely all cheap, dull, and labored endeavors spring from social groupings. Adhering to convention, sacrificing for others, or compromising absolute independence are to be avoided at all costs, including loss of job, career, and even love. Rand's admired characters are all self-made men, examples of Horatio Alger's bootstrap myth.

The protagonist of *The Fountainhead*, architect Howard Roark, views other people, lovers, society, traditions, social conventions, and basically anything social as hindrances that threaten his autonomy and his creative genius. He triumphs by doing things his own way, despite social hindrances. Other central characters include Roger Enright, who, though born to a Pennsylvania coal miner, became a millionaire through his own individual efforts without anyone's help. He represented the quintessential "rags-to-riches" story in America. Having made it on his own, Enright achieved complete independence of others' influence and control. This enabled him to recognize Roark's brilliance, to sneer at social conventions and preferences, and to commission a building from Roark when others shunned Roark for his audacity. Another entrepreneur, Anthony Cord, who "had come from nowhere and made a fortune in Wall Street within a few brilliant, violent years," also commissioned a building from Roark. Gail Wynand lost his father at age 16, leaving him "alone, jobless . . . with sixty-five cents in his pocket."[34] From there, he rose through pluck and determination to become the richest and most powerful man in New York.

Men like these make all of history worth celebrating, according to Rand. Rand's descriptive and prescriptive messages are clear. All accomplishments worth celebrating are the work of lone individuals pursuing selfish ends who triumph over socially imposed adversity. Since the government represents for Rand the epitome of collectivism, it represents part of the adversity that the individual must overcome. This becomes a prescriptive principle: do not accept help from others, including the government, and do not offer it, since it compromises the autonomy of the individual and undermines notable accomplishment.

A belief in the fairness of the political-economic context in which individuals strive, and in the multiple opportunities it offers everyone, today underlies the attribution of sole responsibility for success or failure to individuals. The roots of this belief extend at least to the eighteenth-century Scottish political economist and philosopher, Adam Smith (1723–1790), whose "invisible hand" argument, which appeared in an obscure passage of his *Wealth of Nations* (1776), is often invoked today to defend economic principles and public policies emphasizing free markets and minimal government interference. The passage reads:

> He [each individual] generally, indeed, neither intends to promote the public interest, nor knows how much he is promoting it. . . . He intends only his own security and by directing that industry in such a manner as its produce may be of the greatest value, he intends only his own gain, and he is in this, as in many other cases, led by an invisible hand to promote an end which was no part of his intention. . . . By pursuing his own interest he frequently promotes that of the society more effectually than when he really intends to promote it.[35]

The implications of this argument—that if we simply leave people alone to pursue their individual economic interests, the public interest will emerge as though directed by an invisible hand—suggest that the market is rational, that individual industry will result in just private and public reward, and that all will benefit from free markets.

However, as some critics of free markets note, Smith never advocated such a one-sided approach. *The Wealth of Nations* presupposed his earlier *The Theory of Moral Sentiments* (1759), in which he argued something quite different. In this work, he presumed that the market alone would not guarantee justice and that the government could, and should, intervene to ensure it. Smith acknowledged self-interest, but argued that this hardly paints a complete picture of human motivation. Human capacity for shame and remorse dissuades wholly self-seeking behavior. Even if it were true "that every individual, in his own breast, naturally prefers himself to all mankind, yet he dares not look mankind in the face, and avow that he acts according to this principle." As social beings, most people care how others perceive them. Each person "views himself in the light in which he is conscious that others will view him." Each person also has the capacity for remorse and for compassion. And so, if a man commits an injustice against others, "he is grieved at the thought of it; regrets the unhappy effects of his own conduct, and feels at the same time that they have rendered him the proper object of the resentment and indignation of mankind." The possibility of this social censure "perpetually haunts him, and fills him with terror and amazement." This capacity for compassion, shame, and remorse counters the individual's selfishness and encourages a regard for others and the public interest. Smith also argued that humans possess the capacity for generosity. They feel themselves "to be the natural object of . . . love and gratitude" upon performing "a generous action."[36] This capacity for generosity meets with social approval, thus inspiring more of it. This side of Smith, which emphasizes the need to counter selfish instincts with public-spiritedness and concern for others, in part through government intervention, is rarely cited today since it contradicts the popular and dominant view of Smith as an apologist for self-interested striving without concern for the social consequences.

Proponents of free markets today also cite Friedrich von Hayek (1889–1992) as a supporter of the notion that free markets are fair. And, as in Smith's case, the reality diverges from the perception. Hayek did indeed celebrate the virtues of free markets, but he also acknowledged forthrightly that they cannot guarantee just outcomes. According to Hayek, free markets do not dependably reward merit. Success or failure, he believed, was as much a result of luck as desert. Hayek compared participation in a market economy to a game involving both skill and luck that "proceeds, like all games, according to rules guiding the actions of individual participants whose aims, skills, and knowledge are different." Like a game, the "outcome will be unpredictable" and "there will regularly be winners and losers." And like a game, it makes sense for everyone to play by the same fair rules, but nonsense to insist upon any outcome other than that provided by a combination of skill at playing the game and luck. In short, according to Hayek, "Only the conduct of the players but not the result can be just."

If a free market political economy resembles a game involving luck as well as skill, then sometimes the careless, the ignorant, the untalented, and the lazy will win and, conversely, the careful, the well educated, the talented, and the hardworking will lose. Hayek clearly recognized this, and he concluded that "it is probably a misfortune that, especially in the USA, popular writers . . . have defended free enterprise on the ground that it regularly rewards the deserving." We should instead, he argued, honestly admit that "inevitably some unworthy will succeed and some worthy fail." Moreover, wrote Hayek, we should admit too that "not only the results but also the initial chances of different individuals" vary widely.[37] With this admission, Hayek challenged the prevailing myth of equal opportunity. Not only is the market frequently unfair in its distribution of rewards and punishments, beginning positions in the marketplace are also awarded unfairly. Hayek's recognition of the injustice of a free enterprise economy might suggest a willingness to turn to the instrument of government to correct for it. Hayek refused this course, arguing that the benefits of a free enterprise system nevertheless outweigh its costs. Besides, he argued, any attempt by government to intervene on behalf of social justice opens the door to social engineering and a totalitarian system.

The twin components of belief in the sole responsibility of individuals for their fate and the inherent fairness of the political-economic context converge in the writing on race and poverty of influential contemporary thinkers such as George Gilder, Charles Murray, Lawrence Mead, Richard Rodriguez, Linda Chavez, Thomas Sowell, Glen Loury, and Shelby Steele. These thinkers articulate what has become a dominant perspective on poverty and associated behaviors. According to political economist Gregory Squires (1949–), these authors "reflect and reinforce a common philosophy" with four central tenets. First, poverty, racial inequality, and underclass behavior reflect the values and cultures of poor people. Second, poor people adhere to an inadequate and destructive value system that includes disrespect for work and a live-for-today mentality. Third, offering public assistance welfare to the poor exacerbates the problem by preventing the development of more appropriate values and by breeding dependency. Therefore, fourth, rather than offer public assistance, we must force individuals to take care of themselves in order to overcome the problem of poverty and associated behaviors. These thinkers define the causes and consequences of poverty "as characteristics of selected individuals rather than as structural dimensions of a social system."[38] If, according to this perspective, poverty results from the lack of individual effort alone, so too do wealth and success more generally result from individual effort alone. These thinkers presume throughout that a free market economy offers ample opportunities with fair outcomes to everyone regardless of race. They award government little, if any, role to play beyond setting basic rules and protecting individual rights, including and especially property rights. They believe that government action in the form of public assistance welfare makes the problem worse rather than better.

These elements appear clearly in the work of George Gilder (1939–), a central figure in the efforts during the 1980s to roll back social welfare spending. Individuals alone control their own fate, according to Gilder, and individuals alone bear responsibility for their relative success or failure. Since "real poverty is less a state of income than a state of mind," an individual only needs to acquire the right "state of mind" for success. For black Americans, this right state of mind means abandoning the use of race and racism as an excuse, for the notion that race or racism can explain the continued economic marginalization of black Americans is "false and invidious." Each person can find the cause of success or failure only by looking in a mirror. The poor must learn that "their condition is to a great degree their own fault or choice."[39] A poor person in effect chooses poverty, according to Gilder.

Poor people's failings include a "lack of an orientation to the future." They live "from day to day and from hand to mouth" and fail to "plan or save or keep a job." Gilder attributes this not to economic marginalization and necessity but to individuals' warped value orientation and psychological failings. He further roots these in the breakdown of the urban family, by which he means the shift away from the traditional two-parent, heterosexual family with children. Family breakdown thus causes poverty and unemployment, not vice versa as many social scientists argue. As Gilder recognizes, this begs a deeper question: what underlies the breakdown of the urban family? Gilder poses his answer in psychosexual terms. The urban family is rapidly disintegrating, he argues, because of "the breakdown of family responsibilities among fathers," especially young fathers with their "rhythms of tension and release that characterize the sexual experience." "The key," therefore, to understanding poverty is "the dominance of single and separated men in poor communities," and the "familial anarchy among the concentrated poor of the inner city, in which flamboyant and impulsive youths rather than responsible men provide the themes of aspiration." These men's "links to children and future are too often insufficient to induce work and thrift."

Further compounding the problem, according to Gilder, the loss of their provider role emasculates men. It undermines

> male confidence and authority, which determine sexual potency, respect from the wife and children, and motivation to face the tedium and frustration of daily labor. Nothing is so destructive to all these male values as the growing, imperious recognition that when all is said and done his wife and children can do better without him. The man has the gradually sinking feeling that his role as provider, the definitive male activity from the primal days of the hunt through the industrial revolution and on into modern life, has been largely seized from him; he has been cuckolded by the compassionate state.

Men respond to their loss of dominance within the family with a "combination of resignation and rage, escapism and violence, short horizons and promiscuous sexuality that characterizes everywhere the life of the poor."

Women also choose wrongly, according to Gilder. Any family headed by a woman will find it "almost impossible for it to greatly raise its income" because "few women with children make earning money the top priority in their lives." Gilder's analysis of the roots of poverty thus "begins and ends with family structure and marital status" and the value orientation these breed. These factors explain "far more about the problem than most of the distributions of income, inequality, unemployment, education, IQ, race, sex, home ownership, location, discrimination, and all the other items" used by social scientists to explain it.[40]

Government, in Gilder's perspective, is part of the problem, not part of the solution. Government programs that focus on redistribution, day care provision, schools, and poverty programs will not only not work but will make the problem worse by undermining the motivation to change value orientations. Welfare programs, in particular, *create* poverty rather than alleviate it. According to Gilder, "What actually happened since 1964 was a vast expansion of the welfare rolls that halted in its tracks an ongoing improvement in the lives of the poor, particularly blacks, and left behind . . . a wreckage of broken lives and families worse than the aftermath of slavery." Attempts to help black Americans in particular via government programs such as welfare and affirmative action "account for the worst aspects of black poverty and promise to perpetuate it."

Government assistance "blights most of the people who come to depend on it." It undermines poor families by making it unprofitable for poor men to marry the women with whom they father children. Welfare spending causes "moral hazard," defined as "the danger that a policy will encourage the behavior—or promote the disasters—that it insures against." Housing insurance will increase the likelihood of burning the house down, income supports will reduce recipients' income, and unemployment insurance will increase unemployment. Public assistance welfare increases the number of "families with dependent children" in need of public assistance. The New Deal programs aimed at insuring against joblessness, disability, poverty in old age, absent fathers, and other problems actually cause all of these things.

While Gilder denies that government should act to provide public assistance for the poor, he nevertheless sees a role for government in pushing the central tenets of supply-side economics, including reducing taxes paid by the rich and increasing government spending on corporate welfare. "To lift the incomes of the poor," he argued, "it will be necessary to increase the rates of investment, which in turn will tend to enlarge the wealth, if not the consumption, of the rich ... and the gap between the rich and the poor may grow."[41]

Gilder concludes that the only "dependable route from poverty is always work, family, and faith." The poor must work harder than everyone else. Family provides the psychosexual basis for hard work by motivating the male to assume and keep the role of breadwinner for the family, while poverty provides the spur. Gilder acknowledges the importance of a dependable link between effort and reward. Paraphrasing justice as desert—you get what you deserve—he argues that workers must "feel deeply that what they are given depends on what they give."[42]

The analysis of another influential contemporary thinker, Glenn Loury (1948–), follows many of Gilder's points. Like Gilder, Loury argues that the problems of urban poverty are "connected with the dysfunctional patterns of behavior" adopted by poor people, denies that the solution to poverty lies in governmental programs, and asserts that the problems of the urban poor "require for their solution a language of *values: '*we *should* do this; they *ought* to

do that; decent people *must* strive to live in a certain way.'" Loury acknowledges the presence of institutional barriers to black progress, but denies that
they are determinant. He decries the turn to "familiar intonations of plati-
tudes and empty phrases: 'racism,' 'inadequate funding,' 'no jobs,' 'no hope,'"
and denies that urban poverty can be attributed to "material" explanations
emphasizing economic factors. He calls debates over them "sterile and superficial" because they "fail to engage questions of personal morality. They fail to
talk about character and values. They do not invoke any moral leadership in
the public sphere."[43] If a deficit of values causes the problem, then the obvious
solution is to get more values. Like Gilder, Loury's prescription for change focuses entirely on restoring the social institutions of family, school, and church
that represent the appropriate sources of good values.

No doubt individuals are responsible for their own choices and actions and
must be held accountable for them. Most people would also agree that values
are important. However, a full understanding of human striving and its outcomes requires that we also look precisely at the material factors ignored or
minimized within a wholly individualistic framework. Individuals live in a social context that both enables and constrains them. They exert partial—but
only partial—control over their own fates. Also, attributing responsibility
solely to individuals for their fate runs the risk of blaming the victims of injustice by reducing justice to the simple assertion that, no matter your particular circumstances, you deserve what you get, by definition. In other words, it
inverts justice as desert from "you get what you deserve" to "you deserve what
you get." This simplistic formula represents an ideological assertion that ignores many empirical realities; it cannot serve as an adequate explanation for
the presence and persistence of injustices.

INTERNALIZED OPPRESSION

Apart from forcible repression, why do we sometimes find little or no political
disorder in a context of injustice? Part of the answer to this question can be
found in the idea of internalized oppression. Intellectual and activist Gloria
Anzaldúa (1942–2004) was a prominent figure addressing this issue, focusing
especially on women of color. Four related major themes can be found in her
work. First, according to Anzaldúa, many women of color—or "Third World
women," as she sometimes calls them—occupy the "borderlands" between different peoples, identities, and cultures.[44] Sometimes this can be seen very

clearly, as with Mexican-Americans in Southern California who occupy the borderlands created by the overlap of Hispanic and Anglo cultures. Sometimes, though, the borderlands are less obvious, as with African-American women who occupy a borderlands between black and white cultures in America. Often, these cultures exist in a dominant–subdominant power relationship. To characterize this relationship of power, Anzaldúa employs the language of colonizer and colonized. Thus Anglo norms and beliefs in Southern California represent the dominant, colonizer culture, while Hispanic culture represents a colonized culture. White culture in America represents the dominant colonizer culture and black culture the subdominant, colonized culture. Intrinsic to this relationship of dominant–subdominant are the implicit and explicit norms and beliefs that privilege the dominant culture and its many manifestations. For example, thin white women with straight blonde hair are advanced in many ways as the ideal of beauty in America, while rounder, darker women with kinky, nappy hair are viewed as less desirable.

Second, although at one time the process of colonization occurred through overt uses of force, today it occurs through a subtle process of indoctrination in which the colonized peoples acquire the culture of the colonizers. This involves a denigration of the indigenous cultures of the colonized and a claim of superiority of the colonizers' cultures. Women of color represent one of the major sites where this cultural colonization occurs. Given their position in the borderlands, inevitably women of color internalize at least some of the norms and beliefs of the different cultures represented in the borderlands, including the norms and beliefs of the colonizing culture, the oppressors. This occurs as an "engraving of our bodies" by the oppressors, as an internalizing of the "deadly pollen" of the dominant culture's racism, sexism, heterosexism, and classism. All women of color "have been victims of the invisible violation which happens indoors and inside ourselves: the self-abnegation, the silence, the constant threat of cultural obliteration . . . the privileges, or lack thereof, attached to a particular shade of skin or texture of hair."

Anzaldúa explicitly equates the contemporary cultural colonialism with earlier, more direct forms of colonialism. In the earlier forms, "European colonizers exercise direct control of the colonized, destroy the native legal and cultural systems, and negate non-European civilizations in order to ruthlessly exploit the resources of the subjugated with the excuse of attempting to 'civilize' them." During this phase, "the natives internalize Western culture." They come to accept "the white colonizers' system of values, attitudes, morality, and modes of production." Today, Anzaldúa argues, the "forced cultural penetration, the rape of the colored by the white" continues, with "the colonizers depositing their perspective, their language, their values" in the colonized cultures and peoples. The "external oppression" experienced by dominated peoples and cultures is thus mirrored by the "internalization of that oppression." Since by definition the dominant culture of the colonizer is viewed as preferable and superior, the process is one of "internalization of negative images" of indigenous cultures and identities, and this results in "self-hatred, poor self-esteem." Because historically and presently a specifically white culture dominates and colonizes, the process of colonization results in "internalized whiteness." Having internalized whiteness, some women of color inadvertently help perpetuate the oppression by participating in the privileging of the norms and beliefs about the superiority of whiteness. Even if women of color do not create the oppressive institutions, according to Anzaldúa, "we certainly perpetuate them through our inadvertent support. . . . I see Third World peoples and women not as oppressors but as accomplices to oppression by our unwittingly passing on to our children and our friends the oppressor's ideologies." This process, along with its results, appears "everywhere—it has a stranglehold on everyone. It is cultivated and produced in families, churches, temples and state institutions."[45]

Third, according to Anzaldúa, a major task of women of color in attaining self-respect and freedom is to become aware of their internalized oppression and purge themselves of it. This involves a process of education and criticism. It is not an easy task, this shedding of the norms and beliefs of the oppressors. It may require rejecting part of your own identity. It may be met with hostility. According to Anzaldúa, "When we rebel against the engraving of our bodies, we experience ostracism, alienation, isolation and shame." It may require severing previous loyalties to the norms, beliefs, and practices of the oppressor.

Fourth, Anzaldúa argues that, because of their positioning in the borderlands, women of color represent a category of person distinctive for its *mestiza*, or mixed, character, and this is worth celebrating. Rather than seeking a racially and culturally pure "other" that can be embraced as a worthy contrast to the dominant identity of the colonizer, *mestiza* women should embrace the mixture of diverse cultural elements because it represents inclusivity, a positive mixing of races. Rather than "an inferior being," the *mestiza* represents a "hybrid progeny, a mutable, more malleable species with a rich gene pool."[46]

Cherríe Moraga (1952–), Anzaldúa's coeditor of the best-selling *This Bridge Called My Back* (1981), an anthology of writings by women of color, offers personal testimony of the internal colonization she experienced. Born to a Chicana mother but inheriting the light skin of her Anglo father, Moraga refers to herself as "la güerra," the fair-skinned one. Growing up, she knew that "being light was something valued in my family. . . . Everything about my upbringing (at least what occurred on a conscious level) attempted to bleach me of what color I did have." Her mother viewed assimilation as a desirable goal because she believed it would increase her daughter's prospects for survival and success in an Anglo world. According to Moraga, "It was through my mother's desire to protect her children from poverty and illiteracy that we became 'anglocized'; the more effectively we could pass in the white world, the better guaranteed our future." Her mother avoided teaching her Spanish at home, in hopes of speeding her assimilation.

Moraga acknowledges that she bought into her mother's agenda, seeking assimilation and safety in whiteness. "White was right," she wrote. "Period. I could pass." Although Moraga found growing up that her relatively white skin protected her from overt racial hostility, she experienced direct oppression nevertheless because of her lesbianism, which she referred to as "the avenue through which I have learned the most about silence and oppression, and it continues to be the most tactile reminder to me that we are not free human beings. . . . The joys of looking like a white girl ain't so great since I realized I could be beaten on the street for being a dyke." Moraga also acknowledges that she internalized the subtle privileging of white, middle-class, heterosexual culture. Undoing this internalization required in turn that she "acknowledge that I have internalized a racism and classism, where the object of oppression is not only someone outside of my skin, but the someone inside my skin." Addressing the oppression she experienced thus required that she begin "under the skin." She had to confront the fact that "much of what I value about being Chicana, about my family, has been subverted by Anglo culture and my own cooperation with it." According to Moraga, her experience is characteristic of many women of color: "Each of us—whether dark, female, or both—has in some way internalized this oppressive imagery."

Like Anzaldúa, Moraga came to embrace her *mestiza* character. According to Moraga, "I am a woman with a foot in both [white and brown, Spanish-speaking and English] worlds; and I refuse the split." Rather than denying or privileging one or the other, she "feel[s] the necessity for dialogue" between elements of the two.[47] Choosing one or the other would require privileging one while rejecting the other. This would require that she deny her authentic self.

If, as Thrasymachus argued, the powerful manipulate understandings of justice in their own favor, a first task must be to expose the reality of injustice and the ideologies that legitimize it. Anzaldúa and Moraga help us see that this may not be an easy task. When the injustices are internalized as commonsense beliefs, they may be very difficult to recognize and erase. Although Anzaldúa and Moraga focus on the experiences of women of color, internalized oppression potentially affects anyone who does not conform to dominant beliefs and ideals and who accepts the validity of those dominant beliefs and ideals.

QUESTIONS, PROBLEMS, AND ACTIVITIES

1. Brainstorm a list of injustices. Arrange them in a hierarchy ranging from the relatively trivial to the relatively serious. What injustices have you personally experienced? What makes those experiences unjust? Locate or place your experiences of injustice in the hierarchy you created above.

2. Should the United States give more foreign aid? Why or why not? What kind(s) of foreign aid do you think should be emphasized?

3. Under what conditions, if any, does an adult deserve to suffer material deprivation such as lack of food, shelter, or health care? Under what conditions, if any, does a child deserve to suffer these material deprivations? If your answer to this second question is "none," what would you propose to prevent it?

4. Defend the proposition that a CEO, a college professor, and a garbage hauler should all earn the same wage. Then critique it. Pick three or four other job categories and evaluate the relative justice or injustice of their wage levels. What, in your estimation, are the most essential criteria for determining a person's wage?

5. Should the United States use its power to advance its own interests irrespective of questions of justice? Identify at least one issue that might support a "yes" answer, and at least one that might support a "no" answer.

6. Were the Athenian envoys described by Thucydides correct in arguing that the "weaker should be subject to the stronger" and "the strong do what they can and the weak suffer what they must"? Distinguish between "the way things are" and "the way things ought to be" in answering this question. Give some examples to support your position.

7. Do you agree or disagree with Friedrich von Hayek that luck (good and bad) partly determines a person's success or failure? How, if at all, has luck played a role in determining major achievements, milestones, and directions in your life?

8. Create a work of art (song, sculpture, painting, performance, or other) that expresses your thoughts and feelings about an injustice that particularly interests you.

9. Can you think of examples of internalized oppression as theorized by Anzaldúa and Moraga?

NOTES

1. For a discussion of these issues, see especially Wolfgang Sachs's *The Development Dictionary* (London: Zed Books, 1992) and *Planet Dialectics: Explorations in Environment and Development* (New York: Zed Books, 1999). See also Joseph Weatherby, Emmit Evans Jr., Reginald Gooden, Dianne Long, and Ira Reed, *The Other World: Issues and Politics of the Developing World*, 5th ed. (New York: Addison Wesley Longman, 2003), for a similar use of the terms *North* and *South*.

2. Rick Rowden, "A World of Debt," *American Prospect* 12, no. 12 (July 2, 2001): p. 29.

3. See Thomas Lairson and David Skidmore, *International Political Economy: The Struggle for Power and Wealth* (Fort Worth: Holt, Rinehart and Winston, 1993), pp. 186–90, for a summary of modernization theory.

4. See Lairson and Skidmore, *International Political Economy*, pp. 190–97, for a summary of dependency theorists' critical arguments. For overviews of different development approaches, see Richard Peet, *Theories of Development* (New York: Guilford Press, 1999), and David Stoesz, Charles Guzzetta, and Mark Lusk, *International Development* (Needham Heights, MA: Allyn & Bacon, 1999).

5. See Dianne Long, "Women and Development," in Weatherby et al., *The Other World*, pp. 91–107; Frances Moore Lappe, "Hunger Is Not Caused by a Scarcity of Food but by a Scarcity of Democracy," *Cleveland Plain Dealer*, July 2, 2001; and Sachs, *Planet Dialectics*.

6. Weatherby et al., *The Other World*, p. 354.

7. Rowden, "World of Debt," p. 29.

8. Phillips Foster, *The World Food Problem: Tackling the Causes of Undernutrition in the Third World* (Boulder, CO: Lynne Rienner, 1992), p. 3.

9. United Nations Food and Agriculture Organization, Economic and Social Department, *The State of Food Insecurity in the World, 2005: Eradicating World Hunger—Key to Achieving the Millennium Development Goals* (Rome: Food and Agriculture Organization of the United Nations, 2005), available at http://www.fao.org/documents/show_cdr.asp?url_file=/docrep/008/a0200e/a0200e00.htm.

10. Lappe, "Scarcity of Democracy."

11. Food First Institute for Food and Development Policy, "12 Myths about Hunger," Summer 1998, http://www.foodfirst.org/pubs/backgrdrs/1998/s98v5n3.html.

12. Darryl Fears and Claudia Deane, "Interracial Couples Finding Tolerance," *Cleveland Plain Dealer,* July 6, 2001; Richard Morin and Michael Cottman, "Pulled Over," *Cleveland Plain Dealer,* June 22, 2001.

13. Jonathan Tilove, "Gap Growing Wider in Black, White Views of Racial Relations," *Cleveland Plain Dealer,* July 11, 2001.

14. Lawrence Mishel, Jared Bernstein, and Sylvia Allegretto, *The State of Working America 2004–2005* (Ithaca, NY: Cornell University Press, 2005), p. 319.

15. Marcus Pohlmann, *Black Politics in Conservative America,* 2nd ed. (New York: Addison Wesley Longman, 1999), p. 52.

16. Amnesty International, "Killing with Prejudice: Race and Death Penalty in the USA," http://web.amnesty.org/library/Index/ENGAMR510521999?open&of=ENG-393; Ted Wendling, "Blacks Jailed at 8 Times Rate for Whites, Study Says," *Cleveland Plain Dealer,* July 11, 2001; *Sourcebook of Criminal Justice Statistics* (Washington, DC: Bureau of Justice Statistics, 1996), p. 501; Jesse Jackson Sr., "Liberty and Justice for Some: Mass Incarceration Comes at a Moral Cost to Every American," *Mother Jones,* July 10, 2001, http://www.MotherJones.com/prisons/liberty.html.

17. Amnesty International, "Killing with Prejudice."

18. Mishel, Bernstein, and Allegretto, *Working America, 2004–2005,* pp. 128, 132–33.

19. Bureau of Labor Statistics, U.S. Department of Labor, "Teachers—Preschool, Kindergarten, Elementary, Middle, and Secondary," *Occupational Outlook Handbook, 2002–03 Edition,* available at http://www.bls.gov/oco/ocos069.htm; Bureau of Labor Statistics, U.S. Department of Labor, "Teachers—Postsecondary," *Occupational*

Outlook Handbook, 2002–03 Edition, http://www.bls.gov/oco/ocos066.htm; James Sweeney, "Airport Screeners Get the Lowest Pay," *Cleveland Plain Dealer,* April 10, 2000; "Job Focus: Transportation Security Screeners," *About.com,* http://usgovinfo.about.com/bljobtsa.htm.

20. *Forbes,* http://www.forbes.com/richlist2002; Phil Galewitz, "Living Rich," *Cleveland Plain Dealer,* September 24, 1999.

21. Mishel, Bernstein, and Allegretto, *Working America, 2004–2005,* p. 190.

22. Niccolò Machiavelli, *The Prince* [1513], in *The Prince and The Discourses* (New York: Modern Library, 1950), pp. 66, 56.

23. Ibid., pp. 13, 18, 7–8.

24. Ibid., pp. 24, 27, 29.

25. Ibid., pp. 34–35, 61, 60.

26. Ibid., pp. 64, 63.

27. Ibid., pp. 65, 79.

28. Thucydides, *History of the Peloponnesian War* 1.75–76, 5.89, 5.111.

29. Plato, *The Republic* 1.338c, 1.338e, 1.343d–344c.

30. Plato, *The Republic* 1.362b, 1.361e–362c.

31. Plato, *The Republic* 1.364a–364b, 1.365b–366c.

32. Robert Solomon and Mark Murphy, eds., *What Is Justice?,* 2nd ed. (Oxford: Oxford University Press, 2000), pp. 4–5.

33. Herbert Hoover, campaign speech, New York City, October 31, 1932, in *Campaign Speeches of 1932* (Garden City, NY: Doubleday, 1933), pp. 192–93.

34. Ayn Rand, *The Fountainhead* (1943; repr., New York: Penguin Books, 1952), pp. 308, 405.

35. Adam Smith, *The Wealth of Nations* (1776; New York: Random House, 1937), p. 423.

36. Adam Smith, *The Theory of Moral Sentiments* [1759], ed. D. D. Raphael and A. L. Macfie (Oxford: Clarendon Press, 1976), pp. 83–85.

37. F. A. Hayek, *The Mirage of Social Justice,* vol. 2 of *Law, Legislation, and Liberty* (Chicago: University of Chicago Press, 1976), pp. 71, 70, 74, 84. The contemporary

economist Kenneth Arrow recognized this basic injustice of a market society, and the restrictions it places on human freedom, arguing that "the market in no way prescribes a just distribution of income and the idealization of freedom through the market fully disregards that for many relatively poor people this freedom is circumscribed indeed." Kenneth Arrow, "Distributive Justice and Desirable Ends of Economic Activity," in *Issues in Contemporary Microeconomics and Welfare*, ed. G. R. Feiwel (New York: Macmillan, 1985), pp. 137–38.

38. Gregory Squires, *Capital and Communities in Black and White: The Intersections of Race, Class, and Uneven Development* (New York: State University of New York Press, 1994), pp. 5, 8.

39. George Gilder, *Wealth and Poverty* (New York: Basic Books, 1981), pp. 12, 66, 90.

40. Ibid., pp. 70, 70–71, 114–15, 69, 72.

41. Ibid., pp. 12, 66, 12, 108, 67.

42. Ibid., pp. 68, 69.

43. Glenn C. Loury, "The Role of Normative Values in Rescuing the Urban Ghetto," in *Building a Community of Citizens: Civil Society in the 21st Century*, ed. Don E. Eberly (Lanham, MD: Commonwealth Foundation, 1994), pp. 242, 241–42 (emphasis in original), 243, 244.

44. Gloria Anzaldúa, *Borderlands/La Frontera: The New Mestiza* (San Francisco: Aunt Lute Books, 1987).

45. Gloria Anzaldúa, "Haciendo Caras, Una Entrada," in *Making Face, Making Soul/Haciendo Caras: Creative and Critical Perspectives by Feminists of Color*, ed. Gloria Anzaldua (San Francisco: Aunt Lute Books, 1990), pp. xv, xix; Cherríe Moraga and Gloria Anzaldúa, *This Bridge Called My Back: Writings by Radical Women of Color* (New York: Kitchen Table/Women of Color Press, 1981), p. 5; Gloria Anzaldúa, "En Rapport/In Opposition: Cobrando Cuentas a Las Nuestras," in Anzaldúa, *Making Face, Making Soul*, pp. 142–43; Gloria Anzaldúa, "La Prieta," in Moraga and Anzaldúa, *This Bridge Called My Back*, p. 207.

46. Anzaldúa, "Haciendo Caras, Una Entrada," p. xv; Anzaldúa, "La Conciencia de la Mestiza/Towards a New Consciousness," in Anzaldúa, *Making Face, Making Soul*, p. 377.

47. Cherríe Moraga, "La Güerra," in Moraga and Anzaldúa, *This Bridge Called My Back*, pp. 28, 31, 29, 30, 32, 34.

6

No Peace without Justice

Is there a better way than a wholly individualistic framework of understanding human behavior and individuals' relative success or failure? This section addresses one alternative used frequently by social scientists to understand and explain human thought and action. A social structure refers, first of all, to relatively persistent and patterned social relationships. They exhibit regularities and similarities that endure over time. Humans relate to each other and organize their interactions with others in nonrandom ways. A traditional teacher–student relationship illustrates this. Its constitutive elements include the roles that each adopts in relating to the other, the social status that attaches to each role, and the specific behaviors appropriate within the relationship.

Second, the relationship guides and channels thought and action. Any relationship includes expectations for appropriate behavior, and these find expression in routine and habitual acts. Actions that deviate from the norms, values, and beliefs embodied in a social structure meet with surprise and, sometimes, sanctions. In general, adherence to the norms and guidelines of a particular social structure brings rewards, while defiance of the norms and guidelines brings punishment. The teacher–student relationship guides both teachers and students toward appropriate behavior. Typically, the teacher dominates and the student submits. The teacher identifies knowledge and transmits it to the student using various pedagogical strategies. The relatively passive student records the knowledge and attempts to master it long enough to pass an exam. These characteristics hold relatively true across time and space. A teacher or student in one school district can move to another and retain these expectations about appropriate relationships and behaviors. Taken for granted, they need not be established anew.

Third, a social structure emphasizes the roles that create it rather than the character of specific individuals that inhabit those roles. The properties of the social structure remain relatively independent of the persons actually occupying the roles within it, since one individual can be replaced by another without changing the role. Replacing one college professor with another does not significantly alter the expectations and job description for that professor, even though one may perform the job better or differently than another. The basic relationship remains in place without the need to renegotiate it.

Fourth, people's behavior within a social structure is often driven by unconscious beliefs or assumptions. Teachers assume their authority in the classroom, and so do the students. The practices that occur within the classroom simply presume a relationship of domination–submission and build upon it. The teacher need not establish authority anew with each classroom visit. The basic relationship and its characteristics remain in place because everyone simply expects it.

Fifth, the characteristics of the social structure, and the consequences of the social structure, remain in place over time largely unintentionally, in that people within the structure pursue aims that do not include reproducing the social structure. Each day, students and the teacher engage in routine practices that reinforce and reproduce the relationship. Without intending to, they ensure that the basic relationship persists.

Finally, a social structure both enables and constrains human thought and behavior. It imposes limits on what specific persons can do, while at the same time making thought and action possible. The roles of teacher and student enable the process of education to continue, however imperfectly. Time-consuming questions of authority and responsibility need not be addressed; the correct answers can simply be presumed in order to get to the tasks of teaching and learning. But the roles also limit the range of possibilities within the classroom. The domination–submission norms that partly constitute the traditional teacher–student relationship, for example, rule out democratizing the classroom. The teacher can realistically choose from only a limited array of teaching strategies since factors such as grading policies and requirements imposed by policy makers rule out other alternatives. The net result of this simple social structure of teacher–student is that individual human behavior within the world of education is partly determined in ways that both enable and limit individual volition.

But, one might argue, individual students and teachers can always defy the norms and expectations imposed by a social structure. They therefore retain complete free will and full choice. This objection ignores practical realities that face every student and teacher, however. Saying that any student could defy a teacher is comparable to saying that any person is free to stroll buck naked through a crowded shopping mall. Although superficially correct, it is worth asking why it happens so rarely. Defiance imposes costs sufficiently painful to dissuade certain behaviors. In theory any student is free to bring an accordion to class and play it loudly while the professor is speaking. However, the student would likely face unpleasant repercussions of such an act of willful deviation. In effect the ability of any one individual to deviate from the norms and expectations imposed by the social structure requires breaking out of the relationship entirely. Any student intent on graduation must generally play along with the rules imposed by the social structure; consistent failure to do so would result in expulsion.

Our lives are deeply immersed in ubiquitous social structures in ways that most of us can barely imagine. They structure human behavior and partly determine the character and circumstances of every person's life. All humans live in a web of multiple and overlapping social structures that both enable and constrain their behavior. As contemporary sociologist Earl Babbie (1938–) wrote, social structure "shapes your behavior; it conditions your beliefs, values, and opinions. Social structure is a grid that defines who you are—both in the ways you are identified by others and in how you *feel* about yourself."[1] Yet, a social structure never *fully* determines human possibilities. Humans can become conscious of the ways that social structures shape their lives and can act to reshape a particular social structure, though the ability of any one individual to transform a social structure is in most cases extremely limited.

As an explanatory tool, the concept of social structure offers a powerful means of understanding complex problems such as racism. As described earlier, people of color suffer economic deprivation disproportionate to their numbers and inequitable treatment in the criminal justice system. How can we explain these racial disparities? The explanation proffered by adherents of a wholly individualistic framework emphasizes the individual responsibility of black men and women. If black Americans fare poorly compared to whites in social, political, and economic arenas, it is their own fault, the fault of every individual black person who fails to take advantage of the opportunities that America offers to everyone. Another explanation emphasizes racism in the forms of prejudice, bigotry, bias, and discrimination. According to this view, black inequality and lack of opportunity can be understood as the result of overtly hostile white attitudes that find expression in the denial of jobs, exclusion from matriculation in good schools, and punitive judicial judgments. This explanation emphasizes the conscious, willful denial by white people of opportunities to people of color, based on consciously held beliefs and attitudes that prejudice the treatment of blacks by whites.

While both of these explanations offer some understanding of some cases, neither adequately accounts for the extent and magnitude of racism in America today. Most black people, like most white people, have sufficient talent and motivation to succeed, if given the opportunity. As we saw earlier, black and Latino families now log more work hours annually than do white families. This suggests that, if some of these families remain impoverished, generally it is not due to lack of effort. The second explanation similarly lacks credibility. While some white Americans remain unabashedly prejudiced toward people of color and act on those prejudices, the majority of white Americans today distance themselves from overt expressions of racial hostility and prejudice. Both explanations thus offer partial answers at best.

An alternative answer emphasizes social structures of racism that are more subtle, yet more profound and deeply insinuated into American society. This kind of racism is structural and systemic. Stokely Carmichael (1941–1998) and Charles Hamilton (1929–), two key figures of the Black Power movement of the 1960s, were among the first to distinguish between two kinds of racism. One, an overt individual racism, entails "individual whites acting against individual blacks." It "can be recorded by television cameras; it can frequently be observed in the process of commission." They gave as an example white terrorists bombing a black church. This kind of racism is easily recognized and widely deplored in public. The other kind, which they called "institutional racism," entails "acts by the total white community against the black community." Institutional racism "is less overt, far more subtle, less identifiable in terms of specific individuals committing the acts. But it is no less destructive of human life." This form of racism "originates in the operation of established and respected forces in the society, and thus receives far less public condemnation than the first type." As an example, Carmichael and Hamilton noted that during the 1960s in Birmingham, Alabama, "five hundred black babies die each year because of the lack of proper food, shelter and medical facilities, and thousands more are destroyed and maimed physically, emotionally and intellectually because of conditions of poverty and discrimination in the black community." If a black family moving into a white neighborhood encounters hostility, it experiences the first kind of overt individual racism. For every such incident of overt racism in housing, according to Carmichael and Hamilton, thousands more black people are kept by impersonal economic forces "locked in dilapidated slum tenements, subject to the daily prey of exploitative slumlords, merchants, loan sharks and discriminatory real estate agents."

While individual racism is easily recognized and condemned, institutional racism is not. White America, Carmichael and Hamilton argued, "either pretends it does not know" of institutional racism, "or is in fact incapable of doing anything meaningful about it." Whites can easily absolve themselves of the first kind, individual racism, since "*they* would never plant a bomb in a church; *they* would never stone a black family." Yet, these same people "continue to support political officials and institutions that would and do perpetuate institutionally racist policies." The net result, they argue, is "a racist society" in which racism permeates throughout.[2]

The concept of institutional racism retains its analytical and explanatory power without reference to overt prejudice or hostility by whites toward blacks and other people of color. Institutional racism, as a complex form of social structure, persists in part as an unintended consequence of habitual behavior, as additional illustrations demonstrate.

Redlining refers to a practice once used explicitly by bankers of drawing a line on a map around certain neighborhoods in which they would not make loans. Although Congress declared this practice illegal, it continues, albeit more circumspectly. Looking at the aggregate data for the neighborhood, bankers engaging in this practice deem the likelihood of default on a loan relatively high and the overall rate of profitability relatively low. Based on these economic data, they stop lending in those neighborhoods. Bankers do this to protect profit margins, not to sabotage the lives of anyone in particular. The economic motivation nevertheless produces a racist outcome, albeit unintentionally, since most redlined neighborhoods are inner-city neighbor-hoods with predominately black populations. These neighborhoods, denied access to credit, suffer further declines in their standards of living. The prac-tice penalizes all residents of redlined neighborhoods, regardless of income and credit rating, but black residents disproportionately. Explaining this prob-lem in terms of bankers' overt prejudice against people of color requires dis-torting their actual motivation in most cases.

As described earlier, African-American student and faculty presence on college campuses falls well below their proportionate numbers in the general population. A wholly individualistic framework for explaining this underrep-resentation would emphasize that African Americans simply do not choose to attend college in numbers comparable to white Americans, or perhaps do not try hard enough nor make the requisite sacrifices needed to attend college. Al-ternatively, one could suggest that admissions office staffs are prejudiced against black people and so they sabotage the applications of African Ameri-cans in order to protect the white purity of campus. Neither of these explana-tions is persuasive. Success in America depends substantially on education, and African Americans recognize this as clearly as do white Americans. Also, it is highly unlikely that admissions offices are predominately staffed by prej-udiced individuals. On the contrary, many colleges and universities have within the last two decades tried, sometimes heroically, to diversify their cam-puses by affirmatively considering the racial composition of applicants.

To understand why, despite these efforts by well-intentioned individuals and institutions, most campuses remain bastions of white America in pro-portion to their overall numbers, a different explanation is needed. This ex-planation accounts for the racial disparities in higher education without blaming the individuals who are locked out of participation in higher educa-tion and without misattributing the problem to prejudice among admissions staff. It emphasizes the institutionalized racism in higher education, marked by factors that filter out students of color. The main filters include the quality of K–12 education, college entrance exams, white faculty and curriculum, and financial costs. These filters are relatively patterned and they persist over time, relatively independently of specific individuals, as the unintended conse-quences of routine behavior. And they determine to a large extent the possi-bilities and pitfalls facing potential students of color in higher education. Though unintentional, they nevertheless create stubborn nonrandomized obstacles and gaps in educational attainment that affect some students more than others.

The socioeconomic inequality among white and black Americans offers a final illustration of institutionalized racism. Why, as we have earlier seen, are African Americans approximately three times as likely as white Americans to live in poverty? The wholly individualistic explanation lays the blame entirely on the shoulders of individual African Americans who fail to exert sufficient effort and make bad choices. A second explanation emphasizes the explicit, overt prejudice and hostility that African Americans face in the job market. As in the other illustrations, these explanations fail to explain the relative magnitude of poverty among African Americans.

A systemic, structural perspective that emphasizes institutional racism begins by noting some of the macro changes occurring in the U.S. economy and in urban environments during the last several decades. As the United States switched from a manufacturing and industrial economy to a service economy, many workers lost their jobs. Since black workers were typically the last hired, they are often the first fired. During this period, more and more people with the economic resources to do so began moving from inner cities to suburbs, lured by jobs, better school systems, lower crime rates, and higher property values. Undoubtedly, some also left because they did not want to live next door to people of color. As the jobs and people left the inner cities, the tax base eroded, leaving too little to adequately maintain roads, schools, and other social services. The problem has become a self-perpetuating cycle as inadequate schools and lack of jobs hamstring the next generation. These changes are driven primarily by nonracial motivations. Yet, taken together, they leave a marked racial impact, to the detriment of African Americans left behind in the inner cities.

The same framework for analysis can be applied to global injustices affecting entire nation-states. Global political and economic structures enable and constrain the behavior and options of individual nation-states. They offer development opportunities through selective access to markets, to credit, and to knowledge but also constrain those opportunities through the legacies of colonialism, neocolonialism, debt, the lack of development capital, inadequate infrastructure, and dominant forces arrayed against change. Global justice movements and the promise of alternative development strategies give some Southern nations some hope of escaping crushing debt loads, but at the same time they face constraints imposed by declining terms of trade, by reliance on primary products and cheap labor for comparative advantage, by the relative shortage of indigenous capital, and, again, by dominant states and global institutions opposing changes in the current world order. World hunger could be solved with adequate political will, cooperation among Northern and Southern worlds, and commitment of global resources; however, the solutions are constrained by a global agribusiness community oriented toward profit rather than meeting basic nutrition requirements, elite policy makers firmly committed to the status quo, the persistent belief that the problem can be solved by increasing production of food rather than distributing current production more equitably, and a preference for private property rights over basic food rights.

Other forms of injustice are similarly systematic and structured. Institutionalized sexism, for example, can be found in persistent wage inequalities in which women earn less than men for comparable work; in academic tenure processes that discriminate against women who want to bear children; in careers that track men into senior management and women into "soft" positions in human relations; in the lopsided commitment of financial resources to men's athletic programs while slighting women's programs; and in a culture of "lookism" that subtly pressures women to conform to an unnatural ideal of beauty. Like institutionalized racism, institutionalized sexism both enables and constrains the choices and actions of individuals.

Sometimes these structured injustices intersect in ways that magnify and compound the degree to which individuals' lives are determined by forces outside their control. Black activist and intellectual Angela Davis (1944–) offers intersectional analyses of race, class, and gender. The "triple oppression" faced by working-class women of color makes them the most oppressed human beings in our society, according to Davis:

> Working-class women, and women of color in particular, confront sexist oppression in a way that reflects the real and complex objective interconnections between economic, racial, and sexual oppression. Whereas a white middle-class woman's experience of sexism incorporates a relatively isolated form of this oppression, working-class women's experiences necessarily place sexism in its context of class exploitation—and Black women's experiences further contextualize gender oppression within the realities of racism.[3]

While white, middle-class women may have the luxury of focusing exclusively on gender, working-class women of color must also address injustices rooted in racial and economic issues. They must organize around issues of jobs and adequate education, around plant shutdowns and union-busting, around welfare subsidies and food stamps, around access to health care and violence against women.

In her studies of the U.S. prison system, Davis has extensively analyzed the connections between injustice, crime, and repression and how they disproportionately affect working-class people of color. Naturally, according to Davis, conditions of exploitation and oppression breed discontent, anger, and asocial behavior that sometimes results in crime. Crime is "inevitable," according to Davis, "in a society in which wealth is unequally distributed, as one of the constant reminders that society's productive forces are being channeled in the wrong direction." Crimes are not expressions of bad people but are rather the embodiment of "profound but suppressed social needs which express themselves in anti-social modes of action." In a context of class and racial injustice, at least some individuals "are compelled to resort to criminal acts, not as a result of conscious choice—implying other alternatives—but because society has objectively reduced their possibilities of subsistence and survival to this level."

Policy makers face two general options for responding to crime. They can attempt to redress the injustices underlying the crime, or they can repress the crime symptoms. During the 1960s, the Lyndon Johnson administration attempted to go the former route by increasing social welfare spending. However, since the 1970s, policy makers have increasingly pursued the latter option of increased repression. According to Davis, the effect on black communities of this repressive response can be likened to a police state:

> From Birmingham to Harlem to Watts, black ghettos are occupied, patrolled and often attacked by massive deployments of police. The police, domestic caretakers of violence, are the oppressor's emissaries, charged with the task of containing us within the boundaries of our oppression. The announced function of the police, "to protect and serve the people," becomes the grotesque caricature of protecting and preserving the interests of our oppressors and serving us nothing but injustice. They are there to intimidate blacks, to persuade us with their violence that we are powerless to alter the conditions of our lives.[4]

An ineffective war on drugs replaced the war on poverty. Politicians used the rhetoric of "get tough on crime" to win elections, playing on the fears of white Americans. Legislators in some states passed three-strikes laws mandating life in prison for a third felony conviction, even if those three felonies were non-violent petty theft or victimless crimes. The alleged race-blindness of these laws translates in practice into disproportionate numbers of people of color in jail for life.

After the police come the courts, which have locked African Americans away in staggering numbers. The dominant explanations for this ignore structural factors, especially the economic and political structures of a globalizing capitalism. This failure to account for structured inequality and lack of opportunity for black Americans means that "the racial imbalance in jails and prisons is treated as a contingency, at best as a product of the 'culture of poverty,' and at worst as proof of an assumed black monopoly on criminality." This explanation excuses policy makers from acting to correct the injustices lying at the heart of racial imbalances in incarceration. Instead of attacking root causes of injustices, they have developed a prison-industrial complex that rivals the military-industrial complex first identified by President Eisenhower in the late 1950s. The prison, according to Davis, represents "a key component of the state's coercive apparatus, the overriding function of which is to ensure social control." Prisons serve as "instrument[s] of class domination, a means of prohibiting the have-nots from encroaching upon the haves." Jails and prisons have become "the institutionalized and normalized means of addressing social problems in an era of migrating corporations, unemployment and homelessness, and collapsing public services, from health care to education." Rather than seeking greater racial and class justice, those with wealth and power simply lock up those who act asocially in response to injustice. The result is a "vicious circle linking poverty, police courts, and prison," and this is "an integral element" of life for many black Americans. Davis concludes that black Americans trapped within this vicious circle are "political prisoners" who are "victims of an oppressive politico-economic order."[5]

Defenders of an individualistic framework will respond that every crime is a result of bad choices by bad people, that everyone has options and alternatives other than crime, and that all crime is inexcusable no matter its cause. Undoubtedly, some crime results simply from bad people making bad choices, and in general people should be held accountable for destructive choices.

Davis also arguably romanticizes crime by characterizing it in blanket terms as political protest and by characterizing incarcerated people as political prisoners. Nevertheless, without excusing crime and other antisocial, destructive behavior, we can understand like Davis that the roots of much crime and the political disorder it represents lie in the despair and anger bred from deprivation, lack of opportunity, and generations of injustice. A repressive response deepens the despair and deprivation experienced by many without offering any solution to the root injustices. Understanding the failures of distributive justice in socially structured terms does not excuse individuals from striving, nor does it excuse Americans from assuming responsibility for them.

As Davis argues, simply repressing the results of injustice may not lead to a stable political order. She points toward the need for a just response, rather than a repressive one, as the surest way toward peace and stability. We find a similar argument in Plato's (427–347 B.C.) *Republic* (375 B.C.), where he defined *justice* as "minding your own business and not interfering with other people." This unfortunate translation may mislead contemporary readers familiar with the current idiomatic expression of the same words, meaning simply that a person should not interfere in the affairs of others. Plato meant something more complex: that each of us should know our proper place and role in society, and that we should fulfill that role.

Plato applied this conception of justice both to the state and to the makeup of the individual. The three major elements of the state that will "mind their own business" are the philosopher-rulers, the auxiliaries, and the "businessmen." The philosopher-rulers are the governing class, those who guide the state and make policy decisions affecting the state. Their essential characteristics include intelligence and wisdom. The auxiliaries form the supporting caste, the warriors who lend support to the state and its leaders, guarding it and helping carry out the leaders' directions. Their primary characteristics include strength and courage. Plato puts everyone else in the category of businesspeople, those engaged in commercial pursuits, including farmers, laborers, artisans, and shopkeepers. They form the economic basis of Plato's ideal state. When each of these three classes of people "does its own job and minds its own business, that . . . is justice and makes our state just." On the other hand, "interference by the three classes with each other's jobs, and interchange of jobs between them, therefore, does the greatest harm to our state, and we are entirely justified in calling it the worst of evils."

Similarly, justice within the individual means that each element of the human psyche occupies its appropriate position in relation to other elements and plays the proper role assigned to it. Reason represents the "better element" within the individual, according to Plato, and includes the ability to think, to calculate, to have foresight, and to make decisions. The "worse element" is passion or appetite, which includes the purely instinctive desires such as hunger for food and sex. Between them, and completing the trilogy, lies spirit or emotion that, like its counterparts in the state, plays a supporting role. Plato clearly intended parallel hierarchies of elements in the state and the individual. Within the individual, reason rules over passions, aided by emotion: "So the reason ought to rule, having the wisdom and foresight to act for the whole, and the spirit ought to obey and support it. . . . [Furthermore,] they must be put in charge of appetite, which forms the greater part of each man's make-up and is naturally insatiable."[6] Within the state, the philosopher-rulers govern the businesspeople, aided by the auxiliaries.

One of Plato's central messages was that political order is made possible by justice. In a just state, each part plays its appointed role, wringing discordance and disharmony from the system. It may appear that Plato believed as well that any well-ordered state is a just state. However, a state may be ordered through violence, repression, deceit, and manipulation. In this case, injustice may be simply masked. Though he openly acknowledged the potential need to exercise deceit, censorship, and compulsion to attain political order, and though he valued it highly, Plato did not endorse political order for its own sake. It had to be a particular kind of political order, one with an appropriate arrangement of parts and guided neither by a tyrant nor the common people but by one or more philosopher-rulers.

Several centuries later, Augustine of Hippo (354–430), otherwise known as St. Augustine, echoed elements of Plato's discussion of justice. He applied the same model of different parts forming a harmonious whole as did Plato, both to the individual and to the larger political community. Applied to the individual, Augustine argued:

> The peace, then, of the body lies in the ordered equilibrium of all its parts; the peace of the irrational soul, in the balanced adjustment of its appetites; the peace of the reasoning soul, in the harmonious correspondence of conduct and conviction; the peace of body and soul taken together, in the well-ordered life and health of the living whole.

Augustine distinguished first between body and soul and second between an "irrational soul" concerned with appetites and a "reasoning soul" concerned with belief and will. If applied appropriately to the larger political body, this same division between the reasonable and the irrational would result in "the peace of the political community" marked by "an ordered harmony of authority and obedience between citizens." Augustine also followed Plato's thinking in valuing political order highly, but not just any political order. It had to be a particular kind of political order, a specifically just political order. According to Augustine, "Anyone, then, who is rational enough to prefer right to wrong and order to disorder can see that the kind of peace that is based on injustice, as compared with that which is based on justice, does not deserve the name of peace."

Augustine diverged most obviously from Plato in his infusion of theological interests and intentions. He emphasized theological authority based on religious principle and conviction rather than Plato's secular emphasis on reason. Justice, Augustine argued, is impossible without submission to God's authority. Augustine distinguished between the earthly city and the City of God, each with its own version of justice. Justice in the earthly city, "the virtue which accords to each and every man what is his due," corresponds to Plato's "conventional view" of justice and resembles today's justice as desert. Justice in the heavenly city—what Augustine called "true justice"—can be found only "in that commonwealth, if we may so call it, whose Founder and Ruler is Jesus Christ."[7] Although he apparently believed that both conceptions of justice required submission to God, he emphasized it repeatedly for justice in the heavenly city.

Plato and Augustine both recognized a direct connection between justice and political order captured in the contemporary slogan "No peace without justice." In general, the more just a political order, and the more that people believe in its justness, the more ordered will be the society and state. Though Plato and Augustine both grasped the central insight that legitimate peace is impossible without justice, both attempted to solve the problem of political disorder undemocratically through an authoritarian hierarchy in which everyone knows his or her proper role and faithfully plays it. Also, both saw justice in terms of perfect or near-perfect peace and political order. Departures from that ideal of perfect peace and order marked at the same time a departure from justice. In a democracy, as they well knew, this kind of perfect political order is unlikely. Advocates of democracy must accommodate themselves to a certain level of disorder, because, in a truly diverse democracy, people will disagree over fundamental questions, including the nature of justice, and this ensures a messy and perpetual process of working out differences.

The remainder of this chapter addresses theoretical and practical alternatives for achieving a more just political order and, by extension, greater peace and stability. Because of its fundamental importance in discussions of justice and political order, distributive justice will be emphasized.

JUSTICE AND CARE

In the Book of Genesis of the biblical Old Testament, when God instructs the patriarch Abraham to sacrifice his son Isaac, Abraham dutifully sets out to obey. At the last second, though, God stays his hand and Isaac is spared. Nevertheless, Abraham was willing to kill his son, perhaps the one person he cared most deeply about, because of his stronger allegiance to abstract principles captured in his understanding of a just God.

In ancient Athens, Socrates found himself faced with a similar dilemma, though in this case it was his own life at stake. Convicted on trumped-up charges of impiety and corruption of youth, he was condemned to death via drinking poisonous hemlock. Socrates' friends and enemies expected him to flee into exile rather than drink the hemlock. But Socrates rejected exile, arguing that his allegiance to principles captured in Athenian law and the polity more generally took precedence over his own life. He dismissed as insignificant his friends' arguments about remaining alive to care for his wife and children.

In Mel Gibson's film *Braveheart*, about a Scottish rebel fighting against English domination, the character played by Gibson, William Wallace, leads an unsuccessful rebellion and is caught, tortured, and executed. His torturers offer him an end to his suffering if he will but renounce the rebellion. He refuses, however, and instead shouts, "Freedom!" In the film's grand finale, his fellow countrymen rush into slaughter, in a battle in which they are hopelessly outnumbered and cannot expect to survive. They opt for dying on behalf of the idea of freedom, leaving their wives and children to fend for themselves.

In each of these three cases, men faced a conflict between their dual allegiances to relatively abstract principle and more immediate, concrete principles of filial responsibility. And in each case, they chose their allegiance to abstract principle, essentially abandoning their familial obligations and loyalties. Their choice is widely celebrated as the epitome of honorable men of integrity making noble choices.

Since the early 1980s, some feminist scholars have focused attention on the gendered nature of Abraham's, Socrates', and the Scottish rebels' choice of abstract principle over filial obligation. They concluded that traditional, dominant approaches to questions of justice emphasize a specifically masculine orientation in which abstract principles supersede relational obligations. Harvard University researcher Carol Gilligan (1936–) offered one prominent contribution to this discussion in her response to developmental psychologist Lawrence Kohlberg (1927–1987), who posited a six-stage development process for moral judgment. Though his research focused entirely on boys and men, Kohlberg claimed that the six stages applied to everyone. In higher stages of moral development, according to Kohlberg, "relationships are subordinated to rules (stage four) and rules to universal principles of justice (stages five and six)." Girls and women tend to score low, around stage three, where "morality is conceived in interpersonal terms and goodness is equated with helping and pleasing others," leading to the inevitable conclusion that they are deficient in moral judgment.[8] This conclusion reinforced Sigmund Freud's (1856–1939) earlier observations that what is ethically normal differed for men and women and that women show less sense of justice than men.

Based on her own empirical research, Gilligan responded that girls and women approach the question of justice from different vantage points than boys and men, and they articulate their positions "in a different voice." This different voice emerges from girls' and women's psychological development in relation to their mothers, and from their historically and socially constructed roles as primary caregivers. Gilligan drew the first point in part from the work of Nancy Chodorow, who argued that gender differences are due not to anatomical differences, as Freud argued, but to role differentiation in early childhood. Young girls' mothers represent their primary model of personhood. Growing and developing psychologically requires a girl to emulate her mother and retain a connection to her. By contrast, boys must learn to individuate themselves from their mothers in order to emulate their fathers and develop a specifically masculine identity. This requires that at some point in their development they separate from their mothers. Consequently, feminine personality defines itself in relation and connection to other people, while masculine personality defines itself in separation from others. Gilligan pointed out that the male process of individuation and separation had been defined as the norm for everyone, and this led inevitably to the unfortunate conclusion that something is wrong with women.

Women's "other voice" also develops from women's roles in caregiving. In most cultures, women have long assumed primary responsibility for child care and child rearing. Women also tend to assume responsibility for caring for adult men. Their place "in man's life cycle has been that of nurturer, caretaker, and helpmate, the weaver of those networks of relationships on which she in turn relies." Given their multiple caregiving roles, women "not only define themselves in a context of human relationship but also judge themselves in terms of their ability to care." Thus, if women rather than men are used as the standard, morality becomes a matter of concrete responsibilities rather than abstract rights, and it requires a different approach based on fulfilling relational obligations and duties. While men's conception of morality "ties moral development to the understanding of rights and rules," women's conception of it is "concerned with the activity of care [and] centers moral development around the understanding of responsibility and relationships." Since "the morality of rights differs from the morality of responsibility in its emphasis on separation rather than connection," men worry about interfering with others' rights while women worry about their responsibilities to others and for caring for them.[9]

Gilligan concluded that there are "two ways of speaking about moral problems, two modes of describing the relationship between other and self." She characterized the masculine orientation emphasizing formal rights as an *ethic of justice* and the feminine orientation emphasizing relational obligations as an *ethic of care*. Gilligan viewed both as legitimate and valuable. On the one hand, argued Gilligan, introducing the notion of rights positively moves us from "a bond of continuing dependence to a dynamic of interdependence." Rights help "challenge a morality of self-sacrifice and self-abnegation" and "the interests of the self can be considered legitimate." This helps women avoid traps into which many have fallen historically of self-abnegation and sole attention to the needs of others. On the other hand, an ethic of care helps us move beyond "the paralyzing injunction not to hurt others to an injunction to act responsively toward self and others and thus to sustain connection." Women's "moral strength" lies in their "overriding concern with relationships and responsibilities." Their "sensitivity to the needs of others and the assumption of responsibility for taking care" give women unique grounds for empathy. They "lead women to attend to voices other than their own and to include in their judgment other points of view." Although her language sometimes appears to say otherwise, Gilligan denied that these male and female orientations emerge from inherent traits of men and women. She characterized them instead as socially constructed "in a social context where factors of social status and power combine with reproductive biology to shape the experience of males and females and the relations between the sexes."[10]

While Gilligan stopped at the straightforward conclusion that justice and care simply represent different, separate systems of ethics, Virginia Held (1929–) probed their relation to each other more deeply. While agreeing with Gilligan that care and justice offer "different but equally valid" perspectives, Held argued first of all that care provides a "wider moral framework" for justice. Noting that care persists in families embodying unjust patriarchal relations of domination, she concluded that care can exist without justice. Second, according to Held, without care there would be no persons around to worry about justice. Care makes survival possible. Without mothers caring for their children, survival into adulthood would be impossible. Care is thus more inclusive as a value. Third, Held argued that justice and care both potentially apply in public and private realms. For example, families require greater justice "in a more equitable division of labor between women and men in the household, in the protection of vulnerable family members from domestic violence and abuse, [and] in recognizing the rights of family members to respect for their individuality." At the same time, care is "badly needed in the public domain." Providing care to those who need it should be a political priority, she argued, not one relegated solely to families and charities. In areas such as child care, education, health care, and care of the elderly, the state should provide more effective and inclusive care. Noting that provision of care has largely been the responsibility of women and minorities, who do most of the paid and unpaid work associated with caring for the young and the elderly, she called for a fairer division of responsibility for care both between women and men and between whites and minorities. Care should be a matter of rights, she argued. We should "recognize welfare as something to which each person is entitled by right under conditions of need. Welfare rights would be recognized as basic rights guaranteeing persons the resources needed to live."[11]

Like Held, Joan Tronto (1952–) attempted to politicize the discussion of care. Her "political argument for an ethic of care" emphasized a world "where the daily caring of people for each other is a valued premise of human existence." Following through politically on an ethic of care requires "a political commitment to value care and to reshape institutions to reflect that changed value." An ethic of care can serve both as a moral value and also as a benchmark for "the political achievement of a good society."[12] She argued that an ethic of care can be subdivided into the four ethical elements of attentiveness, responsibility, competence, and responsiveness and the four practical phases of recognizing the need for care, assuming responsibility for care, giving care, and receiving care.

Held's and Tronto's attention to the needs of caregivers as well as care receivers merits special note in politicizing an ethic of care. A more just, careful approach to satisfying the needs of some vulnerable populations, especially children and frail elderly, will focus both on the needs of the vulnerable themselves and also the people who actually deliver the care. As Held notes, historically and traditionally women and minorities occupy most caregiving roles. Tronto's insistence on "reshaping institutions" to reflect an ethic of care points toward policies that support caregiving through wage and benefit supports, family leave, child care supplements, and other family supports.

These theorists agree that attaining greater justice requires that we attend to the care needs of all people, but in particular the most vulnerable. They recommend that an ethic of care be integrated into our considerations of justice and into policy discussions surrounding issues of justice. This need not mean the same kind of care that parents provide their children. It should mean care as used by Held and Tronto in the sense of caring about the welfare of others, especially the vulnerable and those who minister to their needs—and backing it up with policy options providing concrete material support. In this more general sense, care entails greater compassion, empathy, and sympathy. Critics of this approach can be reminded that even Adam Smith (1723–1790), revered godfather of capitalism, integrated such "moral sentiments" into his political-economic philosophy.

Government can play a crucial role, as it already does in many countries of Western Europe, in setting family-friendly policies backed by material commitments. These include, for example, policies supporting paid parental leave when necessary to provide care to children, the frail elderly, and other dependents; extensive child and elder care policies that provide sufficient resources to caregivers to adequately fulfill their care obligations; and living-wage and benefit policies supporting the women and men who opt for careers in caring professions.

Finally, Gilligan, Held, and Tronto agree that abstract principles of justice can sometimes get in the way of providing care for the most vulnerable. One such abstract principle, property rights, requires particular attention. In the United States and elsewhere, property rights often take precedence over the provision of care. This finds expression, for example, in opposition to taxes and social welfare spending. Caring for others may require temporarily and partially suspending property rights, as Lawrence Kohlberg's famous "Heinz" case illustrates. Mr. Heinz's wife has cancer, but Heinz cannot afford the cancer medication. He could steal the drug to save his wife's life, but it would require breaking the law and transgressing property rights. What should he do? Kohlberg, who represents in this discussion a justice-as-abstract-rights position, concurs with the care perspective that Heinz should steal the drug, because human life takes precedence over property rights. A highly developed moral agent would choose this option, according to Kohlberg, because caring for humans takes precedence over property rights when the two conflict.

JUSTICE, PROPERTY, AND THE SOCIAL CONTRACT

In the dominant liberal tradition, justice has historically been deeply wedded to private property and the role of a social contract in securing it. This can be seen clearly in Thomas Hobbes (1588–1679), considered by some the first liberal thinker of the Western canon. Hobbes wrote *Leviathan* (1651) with the prolonged violence and chaos of England's Thirty Years' War in mind. This undoubtedly shaped his political philosophy, which emphasized a selfish, rapacious human nature and a state of nature characterized by lawlessness and violence. In the state of nature, humans are "equall, in the faculties of body, and mind" such that "the weakest has strength enough to kill the strongest." From this natural physical equality "ariseth equality of hope in the attaining of our Ends." Given an assumption of scarcity, when different people start hoping for the same thing that both cannot have, "they become enemies" and "endeavour to destroy, or subdue one an other." Since by definition in a state of nature there exists no "power able to over-awe them all," the result, according to Hobbes, is a "Warre of every one against every one" and life is naturally "solitary, poore, nasty, brutish, and short." Under these conditions, "nothing can be Unjust. The notions of Right and Wrong, Justice and Injustice have there no place," for "where there is no common Power, there is no Law . . . [and] where no Law, no Injustice." With no civil authority to set common laws and force compliance to them, anything goes, and the notion of justice is inconceivable under such circumstances.

What exactly does justice mean to Hobbes? Justice means "that men performe their Covenants made." Justice begins when the "Validity of Covenants" can be ensured, and this is done through "the Constitution of a Civill Power, sufficient to compel men to keep them." To escape the state of nature and remain free of it, Hobbes recommends that humans create a social contract that turns power and authority over to an all-powerful "Leviathan" capable of enforcing compliance to covenants, expressed in laws.

A central reason why justice is impossible in the state of nature is that "the Right of all men to all things" remains intact prior to the establishment of the social contract. Private property cannot be secured except through preponderance of force. According to Hobbes, "Where there is no Own, that is, no Propriety, there is no Injustice." Justice requires establishing and maintaining the right of property. Setting rules of "propriety" also secures the peace:

> This Proprietie, being necessary to Peace, and depending on Soveraign Power, is the Act of that Power, in order to the publique peace. These Rules of Propriety . . . and of Good, Evill, Lawfull, and Unlawfull in the actions of Subjects, are the Civill Lawes.[13]

John Locke (1632–1704) also tied justice directly to property and the social contract. Recall that, in Locke's view, individuals form a social contract to protect their property rights. Locke's formulation clearly takes as given and legitimate the existing inequalities of property and seeks to protect them as they are. As Locke illustrates, while contracts are sometimes useful devices for helping ensure that people get what they deserve, they can also institutionalize existing injustices based on unequal distributions of property or other inequalities.

The central problem with contracts as a basis for justice, as pointed out by contemporary feminist Annette Baier (1929–), is that, assuming self-interest, agreements reached among unequals are likely to favor the strong over the weak and the rich over the poor. Asymmetries of power translate into asymmetrical bargaining leverage, resulting in lopsided agreements. A labor contract enacted under circumstances of rapid capital mobility, declining unions, a rapidly dwindling jobs base, and a race-to-the-bottom dynamic will likely favor the interests of capital. An agreement forged between cash-starved Southern countries and dominant development institutions such as the International Monetary Fund to deal with balance-of-payments crises is likely to favor the dominant institutions. Since dominant states such as the United States control the dominant institutions, the agreement likely affirms existing privilege and power and cements the existing political-economic order. Weaker parties agree to contracts that favor stronger parties because they have little choice. Their desperation makes them vulnerable to exploitation. Citing Hobbes and Locke as prominent examples, Baier argues that many moral philosophers simply presume equality among various parties to the contract, practically ensuring the perpetuation of asymmetries of power and wealth.

Echoing some of the terms of the care-versus-justice debate, Baier emphasized gender in her analysis of the shortcomings of contract as a basis for justice. Males, in particular, fixate on contract, according to Baier. Unlike women, for whom relatively close interpersonal relations are the norm, men "focus their philosophical attention so single-mindedly on cool, distanced relations between more or less free and equal adult strangers." By contrast, according to Baier, women "cannot see morality as essentially a matter of keeping to the minimal moral traffic rules, designed to restrict close encounters between autonomous persons to self-chosen ones." Such an approach "presupposes both an equality of power and a natural separateness from others," both of which are "alien to women's experience of life and morality." For women, whose lives have historically been defined in relationships with less powerful children and more powerful husbands and fathers, a moral code built on the presumption of equality and autonomy will be "at best nonfunctional, at worst an offensive pretense of equality as a substitute for its actuality."[14] For contracts to be fair, according to Baier, the parties to the contract must be at least roughly equal in their power, their level of autonomy, and their level of vulnerability to the other parties to the agreement. Otherwise, the contract institutionalizes a set of unequal relationships.

An adequate approach to justice will acknowledge and address asymmetries of power and vulnerability. This would result in a new social contract, one that protects the least among us rather than the strongest and that would prioritize meeting basic human needs over property rights. This need not entail a wholesale attack on property rights per se, only the simple proposition that property rights should not get in the way of justice and caring for the most vulnerable among us. Sometimes property rights can support both justice and care. Land reform in Latin America to redistribute large holdings to peasant farmers offers one example. One of the most powerful advocates of democracy, Thomas Jefferson, advocated both the desirability of widespread property ownership and redistributing property via policy options such as a progressive income tax. Finally, the mixture of property forms in many Western European countries might serve as an example. While some of the major means of production are owned publicly in order to guarantee their contribution to the general welfare, other means of production are privately owned, and most citizens own property for their private use.

SATISFACTION OF BASIC HUMAN NEEDS

Proponents of an approach to justice that emphasizes the satisfaction of basic human needs justify it on both moral and practical grounds. Morally, persistent deprivation and material suffering represents a profound contradiction of values held dear by most people of the inherent value of each person, the need to protect children and other vulnerable populations, and compassion for those in need. Practically, the satisfaction of basic human needs decreases the likelihood of political disorder in forms such as crime, violence, and rebellion.

The Universal Declaration of Human Rights, adopted in 1948 by the General Assembly of the United Nations, includes rights to basic necessities for survival, in addition to the kinds of rights found in the U.S. Constitution. According to Article 25 of the declaration:

> Everyone has the right to a standard of living adequate for the health and well-being of himself and of his family, including food, clothing, housing and medical care and necessary social services, and the right to security in the event of unemployment, sickness, disability, widowhood, old age or other lack of livelihood in circumstances beyond his control.

Many countries' constitutions now include similar provisions articulating rights to food, medical attention, shelter, clothing, and other provisions deemed necessary for basic survival.

Declaring these to be fundamental human rights does not, of course, guarantee that they will actually be provided. However, it at least puts them on the public agenda, offering policy makers, judicial workers, and activists a practical foothold for organizing to ensure their adequate provision to all residents. Their exclusion from the U.S. Declaration of Independence and Constitution may be one reason why, in one of the richest countries of the world, 36 million Americans suffer shortages of food, 45 million do without medical coverage, and several million live in the streets and under bridges. The needs are even more pressing in Southern countries.

[handwritten annotation: he would make sure people of his country had food. & world Hunger support the UN.]

Justice as Fairness

John Rawls's (1921–2002) *A Theory of Justice* (1971) represents one of the most influential twentieth-century attempts to establish principles of distributive justice that would increase support for those who need it the most. Rawls attempted to move beyond the limitations of the utilitarian liberal approach to justice developed by British political economists Jeremy Bentham (1748–1832), James Mill (1773–1836), and John Stuart Mill (1806–1873) during the nineteenth century. Utilitarians seek "the greatest good for the greatest number." This principle suggests an approach to justice that aims at maximizing the welfare of as many people as possible, which gives it an egalitarian air. However, the principle coexists comfortably with radical inequality and widespread poverty, as a simple illustration will demonstrate.

Imagine a society of ten persons and an aggregate "good" of ten units. If divided equally, each person would hold one-tenth of the aggregate good, or one unit. However, in this society, as in most real societies, one person actually holds five units, and the remaining nine people share the other five. Imagine next that this society experiences an aggregate increase in prosperity, so that the ten units increase to twelve. Superficially, this makes the demands of justice easier to satisfy, since more units can now be distributed among the same number of people. However, too frequently in practice, the one wealthy person increases his share to seven units of the good, while the others still share five units. Although in aggregate this society improves, individually only one person—the one who least needs it—enjoys an improvement in welfare. Yet this increased inequality remains consistent with the principle of "the greatest good for the greatest number," because aggregate welfare increases.

Utilitarianism is also hampered by its inability to distinguish critically among competing wants, desires, and needs. All are considered subjective preferences and thus morally equivalent. Utilitarianism offers no rational basis for distinguishing between good and bad preferences, except to the degree that one produces more utility than another and that a person's actions do not directly harm another. Thus, a rich person's preference for a yacht is morally equivalent to a starving person's preference for food if they produce equal amounts of satisfaction or utility.

Rawls proposed a "difference principle" calling for steady improvement of those most in need. The difference principle "requires that all primary social goods be distributed equally unless an unequal distribution would be to everyone's advantage." Rawls accepted inequality only if it benefits everyone and stressed that "*every* party must gain from the inequality," not just some or even most. To arrive at his difference principle, Rawls began with a thought experiment analogous to the state of nature employed by Hobbes, Locke, and Rousseau. He asks us to adopt an "original position" prior to our assumption of particular identities, needs, and circumstances. The purpose of the original position is "to set up a fair procedure so that any principles agreed to will be just." We are asked in this original position to step behind a "veil of ignorance" that strips us of our particular identities and interests, so that we are not tempted "to exploit social and natural circumstances" to our advantage. Not knowing our own particular circumstances in life, Rawls reasoned, we are forced to "evaluate principles solely on the basis of general considerations" rather than specific circumstances that would bias the decisions on distributive justice toward one principle rather than another. If stripped by this veil of ignorance of our particular identities and the interests that attach to them, Rawls believed that we would rationally choose a "maximin rule" that impels us to "rank alternatives by their worst possible outcomes" and "to adopt the alternative the worst outcome of which is superior to the worst outcomes of the others."[15] This essentially conservative strategy would motivate us to adopt the difference principle as a way of protecting ourselves against worst possible outcomes.

As critics have pointed out,[16] Rawls's difference principle actually defends inequality so long as that inequality benefits everyone. In this way, it resembles supply-side economics, which endorses inequality on the grounds that it benefits everyone through the trickle-down effect.

After *A Theory of Justice* appeared in 1971, Rawls continued to shore up his argument. According to Rawls, the two justice principles that satisfy the requirements for a well-ordered society are:

1. Each person has an equal right to the most extensive scheme of equal basic liberties compatible with a similar scheme of liberties for all.
2. Social and economic inequalities are to meet two conditions: they must be (a) to the greatest expected benefit of the least advantaged and (b) attached to offices and positions open to all under conditions of fair opportunity.

The second of these two justice principles is a restatement of his earlier difference principle. For the first principle, Rawls defines "basic liberties" as "freedom of thought and liberty of conscience, freedom of the person, and political liberty," pointedly excluding "the right to own certain kinds of property (e.g., means of production), and freedom of contract as understood by the doctrine of laissez-faire." Rawls also insists that the well-ordered society that maintains his principles of justice "would attain positive freedom" as well as negative freedom.[17] Together, these mark his attempt to overcome the deficiencies of classical liberal expressions of freedom that emphasize precisely the privileges associated with property and ignore the problem of ineffective freedoms.

Adding a positive freedom component considerably tightens the requirements for a just society. It would have to be one that provides for adequate food, shelter, clothing, health care, education, and basic needs in general because, as we saw in an earlier chapter, positive freedom is impossible without these guarantees. Rawls's commitment to greater equality and to bettering the circumstances for those on the bottom socioeconomically should be apparent. If put into practice, his justice as fairness would mark a departure from the dominant trends of increasing inequality and persistent poverty and deprivation.

To Each According to Need

Many today mistakenly blame the nineteenth-century German political economist Karl Marx (1818–1883) for Stalinism in the former Soviet Union and Maoism in China. Given such unsavory associations, many people might question the validity of turning to him for inspiration on the question of justice. However, a fair appraisal of his work reveals a thinker deeply devoted to principles of justice and democracy. Though Marx wrote little explicitly about the concept of justice, his work is full of language that bears directly on questions of justice. He condemned the "naked, shameless, direct, brutal exploitation" and "subjugation" of workers under capitalism. Though he particularly concentrated on a critique of the political economy of his time, he wrote that "the exploitation of one part of society by the other" characterizes all past ages. In his time, as in previous times, workers had "nothing to lose but their chains" and "have a world to win."[18]

Marx characterized capitalist society as one in which one class lives in luxury at the expense of the majority class, which lives in relative and absolute poverty and wretchedness. He used the term *exploitation* to characterize this form of class domination. Perversely, workers generate wealth that capitalists confiscate and then use against them. The result of this systematic exploitation is concentrated wealth in the hands of the few, workers' poverty and misery, huge inequalities, and failure to meet many people's basic human needs.

In addition to this distributive injustice, Marx argued that capitalism also fails to protect the basic humanity of workers. Capitalism reduces human worth to "exchange value"—the amount each person can command in the marketplace for his or her labor. It makes workers into commodities for exchange along with other factors of production. Workers are commodities who "must sell themselves" to employers in order to survive. They are also "alienated" from the labor process and its products. The worker "becomes an appendage of the machine." Capitalists pay the workers as little as they can—just enough, wrote Marx, to maintain the workers' subsistence. The worker's wage "merely suffices to prolong and reproduce a bare existence."[19] This demeans and dehumanizes workers, who are forced to take menial and unpleasant jobs in order to survive. Workers under these conditions lack the opportunity to develop their creative capacities. Marx recognized, too, the impact of a capitalist political economy on human nature and thus its deeply ethical impact. In transforming the world, he argued, humans also transform themselves. Marx believed that the exploitative, alienating process of production under capitalism distorts human identity, forming us into shallow, ad-driven consumers rather than self-actualized and autonomous agents creating our own destiny.

Marx examined the possibility of ending exploitation by ensuring that workers received the full value of their work, rather than a subsistence value left over after capitalists extracted "surplus value." While this would be an improvement, according to Marx, it nevertheless falls short of justice as he envisioned it. Ensuring that each worker "receives back from society—after the deductions have been made—exactly what he gives to it" remains a bourgeois conception since "here obviously the same principle prevails as that which regulates the exchange of commodities." Under this bourgeois conception, the "equal right" to the fruits of one's labor remains "*proportional* to the labor they supply; the equality consists in the fact that measurement is made with an *equal standard*, labor." Since different people have different capacities for production, they will produce different amounts, resulting in inequality if everyone keeps exactly what they produce. Marx thus characterized a bourgeois conception of justice as "*a right of inequality in its content.*"

Marx also criticized this conception of distributive justice for ignoring differences of need. It fails to take account of the fact that some workers support dependents and others do not. This would magnify inequalities arising from production. To overcome these limitations of a bourgeois conception of distributive justice, Marx offered his own principle for distributive justice: "From each according to his ability, to each according to his needs!"[20] Marx's standard of justice thus emphasizes the satisfaction of all basic human needs, without qualification. To achieve this vision of justice, Marx proposed to replace a capitalist political economy, first with socialism and ultimately with communism. Both would require abolishing private property in the form of ownership of the means of production.

Critics might charge that some people do *not* deserve to have their basic needs met, because they refuse to work hard, preferring to live off the work of others. Moreover, they might argue, any political economy that guarantees basic human provisions is likely to undermine the motivation for hard work and initiative. Marx's response to this challenge emphasized that selfishness is a bourgeois construction determined by a capitalist political economy. Two points might be added. First, whatever can be said about adults' desert, no possible rationale can justify the deprivation experienced by children. They have not earned it. Every child deserves adequate food, shelter, clothing, health care, and education, period. Second, undoubtedly some adults who could work hard will refuse to do so. They will want to live parasitically on the work of others. However, there are ways of encouraging hard work and independence, ranging from the negative income tax proposed by the libertarian economist Milton Friedman (1912–) to Adam Smith's harnessing of social mores of shame and remorse to motivate socially desirable behavior.

A critic might also argue that, whatever the intellectual and moral merits of Marx's approach to justice, and deserved or not, it is wounded beyond redemption by association with Stalinism. Moreover, Marx's approach is simply too extreme to be credible. While the charge of Stalinism may be difficult to shake, the latter charge of extremism can be countered more readily by turning to a thinker whose credibility is beyond question to billions of people in the world today who identify themselves as Catholics.

Preference for the Poor

Like Marx, Pope John Paul II (1920–2005) refused to countenance anything short of meeting every person's basic human needs. He wrote several encyclicals that deal directly or indirectly with issues of justice including inequality, poverty, the exploitation of labor, and asymmetrical development.[21] According to the pope, today we are "faced with a serious problem of unequal distribution of the means of subsistence . . . [and] an unequal distribution of the benefits deriving from them." These inequalities exist within nations and among them.

John Paul II's discussion of inequality within nations can be found in his analysis of contemporary work in a capitalist political economy. He viewed human labor as a key to the question of distributive justice. Work, he wrote, "contains the unceasing measure of human toil and suffering and also of the harm and injustice which penetrate deeply into social life within individual nations and on the international level." Using language similar to that used by Marx, John Paul faulted contemporary work relations for their exploitative, dehumanizing, and alienating character.

First, he condemned the exploitation of workers, all too common in the world today, where "the direct employer fixes working conditions below the objective requirements of the workers, especially if he himself wishes to obtain the highest possible profits." Like Marx, in other words, the pope condemned the payment of wages that are too low to support a decent life. He argued that workers should be paid a living wage and offered decent working conditions. John Paul defined a living wage as "sufficient to enable him to support himself, his wife and his children." Anything less than a wage sufficient to support a family makes the worker "the victim of force and injustice." "There is something wrong," he argued, "with the organization of work and employment" when it condemns so many to exploitive working conditions and wages below subsistence level. He blamed employers for following "the principle of maximum profit" and trying to "establish the lowest possible wages for the work done by the employees."[22]

Second, John Paul criticized the framework of work within a capitalist political economy for subverting human dignity. Human life, he argued, "is built up every day from work, from work it derives its specific dignity." Human labor achieves more than instrumental ends. It is an end in itself since through work "man not only transforms nature, adapting it to his own needs, but he also achieves fulfillment as a human being and indeed in a sense becomes 'more a human being.'" All work carries an ethical dimension because "the one who carries it out is a person, a conscious and free subject, that is to say, a subject that decides about himself." Again echoing Marx, John Paul argued that labor in a capitalist system had become a mere production "input" comparable to other physical resources. It was now "understood and treated as a sort of 'merchandise' that the worker—especially the industrial worker—sells to the employer." This objectifies the worker, when instead the worker "ought to be treated as the effective subject of work and its true maker and creator." It represents a "reversal of order" that makes of the worker merely another "instrument of production." According to the pope, the dignity of work is unrelated to the specific type of work undertaken. All human labor, from sweeping streets to running corporations, should be organized to realize human dignity. This means, too, that remuneration should not be determined solely by market criteria. All work deserves remuneration sufficient to lead a decent life because "the basis for determining the value of human work is not primarily the kind of work being done, but the fact that the one who is doing it is a person."[23]

Third, Pope John Paul II condemned the alienation of workers in a capitalist system. When work is organized "to ensure maximum returns and profits with no concern whether the worker, through his own labor, grows or diminishes as a person," the inevitable result is alienation. Alienation also occurs as a result of the worker's increasing domination by technology, which "tak[es] away all personal satisfaction and the incentive to creativity and responsibility, when it deprives many workers of their previous employment or when, through exalting the machine, it reduces man to the status of its slave."[24]

The pope also condemned inequality among different countries and regions of the world and denounced the poverty forcing billions of humans into precarious living situations. Recognizing the structured, institutionalized nature of global distributive injustice, he identified as causes of underdevelopment the "economic, financial and social mechanisms which . . . often function almost automatically, thus accentuating the situation of wealth for some and poverty for the rest." Among these mechanisms, John Paul included the financial mechanisms that created the international debt crisis and maintain it; the Cold War in which the United States and the former Soviet Union turned Southern countries into pawns to be manipulated and exploited for geopolitical purposes; neocolonialism that reinforces older colonial patterns of domination; "modern imperialism" by wealthy, powerful countries; and arms production and proliferation. The mechanisms "are maneuvered directly or indirectly by the more developed countries" and thus "their very functioning favors the interest of the people manipulating them."[25] Taken together, these attributions of blame make it very clear that he held the countries of the industrialized North responsible and accountable.

In building his case for distributive justice, Pope John Paul began with a presumption of "radical interdependence" and called for "a solidarity which will take up interdependence and transfer it to the moral plane." Since this interdependence, and the solidarity built upon it, is now global in nature, "the demand for justice can only be satisfied on that level." Calling it "one of the fundamental principles of the Christian view of social and political organization," the pope identified "a preference for the poor" as the central principle underlying the demand for justice. If others' interests conflict, they should yield to the needs and interests of the poor.

To act on the principle of preference for the poor, John Paul advocated redistribution from rich to poor. He issued a "call for a leveling out and for a search for ways to ensure just development for all." This would require moving away from a narrow focus on "selfish profit" and abandoning "the all-consuming desire for profit" and the "thirst for power," to focus instead on meeting everyone's physical, cultural, social, and spiritual needs. He recognized that this would require upsetting established priorities that privilege property rights, the unchallenged rule of capital over labor, and market mechanisms that favor the rich over the poor. The pope recognized that redistribution from rich to poor would require that human rights take precedence over property rights. He accepted the legitimacy of private property, but viewed property rights as limited. "Christian tradition," he argued, "has never upheld this right as absolute and untouchable."[26]

Pope John Paul justified the priority of human over property rights, first of all, by arguing for the priority of labor over capital, a principle that "has always been taught by the church." "Capital," he argued, "should be at the service of labor and not labor at the service of capital." He believed that capitalism reversed this priority, to the detriment of workers. Even common, menial labor takes precedence over capital. Every human being who shares in the production process "even if he or she is only doing the kind of work for which no special training or qualifications are required, is the real efficient subject in this production process," while capital is "only a mere instrument subordinate to human labor." The pope acknowledged a "great conflict" between capital and labor, but unlike Marx denied that the conflict represented a fundamental contradiction. Instead, he argued, the conflict represents a historically contingent reversal of the proper order of priority of labor over capital. Any legitimate political economy, he argued, overcomes the apparent contradiction in a way that is consistent with "the principle of the substantial and real priority of labor."[27]

John Paul justified the priority of human over property rights, second, on "the universal destination of the earth's goods." By "universal destination," he meant that God intended for the Earth's resources to be available to all humans. However, when divided as asymmetrically as it is today, private property denies these resources to billions of people. Today we are "faced with a serious problem of unequal distribution of the means of subsistence originally meant for everybody, and thus also an unequal distribution of the benefits deriving from them." Under such circumstances, the right of property must yield since "the possession of material goods is not an absolute right. . . . The 'use' of goods, while marked by freedom, is subordinated to their original common destination."[28]

The pope advocated several concrete practical steps to realize in practice the principle of preference for the poor. First, he advocated the empowerment of workers via employee ownership of the means of production, participation in management, formation and strengthening of worker unions, and solidarity movements among workers.

Second, he advocated government intervention to overcome the limits of the market to achieve justice. He made the preference for the poor the guiding principle for public policy, arguing that "the more that individuals are defenseless within a given society, the more they require the care and concern of others, and in particular the intervention of governmental authority."

Government should provide for basic material needs, "conduct a just labor policy, . . . subject [property and markets] to public control, . . . ensure employment for all," and "ensure wage levels adequate for the maintenance of the worker and his family, including a certain amount of savings."

Third, the pope argued that "one cannot exclude the socialization, in suitable conditions, of certain means of production." He believed that socializing some of the means of production effectively puts property under social control and better ensures that it will be used for public, common ends that benefit everyone, not just the owners.

Fourth, John Paul called for the reform of transnational institutions to better reflect the needs and interests of the poor. He advocated reform of the international trade system to give Southern countries more access to Northern markets; reform of the world monetary and financial system, which burdens Southern countries with excessive debt and unstable currencies; technological exchanges that would put emerging tools and techniques in the hands of those who most need them; and reform of the international division of labor, which locks Southern countries into low wages and the export of low-cost products. The pope viewed these practical steps as "an imperative which obliges each and every man and woman as well as societies and nations" to work to improve the lives of the poor.[29]

What are the consequences of failing to make these changes? Since "peace is built on the foundation of justice,"[30] Pope John Paul II argued that the consequences of persistent and profound distributive injustice, both domestically and globally, include permanent disorder and a perpetual need to repress discontent and unrest. The failure to achieve greater distributive justice ensures ongoing unrest and rebellion. These represent "a just social reaction" to persistent material deprivation, exploitation, and domination of labor by capital. Ignoring the worldwide demand for justice increases "the temptation among the victims of injustice to respond with violence." Ignoring or suppressing these natural outcomes of injustice requires the development of a repressive state, as can be seen in many countries.[31]

Christian Principles of Redistribution

Most Americans draw their primary moral and ethical inspiration, if not from a Catholic pope, nevertheless from Judeo-Christian sources with which the pope is consistent. This consistency can be shown by examining the arguments of Susan Pace Hamill (1961–) in support of a progressive tax system. According to Hamill, a law professor with a graduate degree in divinity, Judeo-Christian principles require that the burden of the tax code increase as income increases and that those most able to pay, pay the highest proportion of their income. Also, a tax code consistent with Judeo-Christian ethical principles provides widely for opportunities by raising sufficient funds for education and other programs that support opportunity.

According to Hamill, three broad moral principles emerge from the Old and New Testaments that "forbid the economic oppression of low-income" people, require that "their basic needs be met," and require that "they enjoy at least a minimum opportunity to improve their economic circumstances and, consequently, their lives." From the Old Testament, Hamill cites Genesis, which teaches that, since all are created in God's image, all are equally important in God's eyes. The commandments to "love the Lord your God with all your heart and with all your soul and with all your strength" and "love your neighbor as yourself" link the proper relationship to God with the proper relationship to other humans. These require that we accept responsibility for others and their well-being, and act as our "brother's keeper." Throughout the Old Testament we find similar expressions of "special concern for vulnerable and powerless persons in the community." The Old Testament forbids economic oppression of poor people and "strongly condemns those who violate this ethical principle." It requires that the poor "enjoy a minimum opportunity to meet their basic needs and improve their economic circumstances" and once again strongly condemns those who violate this principle.[32]

The Old Testament also "creates an infrastructure providing those facing the harshest economic circumstances . . . with an opportunity to achieve economic self-sufficiency." Hamill cites provisions that require the release of servants every seven years, the forgiveness of debts every seven years, the honoring of redemption rights of land sold outside the ancestral family, and the return to the original ancestral owner every fifty years. Acknowledging the vast differences in context and the fact that the Old Testament economic structures do not easily translate into contemporary terms, Hamill nevertheless argues that these Old Testament principles are "genuinely comparable" to today's major provisions for economic opportunity in the form of public education and marketable skills. In both contexts, inadequate attention to the economic structures enabling opportunity and self-sufficiency results in persistent patterns of poverty and economic dependency.

The Old Testament also imposes on people with wealth and power—the priests, prophets, kings, and judges of ancient Israel—a special responsibility and "a greater moral obligation to maintain the general well-being of the entire community, especially a duty to protect the poor from economic oppression and to ensure that they enjoy at least a minimum opportunity to improve their economic circumstances."[33] This greater moral obligation still holds today, Hamill argues, for the contemporary versions of those with wealth and power: politicians, religious leaders, corporate leaders, and the affluent in general.

Hamill argues that the New Testament not only "affirmed and reestablished" the same general moral principles but also "clarified or even strengthened" them. She notes that Jesus himself identified with, and stood in solidarity with, "the least of these" and insisted that "the failure to serve 'the least of these' is the same as failing to serve him." Also, Jesus scathingly criticized hypocritical leaders for "devouring widows' houses," noting that widows were among the most vulnerable and least powerful persons of ancient Near East society. Finally, according to Hamill, the New Testament explicitly demands that the basic needs of the poor be met and that they enjoy at least a minimal level of economic opportunity to improve themselves. The New Testament issues specific instructions

> to share economic resources with those in need, especially those who cannot reciprocate . . . , warns those enjoying an abundance of wealth to avoid the temptation of putting their trust and loyalty in money and possessions rather than God, and makes extraordinarily costly demands on certain wealthy individuals and communities for the purpose of meeting the needs of the poor.

According to Hamill, Jesus' statement that he came "to preach good news to the poor" and "release the oppressed" suggests that Jesus demanded of his contemporaries and of us today a reform of structures and institutions to provide greater justice to the poor, vulnerable, and marginalized. She concludes that a community that operates in a manner consistent with the moral principles of Judeo-Christian ethics must foster the minimum well-being of everyone in the community and cannot be based solely on an economy driven by money and power that only guards the well-being of those with power enjoying access to sufficient money and material possessions.

Calling it a "moral responsibility," Hamill enjoins Christians to support electoral candidates who support a progressive tax system. The force of this "moral responsibility" increases along with wealth, power, and influence. Those who possess "more education, wealth, or status . . . have a greater moral responsibility to foster tax reform."[34]

Supported by supply-side economic philosophy and the ideology of radical individualism, dominant policy makers today generally oppose redistribution as a means to greater distributive justice. Supply-side economics promises gains for everyone in economic well-being without sacrifice to anyone. By reducing taxes on the wealthy, everyone will eventually benefit via trickle down, according to the theory. The individualistic framework for justice as desert excuses policy makers from redistributive action by attributing success or failure solely to the individual. Since the poor have only themselves to blame, the relatively affluent are not obliged to share.

All of the thinkers addressed above agree, first of all, that meeting everyone's basic material needs is minimally necessary for justice and, second, that achieving greater distributive justice will require redistribution of resources from the relatively affluent and powerful to the relatively poor and powerless. Using the tax code to guarantee greater distributive justice has the advantage of being simple and relatively easy to put into practice. The redistribution from rich to poor can occur directly in cash transfers or indirectly through the funding of services such as medical care and education. The same basic mechanisms for redistribution within a country can be used to redistribute globally. The rich countries can do more to ease the suffering of people in other parts of the world. Americans are accustomed to thinking of themselves as already paying a heavy burden in the form of foreign aid. Currently, however, the United States ranks dead last among industrialized countries in giving foreign aid, measured as a percentage of gross national product.

Using the tax code to guarantee greater justice also has drawbacks. Most obviously, it treats symptoms rather than causes. Also, it shares some of the disadvantages of charity, especially the possibility of lingering dependency of the poor on the rich. Far better, most people agree, that those most in need acquire the ability to satisfy their basic needs without undue reliance on others. This suggests the necessity of addressing the issue of self-determination.

JUSTICE AND SELF-DETERMINATION

Self-determination means that individuals control, within justifiable limits imposed by a social context and natural limitations, the circumstances of their own lives. These circumstances include, most obviously, the material factors that enable survival and prosperity. However, they also include most people's wish to go beyond mere survival to develop themselves and their unique capacities, to bloom into fully realized humans, and to make the most of themselves. The concept is sometimes applied to groups under the term *collective self-determination*. This refers to a particular group's ability to determine, again within reasonable social and natural limits, the circumstances of daily life for members of the group. It includes a substantial level of control, which is never absolute, over its own identity and the circumstances of everyday life.

Self-determination requires the presence of opportunities available to everyone to choose and pursue in determining the circumstances of their lives. These opportunities must be real, not simply formal. They include educational, work, career, and enrichment opportunities. Self-determination also requires the possibility and support for self-development—taking advantage of our unique capacities and developing them to their fullness. This requires more than formal or legal guarantees; it also requires the capacity to take advantage of those formal and legal guarantees, to actually act on them to develop our talents and capacities. Self-determination thus requires power, or the possession of sufficient means and resources for critically setting goals and acting on them. This crucial topic of power will be addressed at length in the final section of this book. Finally, self-determination requires the real possibility that people get what they deserve. All of the political thinkers addressed above argue that everyone deserves to have their basic material needs met. Beyond that, self-determination means that within natural and justifiable social limits, motivation and effort will be justly rewarded.

Given the limiting and partially determining social circumstances within which all people live, no person and no group possesses complete power of self-determination. To suggest otherwise would be to ignore the multiple ways that identity and behavior are socially constructed, enabled, and limited. Recognition of the way that a social context both enables and constrains our choices and our behavior directs our attention to that social context. In what specific ways, and to what degree, do existing conditions support or undermine the realization of justice? Answering this question requires that we focus attention on what Rawls called the "basic structure" of society to evaluate how supportive it is of individual and collective self-determination. In the following sections, three defining elements of this basic structure will be addressed: a political economy of capitalism, democracy, and power.

QUESTIONS, PROBLEMS, AND ACTIVITIES

1. Give other examples of social structures, and analyze them in terms of the characteristics of social structures. Draw one or two of them, keeping in mind that social structures both enable and constrain.
2. Apply the concept of institutional racism to two issues not covered in this text. Can you think of examples of institutional sexism?
3. Should public policy be informed by an ethic of care? What would this mean in concrete terms?
4. Do you agree that "Mr. Heinz" is justified in stealing cancer medication to save his wife's life? Can you think of other circumstances where property rights should be, or should not be, set aside in order to protect one or more lives?
5. Develop a simulation that illustrates the problem of bargaining among unequals.
6. Brainstorm ways of ensuring that everyone's basic material needs are met. Which of these, if any, would require others' sacrifice? What specific sacrifices, by whom, would be necessary? Are they worth it?
7. Some people believe that terrorism arises out of real or perceived injustices and an effective strategy for countering terrorism would take this into account. Do you agree? What are the implications of your answer for U.S. foreign policy?
8. What are the implications for Native American collective self-determination of sports team names such as the Cleveland Indians, the Washington Redskins, and the Atlanta Braves?
9. To what degree is your life self-determined? Discuss ways, if any, that others determine the circumstances of your life. Which, if any, of these other determinants are justifiable?

NOTES

1. Earl Babbie, *What Is Society? Reflections on Freedom, Order, and Change* (Thousand Oaks, CA: Pine Forge Press, 1994), p. 35; emphasis in original.

2. Stokely Carmichael and Charles Hamilton, *Black Power: The Politics of Liberation in America* (New York: Vintage Books, 1967), pp. 4–5.

3. Angela Davis, *Women, Culture, and Politics* (New York: Vintage Books, 1990), p. 31.

4. Angela Davis, "Political Prisoners, Prisons, and Black Liberation" [1971], in *The Angela Y. Davis Reader*, ed. Joy James (Oxford: Blackwell, 1998), pp. 45–46, 49.

5. Angela Davis, "Race and Criminalization: Black Americans and the Punishment Industry" [1997], in James, *Angela Y. Davis Reader*, pp. 62, 72; Davis, "Political Prisoners," pp. 45, 49, 47.

6. Plato, *The Republic* 1.433b, 1.434b–c, 1.441e–442a.

7. Augustine, *City of God*, abridged version from the translation by Gerald G. Walsh et al., edited by Vernon J. Bourke (A.D. 426; Garden City, NY: Image Books, 1958), pp. 456, 454, 469, 75.

8. Carol Gilligan, *In a Different Voice: Psychological Theory and Women's Development* (Cambridge: Harvard University Press, 1982), p. 18.

9. Ibid., pp. 17, 19.

10. Ibid., pp. 1, 149, 16–17, 2.

11. Virginia Held, "The Meshing of Care and Justice," *Hypatia* 10, no. 2 (Spring 1995): pp. 131, 129.

12. Joan Tronto, *Moral Boundaries* (New York: Routledge, 1993), pp. x, 178, 9.

13. Thomas Hobbes, *Leviathan* (1651; New York: Penguin Books, 1968), part 1, chap. 13, pp. 183–88; part 1, chap. 15, pp. 201–3; part 2, chap. 18, p. 234.

14. Annette Baier, "Trust and Antitrust," *Ethics* 96, no. 2 (January 1986), pp. 248, 249.

15. John Rawls, *A Theory of Justice* (Cambridge, MA: Belknap Press of Harvard University Press, 1971), pp. 150, 137, 152–53; John Rawls, "Justice as Fairness," *Philosophical Review* 67 (1958): p. 167; emphasis in original.

16. See Marcellus Andrews, " "Liberty *and* Equality *and* Diversity? Thoughts on Liberalism and Racial Inequality after Capitalism's Latest Triumph," in *Race, Liberalism, and Economics*, ed. David Colander, Robert Prasch, and Falguni Sheth (Ann Arbor: University of Michigan Press, 2004), p. 227; and G. A. Cohen, *If You're an Egalitarian, How Come You're So Rich?* (Cambridge: Harvard University Press, 2000), pp. 117–33, 120–29.

17. John Rawls, "A Well-Ordered Society," in *In Defense of Human Dignity*, ed. Robert Kraynak and Glenn Tinder (Notre Dame, IN: University of Notre Dame Press, 2003), pp. 197, 199, 204–5.

18. Karl Marx, *The Communist Manifesto*, ed. Frederic L. Bender (1848; New York: W. W. Norton, 1988), pp. 58, 70, 74, 86.

19. Marx, *Communist Manifesto*, pp. 57, 61, 68–69.

20. Karl Marx, *A Critique of the Gotha Programme* [1875], in *Karl Marx and Frederick Engels: Selected Works* (Moscow: Progress Publishers, 1970), vol. 3, pp. 17–19.

21. See, for example, John Paul II, *Laborem Exercens* (On human work), *Origins* 11, no. 15 (September 24, 1981); John Paul II, *Sollicitudo Rei Socialis* (Encyclical on social concerns), *Origins* 17, no. 38 (March 3, 1988); and John Paul II, *Centesimus Annus* (On the 100th anniversary [of Pope Leo XIII's *Rerum Novarum*]), *Origins* 21, no. 1 (May 16, 1991).

22. John Paul II, *Sollicitudo Rei Socialis*, p. 645; John Paul II, *Laborem Exercens*, pp. 227, 237, 238, 233; John Paul II, *Centesimus Annus*, p. 5.

23. John Paul II, *Laborem Exercens*, pp. 227, 232, 230.

24. John Paul II, *Centesimus Annus*, p. 16; John Paul II, *Laborem Exercens*, p. 229.

25. John Paul II, *Sollicitudo Rei Socialis*, pp. 646–49, 654.

26. Ibid., pp. 649, 645, 656, 652, 653; John Paul II, *Centesimus Annus*, p. 6; John Paul II, *Laborem Exercens*, pp. 228, 235.

27. John Paul II, *Laborem Exercens*, pp. 233, 241, 234.

28. John Paul II, *Centesimus Annus*, pp. 5, 12; John Paul II, *Sollicitudo Rei Socialis*, p. 645.

29. John Paul II, *Laborem Exercens*, pp. 231, 237–38, 235; John Paul II, *Centesimus Annus*, pp. 6, 7; John Paul II, *Sollicitudo Rei Socialis*, pp. 656, 652.

30. John Paul II, *Centesimus Annus*, p. 4.

31. While Pope John Paul II's writings on political economy steadfastly advocate greater justice, some of his stances on homosexuality and the role and status of women undermine it. On the one hand, he supported protection for working mothers, equal pay for equal work, and fairness in career advancements; criticized the emphasis on female external beauty at the expense of intellect and ability; and opposed the use of women's bodies for commercial purposes. However, his opposition to abortion, birth control, and female priests, coupled with his insistence on women's special status as wives, mothers, and handmaidens, reinforce women's submission to men in private and public domains. His designation of homosexuals as "disordered" and homosexuality as an "intrinsic moral evil," positions abandoned long ago in the field of psychology, undermine full acceptance and rights for gay, lesbian, bisexual, and transgender persons. These positions compromise the attainment of full respect and autonomy for women and homosexuals. See John Paul II, "Letter to Women," *Origins* 25, no. 9 (July 27, 1995), and "Letter to the Bishops of the Catholic Church on the Pastoral Care of Homosexual Persons," a letter written by Joseph Cardinal Ratzinger (later John Paul's successor as Pope Benedict XVI) and approved by Pope John Paul II on October 1, 1986, available at http://www.dignityusa.org/1986doctrine/ratzinger.html.

32. Susan Pace Hamill, "An Argument for Tax Reform Based on Judeo-Christian Ethics," *Alabama Law Review* (Fall 2002): pp. 4, 14.

33. Ibid., p. 15.

34. Ibid., pp. 15–16, 4.

IV

DEMOCRACY
AND CAPITALISM

7

An Unhappy Marriage

Democracy is often wrongly viewed in either-or terms. Like a light switch that is either turned on or off, a country is either democratic or it is not. However, democracy is better viewed as a continuum ranging from completely undemocratic to completely democratic. The United States, like all other countries, can be positioned somewhere along this continuum. The degree to which the United States, or any other country, is democratic is an empirical question of existing practices measured against an ideal of democracy drawn from the history of democratic theory and practice. Though there may be many things to admire about the U.S. system of government and about the United States in general, its practice of democracy falls well short of the ideal. This section will address one primary reason offered by democratic theorists why this is so: Americans have attempted to wed democracy with capitalism. And it has been an unhappy marriage in which the demands of capitalism have often taken precedence over the demands of democracy.

A textbook definition of capitalism emphasizes two components of political economy. First, private individuals and entities own the means of production, those resources used to produce other goods and services. Owners control the decisions and operations under which economic activity occurs. Second, goods and services are allocated via markets, which can be thought of as mechanisms for exchange. These components of capitalism can better be appreciated in contrast with socialism. Socialism in its textbook form entails public rather than private ownership of the means of production, and allocation occurs via central planning rather than through markets. Generally, the public owns the means of production through the instrument of the government, which holds the property rights and controls operations in the name of the people. Bureaucrats make allocative decisions by setting goals for supply and demand and then controlling production and distribution to meet those goals.

We can distinguish further between two different kinds of capitalism. Proponents of *free market capitalism* celebrate the role of markets in allocating resources, producing economic growth, and promoting freedom. Free market capitalism allots government a minimal role of protecting property rights, enforcing contracts, managing the supply of money, providing a narrow set of public goods such as national defense, and handling a limited range of side effects produced by markets. A second type of capitalism, *mercantilist capitalism*, involves more cooperation and coordination between the government and economic entities, including large corporations and sometimes entire sectors of the economy. The government proactively supports and advances business interests through cooperative planning, corporate welfare, and policies such as tariffs and subsidies that protect domestic business interests. Both types of capitalism pursue similar goals of increasing economic growth, improving the profitability of domestic corporations and businesses, and ensuring the stability of financial markets.

The United States today pursues a mix of free market and mercantilist strategies. When it appears to advance U.S. business interests, the U.S. government promotes free markets domestically and abroad. But when American businesses call for assistance and protection, the U.S. government often heeds the call by providing corporate welfare and establishing tariffs and quotas to protect domestic manufacturers against foreign competitors. Both free market and mercantilist capitalism allow extensive negative freedom for individuals in economic endeavors. For many people, the promise of wealth acts as a powerful goad to economic enterprise and to economic striving. This contributes to the dynamic character of capitalism, a dynamism equally admired by supporters and critics. Capitalism has also delivered relative material prosperity for a global minority of humans.

Most economies today are mixed forms blending elements of capitalism and socialism. Most socialist countries have abandoned the principle of central planning, partly in response to the dismal record of such countries as the former Soviet Union. Instead, these countries have adopted a blended political economy called *market socialism*. While some of the major means of production are publicly owned and controlled, allocative decisions are made primarily via markets. Most Scandinavian countries, Germany, France, and other Western European countries today can be characterized as market socialist countries. Though typically viewed as socialist, China has in recent years moved aggressively toward the adoption of market principles and increasingly allows some private ownership of the means of production.

On the other hand, though typically characterized as capitalist, the United States' political economy contains some elements of socialism. For example, the government owns and controls a large portion of the means of postal distribution—the U.S. Postal Service—but operates it largely according to market principles. Many utilities are publicly owned. The U.S. government also sometimes uses central planning in areas such as the defense industry, where production relies almost entirely on the planning decisions made by the U.S. Department of Defense.

Every political economy requires making tradeoffs that influence the kinds and degrees of freedom that individuals enjoy. While the United States offers more negative freedom for owners of the means of production than do most socialist or market socialist countries, most socialist and market socialist countries offer more positive freedom in the form of access to basic human necessities for everyone. Also, socialist and market socialist countries are no more likely than capitalist countries to interfere with individuals' use of purely personal property such as homes, household goods, and automobiles.

Readers might wonder how communism fits into this discussion. The simple answer is that it does not. The idea of communism predated Karl Marx (1818–1883), who saw it as an ideal end point of historical evolution beginning in feudalism, passing through both capitalism and socialism, and culminating in communism when the state "withers away." Marx barely developed the details of this ideal, leaving it for the participants in historical struggle to work out the details as befitting specific circumstances. However, he gave clues indicating that he viewed it as a society consisting of voluntary and cooperative relations that would supplant the coercion of the state. Human work would be more creative and satisfying than the exploitative, alienating, and dehumanizing work that he observed. Human relations in general would be democratically ordered, and individuals would enjoy extensive freedom.

This utopian vision stands in sharp contrast to the repressive statist regimes that actually emerged during the twentieth century under the name of communism. In the former Soviet Union, the process of historical evolution became mired in a brutal, bureaucratic form of socialism. Rather than withering away, the state grew into an apparatus for extensive coercion and repression. In China, so-called communism represents a distinctive form of bureaucratic socialism indebted more to Confucius and the revolutionary Chinese leader Mao Zedong than to Karl Marx.

PUBLIC PROBLEMS

Invisible Hand or Invisible Fist?

Earlier chapters addressed ways that Adam Smith's (1723–1790) "invisible hand" metaphor insufficiently accounts for collectively destructive outcomes of individual self-interested behavior, and ways that markets sometimes imprison policy by forcing unpleasant choices upon policy makers. This section addresses a third set of issues. The invisible hand metaphor suggests that markets are the realm of freedom, where individuals freely pursue their self-interests, impeded only by a meddlesome government. It implies that markets themselves are not coercive. However, markets are infused throughout with the possession and exercise of power that favors some while punishing others, that awards extensive freedom to some while constraining others, and that enables a wide range of choice for some while diminishing choice for others. To the degree that this is true, we should consider an alternative metaphor that often more accurately characterizes the operation of markets: the invisible fist.[1]

Milton Friedman (1912–), an influential contemporary libertarian economist, defends capitalism in terms reminiscent of Smith. His *Capitalism and Freedom* (1962) presents "a leading economist's view of the proper role of competitive capitalism." As suggested by the title, his defense of capitalism emphasizes (negative) freedom while leaving both democracy and equality almost unmentioned. Friedman's central argument in the book is that "competitive capitalism"—which he defines as "the organization of the bulk of economic activity through private enterprise operating in a free market"—is both "a system of economic freedom and a necessary condition for political freedom." Competitive capitalism enables political freedom, Friedman argues, because "it separates economic power from political power and in this way enables the one to offset the other." Economic power checks political power, much the same way that the U.S. Constitution uses one institutional power to check another. Friedman endorses this because government "substitutes coercion for voluntary co-operation" and thus poses a threat to freedom.

Friedman defines *freedom* in classical liberal terms as "the absence of coercion." People express their freedom through participation in markets that are not—by definition, according to Friedman—coercive. Friedman equates the market with voluntary cooperation and free choice. People choose freely and voluntarily to participate in a market, or not. In the labor market, this means that workers participate freely in labor exchanges because they have the power of exit: they can take their labor elsewhere, thus guaranteeing their freedom. An employee is thus "protected from coercion by the employer because of other employers for whom he can work." Similarly, people can choose freely and voluntarily to participate or not in consumer markets, and they can select among various consumer options without being coerced. In contrast to markets, according to Friedman, governments are coercive by definition, so they must be minimized in size and role. "The great threat to freedom," Friedman wrote, "is the concentration of power." Like other classical and neoclassical liberals, however, Friedman is only concerned with concentrations of *political* power as represented by government. The obvious way to prevent abuses of political power is thus to limit the reach of government, and Friedman prescribes this throughout.[2]

As we saw in a previous chapter, free choice requires autonomy, critical awareness of one's best interests, access to undistorted information about a full range of options, and freedom from undue vicarious influence. These requirements are deliberately undermined in a capitalist market economy in which the mass media bombard consumers with images and messages designed precisely to manipulate their identity and behavior.

We also saw earlier that freedom requires the presence of viable alternatives. Friedman himself recognizes this, arguing that exchange via a market is voluntary "only when nearly equivalent alternatives exist."[3] In a market economy, the presence or absence of viable alternatives depends very much on how much money a person controls. A millionaire enjoys many more viable options than a person with little or no money. The millionaire can select from myriad attractive options for career, home, leisure, and lifestyle, while the person with no money must choose between sleeping under a bridge or in an abandoned building, and dining at a local soup kitchen or a restaurant dumpster. Similarly, the millionaire can opt out of the labor market entirely and live off investments, while the person of limited means faces the option of flipping burgers or starving. Without money, participation in most markets is at best limited to a few, often unattractive, viable options. At worst, the lack of money makes participation in markets impossible. Millions starve because they have too little money to participate as consumers in a food market.

Moreover, markets sometimes actively eliminate viable options. Each time a corporation responds to market pressures by relocating to China, it takes jobs with it, decreasing domestic options for employment. In some urban neighborhoods, market forces tear out affordable housing, decreasing the living options for low-income residents. Markets may further distort available options as people with significant financial resources systematically bid up the price of items that others need, but cannot afford, and divert production away from the provision of basic necessities for everyone.

According to Friedman, markets offer anyone wishing to participate in a market "full co-operation on equal terms to all." His "equal terms" means simply that the rules of property ownership and control apply equally to everyone, and that one person's dollar is as good as another's. In practice, this means again that individuals with lots of money wield more market power than those without money. It is a recipe, in short, for inequality of outcome. His principle of distributive justice reflects this. In an obvious play on Marx's words, it reads "to each according to what he and the instruments he owns produces." This does not involve the government at all except in guaranteeing property rights and the enforcement of contracts. Friedman acknowledged that such a principle of distributive justice "can be, and in practice is, characterized by considerable inequality of income and wealth." As a principle of distributive justice, it practically guarantees the privilege of the wealthy, and it offers little or nothing for those on the other end of the economic continuum, the impoverished.

Friedman also argued that businesses and corporations should resist any temptation to incorporate concerns for justice since business has only one responsibility: "to use its resources and engage in activities designed to increase its profits." Any "acceptance by corporate officials of a social responsibility other than to make as much money for their stockholders as possible . . . is a fundamentally subversive doctrine."[4] In short, Friedman simultaneously denies a role for government in seeking justice, beyond guaranteeing property rights and enforcing contracts, and at the same time denies that businesses and corporations should concern themselves with issues of justice. Justice in any sense more meaningful than property rights disappears from view. Like equality or democracy itself, it is of little concern to Friedman.

By defining government as the sole realm of coercion, Friedman is unable to appreciate the power wielded through markets and its impact on human freedom. Each time markets limit a person's choices, freedom is diminished. Each time a corporation imprisons policy makers' choices, citizens' freedom to determine the circumstances of their lives is compromised. We should conclude not that markets are inherently undemocratic but that markets, like governments, represent coercive power that citizens in a democracy can legitimately seek to control.

Domination, Exploitation, and Alienation

The relation between labor and capital defines the most fundamental social relationship in a capitalist political economy. Under capitalism, no pretense of democracy is made of this relationship. Rather, it is a straightforward relation of domination of capital over labor. By virtue of its ownership of the means of production, capital controls and exercises power over labor. Ownership confers on owners the right of exclusive use and control of economic resources. Owners can offer or withhold employment. They can remain in one community or country, or move to another. They can enforce "no trespassing" rules on land they control, even in a context of starvation where access to the land would enable the desperate poor to grow food. Owners of capital are independent, to a very large degree, of constraints imposed by communities and governments. Taken together, these privileges confer on owners of capital the ability to significantly determine the circumstances of most people's lives.

Since capital owns the means of production, labor almost always finds itself at a disadvantage in relation to it. When negotiating working conditions and wage and benefit levels, the capitalist can usually drive a harder bargain than can labor. Most workers depend on a weekly paycheck, while capitalists often hold cash reserves on which they can live, sometimes indefinitely. Also, if faced with an intransigent labor force, the capitalist can simply reinvest elsewhere, wherever the labor force agrees to work under conditions preferred by the capitalist. In an increasingly globalized economy, this often means offshore and overseas in Southern countries. Facing the real threat of unemployment, labor often must acquiesce. Its only other option, a mixed blessing at best since it means loss of income, is to withhold its labor power. Although workers are always free to leave a place of employment if the terms of employment are unsatisfactory, their actual effective freedom depends on the existence of other options for decent employment. Workers enjoy no right to employment. Instead they secure employment or not according to the vagaries of the market, at terms dictated by the market.

This power imbalance between labor and capital has been partially offset by government intervention since the late nineteenth century, resulting in laws to protect labor from unsafe working conditions, from exceptionally long workdays and workweeks, and from other forms of abuse. The degree to which the government enforces these worker protections ebbs and flows along with the economy and according to the relative sympathy of succeeding political administrations. Moreover, the government is at least as likely, and often more likely, to intervene on the side of capital against labor. A primary role of the state in a capitalist political economy is to service the needs of capital by safeguarding property rights, enforcing contracts, creating a legal environment conducive to business, providing corporate welfare, and dispatching the CIA and the Marines when necessary to protect U.S. investments abroad. Globalization has increased the difficulty of protecting workers and their rights by increasing the likelihood that capital will simply flee significant attempts to undermine its power, relocating to other countries. Unions also partially offset the power of capital through collective bargaining. However, capitalists employ various means of avoiding unions or undermining their power. The declining influence of unions can be partly measured by the decline in union membership from approximately one-fourth of the workforce in the early 1970s to around 14 percent in 2000.[5]

The dominance of capital over labor might be justifiable if the interests of capital and labor systematically converged, but in general they do not. Most obviously, capital seeks to maximize profits, which entails minimizing costs. Labor represents a cost in a capitalist political economy, like energy and equipment, and so capital naturally seeks to minimize it. By contrast, labor wishes to maximize its wage-and-benefit package. The more that capital wins this battle, the more profit it extracts from labor. Karl Marx called this extraction of profit from workers "exploitation" since, in his view, all profit represents the theft from labor of value they created.

The interests of capital and labor also diverge over issues of working conditions. Profit increases along with the productivity of workers, so capital seeks increases in productivity via an increasing division of labor. An assembly line, where each worker does the same relatively few movements and work tasks repeatedly throughout the workday, represents a quintessential example. Worker productivity increases, but the quality of the worker's day diminishes commensurately as each worker sees less and less of the big picture, plays a progressively smaller role in production, and gradually cedes nearly complete control over the production process to capital and the managers employed by capital to achieve its goals. Marx addressed this characteristic of advanced capitalist economies in terms of the concept of alienation. He noted the increasing objectification of workers in the production process, reducing them to the status of any other commodity. As mere commodities, workers lose their status as free, autonomous, moral agents. Capitalists purchase them like they do a building or a machine, pay them as little as market conditions allow, and discard them when they are no longer useful or profitable.

Alienation takes different forms. First, the worker is alienated from the product of labor. It confronts the workers "as *something alien*, as a power independent of the producer." Having lost control of the production process, and seeing only a small part of it, the worker naturally sees the final product as something distant and separate. The worker cannot identify with the product in the same way as an artisan, who controls the entire process from conception and design through final production. The more the worker produces, "the more powerful becomes the alien world of objects which he creates over and against himself, the poorer he himself—his inner world—becomes, [and] the less belongs to him as his own."

Second, the worker is alienated from the act of production. Capitalist production forces workers into dehumanizing practices that deny innate creativity and require the submission of human worth to the production process. The worker's labor reflects the needs and interests of somebody else—the capitalist. In this context, workers hardly embrace their work as an essential expression of their being. Marx concluded that the worker's labor "is therefore not voluntary, but coerced; it is *forced labor*. It is . . . a labor of self-sacrifice, of mortification."[6]

Third, the worker is alienated from the possibility that work could be fulfilling, an end in itself, not just a means that must be tolerated. Workers submit to mind-numbing toil in order to survive, not because their work excites and satisfies them.

Fourth, the worker is alienated from other workers against whom each worker must compete for the same jobs, the same promotions, and the same favors. It forces on workers selfishness, competitiveness, and indifference to others and undermines their ability to treat each other with respect and in solidarity.

Finally, according to Marx, the worker is alienated from nature, which, like the worker, is treated as an object. Nature and its resources exist as a source of plunder, something to be exploited for profit. This inevitably creates a divide between humans and their natural environments and makes possible the mistreatment of the environment.

While not all work today is as alienating as Marx saw it, much of it is. Disemboweling chickens on an assembly line makes for good profit, but at a steep cost in terms of the quality of work. Much service work, the most rapidly expanding area of employment in the last three decades, numbs mind and body alike. "The customer is always right" may be good for business and profit, but it requires that employees sometimes swallow their pride and sacrifice their dignity, as any experienced service worker can attest. Ironically, the most ugly, demeaning work often pays the least. However, professional jobs can also take their toll in stress, long hours, and a competitive, abusive work environment.

Capitalist Ethics

Like any social system, capitalism embodies a set of values. Proponents argue that capitalism embodies values of hard work, personal initiative, and independence. Hard work is indeed a central feature of capitalism, some of it fueled by positive incentives to succeed, but some of it also by desperation and suffering. Similarly, personal initiative in the form of entrepreneurialism sometimes creates new productive directions in the economy, resulting in economic growth and the creation of new jobs. On the other hand, personal initiative may result in the "creative destruction" noted by Joseph Schumpeter in which entire communities and ways of life are destroyed. It may result in lost productivity as new businesses fail. It sometimes also results in punishment when initiated by nonsupervisory workers who are expected to obey orders within narrow parameters. And capitalism enables financial independence for many, though it also produces financial insecurity for millions of Americans and billions of others globally who experience endemic financial dependence, uncertain employment prospects, and material insecurity and deprivation.

Neoclassical economists endorse free market capitalism because they believe that it advances the goal of efficiency, for them a top value. An efficient economy produces goods and services using as few human, natural, and technical resources as possible and with as little waste as possible. In theory, this minimizes costs to consumers while maximizing profit and protecting the environment. However, in practice the goal of efficiency can undermine important values such as caring for the environment. Firms can achieve greater efficiency in the short term by dumping toxic waste into the river or forgoing pollution control technology. The quest for greater efficiency also can undermine worker dignity and self-fulfillment. Since efficiency entails minimizing inputs, including labor, eliminating labor or increasing its productivity serves the goal of efficiency. Eliminating labor leads to economic insecurity and unemployment for workers. And while increasing productivity can benefit everyone if productivity increases translate into increased wages and not simply into increased profit, it can also magnify exploitation of workers.

The pursuit of greater productivity leads to practices such as "Taylorism," named after Frederick Taylor, a former steel company foreman who in the early twentieth century broke production down into minute parts, analyzed each job, and developed a system of "scientific management" emphasizing detailed division of labor, extensive use of technology and machinery, and piecework wage systems. Taylorism gave management greater ability to micromanage workers in the pursuit of increased efficiency, production, and profits. The costs to workers, measured in terms of the quality of work, have been steep. Taylorism increases the dehumanization of work, further transforms humans into interchangeable and impersonal commodities in a production process, and further purges labor of its creative and fulfilling aspects.

Profit ranks as the top value of a capitalist firm, because without it there can be no capital accumulation needed for investment and no survival of the firm. The goal of profit can and often does override other important ethical values, such as providing secure employment for heads of households, protecting the environment, paying a living wage, and maintaining stable communities. The quest for profit also sometimes leads to excesses and abuses such as the Enron and WorldCom accounting scandals of 2002–2003 in which top managers misled investors in order to protect profit.

If profit is good, more profit is better. This can quickly translate into greed. Many defenders of capitalism affirm rather than deny greed, celebrating it as an engine of dynamism, growth, and innovation. Without greed, they argue, there would be no motivation for striving and for taking risks, two essential ingredients of a dynamic free enterprise system. Greed keeps both capitalists and labor working hard to increase their profits and their income.

Like profit, more consumption is always better than less in a capitalist political economy. Consumption drives production, and if consumption lags, so must production since there is no point in producing goods and services if no one buys them. Even a mild slowdown in consumption produces ripple effects, felt throughout the economy, that reduce profitability, increase unemployment, and potentially lead to recession. This consumption imperative leads to the so-called pig principle: more is always better. The more people consume, the more labor can be employed, and the more profit can be extracted from the process. Producers thus invest billions annually inducing people to go shopping.

The results of this consumption include, first of all, pressures on the environment. To keep up with Americans' appetite for hamburgers, Costa Ricans level their rain forest to make way for cattle grazing. To satisfy Americans' preference for SUVs, coastal areas must absorb oil spills such as the Alaskan Valdez spill. To fuel energy turbines, mining companies level entire mountains to extract the coal. Excessive consumption also results in the commodification and commercialization of all life. Businesses bombard potential consumers with sales pitches at every turn, from highway billboards to product placement in movies to airwaves saturated with advertisements. According to critics, this infects even art, culture, and spirituality, degrading the human spirit and crowding out more creative, ennobling pursuits and interests. Americans also pay a steep price for their consumption habits in terms of loss of leisure. Anthropologists now claim that prehistoric humans enjoyed more leisure than do contemporary residents of the United States and similar countries, who work long hours in order to support their consumption habits.[7]

Competition also ranks highly in the hierarchy of capitalist values. Competition occurs among different producers and sellers who compete against each other for sales and profit. In the theory of competitive capitalism, this forces producers to operate efficiently in order to maintain low prices relative to other producers. Workers also compete against each other for jobs, for higher salaries and benefits, for promotions, and for perquisites. In a competitive context, each individual must do whatever necessary to ensure survival and to guarantee success. Absent guarantees from others or the government, each person must sink or swim through individual effort. Although most Americans routinely look out for each other within individual families, survival and prosperity for most people require that self-interest gain a prominent position in the hierarchy of values. And like greed, supporters of capitalism either implicitly condone self-interest or celebrate it as an inducement for hard work.

Critics of capitalism note that profit, greed, self-interest, competition, efficiency, and acquisitiveness are hardly the values celebrated from the pulpit, which is one good place to look for the values that most people explicitly recognize and cherish. They note that most Americans claim to adhere to spiritual values such as love, compassion, generosity, charity, and the inherent dignity of every human. These values exist, at best, in tension with the central values of capitalism. Critics also point out that the same tension exists between capitalist values and democracy, whose moral meaning emphasizes the inherent dignity of every person and the full realization of every person's unique capacities. Treating humans as discardable commodities, they argue, cannot be reconciled with a view of humans as autonomous moral agents with inherent worth. These spiritual and democratic values suggest that every person deserves to satisfy his or her basic human needs, to work in a satisfying job that pays a living wage, and to be treated with dignity rather than as a commodity to discard if convenient and profitable. As Friedman argued, capitalism shuns these kinds of commitments in favor of profit. Those who seek to achieve these other ethical goals must work outside the framework of capitalism through government and private programs and charities. Since values such as compassion and generosity can gain no secure foothold within capitalism, they must be applied, if at all, in family and religious realms.

Proponents of capitalism defend this shifting of nobler ethical values to other realms. Like political realists who embrace a sole focus on power and interest in political realms, these economic realists embrace selfishness, greed, cutthroat competition, and materialism, arguing that ethical considerations may apply in other realms but not in economics. However, critics note, selfishness, greed, cutthroat competition, and materialism *are* ethical values, just not the ones that most Americans claim to hold dear. Embracing these ethical commitments drives others to the sideline. In effect, according to critics, we are taught to be kind unless it undermines profit; to be generous unless it requires taxes or regulations; to be compassionate unless it hinders the goal of reducing the payroll; to be an active citizen unless it gets in the way of shopping or undermines corporate sovereignty. The separation of realms is an intellectual artifice derived from the liberal segmentation of social space that is difficult, and perhaps impossible, to sustain in practice. Other proponents of capitalism claim that spiritual and democratic values *can* be applied within the framework of capitalism. Although at times this may be true, capitalism at its competitive best makes this a very dubious option, especially in an economically globalized world where compassion and generosity too often result in bankruptcy.

Capitalism, like all other social institutions, induces people to behave in certain ways by responding rationally to the system's incentives. It rewards certain traits while punishing others. And in inducing people to behave in certain ways, it actively forms identities in its own image. We become the things we do. If we opt repeatedly for consumption, we become consumers. If we routinely choose self-interest over the needs of others, we become selfish. Neoconservative Irving Kristol (1920–) acknowledged this conclusion, arguing that capitalism deserves two cheers, but not the third, because of its distorting impact on human development. According to Kristol, capitalism promises material wealth, individual freedom, and "self-perfection—for leading a virtuous life that satisfie[s] the demands of his spirit . . . and that the free exercise of such individual virtue would aggregate into a just society." Kristol believed that capitalism has delivered on the first two but not the third, individual virtue leading to a just society. According to him, capitalism itself "subverted" the third promise by severing the "will to success and privilege . . . from its moral moorings." He argued that capitalism instead has led to "infantile regression" in which selfishness supplants other cherished values.[8]

Making the World Safe for Capitalism

Imperialism is the name given to attempts by one country to expand its territory and influence using aggression, conquest, and violence. Imperialism undermines key values of democracy, especially the freedom, equality, and popular sovereignty of conquered peoples. It also undermines democracy in the imperial power, as power tends to concentrate, and become unaccountable, in the hands of a political and military elite that controls and directs the power. This elite typically maintains a great deal of secrecy within a highly militarized state and often manipulates and controls the knowledge necessary for informed and critical decision making in a democracy.

Is capitalism any more or less prone to imperial tendencies than other forms of political economy? On the one hand, capitalists want peace in order to ensure that business and the flow of profits continue without interruption. Over time, this builds cooperative relations among people of different countries. This can continue so long as it guarantees the mutual satisfaction of national and corporate interests. On the other hand, precisely because capitalists want to ensure the flow of profits, capitalism sometimes breeds expansion, aggression, and violence in order to protect and increase profits. If peace and nonaggression result in diminished profits or lost opportunities for profits, capitalists may harness the instruments of state to ensure profits using whatever means necessary. V. I. Lenin (1870–1924), leader of the Bolshevik Revolution in Russia in 1917, offered one explanation for this.

Lenin called imperialism "the highest stage of capitalism," because for him it represented the logical, culminating expansionist movement of capital overseas and abroad in order to make up for declining profit at home. He attributed the tendency toward declining profit to oversupply–underconsumption crises created by the logic of capitalism in which owners of capital drive wages as low as possible to maximize their profit, but in doing so undermine the purchasing power of labor needed to consume the products created by capitalists. This creates a mismatch of supply and demand in which the system produces more than the workers can consume. Technology exacerbates this contradiction when machines are substituted for human labor in the production process. These mismatches of supply and demand lead to familiar boom-and-bust business cycles in the forms of periodic recessions and depressions. At some point, capital saturates domestic markets, leaving owners of capital with no choice but to seek investment opportunities abroad. This surplus capital "will be used for the purpose of increasing those profits by exporting capital abroad to the backward countries" where profit is high due to the relative scarcity of capital and the cheapness of labor, land, and raw materials. Lenin called this export of capital to Southern countries a "necessity" of late capitalism, arising from the fact that in advanced capitalist countries "capitalism has become 'over-ripe.' . . . Capital cannot find 'profitable' investment" without opening new markets.[9]

Capitalists faced with declining domestic profits and seeking new sources of profit abroad naturally seek the active support of their home states. Since the health of the nation is tied to the health of its economy, the state tends to respond favorably. Some scholars distinguish between instrumentalist and structural views of the state. According to the instrumentalist view, wealthy elites seize control of the state in order to use it to advance their financial and strategic interests. They conspire to seize political power in order to protect their business interests at home and abroad. They back sympathetic candidates, or run for office themselves, in order to secure the political power they need to take control. Once in power, the elites use force to the extent necessary to secure and maintain profit. This may include covert and overt support for sympathetic regimes, including sympathetic dictators. It may also include covert and overt attempts to undermine and destabilize unsympathetic regimes, including unsympathetic democratic regimes. If necessary, it may even include outright invasion in regions where their profits are threatened. One need not adopt this conspiratorial instrumentalist theory of the state to recognize that the state often intervenes in foreign affairs on behalf of business and commercial interests.

According to the alternative structural view, policy makers over time adopt goals and strategies that coincide with the interests of capital, not necessarily because they conspire with capitalists to advance capitalists' interests but because they more broadly view the interests of business as indistinguishable from the larger national interest. Rather than a sole focus on profit, this explanation adds explanatory elements such as ideology, strategic interests, and the national interest that compel much the same state behavior.

Both views of the state arrive at the same conclusion: the quest for profit leads to a competition among advanced capitalist nation-states for control of overseas markets. Capitalists must compete against each other for investment opportunities in Southern countries. This partially explains the history of colonialism and neocolonialism in which powerful countries compete with each other for control of Southern nations. Colonial ownership and control ensures access of national corporations to investment and profit in the Southern world.

In the colonies, argued Lenin, "it is easier to eliminate competition" because of the inequality of power and resources. The imperial power can direct economic activity to conform to the long-term interests of the imperial power itself, even if the costs include distorted development or underdevelopment for the colony. According to Lenin, capitalism forces capitalists and their supporting nation-states "to adopt this method [of dividing the world] in order to get profits." Of course, the territorial division of the world generates violence between colonizer and colonized, and among competing colonial powers. As industrialized Northern nations vie with each other for investment control, conflict and, sometimes, war among them emerges. Consistent with this economic explanation of imperialism, Lenin interpreted World War I as fundamentally imperialist in origin and direction. He viewed it as "an annexationist, predatory, plunderous war . . . for the division of the world, for the partition and repartition of colonies, 'spheres of influence' of finance capital."[10]

From the fifteenth through twentieth centuries, European powers colonized entire continents to plunder them of precious metals, natural resources, and human flesh and also to serve as markets for finished goods manufactured in the European country. In addition to these economic and financial motives, nationalist pressures also came into play as the different European powers vied for strategic advantage. Whether or not this economic expansion is truer of advanced capitalism than it is and was of other economic systems remains a matter of debate. Colonialism and imperialism both predate capitalism by at least two millennia, since we have ample record of imperial aggression and conquest dating to ancient Greece and earlier.

Colonialism in its modern form began during the fifteenth and sixteenth centuries, when economic relations were feudal in nature rather than capitalistic. In modern times, some socialist countries have pursued imperialistic foreign policies that rival those of some capitalist countries. This is especially true of the former Soviet Union, which attempted to counter the power of the United States by maintaining its own sphere of influence. On the other hand, most democratic socialist countries appear disinclined to pursue imperialist foreign policies.

At a minimum, the evidence suggests that capitalism appears to be no less oriented toward colonialism and imperialism than other forms of political economy. Great Britain, with a powerful emerging capitalist economy during the nineteenth century, created and maintained a far-reaching empire. U.S. foreign policy during the nineteenth and twentieth centuries also provides much evidence to support Lenin. This foreign policy has been characterized by overt forms of colonialism and neocolonialism, a willingness to use military force to advance and defend U.S. interests, and a willingness to use undemocratic means when necessary. U.S. expansion was fueled by various factors, including population pressures on the Eastern Seaboard, an ideology of "manifest destiny," racism, strategic concerns, nationalism, and commercial interests. Among these, commercial interests often figured prominently, as a brief discussion of U.S. imperial history can demonstrate.

Most Americans understand in general, if benign, terms that the United States in its earlier years pursued an aggressive, violent foreign policy toward Native Americans. U.S. relations with various Native American tribes show a history of conquest and violence driven at least partly by commercial, financial, and economic interests in acquiring more land and protecting it. Even when land was purchased rather than simply stolen, expansion occurred at Native Americans' expense.

The Mexican-American War of 1846–48 illustrates the central themes of nationalism and commercialism consistently found in U.S. imperial history. Officially, the war originated over a boundary dispute between Texas and Mexico. Unofficially, the war offered the United States an opportunity to acquire what is now the southwest United States, including all or parts of California, Nevada, Utah, Arizona, Colorado, and New Mexico. President James Polk intentionally provoked Mexico into hostilities by ordering U.S. troops to the Rio Grande, occupying the land in dispute between Texas and Mexico. As a U.S. colonel on the front lines wrote in his diary, "It looks as if the government sent a small force on purpose to bring on a war, so as to have a pretext for taking California and as much of this country as it chooses."

Defenders of the land grab justified it on nationalist, commercial, religious, and racist grounds. In mythological-patriotic terms, the Washington *Union* in 1845 expressed the sentiments of the Democratic party and President Polk:

> Let the great measure of annexation be accomplished, and with it the questions of boundary and claims. For who can arrest the torrent that will pour onward to the west? The road to California will be open to us. Who will stay the march of our western people?

Later, the same newspaper posed the United States' motives in blunter terms stripped of the mythological-patriotic veneer: "A corps of properly organized volunteers . . . would invade, overrun, and occupy Mexico. They would enable us not only to take California, but to keep it." The New York *Journal of Commerce* invoked God while adding a racist motivation, arguing that "the supreme Ruler of the universe . . . seems to me to be identified with the success of our arms. . . . That the redemption of 7,000,000 of souls from all the vices that infest the human race, is the ostensible object."

President Polk invoked a host of gods to defend his move, saying that "we are called upon by every consideration of duty and patriotism to vindicate with decision the honor, the rights, and the interests of our country." Earlier, on the night of his inauguration, he confided his interests more bluntly to the secretary of the navy, saying that "one of his main objectives was the acquisition of California."[11] The war itself pitted Mexico against a far stronger foe, with a foregone outcome.

The Spanish-American War at the end of the nineteenth century showed even more clearly the dominant commercial and national interests underlying U.S. imperialism. Like the Mexican-American War, this one had both an official and an unofficial cause. The official reason cited for going to war with Spain was to liberate Cubans from tyrannical Spanish rule, and its immediate provocation was the sinking, allegedly by the Spanish, in 1898 of the American battleship *Maine* in a Cuban harbor. The unofficial reasons were the twin drives of commercial and nationalist interests. Speaking early in the 1890s, Sen. Henry Cabot Lodge of Massachusetts forthrightly outlined a framework of national policy emphasizing commercial interests that would put it on a collision course with Spain:

> In the interests of our commerce . . . we should build the Nicaragua canal, and for the protection of that canal and for the sake of our commercial supremacy in the Pacific we should control the Hawaiian islands and maintain our influence in Samoa . . . and when the Nicaraguan canal is built, the island of Cuba . . . will become a necessity. . . . The great nations are rapidly absorbing for their future expansion and their present defense all the waste places of the earth. It is a movement which makes for civilization and the advancement of the race. As one of the great nations of the world the United States must not fall out of the line of march.

Apologists justified the war explicitly in terms of an oversupply–underconsumption problem in need of resolution. Using language that presaged Lenin, William McKinley, several years before his election to the presidency, said, "We want a foreign market for our surplus products." According to Sen. Albert Beveridge of Indiana in 1897: "American factories are making more than the American people can use; American soil is producing more than they can consume. Fate has written our policy for us; the trade of the

world must and shall be ours." The U.S. Department of State in 1898 placed
the problem of surplus production on the government's agenda, stating:

> It seems to be conceded that every year we shall be confronted with an increas-
> ing surplus of manufactured goods for sale in foreign markets if American op-
> eratives and artisans are to be kept employed the year around. The enlargement
> of foreign consumption of the products of our mills and workshops has, there-
> fore, become a serious problem of statesmanship as well as of commerce.

Several years after the war, the chief of the Bureau of Foreign Commerce of
the Department of Commerce located U.S. involvement in the war directly in
its commercial interests and the need to resolve the problem of oversupply:

> Underlying the popular sentiment, which might have evaporated in time, which
> forced the United States to take up arms against Spanish rule in Cuba, were our
> economic relations with the West Indies and the South American republics. . . .
> The Spanish-American War was but an incident of a general movement of ex-
> pansion which had its roots in the changed environment of an industrial ca-
> pacity far beyond our domestic powers of consumption. It was seen to be
> necessary for us not only to find foreign purchasers for our goods, but to pro-
> vide the means of making access to foreign markets easy, economical and safe.

U.S. investors and policy makers were also intent on protecting existing
commercial interests in Cuba and other Spanish-controlled countries. In
Cuba alone, U.S. investments amounted to between $30 million and $50 million in plantations, railroads, mining, and other areas, and the volume of trade
with Cuba reached $100 million.

What began ostensibly as a war to liberate Cuba quickly became "a splen-
did little war" to expand U.S. possessions. The U.S. Navy attacked Spanish
forces in the Philippines shortly after the declaration of war and moved on
Cuba soon after that. Like the Mexican-American War, the U.S. victory in the
Spanish-American War enabled an expansion of its colonial empire that "was
extensive enough to warm the heart of the most ardent imperialist."[12] The
United States annexed Hawaii, Puerto Rico, Wake Island, Guam, and the
Philippines, justifying the annexations through the same combination of na-
tionalist, deist, racist, and commercial motives used to justify the Mexican-
American War, with prominent commercial interests proclaimed boldly.

Senator Beveridge, representing "the dominant economic and political interests of the country," said to the U.S. Senate on January 9, 1900:

> Mr. President, the times call for candor. The Philippines are ours forever. . . . And just beyond the Philippines are China's illimitable markets. We will not retreat from either. . . . We will not renounce our part in the mission of our race, trustee, under God, of the civilization of the world. . . . The Pacific is our ocean. . . . Where shall we turn for consumers of our surplus? Geography answers the question. China is our natural customer. . . . The Philippines give us a base at the door of all the East.

During the twentieth century, the United States continued to assert, using force when necessary, its economic and strategic interests throughout the world. It declared and enforced an "open door" policy in China guaranteeing access to Chinese markets for American investors. This open-door policy would become a dominant theme of American foreign policy in the twentieth century. When diplomacy failed to grant open-door status to American investments, the U.S. military often forced the doors open. Although somewhat more subtle than its nineteenth-century counterpart, as imperialism it was equally effective in advancing U.S. economic and strategic interests.

If the policies themselves were slightly more subtle, the justifications for U.S. imperial behavior often remained frank and blunt. In 1908, President William Howard Taft announced, "The day is not far distant when the whole hemisphere will be ours in fact as, by virtue of our superiority of race, it already is ours morally." President Woodrow Wilson, who claimed to want to "make the world safe for democracy," stated that "concessions obtained by financiers must be safeguarded by ministers of state, even if the sovereignty of unwilling nations be outraged in the process. . . . The doors of the nations which are closed must be battered down." Prior to World War II, the United States invaded Nicaragua in 1926 to quell a revolution against U.S. interests there, maintaining a Marine presence there for seven years; invaded the Dominican Republic in 1916 for the fourth time, stationing troops there for eight years; intervened in Haiti in 1915 for the second time, leaving troops for nineteen years; and intervened in Cuba four times between 1900 and 1933, in Panama six times, in Guatemala once, and in Honduras seven times.[13]

Since World War II, American interventions abroad have, if anything, increased, as the following partial list of global interventions fueled predominately by commercial and strategic national interests demonstrates: Iran (1953), Guatemala (1954), Indonesia (1957–58, 1965, 1975), Cuba (1960–present), Vietnam (1960s–75), Congo/Zaire (1961–65), Brazil (1964), Dominican Republic (1965), El Salvador (1970s–90s), Guatemala (1970s–90s), Chile (1973), Angola (1975–91), Nicaragua (1979–89), South Korea (1980), Grenada (1983), Libya (1986), Panama (1989), Iraq (1989–present), and Haiti (1991).[14] The same imperialist trends emphasizing commercial and national interests continued, overlaid first with an ideology of anticommunism and, since the collapse in 1989 of the Soviet Union, antiterrorism.

Given the historical evidence, it would be difficult to deny at least some legitimacy to Lenin's argument. The two largest imperial powers of the last two centuries, Great Britain and the United States, have also been dominant capitalist countries. Sometimes their economic motivations have been forthrightly stated, in terms that could have been taken directly from Lenin and that leave no room for misunderstanding.

WHAT IS DEMOCRACY?

Democracy as an idea and a practice can be traced in Western culture to ancient Greece. The word itself comes from two Greek words: *demos*, meaning the common people, and *kratein*, meaning to rule. Thus, for ancient Greeks, *demokratia* meant rule by the common people. Ancient Greece was divided into separate city-states, each an independent *polis*, until united under Alexander. The largest and most prominent of the city-states was Athens, the home of both Plato and Aristotle. Different city-states practiced different forms of government, and political forms changed fairly often within some of the city-states, Athens included.

The Golden Age of Athenian democracy lasted from approximately the middle to the end of the fifth century B.C. It was characterized by widespread participation among citizens who would come to the assembly to discuss and debate. The Athenian assembly met more than forty times per year, and the quorum (the number required for the conduct of public affairs) was six thousand citizens. All major issues came before the assembly for debate and a decision. Consensus was sought when possible, but majority rule sufficed otherwise. Being a citizen meant participating routinely and directly in political decision making in the assembly and in judicial functions.

The Athenians valued political equality highly both for its own sake and as a practical basis for liberty. The ancient Greeks understood freedom partly in terms of freedom to participate in politics. Political equality enabled widespread participation in politics by removing artificial barriers to participation such as class distinctions. The Athenians also viewed civic virtue as an essential trait of citizens. They distinguished between the citizen, who by definition concerned himself with public as well as private matters, and the self-interested *idiote* who shunned public life in favor of private pursuits. Leaders were often chosen for a day only, giving many the opportunity to lead and helping prevent the consolidation of power in one or more demagogues. Rotation in office and term limits made it possible for everyone to participate in positions of responsibility. Leaders were sometimes chosen by lot, essentially pulling names out of a hat.[15]

Many of these elements of Athenian democracy can be found in a famous speech by Pericles (495–429 B.C.), an Athenian citizen, general, and politician. Pericles probably actually delivered his "funeral oration" to the assembled Athenians some thirty years before it was actually recorded by the Greek historian Thucydides. The speech is worth quoting at length:

> Our constitution . . . favors the many instead of the few; this is why it is called a democracy. If we look to the laws, they afford equal justice to all in their private differences; if to social standing, advancement in public life falls to reputation for capacity, class considerations not being allowed to interfere with merit; nor again does poverty bar the way: if a man is able to serve the state, he is not hindered by the obscurity of his condition. The freedom which we enjoy in our government extends also to our ordinary life. There, far from exercising a jealous surveillance over each other, we do not feel called upon to be angry with our neighbor for doing what he likes, or even to indulge in those injurious looks which cannot fail to be offensive, although they inflict no positive penalty. But all this ease in our private relations does not make us lawless as citizens. Against this fear is our chief safeguard, teaching us to obey the magistrates and the laws, particularly such as regard the protection of the injured, whether they are actually on the statute book, or belong to that code which, although unwritten, yet cannot be broken without acknowledged disgrace. . . .
>
> Our public men have, besides politics, their private affairs to attend to, and our ordinary citizens, though occupied with the pursuits of industry, are still

fair judges of public matters; for, unlike any other nation, regarding him who takes no part in these duties not as unambitious but as useless, we Athenians are able to judge at all events if we cannot originate, and instead of looking on discussion as a stumbling-block in the way of action, we think it an indispensable preliminary to any wise action at all.[16]

Democracy, according to Pericles, thus entails dispersal of power among the many rather than the few; political equality, including the elimination of class barriers to participation; active participation by common citizens; freedom both in politics and social life; tolerance; respect for the law; special care for "the injured"; civic virtue; and public discussion and debate.

Another source of information about democracy in ancient Greece is Aristotle (384–322 B.C.), who describes the "attributes of democracy":

There is the election of officers *by* all, and *from* all; there is the system of all ruling over each, and each, in his turn, over all; there is the method of appointing by lot to all offices . . . ; there is the rule that there should be no property-qualification for office . . . ; there is the rule that, apart from the military offices, no office should ever be held twice by the same person . . . ; there is the rule that the tenure of every office . . . should be brief. There is the system of popular courts, composed of all the citizens or of persons selected from all, and competent to decide all cases. . . . There is the rule that the popular assembly should be sovereign in all matters. . . . [There is the rule of] paying all the citizens to attend . . . the courts, the council, and the stated meetings of the popular assembly, and also for serving on any board of magistrates. . . . Another attribute of democracy is to dispense with all life offices—or at least to curtail the powers of any such offices . . . and to make appointments to any life-office depend on the use of the lot and not on election.[17]

Here we see both elections and lot as methods for selecting leaders, popular rule in which the assembly is sovereign, the elimination of class barriers to serving in office and to political participation, rotation in office, term limits, short terms in office, trial by a jury of peers, and the association of democracy with the lower classes and common people. The net effect included a leveling of political power, a heavy emphasis on political participation by all citizens, and the assumption of civic responsibility and civic commitment by average citizens.

While eliminating class barriers to political participation, the Athenians erected other barriers. Athenian democracy counted as citizens only free, adult, Athenian men, excluding women, slaves, and resident foreigners. Slave labor and the domestic labor of women, including wives, enabled the extensive, time-consuming participation in politics by citizens. Athenian democracy could also be deemed unstable, given the frequent mutations from one constitutional form to another, but perhaps no more than the other forms practiced in ancient Greece. Finally, the form of direct democracy practiced in Athens was probably possible only in a relatively small city-state like Athens.

The theory and practice of democracy largely disappeared during the subsequent centuries, reemerging finally in the seventeenth century. The intervening centuries saw the emergence of civic republicanism, which is similar in some ways to democracy. The word *republic* comes from the Latin *res publica*, which means "the public thing" or "public business." We find an early version in the Roman republic, which included a mixed government combining elements from rule by the one, the few, and the many. The many controlled the popular assembly, the few controlled the Senate, and executive consuls implemented the policies adopted by the assembly and Senate. This division of powers prevented one group from seizing too much power. Proponents of republican government believed that it promoted civic virtue and that active participation in politics nurtured in citizens this emphasis on virtue. The Roman republic became an empire under Julius Caesar (100–44 B.C.) who, along with subsequent Roman emperors, emptied the popular assemblies of power and concentrated it in his own hands.

After the collapse of the Roman empire, the Catholic Church assumed secular and spiritual dominance. Self-rule largely disappeared, supplanted by Christian teachings. On the one hand, Christian principles contained a democratic flavor in the teaching that each of us is morally equal in God's eyes and can control our own behavior and thus earn salvation. On the other hand, Christianity required the suspension of critical judgment in favor of adherence to religious doctrine formulated by others. The idea of a political citizen who must exercise his or her own judgment was replaced by that of the true believer who sought communion with God through adoption of beliefs whose origins lay outside the believer. St. Augustine (354–430), with his separation of earthly from heavenly cities and his admonition to Christians to concentrate on the latter, deeply influenced the development of Christianity.

Martin Luther's (1483–1546) "priesthood of all believers" resonated with democratic overtones in its emphasis on individuals controlling their own spiritual fate. However, Luther himself remained wedded to the authority of Scripture as the repository of singular truth, and not just any interpretation of Scripture could suffice. Yet, his work broke the secular and spiritual stranglehold of the Catholic Church and opened a space for individuals to attain salvation without permission of the Church. The American Puritans, heirs to Luther and John Calvin (1509–1564), though deeply undemocratic in some ways, organized their communities along democratic lines as decentralized congregations with elected male elders.

Civic republicanism experienced a revival during the Italian Renaissance. Advocates of republicanism, such as Niccolò Machiavelli (1469–1527) in *The Discourses*, argued for active citizen participation in politics, civic virtue, the rule of law, and mixed government. Republicanism also surfaced in England during the seventeenth century in the writings of James Harrington (1611–1677), especially in *The Commonwealth of Oceana* (1656). While emphasizing the same themes as Machiavelli and the other civic republicans of the Italian Renaissance, Harrington added the need for greater equality so that no citizen would be dependent on another. Harrington also advocated frequent rotation in office in order to prevent one person from acquiring too much power and also to help citizens acquire civic virtue through participation.

Specifically democratic sentiments resurfaced during the sixteenth and first half of the seventeenth centuries among English Levellers, who argued that political authority is derived from the consent of the governed. Taking this to its logical conclusion, the Levellers believed that consent must be offered or withheld by all adult males through voting, without exceptions imposed by property or other qualifications. Levellers sought a society in which all had at least some property, enabling a minimal level of independence and autonomy, and no one had enough property to allow exploitation of others.

Jean-Jacques Rousseau's (1712–1778) *The Social Contract* (1762) outlined his vision of a direct democracy and the conditions needed to bring it into existence and maintain it. Democracy, according to this view, requires rule in the common interest, civic virtue, freedom, political equality, rough economic equality, and extensive direct participation by all citizens. A democratic society, according to Rousseau, is governed by a "general will" that "looks only to the common interest." This general will finds expression in the laws that, by definition in a sound republic, represent the common good rather than any particular interests. To maintain this focus on a general will, Rousseau advocated civic virtue as an essential ingredient. Without civic virtue, citizens would participate with an eye only toward their own private and individual interests rather than public and common interests. This would create "an injustice that would bring about the ruin of the body politic, were it to spread."[18]

Rousseau's vision of democracy also emphasized freedom, especially the positive freedom to participate in the formulation of laws under which everyone lives. So long as citizens obey only laws that they had a hand in making, "they obey no one but their own will." Absent this positive freedom to participate in the formulation of common rules, others determine the rules by which you must live, and they may do so in ways that favor their own interests over the common good.

As this suggests, Rousseau viewed political equality as essential to democracy, since political equality makes a general will possible. In a context of political inequality, some citizens can exert dominating influence over the formulation of laws, resulting in laws that represent their private interests rather than common interests. Political equality also means that the laws obligate everyone equally and award privileges and rights equally:

> The social pact establishes such an equality among the citizens that they all commit themselves under the same conditions and should all enjoy the same rights. . . . Every authentic act of the general will, obligates or favors all citizens equally. . . . In this arrangement, each necessarily submits to the conditions he imposes on others, an admirable concurrence of interest and justice, which gives the common decisions an equitable character.

To guarantee both freedom and political equality, Rousseau further advocated rough economic equality. Like the Levellers, Rousseau believed that ideally everyone would possess some property, but nobody would possess enough to give them power over others that could result in the diminution of the others' freedom. Ensuring rough economic equality would also help ensure political equality by preventing class barriers to participation and influence. Rousseau did not advocate absolute equality, only that "with regard to wealth, no citizen should be rich enough to be able to buy another, and none poor enough to be forced to sell himself, which presupposes moderation in wealth and influence." A society with rich and poor is a class-divided society and, by definition, is a partisan society in which competing interests undercut the general will.

Finally, Rousseau's vision of democracy emphasized political participation by all citizens. Participation makes civic virtue possible as a citizen's "faculties are exercised and developed, his ideas are extended, his feelings are ennobled, his whole soul is so uplifted." Participation maintains freedom and the general will, since it helps guarantee that the laws represent the common interest. Rousseau denied the validity of representation in his vision of direct democracy. He argued that "any law the people has not ratified in person is invalid. . . . In a well-run republic, everyone rushes to the assemblies" to do their part to create a general will.[19]

The American Founders inherited this stew of ideas and practices. The dominant Federalists explicitly rejected the idea of democracy since it represented for them a system of class rule, specifically by the lower classes who could not be trusted to rule responsibly. Since most of the Federalists were drawn from relatively privileged sections of colonial America, they naturally perceived democracy as a direct threat to their interests and rejected it in vivid terms. Speaking to the Constitutional Convention of 1787, Edmund Randolph (1753–1813) opined that the country's problems originated in "the turbulence and follies of democracy" and warned his colleagues of the dangers to be found in "the democratic parts of our [state] constitutions." Elbridge Gerry (1744–1814) called democracy "the worst of all political evils." Articulating a widely held Federalist opinion, William Livingston (1723–1790) said that "the people have ever been and ever will be unfit to retain the exercise of power in their own hands."

Echoing this same distrust of the average American, Alexander Hamilton (1757–1804) said that the "turbulent and changing" masses "seldom judge or determine right." He urged his colleagues to include in the new constitution a permanent governmental body to "check the imprudence of democracy." Gouverneur Morris (1752–1816) said disdainfully, "The mob begin to think and reason. Poor reptiles! They bask in the sun, and ere noon they will bite, depend upon it." According to Jeremy Belknap (1744–1798), a clergyman from New England, "Let it stand as a principle that government originates from the people; but let the people be taught . . . that they are not able to govern themselves." James Madison (1751–1836) bluntly dismissed democracy as unstable and threatening to property rights. "Democracies," he wrote, "have ever been spectacles of turbulence and contention; have ever been found incompatible with personal security or the rights of property; and have in general been as short in their lives as they have been violent in their deaths."[20] As many of these comments suggest, the Federalists' fear and disdain of common people underlay their rejection of democracy.

The Federalists claimed to embrace republicanism, albeit a stripped-down version, rather than democracy. Madison defined a republic as "a government which derives all its powers directly or indirectly from the great body of the people; and is administered by persons holding their offices during pleasure, for a limited period, or during good behavior." Federalist John Adams (1735–1826) even more succinctly defined a republic as "a government in which the people have collectively, or by representation, an essential share in the sovereignty."[21] As these statements show, despite their distrust of common people, the Federalist Founders believed that legitimate political power rests on the consent of the governed. They concluded that the constitution they crafted must give the power of the franchise to citizens. To prevent this from getting out of hand, however, they restricted the franchise to white, male property holders. This restriction gradually yielded during subsequent generations to near-universal suffrage with exceptions based on age, residency status, and criminal record.

The Federalists' constitution also incorporated institutional checks and balances to thwart attempts by the *demos* to seize power. Drawing upon thinkers such as James Harrington and the English constitution, the Founders sought to create a mixed government in which aristocratic and monarchical elements remained. They established the U.S. House of Representatives to represent white, male property-holding commoners, the U.S. Senate to represent the aristocratic class, and the presidency as a monarchical element. The Federalists recognized the need to give the *demos* a say, but sought at the same time to block its unchecked exercise of sovereignty.

The Federalists included other intentionally antidemocratic elements in the Constitution.[22] Indirect election of the president and U.S. senators remained until 1913, and the electoral college system for electing the president, in which electoral votes are apportioned to states based on their total number of U.S. senators and representatives, remains in place today. The Federalists also sought to shield the judiciary from popular pressures by opting for presidential lifetime appointments to the federal judiciary, including the U.S.

Supreme Court. The power of judicial review given to the Supreme Court, along with presidential veto power over legislative decisions, also intentionally set up obstacles to the exercise of popular sovereignty. Taken together, these institutional arrangements signaled the Federalists' abandonment of any hope of civic virtue for common people.

The Federalists' opponents, the Anti-Federalists, more readily embraced democratic principles. They expressed greater fear of centralized power, agreed with Rousseau that a democratic republic must remain small, advocated a judiciary accountable to the people, retained the emphasis on civic virtue, and insisted upon a Bill of Rights as a safeguard to liberty.

The more democratic political philosophy of the Anti-Federalists found institutional expression in some of the state governments of the time. For example, the constitution of Pennsylvania prior to 1790 abolished both an "upper house," or senate, representing the interests of the aristocracy, and the governorship, replacing the latter with an elected executive council that rotated in office. In contrast to the Federalists' property qualifications for voting, the Pennsylvania constitution awarded all male taxpayers and their sons the right of suffrage. Power in the single assembly was checked via short terms in office of one year and by requiring that all legislation be submitted to the voters in annual elections and passed again in the following year. Representatives to the assembly could serve only four out of any seven years. An elected Council of Censors met every seventh year for one year to determine whether or not the actions of the legislature and executive council were consistent with the Pennsylvania constitution and republican principles. This Pennsylvania constitution gave more power directly to all citizens than did the U.S. constitution. While the Pennsylvania constitution erected its own checks on power, the *demos* itself, rather than an aristocratic senate or a monarchical president, provided the necessary checks and balances.

Thomas Jefferson (1743–1826) represents a unique figure of the founding generation. While sympathetic to some of the Federalists' goals and beliefs, he espoused a political philosophy more consistent with the Anti-Federalists. Unlike the Federalists, Jefferson maintained faith in common people and their capacity for civic virtue. "I am not among those who fear the people," he famously wrote. He called the people "the most certain, and the most legitimate engine of government." Rather than throw up obstacles to their political participation as the Federalists intended, Jefferson advocated "educat[ing] and inform[ing] the whole mass of the people. Enable them to see that it is their interest to preserve peace and order, and they will preserve them." The people "are the only sure reliance for the preservation of our liberty."

Although Jefferson agreed with Federalists on the necessity of representative government in an extended republic, he called for direct democracy at local levels. This would give common citizens a direct stake in self-government, develop their civic virtue, and allow them practice in the arts of citizenship. He agreed with Rousseau that political participation protected political equality by ensuring that all citizens' voices were heard in the political process, and this helped protect freedom by ensuring in turn that each citizen had a hand in determining the rules of common life.

Jefferson's description of a system of "ward" government outlined many of his democratic principles:

> Divide the counties into wards of such size as that every citizen can attend, when called on, and act in person. Ascribe to them the government of their wards in all things relating to themselves exclusively. A justice, chosen by themselves, in each, a constable, a military company, a patrol, a school, the care of their own poor, their own portion of the public roads, the choice of one or more jurors to serve in some court, and the delivery, within their own wards, of their own votes for all elective officers of higher sphere, will relieve the county administration of nearly all its business, will have it better done, and by making every citizen an acting member of the government, and in the offices nearest and most interesting to him, will attach him by his strongest feelings to the independence of his country, and its republican constitution. The justices thus chosen by every ward, would constitute the county court, would do its judiciary business, direct roads and bridges, levy county and poor rates, and administer all the matters of common interest to the whole country. These wards, called townships in New England, are the vital principle of their governments.[23]

This is a vision of democracy that the ancient Athenians would have recognized and endorsed. Overall a vision of direct democracy, it integrates local self-government, consent of the governed, political equality, decentralized power and authority, active and extensive citizen participation, an elected judiciary, and civic virtue.

Gradually, the term *democracy* shed its negative connotations. Favorable references to democracy appeared in the media as early as 1794. The

Democratic-Republican Societies active during the founding period offer one example. Yet, most Americans did not embrace democracy until well into the nineteenth century. In particular, the emergence of the Democratic party, which won the presidency under Andrew Jackson in 1828, signaled that the term had gained widespread acceptance and appeal. By that time, the peculiar form of democracy known as *liberal democracy* had begun to take shape in the United States.

LIBERAL DEMOCRACY

According to political philosopher C. B. Macpherson (1911–1987), liberal democracy has historically carried two distinct meanings. First, it refers to "the democracy of a capitalist market society." The term *liberal* in this sense refers to the "freedom of the stronger to do down the weaker by following market rules." In this market society, everything is commodified for sale, value is reduced to money, and most people spend most of their lives engaging in activities that are defined directly or indirectly by the dictates of the market. These observations reflect Macpherson's bluntly critical assessment of the influence on democracy of liberalism and capitalism. The second meaning of *liberal democracy* is "a society striving to ensure that all its members are equally free to realize their capabilities." In this second meaning, the term *liberal* refers to "equal effective freedom of all to use and develop their capacities." While Macpherson held out hope that the second meaning of liberal democracy could become dominant, he noted that it was the first meaning that in fact achieved dominance. Liberal democracy grew up in a context defined by capitalism and liberalism. Democracy had to accommodate itself to those limiting and defining "isms," to what Macpherson called "the underlying structure of society."[24]

Macpherson described four different models of liberal democracy, the first three tracing its actual historical development, the fourth representing an ideal of participatory democracy comparable to the ideal drawn from the Athenians, Rousseau, and Jefferson. The first model, *protective democracy*, bears the liberal footprint most obviously of the three. It originated in the political philosophy of Thomas Hobbes (1588–1679) and John Locke (1632–1704), who both viewed government as playing primarily a role of protecting people's lives, freedoms, and property. Locke, in particular, emphasized the natural right of unlimited property and the need for government to protect it. He also insisted on a point that would become central to liberal democracy: that government must be founded on the consent of the governed.

Jeremy Bentham (1748–1832) and James Mill (1773–1836), two early nineteenth-century British political philosophers, adopted classical liberal assumptions about human nature and applied Locke's idea of consent to elections. Both are best known for developing the philosophy of utilitarianism, with its central maxim of "the greatest good for the greatest number." In practice, "good" was reduced to happiness, then happiness to pleasure, and finally pleasure to acquiring possessions and money. Bentham made the connection directly, arguing that "money is the instrument of measuring the quantity of pain or pleasure." The logical implication is that the more money you have, the happier you are by definition.

Having adopted classical liberal assumptions about human nature, and having equated happiness with money and possessions, Bentham and Mill's society closely resembled Locke's of rational egoists competing for wealth and possessions, with a government needed to protect property. Government protection would enable people to earn money, acquire property, and keep it. Since people differ in talent and effort, obviously some would acquire more property than others. What, if anything, should be done about it? Nothing, answered Bentham, for "equality must yield" to the needs and privileges of property.[25] If government tried to equalize fortunes, he believed, it would undermine the incentive for hard work to attain wealth and happiness. This fateful choice in the history of liberal democracy relegated equality to distant, secondary status relative to negative freedom and property rights.

Bentham was not optimistic that government would refrain from redistributive efforts. He thus faced a double political problem: government must protect private property, but owners of property need protection from government intent on redistribution. He initially solved this problem by advocating limitation of suffrage to people with property—excluding the poor, the uneducated, the dependent, and women. This satisfied both requirements: it would ensure that political power would remain in the hands of property owners, who could use it to protect their property, and the vote itself would make it possible to change the government if it attempted redistribution. Bentham advocated this position for more than two decades. However, by 1820 he had conceded in favor of universal male suffrage, having convinced himself that the poor would not use their votes to attack property. They could see that their interests were better served by maintaining property than by attacking it, since they might one day be rich themselves.

James Mill took a more direct route to universal suffrage. He argued that self-interest and the hunger for power created a need for protection from those with political power. The vote confers political power. Thus, everyone needs the vote in order to protect himself or herself. Though he temporarily hedged these conclusions by appearing to advocate exclusions that included all women, men under 40, and men without property, he eventually turned to universal suffrage. Having made the case for universal suffrage, however, he admitted his true feelings:

> Our opinion, therefore, is that the business of government is properly the business of the rich, and that they will always obtain it, either by bad means, or good. Upon this every thing depends. If they obtain it by bad means, the government is bad. If they obtain it by good means, the government is sure to be good. The only good means of obtaining it are, the free suffrage of the people.

As Macpherson wrote, "this catches nicely the best spirit" of this first model of liberal democracy.[26]

This protective model of liberal democracy fits well with a capitalist political economy. The early liberal conception of unlimited property rights and the role of government in protecting them coincide neatly with the needs of capitalism. Tying happiness to possessions and money provides a powerful stimulus for consumption of the magnitude needed to propel a dynamic political economy based on ever-expanding production and consumption. The presumption of rational egoism complements a political economy based on self-interest and greed. The limitation of government's role to protection offers an expansive private realm for individuals focused primarily on economic pursuits.

The second model of liberal democracy, *developmental democracy*, found expression in the political thought of John Stuart Mill (1806–1873), son of James Mill. J. S. Mill began with a different view of human nature, and this would make a big difference in the direction his thinking would take. Human character, he believed, is not immutable as earlier liberals had presumed. Humans exert themselves and strive to improve themselves and their circumstances, and this gives them the impetus to develop their characters. This character development occurs in part through participation in politics, as voters inform themselves about political issues and discuss and debate them with others.

Between the generations, the working class in England and other countries in Western Europe had begun to appear more dangerous and hostile to propertied interests than Bentham and James Mill had anticipated. The times also saw a deep impoverishment of the working class. This troubled J. S. Mill because, among other things, it undermined the workers' ability to develop themselves. As for the causes of radical inequality and poverty, J. S. Mill refused to blame either private property or the political economy of capitalism itself, choosing instead to locate the problem in an initial unjust distribution of property through conquest and violence. As Macpherson emphasized, in this sense he was not as realistic as his father and Bentham, who both saw that capitalism naturally produced great inequality of fortune and power.

Like his predecessors, J. S. Mill thus faced a dilemma. On the one hand, character development required political participation via voting. This pointed toward the need for universal suffrage so that people had an opportunity to develop themselves. On the other hand, due to their impoverished conditions, many were currently undeveloped and could not be trusted with the vote. Should they get political power via suffrage equal to those already developed? Mill answered no, solving his dilemma by backing away from equal universal suffrage and introducing instead a scheme of weighted voting. According to this scheme, members of the already-developed elite would get more than one vote, while members of the undeveloped working class would get just one vote or, as he argued in some of his writings, none at all.

Mill's addition of a character development dimension gave this second model an ethical component lacking in the first model. By opening the question of human nature, rather than simply assuming an innate and immutable nature as did his liberal predecessors, Mill allowed for the possibility of character development that could include civic virtue. This made political participation a positive good, rather than something grudgingly admitted for the purpose of protecting self-interests. On the other hand, J. S. Mill's developmental model rejected the principle of equal universal suffrage, marking a step back from democracy. Also, like the protective model, it reconciles itself too readily to inequality and concentrated economic power, and it limits political participation for most people to the act of voting.

The third model of liberal democracy is called *pluralist democracy* because it begins from the presumption of a pluralist society defined by multiple competing interests without a common good. It is also sometimes called a democratic elitist model because both descriptively and prescriptively it emphasizes rule by elites. This model represents an attempt made in the early twentieth century to revise the theory of democracy to match actual practice in liberal democracies such as the United States. Developers of the model, including Joseph Schumpeter (1883–1950), Robert Dahl (1915–), Gaetano Mosca (1858–1941), Vilfredo Pareto (1848–1923), Seymour Lipset (1922–), and Walter Lippmann (1889–1974), pointed to the gap between the ideal and the reality of democracy and argued that pretending that the ideal is feasible or even desirable only fosters cynicism. According to these thinkers, the demands of democracy are satisfied if the people's interests are represented in political decision making. This occurs primarily through interest groups that aggregate individual preferences and compete with each other in the political arena for favorable policy decisions. In theory, the government acts as a neutral referee, ensuring that fair rules are in place and that everyone abides by them. Periodic elections foster competition among elites, and this ensures a sufficient level of accountability. Interest groups also provide open, multiple points of access to elite power, according to formulators of the model.

This model once again empties democracy of the ethical dimension of character development. Instead of seeking civic virtue through political participation, adherents of a pluralist model of democracy noted that, empirically, the masses were apathetic and passive. Rather than asking why that might be so, they simply asserted that the masses' apathy and passivity are good because the masses are also inherently incompetent, untrustworthy, prone to passion and irrationality, and easily manipulated. In this, they agreed with the Federalist Founders. The most important decisions are, and should be, made by a tiny minority of intellectually and morally superior elites. What, then, is the role, if any, for average citizens? In answering this question, adherents of this model argued that democracy is *only* a method of choosing leaders. As Schumpeter, an early formulator of this model, put it, "The democratic method is that institutional arrangement for arriving at political decisions in which individuals acquire the power to decide by means of a competitive struggle for the people's vote." Professional politicians "acquire the power to decide," while the rest vote during infrequent elections and stand on the sidelines the rest of the time.

By minimizing the participation of average citizens, this pluralist model represents a return to protective democracy's constriction of public life and the expansion of private life. It restricts public life to decision making by elites, and it effectively bars the majority from any significant role in public life beyond occasional voting for preferred elites. In this model, as noted by Macpherson, democracy gets wedded even more deeply to capitalism until it is almost inseparable.[27] Democracy becomes an entrepreneurial system in which elites assert themselves in public arenas. Like business entrepreneurs, they bring their goods to the marketplace, where they compete for consumers' votes, and they advertise for votes. Since the elites are typically drawn from the ranks of the wealthy, economic and political power merge.

According to Macpherson, the pluralist model fairly characterizes democracy in the United States and other liberal democratic nations today: "As description of the actual system now prevailing in Western liberal-democratic nations, Model 3 must be adjudged substantially accurate."[28] Since he wrote these words in 1977, Model 1—protective democracy—has also returned to prominence in both theory and practice, in the form of libertarianism. Macpherson acknowledged that the current system is stable, but noted too that it is a stable system of inequality and privilege for the few in which economic power buys political power, where elites determine the circumstances of most people's lives, and where average citizens actually participate in politics infrequently, if at all.

The three liberal democratic models described thus far share similar attributes. All three integrate a suspicion of concentrated political power but ignore the problem of concentrated economic power. All accept the likelihood of radical inequality; the third, pluralist democracy, makes a virtue of it. All three presume little faith in average humans, though the developmental model holds out the possibility that this can be partially overcome through education. Each model limits political participation by average citizens to occasional voting and, with the partial exception of the developmental model, views nonparticipation sanguinely; pluralist democracy again makes a virtue of it. All three models value negative freedom more highly than equality, and all equate freedom with property rights—a hallmark of liberal democracy. All three pose government's primary role in terms of making and enforcing rules to protect life, liberty, and estate and assume that this is done in everyone's interest, not just those who actually own an estate. Finally, all three models partition social space in a way that minimizes public life and maximizes private life. Democracy applies only to a narrow realm of government and admits of little or no participation by average citizens outside of occasional voting.

Macpherson's fourth model of liberal democracy, *participatory democracy*, departs so far from the other three that it is debatable whether it can properly be called "liberal." It represented for Macpherson an ideal of what democracy could become, rather than a description of an existing form. It would entail greater "participation in various spheres of society," including "workers' control in industry" as well as "substantial citizen participation in *government* decision-making spread . . . widely." It would also require "a change in people's consciousness (or unconsciousness), from seeing themselves and acting as essentially consumers to seeing themselves and acting as exerters and enjoyers of the exertion and development of their own capacities." In this respect, it required a return to the ethical foundations of the developmental model, emphasizing a view of humans as exerters and strivers who could progressively develop their characters and capacities. Finally, participatory democracy would require "a great reduction of the present social and economic inequality." Since capitalism "reproduces inequality and consumer consciousness, and must do so to go on operating," participatory democracy would require an abandonment of capitalism and a recommitment to human development.[29] This participatory model more nearly resembles the democracy found in ancient Athens and in the thought of Rousseau and Jefferson than it does the three models of liberal democracy.

Macpherson's four models do not adequately account for the welfare liberalism of the New Deal nor of past and contemporary welfare liberal thinkers. Although welfare liberal principles overlap in some ways with Macpherson's other models, they are sufficiently different to warrant a fifth model of liberal democracy. Since the ideas of its principal proponent in contemporary times, John Rawls (1921–2002), have already been addressed in an earlier chapter, here the welfare liberal model will only be summarized.

New Deal legislation emphasized partial redistribution and social welfare spending to increase equality, state regulation of the economy, and the positive government role of providing for the general social and individual welfare. The intellectual principles underlying the New Deal were articulated by early welfare liberal thinkers such as T. H. Green (1836–1882) and L. T. Hobhouse (1864–1929), who emphasized positive as well as negative freedom, the importance of equality in helping guarantee individual freedom and self-development, the need for social control of the economy, and the role of government in providing for the general social welfare, as well as classical liberal principles such as the primacy of the individual, individual rights, and the validity of private property and markets. Contemporary welfare liberals, sometimes called "egalitarian liberals," such as Rawls, Amartya Sen (1933–), Bruce Ackerman (1943–), and Avishai Margalit (1939–), continue to advance these welfare liberal principles.[30]

Most welfare liberals attempt to reconcile their egalitarian commitments with a capitalist political economy. Rawls's difference principle, which concedes inequality if it works to everyone's advantage, epitomizes this effort. Some welfare liberals such as Hobhouse, on the other hand, advocate partial or full socialism as a necessary means of ensuring greater equality. The New Deal, as many have pointed out, in fact represented a partial move toward socialism in the United States. The contemporary dominance of pluralist and protective models of liberal democracy marks a reversal of that direction in U.S. history.

PARTICIPATORY AND LIBERAL DEMOCRACY COMPARED

Contemporary political philosophers generally refer to the variants of democracy found in classical Athens and the writings of Rousseau and Jefferson either as *participatory*, *radical*, or *strong* democracy to distinguish it from *liberal* democracy. Here the term *participatory democracy* will be used, and it will be considered a nonliberal model of democracy.

The variants of participatory democracy share six key features. First, participatory democracy entails popular sovereignty, or rule by the people, where the people include average citizens, not just an elite. Second, participatory democracy requires political freedom, understood to mean the ability and capacity to participate effectively in the processes that determine the circumstances of one's life, and including rights necessary for participation such as free speech and the right of assembly. A third feature, political equality, requires that each citizen exercise equal say over the formulation of laws and that the laws apply equally to everyone. Political equality helps ensure freedom by preventing the more powerful from encroaching on the freedom of others. Many participatory democrats argue further that political equality requires at least a rough semblance of socioeconomic equality. Fourth, participatory democracy requires that concentrations of power, including economic power, be accountable to the people. Fifth, without denying self-interests, participatory democracy requires that citizens cultivate civic virtue, the ability and willingness to balance self-interests against public interests. Finally, participatory democracy requires that average citizens participate routinely in politics.

Participation is both a good in itself, making of politics a positive good rather than a necessary evil, and a means to the other ends of participatory democracy. It helps ensure popular sovereignty and may be the *only* way to ensure popular sovereignty. Rule *on behalf of* the people cannot be substituted for rule *by* the people without running the risk of distorting policy to favor elites who claim to rule on behalf of the people. Participation also helps maintain political equality by increasing the likelihood that each person's voice will be heard in the political process. Participation nurtures civic virtue by making citizens better informed and helping them become more aware of each other's divergent interests and of larger, common interests. Participation helps maintain freedom by ensuring that each person is included in the decision-making processes that determine the rules of common life. Absent widespread participation, elites can impose laws and maintain systems and institutions that limit common citizens' autonomy and independence.

The four models of liberal democracy—protective, developmental, pluralist, and welfare—minimize or abandon the idea of participation in politics. Participation emerges within these four models of liberal democracy primarily as a means of protecting interests, with voting in occasional elections as the specific means. While formally allowing participation in elections by average people, pluralist democracy condones their nonparticipation. Developmental democracy also allows participation in elections by average people, but attempts to minimize their impact through a system of weighted voting that gives more votes to elite citizens. Although the welfare model does not make a virtue of elite rule, as does the pluralist model, it nevertheless coexists relatively comfortably with elite rule in the form of bureaucratic, technocratic management of public affairs and the abandonment of the public sphere by common citizens. With the partial exception of the developmental and welfare models, liberal democracy poses politics as a necessary evil, rather than as something to be embraced both as a good in itself and as a means to other democratic ends. Their minimization of participation follows logically. The liberal democratic models' emphasis on private life over public life also undermines political participation.

Two of the liberal democratic models also abandon any notion of cultivating character. Both protective democracy and pluralist democracy simply assume a fixed human nature and characterize it in terms that are fatal to stronger versions of democracy, for if average citizens can be expected to pursue only their narrowly construed self-interests and if they are prone to passion and irrationality, as the two models posit, then stronger notions of democracy entailing the assumption of political responsibility by common citizens are perhaps impossible and certainly unwise. Developmental democracy holds out hope of developing the characters of average citizens but, in the meantime, views their characters in similarly skeptical terms and takes pains to minimize their political power until the character development process can produce desired changes. Like the developmental model, welfare liberals emphasize a plastic human nature marked by the potential for growth and development. They go further than the developmental model in asserting the necessity of providing social support for this growth and development.

Popular sovereignty, political freedom, and political equality are essential characteristics of liberal democracy as well as participatory democracy.[31] For liberal democrats as for participatory democrats, democracy means that the people should rule. Participatory democrats interpret this principle of popular sovereignty to mean that the people rule at least sometimes directly at local levels, and at all times via active participation by citizens. Liberal democracy's principle of popular sovereignty is satisfied indirectly through representation and leaving open the possibility of—and virtue of, for the pluralist democrats—nonparticipation. Most liberal democrats are satisfied if the people have the formal right to vote, whether or not they actually exercise that right. A participatory democratic understanding of popular sovereignty also means that the people directly assert their interests in politics and effectively determine the circumstances of their lives. For most liberal democrats, popular sovereignty is satisfied if elites represent the people's interests and are held accountable through the vote.

All of the versions of democracy considered above also require political freedom. Participatory democrats emphasize the freedom to participate effectively in the processes and decisions that determine the circumstances of one's life. Precisely through active assertion of oneself in public arenas, a citizen achieves freedom in practice by helping ensure the fairness of rules of common life and preventing domination imposed by elites. The freedoms encoded in the U.S. Constitution help enable this by removing obstacles to participation.

Liberal democrats also see the freedoms enumerated in the Constitution as important guarantees of political freedom. Their commitment to political freedom is undermined, however, by their commitment to the freedoms attached to property. By tying freedom to property, liberal democrats guarantee effective political freedom for the affluent, who can purchase their political freedom in forms such as free speech, adequate legal counsel, and effective voice in the political process. With the partial exception of the welfare liberal model, they award no such guarantees to the nonaffluent. The result is that financial considerations give some people exceptional freedoms and limit the degree to which these freedoms are effective for average citizens. Welfare liberals show greater willingness than other liberal democrats to redistribute and to downgrade property rights in the hierarchy of rights in order to make freedom more effective for more people.

Most liberal democrats also accept as principle that average Americans are denied meaningful participation in some of the most fundamental decisions that determine the character of their lives. Aside from the freedom to exit a particular job, most Americans are not free to participate in decisions that affect their work life, nor can they participate in the decisions that determine the content and quality of media programming. Liberal democrats accept as inevitable and perhaps beneficial that most Americans decline to participate in the political process, thus consigning to elites the power and privilege of determining the rules of common life.

All versions of democracy also include the idea of political equality. In the participatory democratic version, political equality means that each citizen has equal political power, and this is enabled and maintained through citizens' participation in politics. Absent citizen participation, elites develop more political power and this, by definition, undermines the principle of political equality. Liberal democracy reduces political equality to the formal principles of one-person-one-vote and equality before the law. According to a participatory democrat, though, voting and equality before the law cannot by themselves guarantee political equality. Political equality also requires other steps such as severing the link between economic and political power. Welfare liberals are more committed to equality than the other three liberal democratic models. Yet, some welfare liberals' commitment to equality is undermined by their ongoing attempt to reconcile it with a capitalist political economy.

Most liberal democrats remain half-committed to making power accountable. While emphasizing the potential perils of political power and the need to make it accountable via the vote, they make little or no effort to hold economic power accountable. By calling property a natural right and separating economic relations from the political realm, early liberals rendered it politically unaccountable. For the two dominant models today of pluralist and protective democracy, this remains true. Liberal democracy shows the logical result in the form of concentrations of economic power that are rendered invisible and largely unaccountable to the will of democratic majorities. Though they adopt the classical liberal principles of private property, contract, and free markets, welfare liberals are relatively more willing to check corporate power and its basis in private property.

With the exception of some welfare liberals, liberal democrats accept the primacy of property rights, inegalitarian market outcomes, domination by wealthy elites, unaccountable economic power, and other hallmarks of capitalism that drive stronger commitments to democracy from the field. By creating and maintaining radical economic inequality, a capitalist political economy undermines political equality and popular sovereignty. By relying so heavily on the freedoms associated with property rights, it overwhelms other civic and effective understandings of freedom. By emphasizing the pig principle and constantly goading consumption, it turns citizens into consumers. By according so much power to property rights, to capital, and to businesses and corporations, it undermines popular sovereignty and turns it into corporate sovereignty. Capitalism awards exceptional power to those who can pay for it.

These traits of capitalism overwhelm democratic commitments. To maintain the appearance of compatibility between democracy and capitalism, Americans simply redefined *democracy*. In doing so, they emptied democracy of much of its egalitarian, participatory, and developmental content.

QUESTIONS, PROBLEMS, AND ACTIVITIES

1. In what ways, if any, have you directly or indirectly experienced the domination of capital over labor? On what grounds might this be justifiable or unjustifiable?
2. Do you belong to a union? If yes, what do you like and dislike about it? If no, ask a union member to answer the same question. If possible, identify

workers who have participated in a strike, and ask them why they participated.

3. Have you ever experienced alienation at work as described by Marx? Which aspects of alienation, if any, are you likely to encounter in the career you are likely to choose for yourself?

4. Compare and contrast the ethical commitments that you bring to your religious, political, and economic lives, respectively. Do you ever experience tension among these commitments? When in tension, which should yield?

5. Most people take it for granted that work is something that you just have to do in order to pay the bills, and if the work itself is unsatisfying and unpleasant, well, that's the way it is. Can you, like Marx attempted to do, imagine an alternative? What would you like your current or future job to be like in an ideal world? What would you choose for a career if the goal was first and foremost to engage in satisfying, meaningful work rather than primarily to earn money?

6. What do you think are legitimate means for the U.S. government to promote American economic interests abroad? Under what circumstances, if any, should the U.S. government intervene directly in the affairs of another country? Should the United States be willing to use military means of securing and protecting U.S. foreign investments?

7. What do you think of J. S. Mill's weighted voting scheme as a solution to the problem of uninformed voting today? Can you think of better ways to handle the problem of uninformed voting? Some people today argue that the United States employs a de facto weighted voting scheme by allowing economic power to buy political power. Evaluate this claim.

8. As noted above, all models of democracy integrate three essential ingredients: political freedom, political equality, and popular sovereignty. How well is the United States doing on each of these minimum requirements for democracy?

9. Should we be concerned about concentrations of power? Why or why not? Should we be as concerned about concentrations of economic power as we are about concentrations of political power? If your answer is yes, what would you recommend to check corporate power today?

NOTES

1. For an earlier use of this metaphor of an invisible fist, see Samuel Bowles and Herbert Gintis, "The Invisible Fist: Have Capitalism and Democracy Reached a Parting of the Ways?" *American Economic Review* 68, no. 2 (May 1978): pp. 358–63.

2. Milton Friedman, *Capitalism and Freedom* (Chicago: University of Chicago Press, 1962), pp. 4, 9, 39, 14–15, 2.

3. Ibid., p. 28.

4. Ibid., pp. 74, 161–62, 168, 133.

5. Lawrence Mishel, Jared Bernstein, and Heather Boushey, *The State of Working America, 2002–2003* (Ithaca, NY: Cornell University Press, 2003), p. 190. In the early years of the twenty-first century, Wal-Mart has developed a novel way of blocking union-organizing in its stores: it simply closes, or threatens to close, any store where workers vote to unionize.

6. Karl Marx, *Economic and Philosophical Manuscripts of 1844* [1844] (New York: International Publishers, 1964), pp. 108, 110–11; emphasis in original.

7. See Juliet B. Schor's *The Overworked American* (New York: Basic Books, 1991) on overworked Americans and her *Overspent American* (New York: Basic Books, 1998) on the results in terms of strains on family incomes.

8. Irving Kristol, *Two Cheers for Capitalism* (New York: Basic Books, 1978), pp. 257, 262, 268.

9. V. I. Lenin, *Imperialism: The Highest Stage of Capitalism* (1916; rev. trans., New York: International Publishers, 1939), p. 63.

10. Ibid., pp. 84, 75, 9.

11. Howard Zinn, *A People's History of the United States, 1492–Present* (New York: HarperCollins, 1980), pp. 148–49, 152–53, 150, 147.

12. Ibid., p. 291–92, 299, 295; Richard Current, T. Harry Williams, and Frank Freidel, *American History: A Survey*, 3rd ed. (New York: Knopf, 1971), vol. 2, p. 527.

13. Zinn, *People's History*, pp. 306, 355, 353, 399–400; Noam Chomsky, *Year 501: The Conquest Continues* (Boston: South End Press, 1993), p. 158.

14. For histories of U.S. global interventions see, for example, William Blum, "A Concise History of United States Global Interventions, 1945 to the Present," in *Rogue State: A Guide to the World's Only Superpower* (Monroe, ME: Common Courage Press, 2000), pp. 125–67; Chomsky, *Year 501*; Thomas Paterson and J. Garry Clifford, *America Ascendant: U.S. Foreign Relations since 1939* (Lexington, MA: D. C. Heath, 1995); Michael Smith, *Portraits of Empire: Unmasking Imperial Illusions from the "American Century" to the "War on Terror"* (Monroe, ME: Common Courage Press, 2003); and Eugene Wittkopf, Charles Kegley, and James Scott, *American Foreign Policy*, 6th ed. (Belmont, CA: Thomson-Wadsworth, 2003).

15. For a description of the ancient Greek model of democracy, see David Held, *Models of Democracy* (Stanford: Stanford University Press, 1987), pp. 13–35.

16. Thucydides, *History of the Peloponnesian War* 2.37–40.

17. Aristotle, *Politics* 6.1317b–1318a.

18. Rousseau, *The Social Contract* [1762], in *Rousseau's Political Writings*, ed. and trans. Alan Ritter and Julia Conaway Bondanella (New York: W. W. Norton, 1988), pp. 100, 95.

19. Rousseau, *Social Contract*, pp. 103, 116, 95, 143.

20. Quoted in Richard Hofstadter, *The American Political Tradition and the Men Who Made It* (1948; repr., New York: Vintage Books, 1989), pp. 6, 7, 9; James Madison, "Federalist No. 10" [1787], in Alexander Hamilton, James Madison, and John Jay, *The Federalist Papers* (Toronto: Bantam Books, 1982), p. 46.

21. Madison, "Federalist No. 39" [1788], in Hamilton, Madison, and Jay, *Federalist Papers*, p. 190; John Adams, "Letter to Samuel Adams" [1790], in *The Political Writings of John Adams*, ed. George W. Carey (Washington, DC: Regnery, 2000), p. 665.

22. See Robert Dahl, *How Democratic Is the American Constitution?*, 2nd ed. (New Haven: Yale University Press, 2003).

23. Thomas Jefferson, "Letter to Samuel Kercheval" [1816], in Adrienne Koch and William Peden, eds., *The Life and Selected Writings of Thomas Jefferson* (New York: Random House, 1944), p. 615; "Letter to James Madison" [1787], in Koch and Peden, *Selected Writings of Thomas Jefferson*, p. 407.

24. C. B. Macpherson, *The Life and Times of Liberal Democracy* (Oxford: Oxford University Press, 1977), pp. 1, 9.

25. Jeremy Bentham, *Jeremy Bentham's Economic Writings*, ed. W. Stark (New York: Burt Franklin, 1952–54), vol. 1, p. 117; Jeremy Bentham, *The Theory of Legislation*, ed. C. K. Ogden (1802; London: K. Paul, Trench, Trubner & Co., 1931), p. 120.

26. James Mill, "On the Ballot," *Westminster Review* (July 1830); Macpherson, *Life and Times*, p. 42.

27. Joseph Schumpeter, *Capitalism, Socialism, and Democracy* (1942; reprint, New York: Harper & Row Publishers, 1950), p. 269; Macpherson, *Life and Times*, p. 77.

28. Macpherson, *Life and Times*, p. 83.

29. Ibid., pp. 93, 99, 100, 105; emphasis in original.

30. See, for example, T. H. Green, *The Political Theory of T. H. Green: Selected Writings*, ed. John Rodman (New York: Appleton-Century-Crofts, 1964); L. T. Hobhouse, *Liberalism* (New York: Henry Holt, 1911); John Rawls, *A Theory of Justice* (Cambridge, MA: Belknap Press of Harvard University Press, 1971), and *Political Liberalism* (New York: Columbia University Press, 1993); Amartya Sen, *On Economic Inequality* (Oxford: Clarendon Press, 1997); Bruce Ackerman, *Social Justice in the Liberal State* (New Haven: Yale University Press, 1980); and Avishai Margalit, *The Decent Society* (Cambridge: Harvard University Press, 1996).

31. On popular sovereignty, political freedom, and political equality as essential ingredients in democracy, see William Hudson, *American Democracy in Peril: Seven Challenges to America's Future*, 3rd ed. (New York: Chatham House, 2001), p. 20; and Edward Greenberg and Benjamin Page, *The Struggle for Democracy*, 3rd ed. (New York: Longman, 1997), pp. 8–11.

8

Democracy as a Way of Life

Many political theorists have attempted to counter the liberal narrowing of the democratic ideal. Some have sought to maintain and develop a conception of democracy as a whole way of life in which democratic ideals are applied in all social arenas. The Progressive Era thinker Jane Addams (1860–1935) epitomizes this effort. Although best known for establishing Chicago's Hull Settlement House, Addams was also a prolific writer and public speaker. She believed that "although America is pledged to the democratic ideal, the view of democracy has been partial." She argued that democracy should "assert itself in social affairs" beyond the narrow realm of government and the electoral franchise.[1] Like many other democratic thinkers, Addams emphasized human developmental capacity and viewed democracy as the ideal context for development. Why, she asked, limit democracy to a narrow realm of government if in expanding it into all social arenas we can multiply the opportunities for human development?

Addams recognized that everyday life was increasingly shaped by undemocratic economic and commercial forces. The results, most obviously, included endemic poverty, child labor, unsafe workplaces, sweatshop working conditions, and a political system distorted by money. They also included warped human development, the twisting of educational goals toward commercial interests, warped ethics, and the perversion of recreation. In *The Spirit of Youth and the City Streets* (1909), Addams criticized the increasingly dominant commercial interest in the labor and purchasing power of youth, and the corresponding neglect of their development. Increasingly, she argued, youth were offered "only two possibilities, both of them commercial: first, a chance to utilize by day their new and tender labor power in its factories and shops, and then another chance in the evening to extract from them their petty wages by pandering to their love of pleasure."[2] These commercial pressures extended to recreation, as shopping gradually assumed a larger and larger role as a pastime.

Economic and commercial forces, she argued, produced a vocational-technical emphasis in education and dramatically increased truancy as children were forced by the necessities imposed by poverty to enter the workforce at early ages. More broadly, believing that education occurred throughout a person's life as the person is molded by an environment, Addams criticized the society of her time for failing to provide meaningful work and recreation that would foster self-esteem and self-development. Many workers in the industrial system of the United States worked deadening jobs with little or no opportunity to develop their skills, capacities, curiosity, and intellect. Addams observed a "dreary round of uninteresting work, the pleasures narrowed down to those of appetite, the declining consciousness of brain power, and the lack of mental food which characterizes the lot of the large proportion of their fellow-citizens."[3]

Economic and commercial forces also warped ethical considerations. "The present industrial system," she argued, "thwarts our ethical demands, not only for social righteousness but for social order." Moral life, she believed, had been "captured by commercialism." She attacked the widespread assumption that the only possible appeal for motivation is to self-interest and money, two assumptions often taken for granted within a capitalist political economy. Within the workplace itself, Addams criticized the one-sided emphasis on production and the neglect of worker development. "We are apparently unable," she wrote, "to take our attention away from the product long enough to really focus it upon the producer." Finally, Addams criticized the distortion of electoral politics wrought by "the power of money over well-meaning men."[4]

To counter the increasing domination by commercial and economic forces, Addams advocated "socializing" democracy by applying democratic ideals to various social arenas. She sought to "give tangible expression to the democratic ideal" in people's everyday lives.[5] In *Democracy and Social Ethics* (1916), Addams applied this logic to the arenas of philanthropy, the family, household relations between employers and servants, education, the economy, and government. In philanthropy, she argued for an emphasis on social justice rather than charity, and a more systematic, sustained effort complemented by government intervention. In the family realm, she advocated more autonomy, education, and opportunities for girls and women and less domination by the father. In the household realm of employer and servant, she advocated more autonomy and respect for the servant.

Addams believed that education in a democracy should play a far broader role than preparing students for careers. Education should teach a specifically social ethics emphasizing the common lot of everyone in a democracy, rather than an outdated individualistic ethics emphasizing self-interest. It should instill awareness and commitment to key democratic values such as equality, the well-being of every member of the community, and "identification with the common lot which is the essential idea of Democracy." Education should instill an awareness of linked fates, common ground, common histories, and common goals. Education lays the basis for democratic solidarity by requiring us to "mix on the thronged and common road where all must turn out for one another, and at least see the size of one another's burdens."[6]

In economic arenas, Addams advocated more humane work environments, better wages, and a form of workplace democracy. Addams's stance on democratizing workplaces was most vividly revealed in her analysis of the Pullman strike of 1894 in Chicago. The strike began in the Pullman Palace Car Company, where workers struck after five successive wage reductions. The strikers were joined by the American Railway Union, leading to the halting of rail traffic. Eventually President Grover Cleveland intervened with federal troops to break the strike. This strike surprised many, including the owner of the Pullman enterprise, who paid the workers decent wages and provided them amenities such as housing and education. He allotted his workers "so model a town, such perfect surroundings," and still they struck.

Addams pointed out that beneath the veneer of good wages and amenities lay the same undemocratic structure of corporate America. The goal at Pullman, like at other companies, was "commercial and not social." The firm was managed "not for the development of the workman . . . but for the interests of the company owning the capital." Pullman represented "one will directing the energies of many others, without regard to their desires, and having in view in the last analysis only commercial results." The workers were denied any meaningful voice in the determination of their economic and social lives. The owner, despite the best of intentions, failed to appreciate the desire for greater autonomy and control by the workers. Addams concluded that "we are forced to challenge the ideal . . . floating in the minds of all philanthropic employers" of paternalist capitalism. She advocated substituting meaningful participation by workers in "the administration of industry."[7]

Addams pointed in the direction taken by many participatory democrats of broadening and extending the democratic ideal. She sought to make of democracy a whole way of life by breaking through artificial limitations and extending democratic ideals into multiple social arenas. This chapter takes a closer look at attempts to democratize one of those social arenas, the economy. Work dominates most people's time and energy. If Americans want to expand the reach and influence of democracy in their lives, there is no better place to start. Before considering alternatives to the liberal democratic emphasis on capitalism over democracy, several foundational points must be made.

First, capitalism and the bureaucratic socialism of the Stalinist Soviet Union hardly exhaust the possibilities for political-economic forms. As noted in the previous chapter, most contemporary political economies represent a blend of capitalism and socialism. These include relatively democratic forms of socialism as well as potentially more democratic forms of capitalism. Also, human ingenuity offers the possibility of inventing new forms. Different forms of capitalism and socialism represent particular developments under specific cultural and historical circumstances. New times offer new opportunities.

Second, we can distinguish, as C. B. Macpherson (1911–1987) did, between markets as one way of organizing some economic activity, and market society dominated and determined by markets. While markets have existed throughout recorded history, market society is a relatively recent phenomenon. We can use markets without yielding so completely to their dominance.

Third, markets offer only one among potentially many possible ways of organizing economic activity. Political economist Karl Polanyi (1886–1964) has shown that, in precapitalist societies, markets and trade operated, if at all, at the margins of society; that their impact on society was sometimes intentionally circumscribed; and that they handled a relatively small proportion of the overall circulation of goods and services needed for social reproduction. Polanyi identified other distributive mechanisms within precapitalist societies, including the family, the state, the royal court, and the monastery, and showed how these other distributive mechanisms were embedded in society without dominating it as markets do today. These other distributive mechanisms, he argued, also demonstrated other potential values besides profit underlying economic behavior, including reciprocity and redistribution. By historicizing the economy, Polanyi helped show that markets are not the only way of organizing economic activity, nor necessarily the best, and that profit is not the only motive for economic activity.

Fourth, to reaffirm an earlier point, markets should be understood not as neutral mechanisms but as power relationships. While markets sometimes enable mutually beneficial economic exchange, at other times they favor some over others. The means of this favoritism is unequal power. As contemporary political economist Lapo Berti (1944–) argued, the allocation of resources via markets always takes place under conditions of uncertainty, where "one use is preferred over another, not because of a rational ranking whereby *only one* optimum solution is identified, but on the basis of power relationships arising from resource distribution and, more generally, from society's material constitution."[8] Existing power imbalances create unequal opportunities for gain in markets, and result in unequal outcomes. These outcomes reinforce and harden preexisting power imbalances.

Fifth, the argument that economic redistribution and artificial limits on profit will undermine the motivation for work merits critical scrutiny. On the one hand, this argument sells humans short. It ignores an empirical history of human sacrifice, generosity, selfless striving, and hard work for its own sake. On the other hand, accepting the premise of a tie between markets and human motivation, one could argue that this is precisely why we need to alter or abandon capitalism—because, as Friedrich von Hayek (1899–1992) argued, it does not dependably reward hard work and other forms of merit. One-sided characterizations of human nature and human motivation ignore the empirical record that demonstrates a wide range of human traits and capacities. These one-sided characterizations generally mask an ideological orientation more than they attempt to accurately represent the historical record. By simply assuming selfishness and laziness, apologists for capitalism take an active stance in favor of capitalism and against alternatives.

One alternative framework for political economy, described at length in the following section, overturns classical and neoclassical assumptions about humans and motivation. Humanist economics makes a project of human nature and human motivation, rather than assuming the worst. In doing so, it opens new potential alternatives for a democratic political economy.

HUMANIST ECONOMICS

Humanist economics offers one alternative to the dominant neoclassical approach to economics emphasizing free markets, private property with few restrictions, efficiency, economic growth, competition, limited government, an extensive division of labor, comparative advantage, and a view of humans in which self-interest and acquisitiveness play central roles. While retaining or altering some of these elements of neoclassical economic thinking, humanist economics rejects others outright.

A Swiss count, J. C. Simonde de Sismondi (1773–1842), is sometimes identified as the "father" of humanist economics. Sismondi criticized existing political economy practices that simultaneously produced great wealth and widespread unhappiness. After three visits to England in 1818, 1824, and 1826, Sismondi wrote of paradoxes he observed there:

> In this astonishing country, which seems to be submitted to a great experiment for the instruction of the rest of the world, I have seen production increasing whilst enjoyments were diminishing. The mass of the nation here, no less than philosophers, seems to forget that the increase of wealth is not the end in political economy, but its instrument in procuring the happiness of all. I sought for this happiness in every class, and I could nowhere find it.

Sismondi also observed that the existing political economy "tended to make the rich man more rich . . . [and] the poor man more poor, more dependent, and more destitute." He attributed the poverty and suffering he observed in England to a "false economical system" in which profit and the pursuit of wealth took precedence over people's basic well-being and happiness. Self-interest and the invisible hand had conspired not to produce universal prosperity and happiness, as Adam Smith (1723–1790) argued, but to undermine it. They had also produced a new and miserable class of industrial workers, subject to daily exploitation and deprivation, and ongoing disruption via business cycles caused by periodic overproduction and high unemployment.

Presaging Karl Marx (1818–1883), he blamed the problem on the inability of average workers to purchase the products they produced.

Sismondi proposed a different basis for economic activity. In place of material wealth, he proposed that economic activity should be directed "to secure the development of Man, and of all men." This would require focusing on meeting everyone's basic human needs for, without this, the mass of workers would waste away in pursuit of basic survival. According to Sismondi, "No nation can be considered prosperous if the condition of the poor, who form part of it, is not secure" in their basic human needs. He called the provision of these needs "the common right of Man," which "should be secured to all those who do what they can to forward common labour." The relative prosperity of a nation can be judged, according to Sismondi, by the degree to which it achieves the goals of meeting basic human needs and providing the means of happiness for everyone.

Sismondi did not blame private property per se for England's failure to achieve these goals. Instead, like Jean-Jacques Rousseau (1712–1778) and Thomas Jefferson (1743–1826), he blamed it on the huge inequalities of property ownership in which some had fantastic amounts of it while most had none. He believed, however, that private property was legitimate only if it met the twin goals of procuring basic human needs and enabling happiness. As he put it, "The fundamental condition of society is, that no one shall die of hunger; it is *only* on this condition that property is acknowledged and guaranteed."[9] Sismondi proposed that the state intervene to slow industrialization and urbanization, protect the small farmer and artisan, support the formation of unions, guarantee shorter working hours, force employers to support workers during layoffs and in old age, and provide public jobs for the unemployed.

John Ruskin (1819–1900), an English writer of the nineteenth century, challenged the prevailing view that economic prosperity could be founded on self-interest. In the opening paragraph of his *Unto This Last* (1864), he wrote:

> Among the delusions which at different periods have possessed themselves of the minds of large masses of the human race, perhaps the most curious—certainly the least creditable—is the modern *soi-disant* science of political economy, based on the idea that an advantageous code of social action may be determined irrespective of the influence of social affection.

Ruskin criticized the reduction of human motivation to self-interest on both empirical and moral grounds. Empirically, he compared the attempt by classical political economists to found economics on self-interest alone to a gymnast with no skeleton. While it might be plausible to assert that the lack of a skeleton would benefit the gymnast, no amount of tortured assumption could make it so. Classical economists, he argued, overlooked the empirical fact that most people are driven not just by self-interest but also by the motive power of "the Soul," and "the force of this very peculiar agent, as an unknown quality, enters into all the political economist's equations, without his knowledge, and falsifies every one of their results."

Morally, by dismissing motives other than self-interest, Ruskin argued, classical economists placed humans on the same moral footing as "rats or swine." Ruskin denied that self-interest alone provided the best, or most effective, motivation. An ideal employee–employer relationship demonstrates this, he argued. Worker motivation and productivity cannot be achieved based on self-interest alone. It must be based on justice, mutual goodwill, and cooperation. The current situation in England, marked by mutual animosity, hardly met this ideal. He blamed this on the prevailing practice of hiring "a workman at a rate of wages variable according to the demand for labor, and with the risk of being any time thrown out of this situation by chance of trade." In this situation, "no action of the affections can take place but only an explosive action of disaffections." The obvious resolution of this problem, according to Ruskin, was to guarantee a just wage and permanent employment to every worker. Economic security would motivate the worker to strive on behalf of the employer.

Like Sismondi, Ruskin refused to blame "private enterprise" itself. Government, he argued, should intervene only in that private enterprise "which poisons its neighborhood, or speculates for individual gain at common risk."[10] He thus left open the possibility of retaining some features of a capitalist political economy, albeit one required to operate within socially beneficial bounds.

John Hobson (1858–1940), another British political economist, drew much of his inspiration and many of his ideas from Ruskin, while echoing some of the themes of Sismondi. He criticized classical political economy for its myopic reduction of motivation to self-interest and value to money. According to Hobson, "A science which still takes money as its standard of value, and regards man as a means of making money, is, in the nature of the case, incapable of facing the deep and complex problems" of political economy. In place of "making money" as the end of economic activity, Hobson substituted the development of human personality. He distinguished between a lower and higher nature, the former devoted to basic ends of survival and prosperity, the latter to intellectual and spiritual ends. In focusing entirely on the former, Ruskin argued, classical economists reduced the human to a bundle of wants convertible into the standard currency of money. Hobson also faulted classical economists for assuming that all consumption generates positive benefits. Consumption could, and often did, incur costs borne by the consumer distracted from higher pursuits.

Hobson evaluated the political economy of his time according to its effect on the development of human personality. He noted that the menial, monotonous, routine character of factory work undermined this development, as did unemployment, insecurity, and competition that produce anxiety and stress. To rectify this, Hobson followed Sismondi and Ruskin in advocating social control of the economy via government intervention. He was an early advocate of a "living wage" and advocated free public education and public health, old-age pensions, housing, insurance, and sufficient leisure for recreation. Going beyond Sismondi and Ruskin, he also advocated at least partial worker democracy in the form of providing them a voice in management. He called this "an essential condition for the growth of the sense of industry as a social service" and a means toward developing a sense of the common good. "So long as the thoughts of a worker do not, and cannot, go beyond the near implications of his labor-bargain, and his sense of cooperation is confined to his trade-union," he argued, "it is idle to suppose that the more general problems of our economic system can be rightly solved." Worker participation in management would give them "a wider and more conscious sense of the solidarity and social value of the economic system as a whole."

Hobson cited three requirements for the economy if it were to contribute effectively to the development of human personality. First, any legitimate political economy must provide economic security, without which the elevation of human character and personality would be impossible. Regular employment, he argued, "conduces to steadiness of character and provision for the future without anxiety." The inability to count on dependable, regular work "takes out of a man that confidence in the fundamental rationality of life which is essential to soundness of character." Countervailing messages from religion, ethics, or education could have little consequence in countering the effect on workers of "such powerful illustrations of the unreason and injustice of industry and of society." In response to the claim that economic security would undermine workers' motivation to work hard and thus undermine character, Hobson asserted that economic security would elevate workers' characters by drawing them out of a numbing and mindless struggle for bare survival. It would give them "that confidence in the fundamental rationality of life that is essential to soundness of character." The result, he believed, would be greater civic virtue and social solidarity contributing to sustained effort:

> All proposals by organized public effort to abolish destitution give rise to fears lest by so doing we should sap the incentives to personal effort, and so impair the character of the poor. Among such critics there is entertained no corresponding hope or conviction that such a policy may, by the better and securer conditions of life and employment it affords, sow the seeds of civic feeling and of social solidarity among large sections of our population where life hitherto had been little else than a sordid and unmeaning struggle.

Workplace democracy, he argued, would reinforce the positive effects of economic security by increasing workers' sense of social solidarity.

Hobson's second requirement for a political economy to contribute to human personality development was economic justice. Economic fortune disconnected from merit left many with little or nothing to show for their best efforts. Workers' independence and motivation depended on overcoming this injustice. "Only by resolving unearned into earned income," Hobson wrote,

> so that all Property is duly earned either by individuals or by societies, can an ethical basis be laid for social industry. So long as property appears to come miraculously or capriciously, irrespective of efforts or requirements, and as long as it is withheld irrationally, it is idle to preach "the dignity of labor" or to inculcate sentiments of individual self-help.

This passage suggests three separate points: that workers must feel confident that their efforts will result in decent wages and economic security, that unearned wealth inherited by some is incompatible with a just economy, and that complete private control over wealth is "irrational." A more just political economy would elevate human personality by making it possible for workers to consider the larger social good, and also to concentrate on aspects of the self beyond motives for survival:

> It is evident that this justly-ordered environment would do much to raise the physical, and more to raise the moral efficiency of the individual as a wealth producer and consumer. But its most important contribution to the value and the growth of human welfare would lie in other fields of personality than the distinctly economic, in the liberation, realization and improved condition of other intellectual and spiritual energies at present thwarted by or subordinated to industrialism.[11]

Third, Hobson argued that workers must have access to meaningful work if it is to develop their personalities and characters. His discussion of meaningful work again included a consideration of participation by workers in the management of industry. According to Hobson, work was increasingly organized in a way that engaged only a small part of the individual worker's overall self. Echoing both Marx and John Dewey (1859–1952), Hobson argued that this inevitably resulted not just in a division of labor generally, but a division of the laborer as well. It also ensured that much of the human personality remained undeveloped.

Hobson advocated participatory democracy in the workplace as a solution. Workplace democracy necessarily engages more of the self. It requires that workers employ, and thus develop, their intellectual faculties in helping manage a firm. According to Hobson, it also develops the social and spiritual parts of the self, as workers develop more awareness and concern for others. Social solidarity would increase among workers as a more communal, cooperative orientation based on shared work and common goals would replace competition against each other for jobs and wages.

Richard Tawney (1880–1962) outlined his contribution to humanist economics in *The Acquisitive Society* (1920). As the title suggests, Tawney portrayed his times in terms of an all-encompassing drive to acquire possessions and consume. This, he argued, distracted attention from more noble ends and ensured that many would not have access to basic necessities. He asked a "simple question" of defenders of the existing political economy:

> To those who clamor, as many now do, "Produce! Produce!" one simple question may be addressed—"Produce what?" Food, clothing, house-room, art, knowledge? By all means! But if the nation is scantily furnished with these things had it not better stop producing a good many others which fill shop windows in Regent Street?

Tawney's substitute for the acquisitive society was a "functional society," one oriented first toward satisfying basic human needs. Like others in the humanist economics tradition, Tawney submitted private property to a test: does it advance the end of satisfying everyone's basic human needs? If not, he was willing to sacrifice it to more important social ends. "Property," he argued, "is the instrument, security is the object, and when some alternative way is forthcoming of providing the latter, it does not appear in practice that any loss of confidence or freedom or independence is caused by the absence of the former." Tawney noted that absentee ownership of property[12] increasingly characterized advanced capitalism. He believed that this "undermine[d] the creative energy which produced property and which in earlier ages it protected" and justified the nationalization of industry with workers given partial control in its management:

> If the abolition of functionless property transferred the control of production to bodies representing those who perform constructive work . . . [employees'] associations which are now purely defensive would be in a position not merely to criticize and oppose but to advise, to initiate and to enforce upon their own members the obligations of the craft.

Tawney denied that we could rid the species of negative qualities such as selfishness and greed and their antisocial effects. However, reorganizing industry along the lines he proposed would "create an environment in which those are not the qualities which are encouraged."[13]

Mahatma Gandhi (1869–1948), who attributed many of his ideas to Ruskin, applied humanist economic ideas to India and other developing countries. Like Hobson and Ruskin, Gandhi rued the separation of economic activity from humanist ethical values. He argued that the end of any economic system should be "human happiness combined with full mental and moral growth." An economy must, of course, produce the goods needed to provide for basic human necessities. Beyond that, it must produce in accordance with the values of equality, nonviolence, and creativity. In words presaging those of Pope John Paul II (1920–2005), Gandhi argued that "any economic development had to be primarily oriented to raising the poorest to subsistence." But it also had to meet higher social needs as well as physical needs. To achieve these ends, Gandhi called for the destruction of the colonial system, and an economic restructuring based on "self-reliant, egalitarian village economies in the rural areas."[14] This suggested that industry must be small scale, using appropriate human-scale technology that would not alienate workers.

Like Gandhi, E. F. Schumacher (1911–1977) applied humanist economics to developing economies. He proposed an economics "as if people mattered." Schumacher oriented his ideas toward small-scale and labor-intensive development, relying on local, indigenous technology that came to be known as "appropriate technology." He believed that the goal of development economics should be to create "millions of new workplaces in the rural areas and small towns" of Southern countries.[15] This would require four basic components. First, workplaces must be created where people now live, not primarily in metropolitan areas to which people must migrate. Second, the workplaces must be small enough so that they could be created with little capital. Third, production technology must be simple, minimizing the requirements of production, organization, finance, and marketing. Fourth, production must be oriented toward meeting local needs, created from local materials. Schumacher emphasized economics on a local scale, cooperative and social ownership of the means of production, the necessity of meaningful, satisfying work, and conservation of resources. His book *Small Is Beautiful* (1973) enjoyed enormous success and was translated into at least fifteen different languages. This suggests that the ideas of humanist economics remain vital and appealing to many.

Humanist economics can now be summarized. First, humanist economics criticizes capitalism for organizing work in a dehumanizing way, stunting and distorting human development, undermining basic material security for many, and depriving individuals of democratic participation in the workplace.

Second, the satisfaction of basic human needs and the development of human personality replace profit and aggregate production as the measures of validity of any economic system. Implicitly and explicitly, humanist economics begins from the view that human nature includes traits that range from base instincts to higher intellectual, psychological, and spiritual aspirations. Humans clearly need to meet their biological needs, but they also need to develop their personality into its full capacity. Toward this end, a properly structured society is essential, since humans are learners whose identities change with their environment. Humanist economics substitutes an emphasis on factors such as moral development, higher consciousness, and community for the classical and neoclassical emphasis on economic growth and consumption.

Third, humanist economics endorses both private property and the market only to the degree that they advance social goals and meet everyone's basic human needs. If they fail to advance those goals, then we can and should interfere with them, potentially transforming them. Returning control of private property, markets, and economic forces more generally to common people in their everyday lives entails minimally some measure of social control over the economy and the workplace.

Humanist economics thus endorses, fourth, some measure of workplace democracy and democratization of the economy. This might entail decentralization of economic forces, worker participation in management, or community control over economic forces.

Fifth, humanist economics rejects the dominant view in classical and neoclassical economics of human nature composed primarily of self-interest, acquisitiveness, and competitiveness. This view of human nature assumes away empirical examples of virtue in various forms, and treats as a given what ought to be a theoretical and practical project: the development of human character. Defenders of the dominant view of human nature deliberately purge economics of any ethical or moral content—at least in pretense, if not in fact, since their descriptions quickly become prescriptions. The classical and neoclassical view of human nature is thus, according to humanist economics, both empirically wrong and morally corrupt. While humanist economics does not deny self-interest, it constrains it within the need to advance a common good, understood to mean material sufficiency, dignity, and personal development for all.

Sixth, humanist economics posits objective needs shared by all humans. As we saw earlier, by calling all human needs morally equivalent subjective "preferences," the utilitarian liberal foundations of neoclassical economics disallow the possibility of making critical distinctions between "wants" and "needs" and of identifying objective needs. These objective needs begin with biological needs for survival and sustenance such as food, shelter, and medical care. The humanist economists' insistence on curtailing expenditures on luxury goods when necessary to divert resources toward meeting everyone's basic human needs is founded on this point. Stop pretending, the humanist economist argues, that "a rising tide will lift all boats" or that benefits will "trickle down" to satisfy people's basic needs. Instead, go straight at them; make their satisfaction the first and primary goal and allow luxury goods only as secondary products of political economy. Humanist economics also forthrightly asserts objective needs for personal development, including the "higher" needs of self-awareness, moral capacity, and social consciousness. A humane economy should satisfy both physical and psychological needs.

Finally, humanist economics ties human character and personality to the political economy in which humans live. If you want to encourage selfishness, greed, and acquisitiveness, then capitalism in its current form can reasonably be your choice. If you want average people to imagine and attend to a common good in addition to their self-interest, then the political economy must support this via conducive incentives. If you want workers to commit to the well-being of others and to the economic enterprise for which they work, then the political economy must be just and must guarantee a secure living wage. If you want the political economy to encourage the creation of responsible democratic citizens, then it must offer ample opportunities for practicing the arts of democratic citizenship within the workplace itself.

AN ECONOMY OF SUFFICIENCY

Ecologist and development theorist Wolfgang Sachs (1946–) builds upon some of the humanist economists' ideas while extending them to encompass ecological concerns. Like the humanist economists, Sachs both criticizes the existing political economy and offers an alternative vision. Sachs focuses his critique on "developmentalism," his term for the dominant approach to development considered earlier as modernization theory. However, he intends his critique to encompass the underlying framework of neoclassical economics with its emphasis on materialism, production, consumption, continuous growth, and free markets. Developmentalism, according to Sachs, aims at developing the world along the lines of a single image offered by neoclassical economics and represented by the "overdeveloped" industrialized countries. These countries, he argues, are part of the problem, not the solution. The economistic values they represent "distract attention from the urgency of public debate on our relationship with nature, for they preclude the search for societies that live graciously within their means, and for social changes that take their inspiration from indigenous ideas of the good and proper life." According to Sachs, developmentalism "is fundamentally at odds with both the quest for justice among the world's people and the aspiration to reconcile humanity and nature."[16] It pays too little attention to the causes of poverty and to alternatives more consistent with ecological concerns. He identifies a dual crisis and a dilemma within developmentalist thinking: any attempt to solve the crisis of nature threatens to aggravate the crisis of justice, and vice versa. Solving the crisis of nature, if it requires reducing economic growth, undermines growth-oriented strategies for battling poverty; solving the crisis of justice through growth exacerbates ecological problems. Sachs's work represents an attempt to resolve this dual crisis and dilemma.

Developmentalism poses continuous economic growth as the solution to injustice. Expanding the economy opens the theoretical possibility of increasing each person's share of material wealth, thus reducing poverty worldwide. This dedication to a growth strategy represents, according to Sachs, an attempt to sidestep the difficult questions of justice by making redistribution unnecessary. As a solution to injustice, Sachs argues, a growth strategy empirically has failed, as poverty continues to increase along with production.

Greater production and continuous economic growth also continue the assault on nature. The ecological costs of the growth approach have been rendered invisible by shifting them onto future generations, distant countries, and poor people. Environmental concerns have been assimilated into the rhetoric and practice of developmentalism in the guise of "sustainable development." However, this form of sustainable development has not abandoned growth as the solution. It seeks greater resource efficiency, but gains are swamped by growth. For example, improvements in automobile fuel efficiency have been overwhelmed by increases in the number of cars on the road. Developmentalists view growth as the cure for the problems caused by development. In theory, growth allows us to pay for environmental cleanup. In practice, it means perversely that we need to pollute the environment in order to clean it up.

Sachs also rejects the developmentalist emphasis on technology as a cure for poverty and degraded environments. He calls technology a "Trojan horse" because, in adopting a particular form of technology, a whole way of life accompanies it. If you buy an electric mixer, you must also acquire the outlet in the wall and link up to the extensive systems of material infrastructure that bring electricity to that outlet. If you buy a car, you soon find yourself immersed in car payments, automobile insurance, ever-increasing traffic, road rage, and the multiple hassles associated with maintaining it. If you buy hybrid seeds, you must also buy expensive fertilizers, pesticides, and irrigation systems to make them grow.

Most fundamentally, Sachs argues, developmentalism advocates the wrong values. Under developmentalism, the economy dominates society rather than the more rational opposite. Developmentalism precludes consideration of other less material or nonmaterial paths to development and obliterates more holistic approaches that recognize nature's intrinsic value. The pursuit of rich spiritual and aesthetic lives yield to the developmentalist emphasis on materialism and consumption. Under developmentalism, "well-being . . . is recast as well-having" in which "the many different ways to the good life are implicitly reduced to the one single race-track towards a higher standard of living." "The Utopia of affluence undercuts the Utopia of liberation" by loading us up with material aspirations that decrease our time for other pursuits.[17]

Sachs's vision for change departs fundamentally from developmentalism. "Tinkering here and there will not do," he argues. "It will not be possible that all citizens of the world will share in the fossil fuel-based, money-driven development model," because this model precludes both distributive justice and long-term ecological sustainability. Turning a core assumption of developmentalism on its head, Sachs argues that the search for justice and ecological sustainability must "start with changing the rich—not with changing the poor" as developmentalist economics assumes. Turning the affluent, industrialized countries into "good global neighbors" requires "building economies which weigh much less heavily on the planet and on other nations." The scale of this change must be enormous in order to be effective: the affluent, industrialized countries "will have to bring down their throughput of energy and materials by a factor of 10 within the next 50 years . . . to reduce their resource weight by 80–90 per cent with respect to the year 1990." Sachs acknowledges that this amounts to a "civilizational transition."[18]

In place of developmentalism, Sachs advocates an economy of sufficiency. This economy of sufficiency is characterized, first of all, by a norm of frugality. Frugality means "good housekeeping" in which

> food is stored, tools are carefully maintained, furniture is handed down from generation to generation. Necessary possessions are fully used, while outside purchases are kept to a minimum. Each coin is turned over twice before it is spent, each transaction is carried out prudently, sometimes even with misgivings. However, the point of good housekeeping is not economizing for the sake of investment, but saving for the sake of independence.

Frugality is "a mark of cultures free from the frenzy of accumulation."[19] Although developmentalists often mistake frugality for destitution, destitution occurs only in situations of injustice when people are deprived of access to land, water, wood and other means of subsistence.

An economy of sufficiency is characterized, second, by simplicity of means and richness of ends. Developmentalism focuses on means without critically scrutinizing goals. It advocates more growth, more consumption, higher speeds, and more advanced technology without considering the possibility that the direction in which these aim may be fundamentally flawed. Sachs advocates a critical focus on basic values and goals, as well as the means of getting there. The emphasis in Western culture on materialism, production, and consumption reveals a commitment to "the cult of things." At the heart of Sachs's ideal lies a willingness to make do with less material goods. Unlike developmentalists and neoclassical economists, he asks, "How much is enough?" This question "leads without much detour to the question 'What do we want?' Sustainability in the last instance springs from a fresh inquiry into the meaning of the good life." He advocates that we seek "wealth in time rather than wealth in goods," and that we pursue "well-being instead of well-having." We need a "prudent moderation of ends" more consistent with ecological sustainability, and "new models of wealth" consistent with distributive justice in which every person has sufficient means of leading a good life. A focus on efficient means of achieving our ends is also important. However, "while efficiency is about doing things right, sufficiency is about doing the right things." Sachs does not advocate a return to pretechnological society where people live in caves and cook over open fires. He favors creating "sophisticated but moderate-impact technologies" that are "resource-light."[20]

Third, an economy of sufficiency is characterized by greater attention to the diversity of cultural approaches to sustenance. Not all cultures favor material accumulation and "overdevelopment" over other forms of being in the world, and these should be recognized and valued. Some of these other cultures "intentionally live on intermediate levels of material demand." The affluent, industrialized countries can learn from them.

Fourth, an economy of sufficiency is characterized by a willingness to accept limits to growth, to materialism, and to consumption. Sachs advocates "societies that are able to cope gracefully with finiteness," that adopt a mode of "lean consumption," that function at "an intermediary level of performance," and that are "able not to want what [they] would in fact be capable of providing." Embracing limits, he argues, need not mean a reduction in the quality of life. A "prudent moderation of ends" can lead to self-liberation, as an emphasis on the quality of life replaces the current emphasis on consumption. We can "live with elegance" inside limits.[21]

An economy of sufficiency resolves the dual crisis of ecology and justice, and the dilemma that accompanies them, according to Sachs. Living within limits better ensures ecological sustainability. By calibrating our ends to the ability of nature to provide for them over the long term, we ease the pressure currently placed on ecological systems. Abandoning the fiction of continuous growth in which everyone eventually prospers forces us to confront distributive injustice head on and move toward effective redistributive policies. We can all live well within a culture of frugality, if the affluent countries lighten their footprints on Southern countries and the environment, and steps are taken to ensure material security for everyone.

A DEMOCRATIC ECONOMY

Political theorists offer both consequentialist and rights-based rationales for democratizing the economy. One consequentialist argument, previously considered, emphasizes the educative impact of a political economy on human identity. According to John Dewey and the humanist economists, humans acquire a substantial portion of their character, skills, motivations, and overall identity from their social environment. If we accept that argument, the rest follows logically. If we want to nurture specifically democratic identities and capacities, we must create specifically democratic social environments that nurture democratic skills and dispositions.

We also find consequentialist arguments for democratizing the economy in Rousseau and John Stuart Mill (1806–1873). Participation plays three main roles in Rousseau's thinking. First, like other participatory democratic theorists, Rousseau believed that citizens develop their character through political participation. They acquire capacities and skills such as civic virtue, critical thinking, leadership, and debate skills. Participation educates citizens through practice. Second, according to Rousseau, participation maintains the freedom of individuals by preventing others from imposing laws undermining their autonomy and independence. Third, participation helps maintain a general will of common interests. If everyone participates, then everyone's interests are represented and the result will be policies that advance a common, rather than particular, good. To maintain this general will, it is important that "each citizen speak only for himself."[22] Ongoing participation allows for constant vigilance against seizure and distortion of the general will into a particular will.

Rousseau's arguments apply as much in economic as political arenas. If a social order partly determines human identity, and if the economy is part of the social order, then participation in an economy has specific consequences for the development of human attitudes, skills, and dispositions. Ideally, economic practices will support, rather than undermine, democratic character. The way to ensure that they do is to democratize the economic environment. Second, the question of maintaining the freedom of each individual is as germane to economic as political practices. Direct participation in the management and operation of economic firms enables the individual worker's freedom. Absent this participation, the worker is subject to the domination imposed by those who own and control the firm. Third, participation in economic decisions encourages the development of a general will of sorts within firms and the economy as a whole. As some of the humanist economists argued, it increases workers' commitment to the common good within firms and in the larger economy. Participation enlarges the workers' perspectives beyond their immediate interests in better wages and working conditions to include, for example, the impact on the environment of economic practices and the long-term viability of their firm.

J. S. Mill also emphasized the effect of political participation on the development of citizens. He argued that political institutions can be judged according to "the degree in which they promote the general mental advancement of the community, including under that phrase advancement in intellect, in virtue, and in practical activity and efficiency." Even if a benevolent despot could govern more effectively and wisely, the option still ranks second best to popular government in which average people participate and, in the process of participation, develop themselves. Like Rousseau, Mill was especially concerned that citizens develop the capacity for civic virtue. When a person does not participate in public affairs, he or she "never thinks of any collective interest, of any objects to be pursued jointly with others, but only in competition with them, and in some measure at their expense." Political participation forces the citizen to "weigh interests not his own; to be guided, in case of conflicting claims, by another rule than his private partialities; to apply, at every turn, principles and maxims which have for their reason of existence the common good."

Mill applied this logic to the economy as well. Moral, intellectual, and practical development, he argued, requires that the workplace be democratized. Participation in the management of collective affairs within industry could, like participation in political affairs, lead to a "moral transformation" of individuals in which they develop their "social sympathies and the practical intelligence." "If mankind is to continue to improve," Mill argued, the organization of the workplace must be conducive. A workplace divided between "a capitalist as chief, and workpeople without a voice in the management" hardly qualifies. He proposed instead "the association of the laborers themselves on terms of equality, collectively owning the capital with which they carry on their operations, and working under managers elected and removable by themselves."[23]

In his *Preface to Economic Democracy* (1985), contemporary democratic theorist Robert Dahl (1915–) presented a second kind of rationale for democratizing the economy based on human rights. According to Dahl, a rational belief in democracy entails "the view that in a certain kind of human association, the process of government should as far as possible meet democratic criteria." The reason for this is that "people involved in this kind of association possess a *right*, an inalienable right to govern themselves by the democratic process." The validity of this right rests upon certain assumptions about the nature of a democratic association and the people in it. These include the need to reach collective decisions, that binding collective decisions should be made by those they bind and not by others, that the good of each person is entitled to equal consideration, that each person is the best judge of his or her interests, that each is equally qualified to deliberate and decide, and that valued things should be fairly distributed. Assuming the validity of these assumptions, it establishes "a claim to democracy *as a matter of right* in *any* association of any kind for which the assumptions are valid."

Whether or not citizens choose to exercise it, they have an "inalienable right to govern themselves by means of the democratic process" in any association for which the assumptions hold. This includes the "*right* to govern ourselves democratically within our economic enterprises." According to Dahl, "*If* democracy is justified in governing the state, then it must *also* be justified in governing economic enterprises; and to say that it is *not* justified in governing economic enterprises is to imply that it is not justified in governing the state." This right overrides the property rights that currently award complete control to owners of property. The right to property is merely utilitarian or instrumental, while self-government is a "fundamental and inalienable right." Therefore "any legal entitlement to private ownership of the economy is *subordinate* to the right of self-government." Dahl recommended a "system of economic enterprises collectively owned and democratically governed by all the people who work in them."[24] Dahl wanted to democratize each individual firm, but retain the market as the primary mechanism of allocation.

Even though he justified workplace democracy primarily on the basis of rights, Dahl also included some consequentialist arguments. He argued that workplace democracy would overcome the problem of minority tyranny in which a wealthy elite exercises disproportionate political power in America. Give workers democratic control of corporations, he argued, and this would counter the disproportionate power currently held by the wealthy. He also argued that workplace democracy would improve democratic government of the state by educating us into better citizenship and increasing political equality. It would make us better citizens by giving common people extensive practice in the arts of democratic citizenship. It would increase political equality by leveling power across society, and by increasing the likelihood that common people would participate effectively in politics.

Having considered two kinds of rationales for democratizing the economy, what are some specific practical ways of doing so? Democratic theorists identify at least four practical directions for thought and action: equalizing power between labor and capital, democratizing the workplace, making economic power socially and publicly accountable, and decentralizing economic power.

Equalizing Power between Labor and Capital

Power between labor and capital can be equalized, first, by increasing the role and power of labor unions. Unions offer strength in numbers, absent when workers face management as lone individuals. Collective bargaining enables labor to drive harder bargains with capital. Unions play a much larger role in Europe and are one of the major reasons for the greater equality in European countries.

Second, and closely related, increasing the credibility and effectiveness of their major weapon against capital, the strike, can increase the power of unions. Most importantly, legislation can be passed banning replacement workers and lockouts. The ability to hire replacement workers undermines the credibility and effectiveness of strikes by allowing management to simply say to workers "if you strike, we will replace you." Management uses lockouts to maintain the submission of workers by depriving them of their income. Legislation that currently prevents secondary boycotts and strikes can also be dismantled. Members of one union use these to support members of another union. For example, members of a truckers' union might refuse to deliver grocery products to a grocery chain whose meat cutters are striking. Secondary boycotts and strikes offer workers a means of increasing their power by presenting an even more united front against capital.

Third, the mobility of capital can be slowed down. Currently, capital can credibly threaten labor with relocation should workers not bow to management's demands. This decreases labor's ability to negotiate living wages and a safe working environment. There are several credible proposals for slowing capital's mobility, including most prominently a proposal to tax capital mobility. This proposal has the advantage of slowing capital mobility while at the same time raising funds to support workers who lose their jobs.

Fourth, the Federal Reserve Board can be required to reverse its preferential treatment of capital over labor. As seen earlier, the Fed ranks inflation-fighting among its highest priorities, in part because inflation erodes the value of investments and other forms of capital. In pursuing this goal, it implicitly accepts the likelihood of relatively high unemployment. A policy of full employment would increase the bargaining power of labor by shrinking the pool of unemployed.

Democratizing the Workplace

The second practical direction, democratizing the workplace, is closely related to the first general option of equalizing power between labor and management, since most proposals for a democratic workplace entail some equalization of power. First, at a very minimal level of democratization—if it can even be called democratization—management can solicit workers' opinions when making decisions that affect the company or the workers themselves. Management will then make the actual decision, taking into account the workers' contribution, or not. Since this leaves the hierarchical management structure of the corporation untouched, workers do not gain any power. Some firms already routinely consult their workers as a way of showing respect, of genuinely seeking contributions from their workers, of seeking to improve worker morale, or simply of adding a patina of power-sharing to deflect workers' disgruntlement.

Second, Employee Stock Ownership Programs (ESOPs) can partly democratize the workplace and increase the power of labor by making them owners. If labor's share of ownership grows large enough, workers gain the ability to influence, and perhaps control, decisions affecting the firm and their livelihood. This has the added advantage of giving workers a deeper stake in the health of their firm, increasing their commitment to it and the likelihood that they will make responsible long-term decisions regarding the firm. The democratic nature of ESOPs is undermined if one vote is tied to each share of stock and workers own variable amounts of voting stock leading to political inequality within the firm.

Third, workers can be given the authority to make workplace decisions, which gives them increased control over their work life. Some firms already experiment minimally with this, generally not in the name of democratization but as a way of hopefully increasing worker satisfaction and productivity. The kinds of decisions granted to workers can range from minimal to extensive. Minimally, workers can control issues such as how best to run a machine, how to manage work breaks, how to best assemble a product, or how to divide work responsibilities among themselves. More extensive democratization occurs when workers gain control over more fundamental issues such as their work schedules and their salary and benefit mix. Management might still retain ultimate control by, for example, setting aggregate figures for wages and benefits while letting the workers work out the details.

Fourth, workers could be organized into work teams or units in which each worker participates fully and equally in making decisions and carrying out work responsibilities. This does not mean that they could do just anything they wanted to do; workers would hold each other accountable to standards of excellence and effectiveness, in the same way that management holds workers accountable in a traditional, undemocratic firm.

Fifth, co-management schemes offer workers real, effective decision-making authority. One strategy involves putting workers' representatives on boards of directors and management teams in sufficient numbers to make a difference and to offset capital's voice. Whether or not these result in significant democratization of the workplace depends on the level of representation afforded to workers. If the workers have only one representative and no veto authority, it is unlikely that workers' interests will be significantly advanced, and in this case the level of democratization is relatively minimal. On the other hand, if workers secure equal voice in policy making, planning, and day-to-day operations, a greater degree of democracy within the firm is achieved.

A related, sixth proposal is to form separate employee assemblies, modeled on the Workers Councils of Germany, that must approve all significant corporate decisions. This proposal builds into economic organizations an institution taken for granted in the U.S. system of government: bicameral decision-making authority. It increases the power of labor by affording workers the institutional means of effective participation in decision making.

Finally, workplaces can be completely democratized through buyouts in which workers gain both complete ownership and full control. Of course, democracy is consistent with the delegation of responsibility. Nothing in principle would prevent workers from hiring expertise in management and in technical areas. The key point is that workers would retain ultimate authority for retaining or firing the managers and for setting overall policy for the enterprise.

Making Economic Power Socially and Publicly Accountable

A third practical direction for democratizing the economy is to make economic power more socially and publicly accountable. Currently, economic actors often determine the behavior of policy makers, rather than the other way around. In a representative democracy, this is wholly unacceptable, since it is through elected and accountable policy makers that the people exercise their sovereignty. So long as policy makers are accountable to owners of capital, rather than vice versa, democracy is undermined. If capital determines the quality of life within a community, rather than a community determining the behavior of capital, democracy suffers.

To address this problem, first of all, the tax on capital flight already noted would help make economic power accountable by exacting costs on corporations' socially destructive relocation. At a minimum, it would force owners of capital to think twice before abandoning one locale for another. It would allow a local community to say to capital, "We will make you pay for pulling out," and this increases the bargaining position of community members.

A second proposal, taxing currency transactions, attains the same end by increasing the costs to corporations of economic globalization. Any firm that operates in more than one country must sooner or later exchange home currency for another currency. Taxing these currency exchanges would impose a cost on economic behavior that has been deemed socially destructive by destroying local jobs. Taxing currency transactions would also impose costs on socially destructive currency speculation. At present, currency traders buy and sell trillions of dollars' worth of currencies every day, much of it in the form of currency speculation. In recent times, they have brought entire national and regional economies to their knees. Imposing a tax on currency transactions would help rein in their sometimes-destructive behavior.

Third, policy makers can pass and enforce regulations protecting workers and the environment. World Trade Organization (WTO) critics have especially raised this issue. WTO rules currently favor capital by increasing its mobility without imposing balancing costs. WTO critics propose fair trade rules, or side agreements, that offset capital's power. These rules and agreements would increase local, regional, and national actors' ability to control the behavior of capital. Legislation can help ensure that American firms think twice before relocating in order to avoid environmental cleanup costs, taxation, and living-wage levels. These regulations and agreements would be more effective if enacted transnationally. Otherwise, one nation can play off another in a competition for economic investment, resulting in a "race to the bottom."

Fourth, shareholder actions and consumer boycotts offer proven tools for controlling the behavior of corporations. Though often difficult to initiate and sustain, both can be effective.

Fifth, individual investors can help control corporations' behavior through socially responsible investing. By rewarding socially responsible corporations and punishing socially irresponsible ones, investors can make at least some impact on corporate decision making. Many investment funds now routinely include a list of socially responsible investments in their portfolio.

Sixth, various corporate governance reforms such as community stakeholder representation on boards would increase community control of corporations. Currently, corporate boards of directors are stacked one-sidedly with directors representing the interests of capital. Other stakeholders, including labor, the environment, and local communities, can also be independently represented. Community representation on corporate boards of directors offers a direct road to community control of corporate behavior.

Seventh, the current emphasis on property and corporate rights over human rights can be reversed. Sometimes profit must be sacrificed in order to guarantee basic human rights to food, shelter, and medical attention and to guarantee the long-term viability of the environment. This strategy can be pursued through a combination of a progressive taxation scheme, government regulations, and public confiscation of private property when necessary to ensure basic human rights and the protection of the environment. Proposals by capital's proponents to achieve human rights and ecological sustainability precisely through property rights are worth considering and implementing selectively if and when they actually attain socially desirable ends.

Finally, the public could retain ownership and control of capital. This option, known as democratic socialism, would require public ownership of the major means of production and would enable community control via the mechanism of government. It would necessarily entail moving away from capitalism as we know it, though not necessarily abandoning markets. A partial step in this direction would be to selectively, rather than completely, socialize the means of production.

Decentralizing Economic Power

The fourth practical direction for democratizing the economy is to decentralize economic power. This is related to the third strategy of making economic power accountable, but sufficiently different to warrant separate treatment. As a general principle, the larger an economic actor grows, the more powerful it becomes. One hallmark of a capitalist political economy is just such a tendency toward concentrations of power as one firm consolidates market power, drives competitors out of business, and acquires other firms with or without their consent.

One way to pursue a decentralizing strategy is to strengthen and enforce government prohibitions against concentrations of market power. Though the United States has had antitrust legislation on the books for many years, it has been a history of too little and too ineffective. The result, as seen in the 1990s and the early years of the twenty-first century, has been a surge in mega-corporations. In 1996, fifty-one out of the world's hundred largest economic entities were corporations and only forty-nine were nations.[25] Stronger legislation aimed at preventing concentrations of economic power can be passed and enforced.

Second, interlocking boards of directors can be broken apart. Interlocking corporate boards means that the same people sit on various boards of directors. This increases the concentration of power by reducing the number of decision makers with control over corporate policy. Especially when added to the predominance of directors representing the interests of capital, this increases the overall concentration of capital's power.

Third, legislation can be passed awarding preference to locally owned and controlled businesses over chains. One dominant trend in recent years is the encroachment by Wal-Mart and other huge chains through the United States and other countries. While consumers may pay lower consumer prices in the short term, they pay high costs in terms of loss of local autonomy, loss of local sovereignty as chain stores hold residents hostage with various direct and indirect threats, bankruptcy of locally owned businesses, and loss of capital as profit is expropriated to the corporate headquarters. A statutory preference for locally owned and controlled businesses would help restore local autonomy, revive downtowns devastated by the development of chain box stores in suburbs and in rural areas, and help maintain the long-term viability of local economies.

Many of these ideas for economic democracy have already been successfully put into practice. Among the best-known examples of democratized workplaces are the Mondragon cooperatives in Spain, worker self-management in the former Yugoslavia, and the Washington state plywood cooperatives. Others such as the Upper Midwest's "new wave" co-op federation can be found scattered throughout the United States and other countries. Each of these examples provides empirical validation of the practical potential for democratizing the economy.[26]

Some critics would charge that the various proposals for democratizing the economy are anticapital and that they would ensure the destruction of capi-

talism. These critics are undoubtedly partly correct in that some of the proposals would entail fundamental transformation of the current political economy from capitalism to something else, possibly democratic socialism.
However, many of the proposals are no more anticapital than speed limits are
anti-automobile. For example, a tax on capital mobility or currency transactions can be viewed as a speed limit intended to slow down the movement of
capital. It attempts to control the behavior of capital by forcing it to adopt socially responsible policies.

Some critics would likely argue that turning power over to the workers
would destroy the firm, since workers would behave irresponsibly, squeezing
higher wages out of it at the expense of long-term viability. This argument
parallels the arguments of the Federalist Founders that common citizens cannot be trusted with political power. There are certainly many examples from
history where citizens have chosen badly in the electoral arena, and undoubtedly there would be instances where workers choose badly in the workplace.
However, in general, giving power to average citizens has not wrecked the U.S.
Constitution nor spelled disaster for political stability, nor would giving workers more power and control within the workplace necessarily wreck the firm
or the economy. Empirical evidence suggests that workers choose responsibly
when they know that their short-term and long-term interests are intertwined. It should also be emphasized that, under the current regime, poor
choices by owners of capital and their managers occur with some frequency.

Other critics would argue that private property and the prerogatives of capital are more important than democracy. In other words, capitalism is more
important than democracy. This intellectually defensible position can be
made coherently and logically. It acknowledges the tension between democracy and capitalism and makes a value judgment in favor of capitalism. The
key point here is that capitalism may be defensible on certain grounds, such
as its dynamic character, the myriad consumption opportunities it offers to
many, and the freedom it allows for a minority to get rich, but the defense cannot plausibly rest on a foundation of its alleged compatibility with democracy.

Some critics might argue that too much has been made of the incompati-
bility of capitalism and democracy. In fact, they might argue, the two are compatible. This stance requires either ignoring the empirical evidence drawn
from history and from contemporary times, or distorting the meaning of democracy. The latter strategy is a popular one. Calling the United States "fully

democratic" requires altering the meaning of *democracy* to make it more compatible with rule by the wealthy—what the ancient Greeks called an *oligarchy*. It requires that we sever words from their historical moorings. Adopting this strategy opens dangerous worlds, as George Orwell and many others have noted, where language corruption both mirrors and enables the corruption of political ideals.

Finally, a critic might charge that adopting these proposals for democratizing the workplace and the economy would lead to economic breakdown and chaos, plunging us into an economic depression without end. This argument rests on a host of assumptions: that humans are only selfish, competitive, and acquisitive; that most people will strive only if they are bribed monetarily to do so; that the only two possible political economic systems are capitalism or Stalinism; that humans have already exhausted the possibilities for political-economic forms and that capitalism is far preferable to the alternative of Stalinism; that capitalists and managers will make decisions that advance everyone's best interests; that average people cannot handle significant responsibility in their work lives; that communities cannot responsibly exercise their sovereignty over corporations; and that stability and the status quo are more important than democratic change. Indeed, if the choices are capitalism and Stalinism, let us choose capitalism. However, to assume that only two options exist—the democratic socialist countries of Western Europe refute such a claim—and that humans have already exhausted the possibilities, is to radically underestimate the power of human ingenuity and imagination. To one-sidedly emphasize the selfish, competitive, and acquisitive traits of humans is to ignore the empirical frequency of unselfish, generous, cooperative, and nonmaterial choices of average humans. To assume that average people cannot handle significant responsibility in their work lives is to uncritically adopt the elitist argument that all managers and capitalists are a special breed who alone can act responsibly; it also ignores the empirical reality that owners of capital and their managers consistently make choices that advance their own interests at the expense of other people and entire communities. To assume that stability and the status quo are more important than democratic change is to engage in remarkable historical amnesia in which key events in U.S. history such as the American Revolution and the civil rights era are swept from memory. Many of the proposals for democratizing the economy require new assumptions, new ways of thinking about humans and their capabilities, and new ways of thinking about the economy, how it works, and toward what ends.

Critics and supporters alike should avoid reducing this discussion to a battle between liberal and conservative or between left and right. They should focus on democracy and its possibilities, something that hopefully Americans can unite behind. It is possible to be probusiness while ensuring democratic accountability and fairness. Government is the major instrument through which the people exercise their sovereignty, and it does so through laws and regulations. When the people exercise their sovereignty in the economic arena, they are simply carrying out the logic of democracy. Though we need not assume that efficiency will be sacrificed, a democratic people may well choose to do so when necessary to achieve other ends such as effective freedom, equality, and popular sovereignty.

QUESTIONS, PROBLEMS, AND ACTIVITIES

1. Defend the proposition that democracy *should* yield to capitalism, since capitalism is more important and valuable than democracy. Evaluate this argument for its merits, and for what it says about values.
2. According to Simonde de Sismondi, "The fundamental condition of society is that no one shall die of hunger; it is only on this condition that property is acknowledged and guaranteed." Do you agree? What would this mean in practical terms?
3. Make a list of everything you consume in a week. Be sure to include nonobvious things such as shower water and hair products as well as the obvious things like gasoline, clothing, and food. Distinguish between "wants" and "needs" on your list.
4. Do you agree with Wolfgang Sachs that "well-being" has been transformed into "well-having" in American culture? What are the costs and benefits of a highly materialistic lifestyle?
5. Should we extend the logic and practice of democracy into other aspects of our lives? Which, if any? Economic? Cultural? Religious? Educational? Why or why not?
6. What are some possible ways to democratize education? The media? Foreign policy? The world of art? For each case, arrange the possibilities on a continuum from less to more democracy. Which, if any, of these would you support? Why?

7. List the strengths and weaknesses of humanist economics as you see them. Do the same for an economy of sufficiency. Would you favor partial, or entire, adoption of these alternative economic frameworks?

NOTES

1. Jane Addams, "The Subjective Necessity for Social Settlements" [1892], in *Jane Addams on Education*, edited by Ellen Condliffe Lagemann (New York: Teachers College Press, 1985), p. 50.

2. Jane Addams, *The Spirit of Youth and the City Streets* [1909], in *The Social Thought of Jane Addams*, ed. Christopher Lasch (Indianapolis, IN: Bobbs-Merrill, 1965), pp. 87–88.

3. Jane Addams, *Democracy and Social Ethics* (New York: Macmillan, 1916), p. 3.

4. Ibid., pp. 166, 264, 265, 210, 247.

5. Addams, "Subjective Necessity," p. 52.

6. Addams, *Democracy and Social Ethics*, pp. 11, 6.

7. Addams, *Spirit of Youth*, pp. 109–11; Addams, *Democracy and Social Ethics*, p. 139.

8. See Karl Polanyi, *The Livelihood of Man* (New York: Academic Press, 1977), *The Great Transformation* (New York: Farrar & Rinehart, 1944), and *Dahomey and the Slave Trade* (Seattle: University of Washington Press, 1966); Lapo Berti, "Society and the Market: Remote and Less Remote Sources of a Present Issue," in *Economics, Culture and Society—Alternative Approaches: Dissenting Views from Economic Orthodoxy*, ed. Oscar Nudler and Mark Lutz (New York: Apex Press, 1996), pp. 66–67; emphasis in original.

9. J.-C.-L. Simonde de Sismondi, *New Principles of Political Economy: Of Wealth in Its Relation to Population*, 2nd ed. (1826; New Brunswick, NJ: Transaction Publishers, 1994), pp. 8, 7, 140, 127, 222; emphasis in original.

10. John Ruskin, *Unto This Last* (1864; New York: John Wiley & Son, 1988), pp. 1, 28; John Ruskin, "Letters on Political Economy," in *Arrows of the Chace* (Boston: Colonial Press, 1880), vol. 2, p. 282.

11. J. A. Hobson, *The Social Problem* (London: Nisbet, 1901), p. 38; J. A. Hobson, *Economics and Ethics: A Study in Social Values* (Boston: D. C. Heath, 1929), pp. 266,

267; J. A. Hobson, *Work and Wealth: A Human Valuation* (1914; repr., New York: Augustus M. Kelley, 1968), pp. 199, 284, 297–300.

12. In its contemporary form, "absentee ownership" occurs routinely in the form of stock ownership of public corporations. As Marjorie Kelly points out, dominant economic thinking awards complete autonomy and control to these absentee owners, while awarding none to the people who actually physically do the corporation's work. This, she argues, is inconsistent with democratic values. It erects and sustains a "corporate aristocracy" whose interests take precedence over the majority population composed of the corporation's workers and community members whose lives are affected by the corporation's behavior. Marjorie Kelly, *The Divine Right of Capital: Dethroning the Corporate Aristocracy* (San Francisco: Berrett-Koehler, 2001).

13. Richard Tawney, *The Acquisitive Society* (New York: Harcourt, Brace, 1920), pp. 39, 73–74, 81, 154, 180.

14. A. M. Huq, "Welfare Criteria in Gandhian Economics," in *Essays in Gandhian Economics*, ed. Romesh Diwan and Mark Lutz (New Delhi: Gandhi Peace Foundation, 1985), p. 67; Mark Lutz, "The Reforming of Economics: Retrospect and Prospect," in Nudler and Lutz, *Economics, Culture, and Society*, p. 105.

15. E. F. Schumacher, *Small Is Beautiful* (New York: Harper & Row, 1973), p. 164.

16. Wolfgang Sachs, *Planet Dialectics: Explorations in Environment and Development* (New York: Zed Books, 1999), pp. 28, x.

17. Ibid., pp. 52–53, 193.

18. Ibid., pp. xi–xii, 174.

19. Ibid., pp. 54, 10.

20. Ibid., pp. 12, 186, 207, 209, 185, xi–xiii.

21. Ibid., pp. 42, 49, xii, 88–89, 195.

22. Rousseau, *The Social Contract* [1762], in *Rousseau's Political Writings*, ed. Alan Ritter and Julia Conaway Bondanella (New York: W. W. Norton, 1988), p. 101.

23. J. S. Mill, *Representative Government* (1860; New York: Liberal Arts Press, 1958), pp. 27–28, 54–55; J. S. Mill, *Principles of Political Economy with Some of Their Applications to Social Philosophy* (1884; Fairfield, NJ: Augustus M. Kelley, 1987), pp. 789, 147.

24. Robert Dahl, *A Preface to Economic Democracy* (Berkeley: University of California Press, 1985), pp. 56–57, 61, 135, 111, 63, 91; emphasis in original. For another articulation of a right to workplace democracy, see Carol Gould, "Feminism and Democratic Community Revisited," in *Democratic Community*, ed. John W. Chapman and Ian Shapiro (New York: New York University Press, 1993).

25. Chuck Collins and Felice Yeskel, *Economic Apartheid in America: A Primer on Economic Inequality and Insecurity* (New York: New Press, 2000), p. 74.

26. See Robert Dahl's discussion of the Mondragon cooperatives in his *Preface to Economic Democracy*, esp. pp. 123–25, 157–58. On worker self-management in the former Yugoslavia, see Carol Pateman, *Participation and Democratic Theory* (Cambridge: Cambridge University Press, 1970), pp. 85–102. On the Washington plywood cooperatives, see Edward Greenberg, *Workplace Democracy: The Political Effects of Participation* (Ithaca, NY: Cornell University Press, 1986). See also Jane Mansbridge, *Beyond Adversary Democracy* (Chicago: University of Chicago Press, 1980), esp. part 3, "A Participatory Workplace," pp. 139–232. On the Upper Midwest's co-op federation, see Craig Cox, *Storefront Revolution: Food Co-ops and the Counterculture* (New Brunswick, NJ: Rutgers University Press, 1994).

V

POWER AND CITIZENSHIP

9

Power and the
Disappearing Citizen

Contemporary political theorist and social critic Carl Boggs (1937–) characterized the current state of citizenship in the United States as "the most pressing crisis of our time."[1] His dismal description can be added to the chorus of agreement that citizenship is in decline in this country. The problems of citizenship in the United States, though complex in nature, can be easily summarized: there is too little of it, it is based on one-sided commitments to individual and private interests, and basic trends tend to favor the already privileged.

Various polls in the last two decades show low and declining interest in public affairs and low rates of awareness of key issues in public affairs. The levels of direct participation in politics have been dropping steadily for decades. Declining voting rates, addressed below in a section on elections, offer but one prominent example. Some observers raise the concern that average citizens today participate less in civic associations, the backbone of nineteenth-century U.S. democracy, according to the French observer Alexis de Tocqueville (1805–1859). These civic associations—unions, fraternal organizations, volunteer fire departments, literary societies, mutual aid societies, and a host of others—have historically provided a means of direct involvement and participation by average citizens in civic matters. They offer citizens an occasion and a means for gathering together to engage in collective pursuits. Citizens learn some of the arts of citizenship in these civic associations.

They learn to listen to others and to balance their own needs and interests against others'.

But what about the proliferation of interest groups, social movement activism, and increasing use of initiative and referendum that also mark contemporary times? Do these signal hopeful signs of civic renewal? The modern era has indeed seen the rapid rise of each of these forms of civic involvement. However, their overall impact must be qualified. Many interest groups and activist organizations rely increasingly on paid organizers, rather than active citizen volunteers. They hire signature-gatherers and lobbyists and buy media time. While these organizations may find these tactics necessary to mount effective political campaigns, they tend to sideline the average citizen. Also, many of these organizations address only single issues, and they integrate participation only for that one issue. Many ask for citizen participation only in the form of writing checks to help fund the organization and its political organizing. These same problems also afflict many contemporary initiative and referendum efforts. Social movements, though potentially powerful expressions of citizenship, provide relatively little framework for ongoing participation in politics, and many suffer outsider status that limits their effectiveness.

Most citizens watch passively while elites make decisions that determine the circumstances of their lives. If the local corporation decides to move overseas taking local jobs along, most citizens just shrug their shoulders, thinking there is little or nothing they can do about it. If Congress passes another tax cut for the wealthy while shifting the burden for funding social services onto cash-strapped state and local governments, citizens may react with disgust and anger, but also with a sense of futility. As their sense of political efficacy declines, citizens increasingly abdicate any sense of responsibility for addressing public problems. They shift the entire responsibility over to elected representatives, and when the representatives cannot or will not fix the problems, it understandably fuels further anger and cynicism. Disinterest in politics might be more understandable if it were tied to confidence among citizens in government. "I don't need to pay attention," a citizen might say, "because the government is doing a good job of taking care of things for me." However, matching the increased cynicism about politics, confidence in the federal government declined from 75 percent in 1964 to 35 percent in the late 1980s and less than 25 percent in the late 1990s—lower by far than any other industrialized country.[2]

If average Americans are not paying close attention to politics, to what are they tuning? People spend far more time and energy today on work-related pursuits, entertainment, and other diversions than on politics. Most sports fans find enough time, energy, and financial resources to merit a trip to the ballpark or at least to watch the game on television. More people watch the Super Bowl than election returns. Most people watch far more television in a single week than they invest in political participation during an entire year. The same can be said for visits to the shopping mall and to surfing the Internet. In light of Americans' extensive pursuit of these pastimes, we can react skeptically to claims that "I just don't have the time and energy" to participate in politics. Yet, this merits a caveat: many Americans *are* stretched thin trying to make ends meet, sometimes working two or more jobs and juggling child care and other responsibilities. For them it is understandable that weekends are greeted with a sigh of relief as a time to relax in private pursuits and entertainments.

Why are Americans tuning politics out? One frequently cited reason is that most Americans now view politics with disdain as a corrupt, venal, irrelevant, and unprincipled pursuit of power, a forum for bickering among elites who are far out of touch with the everyday lives of average people. Unfortunately, their cynicism is not entirely unfounded. The electoral arena, and the behavior of some politicians, does often appear corrupt, venal, and irrelevant to most people's everyday lives. Politics seems to be more about sex scandals, bickering among politicians, attack ads, ethical lapses, campaign deceit, and the blatant purchase of political power by wealthy individuals and groups than about solving real problems. The media make it worse by reducing politics to the equivalent of a game show or car chase.

The little active participation that remains tends to be focused too heavily on the pursuit of private and self-interests. While some focus on private and self-interests is legitimate, without some sense of the public interest we are left with what Boggs calls the "quasi-Hobbesian character of contemporary society" marked by extreme individualism, competition, and distrust.[3] From a practical standpoint, we are left with a politics of zero-sum maneuvering for partisan advantage that sabotages real solutions to public problems. Politics in the United States seems decreasingly about addressing shared problems. Many politicians and activists aim primarily to beat the other side, doing whatever it takes in the short term, even if it means sabotaging solutions to shared problems. They emphasize issues that inflame passions, confuse voters, and distract voters from the pressing public problems that need attention.

If most people do not participate in politics, and if the ones who do participate focus squarely and solely on their own interests, then the participants are likely to create public policy that advances their own particular interests, often at the expense of others'. Participation and nonparticipation in U.S. politics has always been nonrandom. As political scientists have extensively documented, participation increases with income and education, resulting in a distinct class bias in U.S. politics, with upper-income Americans better represented in politics than lower-income Americans. Public policy inevitably tends to advance the interests of the relatively affluent. The political agenda itself reflects this domination by corporate and elite interests. Issues such as global hunger, homelessness, radical inequality, and declining job security for average Americans rarely garner the attention they deserve, shouldered aside by issues such as tax relief for the wealthy, corporate welfare, deregulation, and the dismantling of the welfare state. Most Democratic and Republican politicians now support free trade, corporate welfare, limited social spending, downsizing government, personal responsibility, and getting tough on crime. Neither party wants to take on jobs flight, urban decay, poverty, or bloated defense spending for fear it will undermine their chances of winning the next election.

An apologist might characterize the decline of citizenship as a post-politics age where citizens rightly turn over responsibility for governing to elected representatives who, at least in theory, are better qualified to govern. These representatives are more informed, have more political aptitude, and have more skills for governing. In addition to the country running more efficiently and effectively, this frees up citizens for private pursuits. In this view, politics is a necessary evil, and the more we can free people from it, the happier and better off they will be.

Whatever the merits of this sanguine view as an ideal, in practice it has at least two major shortcomings. First, it fails as measured by our collective ability to recognize, address, and solve our shared public problems. If citizens elect the president and representatives to do the business of politics for them, it is a business headed for bankruptcy. Major public problems are increasingly ignored or set aside for the more pressing work of sabotaging the other side.

Second, even if this corporate model of governance actually worked in practice, it nevertheless cannot easily be reconciled with democracy, which requires a leveling of power and responsibility, and active participation by common citizens.

Apologists might also argue that nonparticipation by most citizens affords more stability, demonstrates citizen satisfaction with politics as it is, and reflects people's preference for private life. Nonparticipation may indeed increase stability. At least at a superficial level, the most stable political system might very well be an authoritarian system led by an all-powerful autocrat. As argued earlier, however, the surface stability may simply hide seething resentment and anger that could erupt into instability, violence, and crime. That said, it must be acknowledged that democracy is a messy system. Fans of quiet harmony may celebrate the flight from politics of average citizens, but they should defend it on the basis of order and not on the basis of democracy.

As for the second argument, a more accurate reading of nonparticipation would acknowledge the possibility that it reflects citizen *dissatisfaction* with politics, rather than satisfaction. Average citizens view politics as corrupt, dominated by rich and powerful people. Their flight from politics reflects their dismay with the petty rivalries, the failure to address real problems, the partisan bickering, and the nasty, corrupt character that electoral politics tends to assume. This cynical view of politics may be most justifiable among the most marginalized Americans, who have for generations watched politicians ignore their interests or use them selectively and strategically during electoral campaigns but ultimately turn their backs on them once elected. For these people, politics-as-usual offers little in the way of hope or redress for the injustices they take for granted in their lives. Their dissatisfaction with politics thus emerges from their understandable, if unfortunate, conclusion that politics has little to offer them.

The third response, that nonparticipation simply reflects citizen preference for private life, may be partly true, but again must be qualified. The abandonment of public life may be driven by the disgust and cynicism noted above. It avoids reckoning with the multiple ways that public life determines the character of private life as policy makers and corporate elites make decisions affecting everyone. It allows the persistence and deepening of public problems left unattended by those in power who are pursuing their own agendas.

PUBLIC PROBLEMS

Voting and Elections

Participation in elections reflects the trends identified above: turnout is low, voting is based primarily on self-interests, and the process is controlled to a large degree by the affluent and powerful in their own interests. In a representative democracy, perhaps the single most important form of citizen participation is voting for representatives and other leaders who will set policy. Increasingly, voters are also asked to vote directly on legislation put on the ballot through the initiative and referendum processes. Voter turnout in the United States is among the lowest of industrialized countries. With rare exceptions, turnout for presidential elections hovers around 50 percent of eligible voters, compared to 70 to 90 percent in most other industrialized countries. Midterm, nonpresidential election turnout falls even lower, between 35 and 40 percent in recent elections. The midterm elections of 1994, which swept a new generation of conservative Republicans into office, was decided by a mere 38.6 percent of registered voters, approximately half of whom voted for the Republicans. In other words, this major shift in party power was actually endorsed by approximately one-fifth of registered voters. In 1996, 196 million Americans were eligible to register and vote. Ninety-six million (48.8 percent) actually were registered. Of these registered voters, 23.9 percent backed Clinton's reelection, meaning that he won with the support of less than one-fourth of the population. The notion of a mandate to govern rests on insubstantial foundations under these circumstances.

Consistent with a liberal democratic framework, contemporary voting emphasizes the protection of self-interests. If voters think only in terms of their self-interests, politicians must follow suit, assuming they want to keep their jobs. Many politicians pander to the self-interests of voters by emphasizing issues such as tax reduction, personal safety, and pork barrel issues that bring money and jobs to the voters. Their reelection often depends on it. While attention to self-interests is legitimate, a sole focus on self-interests undermines the likelihood of addressing public interests. These require an enlarged focus of attention and a willingness to potentially accept some sacrifice and inconvenience.

Political theorist William Hudson (1948–) identifies two kinds of factors that determine voter turnout. First, social-psychological factors, especially socioeconomic status, increase or decrease the likelihood of voting. Generally, the propensity to vote increases with income. Voting rates thus reflect class divisions, with turnout among the least affluent lagging considerably behind turnout among the affluent. For example, while only about 35 percent of eligible working-class voters cast ballots in 1996, 75 percent of eligible affluent voters did so. The class bias ensures that the interests of affluent Americans are better represented among policy makers than are the interests of lower- and lower-middle-class Americans. Turnout also increases with educational attainment, and the type of job one holds partly determines voting turnout, as well. Professional positions in general afford greater work flexibility, and this makes it easier to find time for voting, as compared to many working-class jobs that require stricter adherence to the clock.

Second, according to Hudson, legal-institutional factors partly determine voter turnout. These factors include registration requirements that, in some states, require advance planning and may be stringent. Unlike many Western industrialized countries whose citizens vote on Saturdays or voting holidays, in the United States voting traditionally occurs on Tuesday, a workday. This makes it inconvenient and, for many, difficult to get to the polls. Hudson concludes that "the electorate is not representative of all citizens."[4]

The plurality system of voting used in the United States magnifies the consequences of skewed voting rates. In a plurality system, the person with the highest number of votes, whether or not it constitutes a majority, wins the election. Also, no matter how many candidates vie for office in a particular district, only one candidate wins. Nationwide, plurality voting practically ensures that only two parties can effectively vie for power, since third parties rarely win more votes than the Democrats or Republicans. This can be better understood by contrasting it with a proportional system of elections used in some parliamentary democracies. In a proportional system, candidates are elected proportionate to the number of votes their party receives. If Party X receives 25 percent of the total votes, then Party X gets 25 percent of the seats in the assembly or other representative body. If Party Y receives 10 percent of the total votes, it assumes 10 percent of the seats. In this way, smaller political parties, representing alternative political perspectives, are better able to secure a seat at the table. Proponents of a proportional system list among its virtues the fact that it ensures the representation of minority voters in a way that a plurality system does not.

In some states, voters are increasingly taking matters into their own hands by using the initiative and referendum processes. This route typically requires securing a certain number of signatures to put a policy question on the ballot, circumventing the legislature. The democratic potential of these tools should be obvious, for in principle they require participation in direct democracy by average citizens. However, as currently practiced, the corrupting influence of money distorts their impact. Increasingly, initiators of the process simply hire professional signature-gathering firms rather than relying on volunteers and activists. If they can afford to purchase signatures, they are also likely to enjoy sufficient backing to bombard voters with advertisements, some of which may be more persuasive than accurate. In short, the initiative and referendum processes may reproduce, and even magnify, the problems of class bias present in the voting for representatives.

Apart from voter turnout problems, Hudson calls elections in America "trivialized." According to him, for elections in a representative democracy to be democratic, they must meet three "essential criteria":

1. They must provide for equal representation of all citizens.
2. They must provide mechanisms for deliberation about policy issues.
3. They must control what government does.

Hudson argues that elections meet none of these criteria in the United States. Rather than equal representation, as we have already seen, the socioeconomic and other determinants of voter turnout bias the outcomes of elections in the interests of higher socioeconomic categories. Since class and race intersect, elections are biased in favor of specifically white, affluent class interests. Other mechanisms of unequal representation include hidden elections (in which wealthy campaign contributors determine the viability of candidates) and mass media that play a gatekeeper role of selling expensive ads to the highest bidder and only providing coverage of candidates that they themselves deem credible or electable.

Election season increasingly offers a corrupted version of deliberation marked more by sound bites and attack ads than actual debate. Carefully sculpted candidates portray themselves in terms suggested by public relations teams, where image takes precedence over substance. The most prominent opportunities for deliberation offered by the election process—the candidates' debates—have themselves become opportunities for candidates to manipulate sound bites and offer carefully rehearsed speeches rather than engage in genuine debate.

Finally, elections often have little impact on politicians' positions, which are determined by the need to please major funders and to beat the other side, in addition to representing constituents' interests. Incumbents can rely on name recognition and other advantages of incumbency without having to respond materially to constituents' needs and wishes. Also, policy is increasingly made in government bureaucracies, the courts, and congressional committee rooms where the committee chair representing the majority party can singlehandedly make or break a legislative proposal by denying it a place on the agenda.[5]

Even if voter turnout in the United States averaged 90 percent or higher, it must be noted that voting requires relatively little of citizens. A trip to the polls every two years requires little of a citizen's time. Of course, some citizens spend much time staying informed about political issues so that they can cast their votes intelligently. Many, though, invest relatively little time in staying informed. Simply increasing turnout, in this case, hardly solves the problem; it merely increases the problem of uninformed voting.

Media Are Part of the Problem

If citizens are to play responsible roles in public life, they must do so from an informed position. In democratic theory, the media play an essential role of providing information to citizens about public issues and political candidates. In the United States the media are vast and varied. With a little effort and sometimes money, citizens can avail themselves of ample sources of good quality information. That said, the overwhelming majority of Americans rely exclusively or nearly exclusively on major corporate media for their information, if they pay attention to public issues at all. They get their news and information from their local newspaper or from one or more local television channels affiliated with one of the major broadcast television networks. Many Americans increasingly supplement these sources with information taken from the Internet, but without replacing newspapers and television as primary sources.

The quality of the news and information available from these sources ranges considerably. Overall, information available from major media players increasingly appears in sound-bite format with little or no critical analysis, while car chases, crime, and scandals often dominate the news. Coverage of election campaigns, surely one of the most important elements of a representative democracy, has declined steadily in length and quality. In one study of more than ten thousand top-rated evening news broadcasts on 122 stations during the seven weeks leading up to the 2002 elections, only 44 percent of those broadcasts contained any campaign coverage at all. Most of the stories that did find their way on the air addressed campaign strategy or the latest polls, rather than candidates' positions on the issues. While viewers of these broadcasts had less than a 50 percent chance of watching any campaign coverage, approximately half of the broadcasts contained three or more political ads and more than 80 percent of them aired at least one ad.[6] These ads present biased views about candidates rather than reliable, balanced information. The promise of a democratic media is largely unfulfilled.

Edward Herman (1949–) and Noam Chomsky's (1928–) "political economy of the mass media" helps us to understand why. They argue that the mainstream media systematically filter certain news and information out of the public domain.[7] The first filter is the size, ownership, and profit orientation of the mass media. Without exception, the major media are large corporations, attached to even larger corporations, which exert extensive influence over mass culture, news, entertainment, and the dispersal of information. Approximately twenty media corporations now dominate the worldwide mainstream media. The largest of these include Time Warner, Disney/ABC, Bertelsmann, Viacom, and Rupert Murdoch's News Corporation. It is worth listing the affiliates of just one of these, Time Warner just prior to its merger with AOL in 2000: Warner Bros. Pictures, Morgan Creek Productions, New Regency Productions, Warner Bros. Animation, Savoy Pictures, Little, Brown & Co., Bullfinch, Back Bay, Time-Life Books, Oxmoor House, Sunset Books, Warner Books, the Book-of-the-Month Club, Warner/Chappell Music, Atlantic Records, Warner Audio Books, Elektra, Warner Bros. Records, Time-Life Music, Columbia House, Seattle's Sub Pop Records, *Time, Fortune, Life, Sports Illustrated, Vibe, People, Entertainment Weekly, Money, In Style, Martha Stewart Living, Sunset, Asia Week, Parenting, Weight Watchers, Cooking Light,* DC Comics, Six Flags theme parks, Movie World and Warner Brothers parks, HBO, Cinemax, Warner Bros. Television, Comedy Central, E!, Black Entertainment Television, Court TV, the Sega channel, the Home Shopping Network, Turner Broadcasting, the Atlanta Braves and Atlanta Hawks, World

Championship Wrestling, Hanna-Barbera Cartoons, New Line Cinema, Turner Classic Movies, Turner Pictures, Castle Rock Productions, CNN, CNN Headline News, CNN International, CNN/SI, CNN Airport Network, CNNfi, CNN radio, TNT, WTBS, and the Cartoon Network.

The size of media conglomerates ensures their market power, which helps them maintain a monopoly position in any particular local market. Most major cities in the United States now have only one daily newspaper, compared to the two or more in most medium-size cities as recently as the 1970s and 1980s. Potential competitors find it difficult or impossible to enter the market to effectively compete against media giants. The size of media conglomerates, and the sheer number of media affiliates gathered under one media giant, also helps them concentrate control over content. Like other large corporations, media conglomerates are owned by a relatively few wealthy individuals and managed by individuals beholden to those owners. Their ownership and control of the major means of communication confer enormous power on the owners. These owners, taken together, constitute a relatively small wealthy, white, male, conservative elite whose influence over U.S. public culture is difficult to overestimate. Their consolidated power "has clearly had a deleterious effect—lessening competition, squelching dissent, choking off debate, and elevating profit over the public good."

Another consequence of the concentration of media ownership is the inevitable narrowing of public debate and discussion. Instead of multiple, diverse perspectives from all points on the political compass, corporate headquarters approves a relatively narrow band of sanctioned news and opinion, the "same narrow, conventional wisdom" repeated ad nauseum.[8] Also, media affiliates rarely criticize the corporate parent or other affiliates, as bluntly admitted by Michael Kinsley, founding editor of Slate.com, funded entirely by Microsoft Corporation, who admitted that "*Slate* will never give Microsoft the skeptical scrutiny it requires as a powerful institution in American society—any more than *Time* will sufficiently scrutinize Time Warner. No institution can reasonably be expected to audit itself."[9]

Like other corporations, media corporations aim first and foremost to earn a profit. This goal sometimes conflicts with other, more democratic goals of the media, including providing unbiased news and information. As contemporary media critic Robert McChesney (1952–)writes, a media system oriented toward maximizing profit "works well for them [the media corporations], but it is a disaster for the communication needs of a healthy and self-governing society." Or, as James Fallows (1952–) writes, "Media companies, like banks or fast-food chains, are basically under pressure to do more of whatever makes money and less of whatever does not."[10]

If the media are profit-making entities, they will generally support policies that favor profit making. Their editorial positions will reflect this in, for example, support for free markets (unless a regulated market guarantees more profit) and free market capitalism more generally, corporate welfare, freedom of expression where freedom means the right to buy public expression, consumerism, and deregulation. Their selection of news and information worthy of publication or broadcast will also tend to reflect this support for the basic institutions and mechanisms of profit making. The net result is a very business-friendly media, and one profoundly hostile to any open discussion of issues counter to its interests, such as the potential benefits of democratizing ownership and control of the mass media.

Another consequence of profit-driven media is the pressing need to gain and keep the public's attention, no matter what the costs in terms of the quality of news and information. To ensure their profitability, media corporations must attract and keep viewers, listeners, and readers. Among popular methods of doing this in modern times, we see news increasingly presented as entertainment, and a focus on "human interest" stories rather than hard news. Both broadcast and print news media increasingly lead with the latest car chase or murder, then turn to human-interest stories ranging from the rescued kitten to the latest celebrity scandal. This corruption of news is especially evident in prime-time broadcast news presented by the major networks, which increasingly favors repartee among glamorized anchors over hard news.

Another favorite contemporary method of attracting and keeping the public's attention is to appeal to the lowest common denominator in programming and publishing. This means that the public is fed a steady diet of reality television, trashy daytime talk shows, celebrity fashion and scandal, sports, and anything else that can capture and hold an allegedly short public attention span. If one media giant offers these elements of programming and finds that they sell well, every competitor quickly follows suit with its own version. As competitors in a market economy, the major media corporations inevitably emulate each other's successes. They perceive it as necessary to protect their profitability. Meanwhile, public concerns and issues of real substance are driven from the field.

An additional problem tied to the profit orientation of the media is the perception among the mass media that the contemporary consumer of news and information is incapable of sustained attention and must be fed in tiny sound bites. The average news story consequently has declined substantially in length. Illustrating this decline, the average length of presidential candidates' statements aired on the evening network news declined from 42.3 seconds in 1968 to 9.8 seconds in 1988 and further to 7.3 seconds in 1992.[11] A sound-bite format makes critical analysis by the media impossible, and it makes the possibility of critical understanding by citizens who are reliant upon the mainstream media increasingly remote. Another element of this alleged short attention span is sometimes referred to as "hit-and-run" journalism, where stories are presented to the public but little effort is made to follow up on them and little effort to sustain focus on the issues raised in the stories. Rather than sustained attention and the potential critique that could accompany it, media consumers are treated to a constant parade of changing headlines, many of them of little value to a democratic citizen seeking reliable news and information about public affairs.

Another potential conflict with the media's bottom line arises because advertising provides the major source of revenue. This is Herman and Chomsky's second filter. Since advertising provides the means of profit, it exerts a pronounced impact on the content of news and information presented by the mainstream media. The media must please advertisers by claiming market share—hence the perceived need to appeal to the lowest common denominator—and by running news and information that minimally does not conflict with the advertisers' own profit-making goals. Although most media representatives will insist that they maintain a strict firewall between their editorial and business departments, the likelihood that this is true is exceedingly small. As one media critic put it, the wall between news and business "was always a porous wall, and now . . . they run a bulldozer through it."[12]

Occasionally, examples emerge of explicit censorship of certain news stories because they conflict with the wishes of advertisers and owners. Usually, however, the censorship is very difficult to document. Most alternative print magazines are ad-free. While this may represent a choice in some cases, in many cases it simply means that advertisers shun it because of the publication's critical stance.[13] Most businesses will understandably put their advertising dollars in media outlets that run stories that burnish their image and favor their interests, and will pull their advertising dollars from critical media.

Advertisers tend to be ideologically and culturally conservative. This helps explain the generally conservative, probusiness slant of the media.

The sources of mass media news create a third filter. Since reporters have limited time and resources, they favor established sources for their news. These established sources include public relations departments of major corporations. Estimates of news content derived from these PR departments range as high as 40 percent for newspapers. We should not expect unbiased information to be fed to reporters by corporate PR departments whose job it is to positively raise the profile of the corporation by projecting an image of good corporate citizen, whether it matches actual corporate behavior or not. Much of what passes for news is thus little more than propaganda fed to the news media by large corporations.

Other major established sources of news include the institutions of government and public officials in general. Government institutions include, for example, the White House, Congress, the Pentagon, governors' offices, most state and federal agencies, city halls, and police and fire departments. Reporters treat representatives of these institutions as routine sources of news and information. Pronouncements issued by institutional spokespersons are typically awarded automatic credibility, making it more likely that they will be published. Most public officials can secure a public forum simply by calling a press conference. Reporters faithfully record the event and publish its essential message and selected quotes. Like the reporting based on corporate sources, the information gathered from public officials is typically reported with little or no attempt made to sift it critically for the plausible and implausible. The very act of reporting the pronouncements increases their credibility and plausibility. Once reported, they take on the character of factual information. These sources automatically confer credibility on the news and information that emanates from them, and the way that the media treats them increases their credibility. White men in business suits are treated as automatically worthy of credibility, whatever might come out of their mouths.

Herman and Chomsky call their fourth filter "flak and the enforcers." This refers to the ability of powerful corporations and other groups to respond punitively to news and information that they dislike, sometimes but not always in the form of a lawsuit. This increases the reluctance of the media to publish news critical of these powerful organizations. In one example from 2001, media giant Gannett was forced to pay a $14 million settlement to Chiquita Brands International in restitution for a series run by a Gannett newspaper, the *Cincinnati Enquirer*, criticizing Chiquita's economic policies in Central America. Another example was the October 1995 squelching by CBS of a *60 Minutes* segment critical of the tobacco industry in response to fears by the corporate owner of litigation. The fears were not unfounded: only a few months earlier, in the summer of 1995, ABC had been forced to capitulate to a $10 billion libel suit by tobacco company Philip Morris.[14] Two more recent examples include the pulling of a film biography of Ronald and Nancy Reagan in response to opposition by conservative groups concerned about the potentially negative portrayal, and Disney Corporation's refusal in 2004 to release Michael Moore's documentary *Fahrenheit 9/11*. In both cases, powerful groups successfully pressured the parent company to censor material they deemed hostile. An actual punitive response is often unnecessary when the simple threat of one is credible. The threat of a lawsuit may work as effectively as a lawsuit itself, since a lawsuit of this kind is very expensive to defend against, whether successfully or not. The cost in terms of the free flow of information in a democracy is high.

Writing prior to the breakup of the former Soviet Union, Herman and Chomsky identified anticommunism as the fifth filter. One might argue that the "war on terrorism" has replaced anticommunism as the ideological straightjacket that now filters the news. The news media are reluctant to cut against the grain of prevailing public opinion, since doing so would threaten profit. If most Americans are backing their president in a war against Iraq as an alleged source of terrorism, the many media corporations are more likely to act as cheerleaders for the war than as independent sources of critical news and information. One prominent newspaper, the *New York Times*, in 2004 published a written apology for its cheerleading role in the early stages of the Iraq war.

The ideologies that act as filters of news and information can be considerably broadened to include many of the central tenets of liberalism—the individual is more important than the community, freedom is more important than equality, rights are sacred, property rights are most sacred of all—and other articles of faith in the United States, including that the United States is the greatest country on Earth, that the United States is democratic and anyone who disagrees with us is wrong and perhaps evil, and belief in a Christian god. Very rarely do the major media in the United States publish news and information running contrary to these central and foundational components of public opinion and public culture. Taken as articles of faith, challenges to them are viewed as too incredible for publication.

This discussion suggests a skeptical response to the often-heard criticism that, with few exceptions such as the Fox News television network and the *Wall Street Journal*, mainstream news is slanted with a left-liberal bias. Media critic Eric Alterman (1960–) calls this the myth of the "so-called liberal media," or SCLM for short. The myth is more a result of conservatives successfully "working the refs," according to Alterman, than it is grounded in reality. While a truly liberal media segment does exist, according to Alterman, it is "tiny and profoundly underfunded compared to its conservative counterpart." Moreover, this tiny liberal media segment is "filled with right-wingers" who are offered a space to present their views, while overtly conservative publications such as the *Wall Street Journal* make relatively little effort to reciprocate. Conservatives are thus "extremely well represented in every facet of the media." What few truly liberal media exist are "no match—either in size, ferocity, or commitment—for the massive conservative media structure that, more than ever, determines the shape and scope of our political agenda."[15] Alterman's explanation for the conservative bias in the media parallels Herman and Chomsky's in its essential elements. Most importantly, like Herman and Chomsky, Alterman emphasizes political economy elements of size, ownership, profit ownership, and dependence on advertising for profits, while acknowledging the importance of ideology.

Herman and Chomsky's discussion emphasizes systemic problems of the mainstream media rather than the failure of specific individuals. Individual reporters and editors may strive for objectivity and balance, yet find their efforts stymied by the larger systemic forces. A truly thriving media sector that does its job in a democracy would include a diversity of views spanning the political spectrum. This means drawing on views both to the left and right of Democrats and Republicans. It should also include extensive critical analysis inconsistent with a sound-bite format. Conservatives and liberals alike should be concerned about media concentration and its stultifying and narrowing effect on political discourse.

Private Opulence and Public Squalor

In dominant economic theory, supply follows demand, in that producers respond to the demands set by consumers. This may sometimes require that

producers attempt to anticipate consumer demand in order to position themselves favorably to respond quickly. In other words, the production of a new
good or service may actually precede consumer demand in time. Anticipating
consumer preferences does not, according to this view, mean creating or shaping consumer preferences. If this theory holds true, then consumption patterns simply represent the preferences of consumers, expressed through the
marketplace. Producers do not create or distort those preferences in any way;
they simply respond with products and services to satisfy them. Neoclassical
economists make this stipulated primacy of the consumer a normative principle, expressed as consumer sovereignty. This means that consumers are, and
should be, autonomous choosers who know best what is in their interest.
Consumers act on their preferences by making choices in the marketplace that
satisfy their preferences and advance their self-interest. Producers offer information through advertising that will enable these sovereign consumers to
make the best possible choices.

Political economist John Kenneth Galbraith (1908–) challenged these presumptions of dominant economic theory. In place of the idea that demand
drives supply, he offers the concept of "the dependence effect," and in place of
consumer sovereignty, he offers producer sovereignty. The dependence effect
refers to the inversion of the relationship drawn by mainstream economists:
instead of demand driving supply, according to Galbraith, supply drives demand. "As a society becomes increasingly affluent," he argues, "wants are increasingly created by the process by which they are satisfied. . . . Wants thus
come to depend on output." They come to "depend on the process by which
they are satisfied."

This pumping up of consumer demand occurs in two ways, according to
Galbraith. First, "Increases in consumption, the counterpart of increases in
production, act by suggestion or emulation to create wants." Another political
economist, Thorstein Veblen (1857–1929), had earlier dubbed this process of
increased consumption via emulation "conspicuous consumption," referring
to the way that the wealthy demonstrate their wealth and thus gain prestige,
and "pecuniary emulation," referring to people's imitation of the spending
habits of their peers and those above them socioeconomically. Today we refer
to this process of "pecuniary emulation" as "keeping up with the Joneses." Second, producers actively "create wants through advertising and salesmanship."
They devote their extensive resources to advertising in order to create new
consumer demand necessary to sell their new products. Producers not only

react to existing consumer demand—they also actively create and shape consumer demand.

If this is true, it calls into question the assumptions underlying the notion of consumer sovereignty. If producers' advertising creates and manipulates consumers' preferences, the notion of an autonomous chooser becomes a fiction. This process of want formation may detract from, rather than add to, the quality of life. According to Galbraith, increases in consumption may yield lower rather than higher levels of satisfaction and overall quality of life. As people stretch their budgets to buy new things, they are forced to work harder and longer to fund their ever-increasing consumption. The materialism this engenders also distracts people from other, perhaps more satisfying and ennobling, pursuits.

Galbraith's critique of consumerism can also be found in his theory of social balance. According to this theory, a healthy society balances private and social investment. In a healthy society, investment in public goods such as parks, environmental cleanup, and public education more or less balances investment in private goods such as automobiles, homes, and home appliances. If public investment too far exceeds private investment, individual freedom may be compromised. On the other hand, if private investment too far exceeds public investment, the common good is diminished or even obliterated. Galbraith left no doubt about which was the worse problem in the United States: private investment far outweighs public investment, with disastrous consequences for the common good overall and for specific public goods such as public education and environmental quality.

Galbraith's two critiques are directly related: advertising that drives producer sovereignty pumps up private investment that overwhelms and displaces public investment and spending. The consumer, he argues,

is subject to the forces of advertising and emulation by which production creates its own demand. Advertising operates exclusively, and emulation mainly, on behalf of privately produced goods and services. Since management and emulative effects operate on behalf of private production, public services will have an inherent tendency to lag behind. Automobile demand . . . will inevitably have a much larger claim on income than parks or public health or even roads where no such influence operates. The engines of mass communication, in their highest state of development, assail the eyes and ears of the community on behalf of more beer but not of more schools. . . . The competition is especially unequal for new products and services. Every corner of the public psyche is canvassed by some of the nation's most talented citizens to see if the desire for some merchantable product can be cultivated. No similar process operates on behalf of the nonmerchantable services of the state.

The result, according to Galbraith, is inevitably a social imbalance leaving members of a community with too little rationale for public investment. The impetus for private investment will swamp rationales for public investment in any society that views individual spending and investment as expressions of personal freedom, and public spending and investment reliant on taxes as an abridgment of individual freedom:

> A community decision to have a new school means that the individual surrenders the necessary amount, willy-nilly, in his taxes. But if he is left with that income, he is a free man. He can decide between a better car or a television set. . . . The difficulty is that this argument leaves the community with no way of preferring the school. All private wants, where the individual can choose, are inherently superior to all public desires which must be paid for by taxation and with an inevitable component of compulsion.[16]

The social imbalance created by a one-sided emphasis on private investment contributes to the "tragedies of the commons" discussed earlier. The tendency to favor private over public investment is deeply tied to a capitalist political economy in which producers must convince consumers to purchase their products. If they fail to do so, bankruptcy and recession will soon follow. The unfortunate result, according to Galbraith, is a society marked by "private opulence" and "public squalor."

Two consequences for citizenship can be identified. First, consumerism undermines the practices of citizenship by distracting people into private consumption pursuits. Shopping assumes the character of a leisure activity, in addition to the requisite time and energy people invest in shopping simply to maintain a household. People are not simply distracted, however. At some point, many become trapped by their consumption, especially when, as with millions of Americans, their spending exceeds their means. They have to work harder and longer to pay for excess consumption.[17] But, a critic might respond, Americans love shopping. They are simply maximizing their freedom and their satisfaction through their choices. Galbraith raises the possibility instead that consumers are not as free as they think they are—that they are manipulated and their choices distorted to reflect the needs of producers in a capitalist political economy.

A second consequence is the impoverishment of public life in general and the corroding effects this has on citizenship. If structural and institutional forces create private opulence and public squalor, is it any wonder that individuals opt for private life while abandoning public life? Time and energy invested in private life result in a more attractive payload. The "social imbalance" identified by Galbraith arises from forces that actively drive people from public life, impelled by producers to spend and invest privately, with no corresponding structural and institutional forces impelling us to spend and invest publicly. Americans embrace three-car garages and glitzy shopping malls on the one hand, while tolerating degraded public transit systems and public schools literally in ruins on the other. They invest heavily in new cinemaplexes, but close public beaches due to inadequate waste treatment facilities. They fill their homes with luxury gadgets, but tolerate a health care system that systematically excludes millions from basic care. They lavish care and resources on private lawns, while gutting funding needed to maintain clean, safe public parks. They buy up the latest gas guzzlers, while tolerating air pollution at levels increasing the incidence of lung cancer.

If Galbraith is correct, we make these choices at least in part because of deep structural and institutional forces at work that systematically distort our choices, driving us from public life and more deeply into private life. Even public space eventually serves private needs: freeways serve the needs of individual drivers and, not incidentally, automobile manufacturers who actively conspire to block public transportation systems. Public sports arenas are increasingly dominated by advertisers. There is nowhere we can go, except perhaps to wilderness areas, to escape the messages of producers aimed at manipulating our desire.

The Anemic Liberal Citizen

Contemporary political theorist Ruth Lister (1949–) identifies "two great historical traditions of citizenship" in the Western world: liberalism and civic republicanism.[18] This book has repeatedly addressed each of these political traditions, and it will come as no surprise to learn that liberalism today defines the dominant mode of citizenship. Recall that, as defined by thinkers such as Thomas Hobbes (1588–1679) and John Locke (1632–1704), liberals begin with a vision of humans in their natural state with fundamental rights to life, liberty, and estate. Absent an overarching authority, naturally selfish, aggressive, competitive humans threaten each others' fundamental rights, leading to the need to form a protective government. This dominant liberal framework casts government and politics as necessary evils rather than positive goods. It also frames private life as natural and public life as an artificial creation. Individuals' assumed rational egoism propels them primarily into the pursuit of private, selfish ends. These individuals enter public life, if at all, to protect those private interests. And the private realm, the realm of freedom within this view, should be maximized, while the public realm, seen as the realm of necessity, should be minimized. Minimizing participation in politics thus flows naturally and logically from liberalism. Although some liberal thinkers such as John Stuart Mill (1806–1873) believed that participation in public life could develop the civic and moral capacities of individuals, making politics a potential good, their view never attained dominance.

For liberalism, membership within a particular nation-state bestows citizenship. Any individual who meets certain criteria of residency qualifies as a citizen for the purposes of drawing upon the state's resources and protections. The history of liberalism can be viewed in part as a history of the progressive inclusion of more and more people in the category of "citizen." As a means of inclusion, citizenship has thus been a powerful tool for the marginalized to organize to gain membership and the privileges and rights that go with it. However, despite the shattering of many formal barriers to full membership, many informal barriers tied to factors such as class, race, gender, and disability continue practically to exclude some from full participation in citizenship. Who qualifies as a citizen remains a potent, politicized question. Witness, for example, current battles over the status of undocumented immigrants. Some European countries also struggle with this issue of membership as émigrés and refugees from other parts of the world seek permanent citizenship status in their new homes.

Though liberal citizens enjoy many rights, they incur few obligations beyond obeying the law in its many manifestations. Despite their shortcomings, rights have played an important role in the protection of individuals against various forms of domination. They have historically offered a framework for increasing the inclusiveness of citizenship and for protecting individuals of various identities against encroachments by others and the state. Struggles for greater rights, and the extension of rights to excluded groups, have served as a basis for organizing among marginalized people. In the United States during the twentieth century, these individuals and groups included women, African Americans, the disabled, Native Americans, and gay, lesbian, bisexual, and transgender persons.

Since most liberal citizens become members simply by being born that way, liberal citizenship requires literally nothing practical of the citizen. Assuming only a protective interest in public life, many liberal citizens naturally transfer that responsibility to elected representatives and interest groups, leaving little or no reason for political participation. Liberal citizens can spend their entire lives forgoing political participation, and many take precisely this route. Most of those who do participate do so by voting, a political action that requires only at most several hours every two years. In the interim between elections, citizens watch politics as spectators who observe and complain when things go against their interests. The passive citizenry that naturally results contributes to the crisis of citizenship.

The shortcomings of the liberal model of citizenship can be better appreciated by comparing it with the second model identified by Lister, civic republicanism. Like liberalism, civic republicanism initially limited membership in the category of citizenship to select groups, especially freeborn males. Unlike liberalism, the civic republican citizen's identity does not one-sidedly emphasize the pursuit of individual self-interests. Civic republicans expect citizens to balance self-interest with civic virtue. They view citizen identity as malleable rather than fixed and inherent. The character of individuals develops through participation, as individuals encounter others with whom they must accommodate their own private interests. In contrast to the radical individualism of liberalism, civic republican citizens develop mutual bonds and shared points of identity, including and especially a commitment to the common good and to the political community. Civic republicans view politics as a positive good, an end in itself, not just a necessary evil and a means to other ends of protecting individual rights and private interests. The civic republican tradition, unlike liberalism, requires extensive participation in public life by citizens, partly as an expression of positive freedom. Unlike a liberal citizen, the civic republican citizen assumes significant obligations.

Foremost among these are the obligations to participate in the work of public life and to seek the common good as well as individual and private goods.

Some political theorists have criticized civic republicanism for its narrow, exclusionary definition of who counts as a citizen, its narrow conception of the political realm founded on a rigid separation of private and public, the demanding nature of the obligations it imposes, and the exceptional amount of time and effort it requires of citizens. Defenders have subsequently broadened membership to include previously excluded groups and expanded the application of citizenship to encompass other realms, including the workplace and the family. The demanding nature of its obligations and the extensive time and energy they impose on citizens remain a concern, especially for individuals and families living in relatively marginal economic circumstances whose political participation diverts time and energy from income-producing efforts.

The most promising proposals for revitalizing citizenship draw from both of these traditions.[19] The liberal emphasis on the fundamental importance of each individual and the individual's freedom represents a historical accomplishment worth retaining and celebrating. The ability and freedom of each individual to develop unique capacities, emphasized by some liberals such as J. S. Mill, is also worth emphasizing. Rights, the specific means of protecting individuals and their freedom, have generally served well. The one exception most often cited by political thinkers, including some welfare liberal thinkers, is property rights, which sometimes override other more essential rights. Property rights need not be eliminated in order to make them more consistent with other highly valued rights and freedoms, however; their value can be calibrated to other pressing needs.

But citizenship in a democracy requires more of the citizen than liberalism alone can offer. Despite their practical usefulness, rights are necessary but insufficient for citizenship in a democracy. If the current problems of citizenship can be summarized as too little of it, focused on one-sided private and self-interests and biased in the interests of the already privileged, then citizenship in a democracy must expand the idea of citizen to include a more dynamic, active citizen who participates more in public life—who participates to protect private self-interests but who also maintains a commitment to common, public interests—and to effectively integrate the participation of, and represent the interests of, the marginalized and excluded to a degree necessary to offset the power wielded by privileged individuals and groups. This conception of citizenship will draw from the civic republican tradition a greater emphasis on political participation by all citizens, an active commitment to public as well as private interests, and a more equal dispersion of effective political power.

POWER AND THE IMPOVERISHMENT OF CITIZENSHIP

John Kenneth Galbraith argued persuasively that institutional and structural forces systematically shape, distort, and manipulate individual choice and desire, with ruinous consequences for public life in a democracy. He saw clearly that autonomous individual choice represents a promise of democracy, but not necessarily a reality; that individual autonomy and freedom are systematically compromised; and that the decline of citizenship is only partly the result of free choice. Individuals have abandoned the public realm in part, he recognized, because they have been forced out by the workings of power. The fault for an anemic public life thus lies not entirely with apolitical, apathetic individuals. Power has been exercised in multiple ways to undermine active citizenship in the United States.

Political theorists distinguish between power as a means of domination and power as a positive capacity. The former refers to uses of power to control the thoughts and actions of others. This carries negative connotations since it entails one individual or group impinging on the autonomy of another individual or group. Power-as-capacity refers to the means and resources both for overcoming domination and more generally to support critical thought and effective action. This kind of power "empowers" individuals and groups.

Theorists distinguish further between different dimensions, or faces, of power-as-domination.[20] The first face of power is the most obvious and most easily recognized. It refers to explicit, observable uses of power to control the behavior of others. As political theorist Robert Dahl (1915–) put it, in the first face of power, "A has power over B to the extent that he can get B to do something that B would not otherwise do."[21] Employers exercise this form of power when they require their employees to work overtime or on a holiday. Legislators exercise it when they pass legislation requiring that citizens pay additional taxes, reduce their driving speed, or wear seat belts. A real estate developer may use this form of power to buy influence over local planning boards. A bully exercises it in pushing another around, and a rapist wields it in forcing himself upon his victim. As these examples illustrate, the first face of power is easily recognized and understood. Its presence and use can be observed.

The two major institutions in contemporary life most able to exercise the first face of power to influence the nature of citizenship are government and the modern corporation. As governments grew in size and scope during the twentieth century, the roles allotted to citizens shrank commensurately. Elected representatives and bureaucrats assumed more and more of the responsibility for civic matters. Elected officials also exert direct and determining influence over the character of citizenship by establishing rules for elections. Registration requirements can be stiffened to decrease participation in elections or relaxed to increase participation. Elected officials mandate the days and times of elections. The state party in power often engages in gerrymandering, the practice of redrawing congressional boundaries after each census in such a way as to intentionally marginalize a group of voters. Policy makers can shatter a fragile coalition of activist neighborhood groups by routing a new freeway through the heart of the neighborhoods or by approving an urban redevelopment project that effectively destroys existing communities. They hasten the decline of participatory citizenship by approving exurban development that further isolates citizens from each other and separates them from the possibility of civic awareness and participation. Each of these can be viewed as exercises of the first face of power in which one actor exerts controlling influence over others. They are observable uses of tools and resources held by dominant policy makers to control or influence the nature of civic engagement by common citizens.

Modern corporations exert profound influence over citizenship in myriad ways. Author William Greider (1936–) describes the political impact of just one huge corporation:

General Electric . . . not only manufactures light bulbs, jet engines, and nuclear power equipment but also plays a significant role in the mass media (it owns NBC and CNBC), the military, the environment, foreign trade, and of course the larger expanse of the international economy. It devotes huge resources to advertising, controls important segments of media programming, and influences election campaigns along with legislation, not only through its enormous power and wealth but through its ubiquitous institutional presence. . . . Such quasi-governing institutions hire large teams of lawyers, lobbyists, public relations agents, and advertisers to protect their interests and propagate their values. . . . General Electric has worked aggressively, often ruthlessly, for a strong military, a fiercely nationalistic foreign policy, free trade, reductions in taxes and social programs, and loosened environmental regulations. As a major producer of nuclear power equipment it has, not surprisingly, been in the forefront of a pronuclear agenda.[22]

Corporations use the property rights they control to directly influence policy makers. Possession of property rights often makes successful citizen action against a corporation exceptionally difficult. Large multinational corporations exercise extensive power over resource allocation, investment patterns, commerce, and trade. Common citizens find it difficult or impossible to exercise their sovereignty in these areas. Corporations also directly influence citizenship through their massive commitments to public relations campaigns in which they whitewash their own behavior, successfully deflecting needed criticism and undermining the possibility of citizen action. These large corporations use their vast economic and political power to extract various concessions such as deregulation, tax abatements, privatization, and fiscal austerity from governments at all levels. Since each of these tactics shifts power and control from public to private arenas, each reduces the potential range of citizens' participation and control over their lives.

Sometimes individuals and groups are controlled in less overt and observable ways than suggested by the first face of power. A can also exercise power over B through the use of threats, fear, control of access to decision-making arenas, and control of the political agenda, rather than through explicit and observable means such as physical force, votes, or money. When this happens, the second face of power is exercised. An employer may block the union-organizing efforts of employees without having to make use of direct force or other forms of the first face of power but simply through the use of implicit threats of retaliation. A homosexual may refrain from running for political office because his opponent has threatened to "out" him. The threat of violence prevents some women from walking alone at night because of the potential costs. The second face of power may also prevent a woman from leaving an abusive relationship because of the fear of a violent reaction.

Marginalized groups often find it difficult to enter traditional decision-making arenas such as city councils, planning boards, and legislatures because entrance often requires significant money, expertise, and experience that they lack. They inevitably watch from the sidelines as more privileged insiders make decisions that directly influence their lives. Mandatory overtime imposed by an employer makes participation relatively difficult or, in some cases, impossible. Minimum-wage jobs undermine participation by providing too few resources supporting active involvement in public life. An employer might dissuade participation by threatening reprisal for union organizing, or for taking time off to vote. The exclusion of these groups from participation marks the successful exercise of the second face of power.

The second face of power also finds expression in the control of public agendas. Groups that wish to press for political change may find their efforts stymied by their inability to get their issue onto a public agenda. For many years, proponents of equal rights for African Americans found it impossible to secure the attention of policy makers who either opposed it outright or feared a backlash from constituents. In the language of Peter Bachrach (1918–) and Morton Baratz (1923–1998), who initially outlined the second face of power, biases against equal rights or even a public discussion of it were successfully mobilized to keep the issue off public agendas.[23]

If they want to, policy makers can simply ignore the concerns of marginalized constituents with little means of gaining public attention. By limiting the specific topics and issues that can be addressed in a public forum, policy makers control the range and character of potential citizen action. Congressional rules institutionalize some of this control of the political agenda. For example, committee chairs can successfully block consideration of a particular issue. For some issues, existing norms make intentional action to block particular issues unnecessary. This is true for issues such as property rights, which are not on the table for debate and are unlikely to get there in the near future. More broadly, the liberal depoliticization of the economic realm effectively removes from the public agenda a whole range of issues and problems that might otherwise fall comfortably within the purview of citizens' organizing efforts.

The media play a highly influential role in determining what is or is not on the public agenda through their selection of newsworthy issues and how they run them. Does the issue merit front-page coverage or is it buried in the back of the sports pages? Is attention to the issue sustained over days and weeks, or is it dropped from view after an initial sensational splash?

Overall, the growing concentration of economic and political power in fewer and fewer hands limits the range of topics that can be publicly debated.

As large, powerful economic and political entities seize control over successive reaches of daily life, the range of issues and practices that are subject to citizen discretion diminishes.

The exercise of the second face of power often occurs in the form of a nonaction or nonbehavior by the policy makers. Unlike the first face of power, in which A *makes* B do something that B would not otherwise do, in the second face of power A *prevents* B from doing something that B would *like* to do. This does not make the exercise of power any less decisive. In each of these cases of the second face of power, power is exercised in relatively subtle ways in comparison to the first face of power. Its exercise often cannot be observed or measured empirically.

The first and second faces of power cover cases in which actor B is aware of the power and control exercised by actor A. However, power may be used to control actor B in ways of which B is unaware. Steven Lukes (1941–) proposed a third face of power in which people are controlled by the manipulation or distortion of their self-understandings and their perceptions of their interests.[24] Here the exercise of power occurs via means such as propaganda, manipulation of symbols, media distortions, and ideology. People sometimes believe the myths and stereotypes about themselves or accept others' stories and descriptions about them. Marginalized people may adopt the worldview of their oppressor; it becomes part of their own view and their common sense. This increases the likelihood that victims of the third face of power will unwittingly collaborate in their own oppression. When this occurs, actor B willingly does what actor A bids, even though objectively it contradicts B's interests.

The third face of power has been successfully exercised if a battered woman blames herself for the violence perpetrated against her, internalizes the perpetrator's demeaning view of her, or accepts the perpetrator's justification that she deserves it. As described by John Gaventa (1949–), the third face of power is exercised to persuade Appalachian miners that they are "hillbillies" and therefore incapable of accomplishment or resistance to economic oppression.[25] The third face of power is exercised to persuade working-class Americans that supply-side tax cuts for the wealthy are good for everyone, though the empirical evidence suggests skepticism. Of course, many battered women, Appalachian miners, and working-class Americans are well aware of the attempted manipulation of their self-understanding and successfully resist it. Others, however, are not, and in their case the third face of power may be successfully exercised against them.

The same powerful economic and political actors that exercise the first and second faces of power are positioned especially well to make use of the third face of power. Access to financial means allows these actors to purchase media time, or media outlets themselves, in order to popularize their version of the world and of specific events. Governmental actors who enjoy privileged access to the media need only call a press conference to capture the public's attention. A relatively small elite thus can significantly control the range and character of public debate available to common citizens. The beliefs and perceptions of common citizens inevitably reflect these trends.

If common citizens see only the information and debate fed them via dominant channels, their self-understandings and perceptions of their interests might plausibly be distorted. Thus, in the absence of any debate over the relative merits of economic democracy, most people dismiss it as incredible. The relentless media portrayal of black men as criminals sets a psychological tone for profiling, for irrational fear of black men, and for accepting uncritically the high incarceration and unemployment rates among black men. The relative nonparticipation by Latinos in Southern California is tied to the acceptance by some Latinos of the dominant explanation of their status as "aliens" and therefore unwanted. Some have come to accept their marginal status as deserved, and this motivates against assertion in public arenas. At least some of the low voting rates of lower-income people is tied to this third face of power, in that many have internalized justifications for their marginalized status.

When moving from the first and second to the third face of power, the focus of attention moves from a concern with the action or inaction of actor B to the beliefs of B prior to action or inaction. This means that the focus of attention broadens to include some consideration of the identity of actor B. Peter Digeser (1958–) proposed a fourth face of power, based on the work of French social critic and theorist Michel Foucault (1926–1984), that deepens this focus on B's identity while also raising questions about the nature and identity of A.

Although the third face of power partially addresses the identity of subjects through reference to a person's or group's objective interests and beliefs about them, it does not inquire *deeply* into that identity. It largely takes for granted the identity of actor B, while focusing on whether or not B's objective interests are violated and also on B's self-perceptions and self-understandings. The fourth face of power concerns the process by which actor B is formed as a subject with specific interests and beliefs. It focuses on the work of power in shaping the beliefs, self-understandings, and other constituent elements of B's identity. It challenges the notion of stable, autonomous identities with a set of coherent interests apart from their power-laden and power-implicated social construction. It draws attention to a social context, shaped by relations of power, that exerts profound and extensive influence over our identity.

According to Digeser, "All of our political, economic, legal, and religious practices are planted in a social context governed by various rules and discourses forged by relations of [the fourth face of] power." We learn to think and behave in certain ways, and thus become certain kinds of people, as a result of living within this social context. We are "subjected" to the beliefs, rules, and practices of normality within that social context. The fourth face of power thus operates through an authoritative cultural context in which dominant normalized beliefs, behaviors, and ultimately identities are shaped.

The third face of power is implicated when our beliefs and self-understandings are distorted counter to our objective interests. The fourth face of power calls into question the very possibility of normal, undistorted self-understandings and poses instead the likelihood that our identity is always the result of a process of discipline and subjectification. Although this process of subjectification may create resistance, according to Foucault we can exercise only partial control, at best, over this face of power and its impact on our identity. However, we can achieve critical awareness of it through a "genealogy," or a "historical recovery of the struggles and conflicts that ultimately forge a norm," and exercise some control over it in the future by exerting partial control over the social context of rules, beliefs, and behaviors that forge identities.

Although Digeser does not emphasize this point, to talk about how actor B is socially constructed and subjectified does not rule out the possibility—nor perhaps the necessity—of reference to a set of interests. In determining whether or not power is present benignly or malignantly in relation to B, some standard is required. Without it, we have no critical foothold for determining the relative well-being of actor B. Seizing that critical foothold requires that we refer to some notion of what is, or is not, in the interests of actor B. Similarly, though Digeser does not make this point, what changes the most as we move from the third to the fourth face of power is not the identity and behavior of B, but the nature and identity of A. We shift from a coherent, identifiable actor A that exercises power to a relatively diffuse social and cultural environment in which power is embedded and through which it operates. As Digeser notes, we find that the fourth face of power "lies at the bottom of all our social practices. . . . These practices are situated in a context in which [the fourth face of] power is everywhere. There is no escaping it."[26]

Many of the elements of the fourth face of power that affect citizenship have already been considered elsewhere. Consumerism both distracts people from their citizenship obligations and sometimes forecloses participation as more and more people sink under the debt created by their spending, leaving pressing bills to pay and pressures to work harder and harder. Corporate power increasingly infuses all of culture, saturating everything with distracting messages to consume. Similarly, a culture marked deeply by competitive sports eats up huge chunks of time for the average person and family. At least some of this time could be devoted to civic pursuits. A liberal civic culture emphasizes the primacy of private life and the pursuit of economic gain over public life, motivating many to ignore politics. Radical individualism motivates participation only if directly necessary to protect self-interests. These deeply ingrained features of contemporary U.S. culture appear natural and normal, and they shape individuals' thoughts and behaviors.

What options do citizens have for overcoming the various forms of power-as-domination? If the presence and exercise of power partly explain the decline of citizenship, they also present possibilities for the reinvigoration of citizenship. The following chapter addresses these possibilities by focusing on power-as-capacity.

QUESTIONS, PROBLEMS, AND ACTIVITIES

1. Hold a mock election to determine what brand(s) of soda will be available on campus, using first a plurality ("winner-take-all") and then a proportional system. Which system do you think better represents students' interests? Would you be in favor of abandoning our plurality system of voting and turning to a proportional system of representation? What would be the advantages and disadvantages of this shift?

2. Can you suggest ways of increasing voter turnout? Would you be in favor of mandating voting and backing up the law with a penalty for nonvoters?

3. Which do you find more plausible: consumer sovereignty or producer sovereignty?

4. How much time each week or month do you spend shopping? Watching television? Engaging in sports? Other leisure activities? What would it take, if anything, to get you to substitute civic and political involvement for some of that time?

5. What are the obstacles to your own more active participation in politics? Can you imagine others that do not apply to you?

6. Do an inventory in your city of "private opulence and public squalor." What evidence can you find of each? In your estimation, is Galbraith's thesis of a social imbalance, in which public investment lags, correct? Count the number of invitations you encounter in a day to invest privately versus publicly.

7. Investigate the political economy of the media from which you get most of your news, using Herman and Chomsky's analysis as a guide.

8. Think of additional examples for each of the different faces of power and their impact on citizenship.

9. Draw each of the four faces of power-as-domination.

NOTES

1. Carl Boggs, *The End of Politics: Corporate Power and the Decline of the Public Sphere* (New York: Guilford Press, 2000), p. 47.

2. Ibid., p. 3.

3. Ibid., p. 19.

4. William Hudson, *Democracy in Peril: Seven Challenges to America's Future*, 3rd ed. (New York: Chatham House, 2001), pp. 104, 106.

5. Ibid., pp. 123–57.

6. "Local TV News Coverage of the 2002 General Election," *The Lear Center Local News Archive*, http://www.localnewsarchive.org/pdf/LocalTV2002.pdf.

7. Edward Herman and Noam Chomsky, *Manufacturing Consent: The Political Economy of the Mass Media* (New York: Pantheon, 1988).

8. Arianna Huffington, "Blog Heaven," *American Prospect* (July 2004): pp. 28–29.

9. Quoted in Eric Alterman, *What Liberal Media? The Truth about Bias and the News* (New York: Basic Books, 2003), pp. 23–24.

10. Robert McChesney, "Waging the Media Battle," *American Prospect* (July 2004): p. 24; James Fallows, "The Business Motive," *American Prospect* (July 2004): p. 29.

11. National Environmental Education Advancement Project, "Crafting Your Messages with Soundbites," *EE and the Media Gazette*, June 29, 2004, http://www.uwsp.edu/cnr/neeap/media/crafting.htm.

12. Interview of Ben Bagdikian, supporting material for "Smoke in the Eye," PBS *Frontline*, April 2, 1996, www.pbs.org/wgbh/pages/frontline/smoke/interviews/bagdikian.html.

13. See Gloria Steinem's account of her ongoing battle with advertisers as editor and publisher of *Ms.* magazine in "Sex, Lies, and Advertising," chapter 3 of her *Moving beyond Words* (New York: Simon & Schuster, 1994), pp. 130–68. *Ms.* eventually resolved its dilemma the way most alternative magazines do: it switched to an ad-free format wholly reliant on subscriptions and donations for revenue.

14. See Lawrence Grossman, "Lessons of the *Sixty Minutes* Cave-In," *Columbia Journalism Review* (January/February 1996), available at http://archives.cjr.org/year/96/1/60minutes.asp.

15. Alterman, *What Liberal Media?*, pp. 9–11.

16. John Kenneth Galbraith, *The Affluent Society* (Boston: Houghton-Mifflin, 1958), pp. 158, 260–61, 267; Thorstein Veblen, *The Theory of the Leisure Class* (New York: Modern Library, 1934), pp. 68, 22.

17. On this point, see Juliet Schor, *The Overworked American* (New York: Basic Books, 1991).

18. Ruth Lister, *Citizenship: Feminist Perspectives*, 2nd ed. (Washington Square, NY: New York University Press, 2003), p. 3.

19. For example, Ruth Lister argues that the two traditions can be "mutually supportive" (*Citizenship*, p. 36). See also Chantal Mouffe, "Feminism, Citizenship and Radical Democratic Politics," in *Feminists Theorize the Political*, ed. Judith Butler and Joan Scott (New York: Routledge, 1992), pp. 369–84; and David Held, *Democracy and the Global Order: From the Modern State to Cosmopolitan Governance* (Stanford: Stanford University Press, 1995), esp. pp. 143–58.

20. For a discussion of the distinction between power-as-domination and power-as-capacity, see Thomas Wartenberg, *The Forms of Power: From Domination to Transformation* (Philadelphia: Temple University Press, 1990). For a summary of the different faces of power, see Wartenberg, *Forms of Power*, pp. 51–70, and John Gaventa, *Power and Powerlessness: Quiescence and Rebellion in an Appalachian Valley* (Urbana: University of Illinois Press, 1980), pp. 3–32. For his summary of the first three faces of power and his addition of a fourth face of power, see Peter Digeser, "The Fourth Face of Power," *Journal of Politics* 54, no. 4 (November 1992): pp. 977–1007.

21. Robert Dahl, "The Concept of Power" [1957], in *Political Power: A Reader in Theory and Research*, ed. Roderick Bell, David M. Edwards, and R. Harrison Wagner (New York: Free Press, 1969), p. 80.

22. William Greider, quoted in Boggs, *End of Politics*, pp. 72–73.

23. Peter Bachrach and Morton Baratz, "Two Faces of Power," *American Political Science Review* 56 (1962): pp. 947–52.

24. Steven Lukes, *Power: A Radical View* (New York: Macmillan, 1974).

25. See Gaventa, *Power and Powerlessness*, for the application of this third face of power to a case study of miners in Appalachia.

26. Digeser, "Fourth Face of Power," pp. 982, 980.

10

Power and the
Revival of Citizenship

Power undermines democratic citizenship, but it is also a crucial requirement of citizenship. Without power as a capacity that enables critical thought and effective action, individuals can do little as citizens. Power-as-capacity requires, first of all, access to concrete material resources. The most obvious and perhaps most important of these, because it is convertible into other forms of power, is financial capital. Financial capital enables political actors to purchase resources for influence and control. With sufficient financial capital, political actors can secure political office, buy access to policy makers, purchase a seat at the policy-making table, push effectively to see that their interests are positioned favorably on the public agenda, hire the best lawyers, and publish or broadcast their views in public. Lack of financial capital leaves other political actors at a disadvantage. This disadvantage may be difficult, though not impossible, to overcome.

Social capital, according to its proponents, also increases the capacity of political actors. "Social capital" refers to "features of social organization, such as networks, norms, and social trust, that facilitate coordination and cooperation for mutual benefit." Social capital supports community-building and public problem solving. According to political scientist Robert Putnam (1941–):

> Networks of civic engagement foster sturdy norms of generalized reciprocity and encourage the emergence of social trust. Such networks facilitate coordination

379

and communication, amplify reputations, and thus allow dilemmas of collective action to be resolved. When economic and political negotiation is embedded in dense networks of social interaction, incentives for opportunism are reduced. At the same time, networks of civic engagement embody past success at collaboration, which can serve as a cultural template for future collaboration. Finally, dense networks of interaction probably broaden the participants' sense of self, developing the "I" into the "we."

Putnam's analysis of trends in the United States offers little room for optimism about the contemporary vitality of social capital. He concludes from declining voter turnout, declining newspaper readership, increasing distrust in government, increasing social alienation, decreasing interaction among neighbors, declining social trust, and trends in group membership that social capital is waning in the United States. According to Putnam, changes such as fewer marriages, more divorces, fewer children, and lower real wages have contributed to the decline by undermining the material bases for civic engagement. However, as the major culprit Putnam identifies "deep-seated technological trends" that are "radically 'privatizing' or 'individualizing' our use of leisure time and thus disrupting many opportunities for social capital formation." Television, he argues, is "the most obvious and probably the most powerful instrument of this revolution."

Other than shooting our televisions, ways to revitalize social capital, according to Putnam, include increasing the civic engagement of youth in service organizations and projects, making the workplace more family-friendly and community-congenial, spending less time traveling and more time with neighbors, designing more community-oriented neighborhoods and public spaces, increasing and deepening Americans' engagement in "spiritual communities of meaning," spending less time in passive entertainment, participating more actively and more frequently in participatory cultural activities such as social dancing and songfests, and participating more in electoral politics.[1]

Putnam's critics[2] have pointed out that if people are less inclined today to gather in the traditional associations studied by Putnam, they nevertheless continue to congregate in different kinds of associations such as churches and other religious organizations, youth service organizations, and others. Putnam and his critics agree that membership in interest groups such as the American Association of Retired People (AARP), the National Rifle Association (NRA), or the National Organization for Women (NOW) does not substitute for the deeper association that creates social capital, since these organizations require nothing of members beyond an annual membership check. Others have pointed out that Putnam's analysis largely reproduces John Dewey's (1859–1952) with different language. Like Dewey and later the communitarians, Putnam views rich communal ties as a precondition to vital, participatory democracy. Isolated individuals ensconced in their private lives cannot solve pressing public problems. They must knit ties of recognition, awareness, and commitment as a precondition for collective political action. It should finally be noted that social capital, like financial capital, can serve undemocratic as well as democratic ends. As Putnam notes, social capital is a feature of white power movements, terrorism, and NIMBY (Not In My Back Yard) campaigns.

Psychological factors in the form of self-esteem or sense of efficacy may also contribute or detract from power-as-capacity. In attempting to explain why some African Americans in the early 1960s were politically inactive, Martin Luther King Jr. (1929–1968) argued that some, "as a result of long years of oppression, have been so completely drained of self-respect and a sense of 'somebodiness' that they have adjusted to segregation."[3] Oppressed people may grow accustomed to the situation and internalize it in part as a lack of self-respect or self-esteem. They may believe that they have little to offer and that they merit their oppression. In these cases, it may be difficult to muster the confidence to assert oneself in public arenas. A sense of efficacy also plays a role in propelling some into public life. A "sense of efficacy" means that people reasonably believe that their efforts will achieve results. Without this sense of efficacy, it may be easy to lapse into indifference, cynicism, and a sense of futility.

Self-esteem in particular merits a cautionary word. An emphasis on self-esteem as a basis for active citizenship can quickly lapse into private narcissism and a therapeutic, rather than political, orientation. Self-esteem may be necessary, but is not sufficient, for active citizenship. Also, self-esteem might in some cases be a result of active citizenship, rather than a cause, if active citizenship leads to favorable results that stoke the confidence and self-respect of participants.

Emotion, too, can contribute to capacity. Plato (427–347 B.C.) hinted at this in his *Republic*, awarding emotion a supportive role to reason. In recent times, Jill Gregory and her colleagues developed the notion of affective power that supports practical power by amplifying it.[4] Noting that many political actors feel a passionate commitment to their cause, they argued that tapping into that passion increases the effectiveness of organizing. They argued that political philosophers and political scientists err by one-sidedly emphasizing rational calculation, reason, and cognition while ignoring passion and emotion. Tapping into the affective power experienced by many people around a host of issues magnifies experience, increases courage and resolve, and deepens the commitment to change. Drawing on the whole person more effectively motivates people to participate. They added that affective power can be used for destructive as well as constructive ends and that it is relatively impotent by itself, prone to quick dissipation if unaccompanied by practical action.

EDUCATION FOR CRITICAL CONSCIOUSNESS

Effective citizens must be critically aware of power and its impact on their lives. To participate responsibly in politics, they must correctly perceive their own interests and the larger, public interest, as well as the role of the third face of power in distorting perception. Their ability to do so is itself a form of capacity.

This topic of critical consciousness has long preoccupied political thinkers. An early discussion of it occurs in Plato's *Republic* (375 B.C.). Plato presumed that, for the average person, a gap exists between reality and that person's perception of reality. To make his point, he asked the reader to imagine an underground cave, with a long entrance open to the daylight. Within the cave sit men who have been chained since childbirth. Their heads are immobilized so that they can only look straight ahead. Higher up, closer to the entrance, burns a fire. Between the fire and the prisoners, a curtain has been erected so that the prisoners cannot see the fire. On the far side of the curtain, people move around and the fire projects their shadows onto the curtain. Since the prisoners can only see the shadows and not the real figures, they mistake the shadows for the real thing. "And so in every way," Plato concluded, "they would believe that the shadows . . . were the whole truth."

Plato asks us to further consider what would happen if one of the prisoners were suddenly released. Initially, it would be difficult for the prisoner to accept the fact that he had mistaken a shadow world for the truth. The new experiences "would be painful and he would be too dazzled to see properly the objects of which he used to see the shadows." The light from the fire would initially blind him. This former prisoner would prefer to look at the familiar shadows and would be reluctant to accept the new experiences as real. If the captors persisted and dragged the former prisoner out into the daylight, "the process would be a painful one" and the former prisoner would be too blinded by the sunlight to see clearly. It would take a period of adjustment to the new reality for the former prisoner to correctly perceive and accept it. At first he would want to look at shadows, then at reflections in water, and eventually at the moon and stars at night. The most difficult of all would be to look directly at the sun. Eventually, Plato argued, the former prisoner would fully accept a new, more accurate understanding of the world made necessary by a confrontation with empirical evidence inconsistent with his old understanding.

Plato believed that the former prisoner had a responsibility to return to the cave to share his new knowledge with the other prisoners. This would not be an easy process, however. Upon returning to the cave and resuming his former seat, he would again have difficulty seeing clearly until his eyesight adjusted to the darkness of the cave. The other prisoners "would say that his visit to the upper world had ruined his sight." His stories of new experiences and insights would be met with scoffing and even ridicule since they diverged so fundamentally from accepted understandings of the world. The prisoners would consequently view the ascent out of the cave as pointless, and "if anyone tried to release them and lead them up, they would kill him if they could lay hands on him."[5]

Plato was arguing, first, that average people are prone to misperception of reality and, second, that they are reluctant to abandon their misperceptions, even in the face of contrary evidence. A contemporary version of the simile of the cave might focus on television. Many people watch television for hours on end, sitting immobilized as images flash on the screen. Eventually, many begin to believe in the truth of the images flashed on the screen and mistake them for reality. For example, the plethora of crime shows on television today give many viewers the misperception that crime is ubiquitous and that it is patently unsafe to leave their homes, even though violent crime overall has been decreasing. The tendency to use African-American actors to portray criminals on television arguably increases the likelihood that some viewers will begin to equate African Americans with crime. The claims made by a dishonest political candidate on television might be taken at face value rather than as a politically motivated statement devoid of factual content. The ubiquity of thin women with large breasts that dominate prime time might also mislead many to the perception that such women are, or should be, the norm.

Brazilian educator Paolo Freire's (1921–1997) *Pedagogy of the Oppressed* (1970) is a classic in education for critical consciousness. The pedagogy of the oppressed is a means of "critical discovery" with a goal of *conscientização*, which refers to "learning to perceive social, political, and economic contradictions, and to take action against the oppressive elements of reality." Freire recognized that a context of oppression may result in a distortion of consciousness in which the oppressed believe in the legitimacy of their oppression. He called this a relationship of "prescription" that "represents the imposition of one man's choice upon another, transforming the consciousness of the man prescribed to into one that conforms with the prescriber's consciousness." The oppressed thus "internalize . . . the image of the oppressor and adopt . . . his guidelines." They have "adapted to the structure of domination in which they are immersed, and have become resigned to it." Internalization of the opinions and views of the oppressor also results in "self-depreciation." To overcome this internalized "self-depreciation," they must "find the oppressor out and become involved in the organized struggle for their liberation." Only then will they "begin to believe in themselves."[6]

To break through internalized oppression, Freire called for a "pedagogy of the oppressed" that "must be forged *with*, not *for*, the oppressed." Freire's "pedagogy of the oppressed" aimed at making it possible for people to "enter the historical process as responsible Subjects" capable of knowing and critical action, as opposed to "objects" that are known and acted upon. Oppressors will not willingly yield their privilege, however. They will attempt to discount and discredit change by labeling change advocates with dismissive titles such as "the blind and envious masses," "savages," "natives," or "subversives."[7]

Freire contrasted his pedagogy of the oppressed with the traditional "banking" model of education in which the expert teacher deposits knowledge in the essentially empty minds of the students. This approach to education actively constrains the process of awakening and critical consciousness. According to Freire:

> The more students work at storing the deposits entrusted to them, the less they develop the critical consciousness which would result from their intervention in the world as transformers of that world. The more completely they accept the

passive role imposed on them, the more they tend simply to adapt to the world as it is.

Rejection of the banking model requires that teacher must become student, "one who is himself taught in dialogue with the students," and students become teachers, "who in turn while being taught also teach." The students give up their role as "docile listeners" and become "critical co-investigators in dialogue with the teacher." This process is dialectical, or Socratic, in that "the teacher presents the material to the students for their consideration, and reconsiders his earlier considerations as the students express their own." This is "education as the practice of freedom—as opposed to education as the practice of domination." Freire contrasted the "banking" model of education to his "problem-solving" model:

> Banking education resists dialogue; problem-posing education regards dialogue as indispensable to the act of cognition which unveils reality. Banking education treats students as objects of assistance; problem-posing education makes them critical thinkers. Banking education inhibits creativity and domesticates (although it cannot completely destroy) the *intentionality* of consciousness. . . . Problem-posing education bases itself on creativity and stimulates true reflection and action upon reality.[8]

Freire also emphasized the importance of the oppressed "naming the world" in their own terms rooted in their everyday lives. Renaming the world is a first step in transforming it.

Beginning in the 1960s, feminists developed "consciousness raising," a form of education that resembles Freire's pedagogy of the oppressed in its aims and methods. Its importance in the feminist movement has been noted by contemporary feminists Lisa Disch, for whom consciousness-raising represents "the most distinctive political practice of women's liberation in the United States"; Anita Shreve, who called it "one of the largest ever education and support movements of its kind for women in the history of this country"; and Debra Michals, who dubbed it "the engine that drove the women's movement from disjointed liberal-versus-radical factions to a major movement."[9]

Consciousness-raising grew out of the experience of many U.S. women who, during the mid-twentieth century, felt dissatisfied with having their roles limited to being housewives and mothers. Many had read Betty Friedan's

(1921–2006) *The Feminine Mystique* (1963), a book that helped galvanize the feminist movement. Friedan identified a widespread problem that

> lay buried, unspoken, for many years in the minds of American women. It was a strange stirring, a sense of dissatisfaction, a yearning that women suffered in the middle of the twentieth century in the United States.

In large numbers, Friedan wrote, women began to ask, "Is this all?!" "This" was the social norm and expectation that women could and should find fulfillment solely in their roles as mothers and wives. But, as Friedan discovered in her interviews, many women in the United States were not finding fulfillment by pursuing this "feminine mystique."

According to the feminine mystique, "the highest value and the only commitment for women is the fulfillment of their own femininity," which they should seek inside the home in domestic roles. The root of women's troubles in the past, according to the mystique, "is that women envied men, women tried to be like men, instead of accepting their own nature, which can find fulfillment only in sexual passivity, male domination, and nurturing maternal love." To conform to this feminine mystique, millions of girls and women suppressed any ambitions they may have had for careers outside the home. They attempted to look and act in ways that would garner approval from the experts, their friends, their relatives, and their potential husbands, all of whom had bought into the norms of the feminine mystique. Any woman who found it difficult to conform was told to locate the source of the problem within herself. Women thus inevitably blamed themselves for the emotional and psychological problems they encountered trying to conform to the feminine mystique. As Friedan wrote, "The chains that bind her in her trap are chains in her own mind and spirit. They are chains made up of mistaken ideas and misinterpreted facts, of incomplete truths and unreal choices. They are not easily seen and not easily shaken off."[10] Friedan concluded that women had been brainwashed into accepting the feminine mystique.

Consciousness-raising provided a tool for overcoming this brainwashing. It emerged initially in informal kitchen chats and discussions among neighborhood friends. Through these discussions, women realized they shared the same problem, and they began to talk about it. As described by contemporary feminist Jo Freeman:

Women came together in small groups to share personal experiences, problems, and feelings. From this public sharing comes the realization that what was thought to be individual is in fact common: that what was thought to be a personal problem has a social cause and a political solution. The [consciousness-raising] group attacks the effects of psychological oppression and helps women to put it into a feminist context. Women learn to see how social structures and attitudes have molded them from birth and limited their opportunities. They ascertain the extent to which women have been denigrated in this society and how they have developed prejudices against themselves and other women. They learn to develop self-esteem and to appreciate the value of group solidarity.

The consciousness-raising groups offered a "healing ritual" in which "women gained the strength to challenge patriarchal forces at work and at home."[11] But they also added an analytical component, allowing women to begin understanding the sources of their oppression, naming their victimization, identifying the sources of their frustrations, and critically examining their own beliefs and attitudes that helped perpetuate their own oppression. Many proponents of consciousness-raising emphasized a final step of political action. Without political action, they argued, consciousness-raising is merely therapeutic, a form of self-indulgent escapism. These proponents hoped that consciousness-raising would link self-discovery to social discovery and political transformation. Gradually, consciousness-raising became more formalized, with some groups following formal group process guidelines. Consciousness-raising in small, informal, private groups was replaced or augmented by consciousness-raising in women's studies programs that emerged during the 1980s and 1990s in many colleges and universities. This effectively institutionalized it.

These approaches to education for critical consciousness share several themes. First, Plato, Freire, and feminists agree on the reality of oppression faced by certain groups in which the oppression assumes the character of common sense. It appears natural and right to Plato's prisoners, Freire's knowledge "depositees," and women limited to housewife roles. Second, they agree that the self-understandings of the oppressed sometimes represent a misperception, a case of false consciousness. Third, if the oppressed accept the legitimacy of their own oppression, they unconsciously and unwittingly collaborate in that oppression by fulfilling the roles allotted to them by their oppressors. In some cases, as in Plato's prisoners, they actively resist attempts to shatter their misperceptions. Fourth, each poses the necessity of a critical awakening to break through denial and misperception. Plato's returning ex-prisoner, Freire's pedagogy of the oppressed, and feminists' consciousness-raising each offers an educative process for achieving critical consciousness. Finally, in each case critical consciousness is viewed as a crucial step toward active citizenship. Plato imposed a burden of responsibility on enlightened prisoners to return to the cave to educate others. Freire and feminists viewed critical consciousness as only a first step toward practical action to eliminate material forms of oppression.

DEMOCRATIC CULTURE

If power insinuates itself throughout culture in ways that undermine demo-cratic citizenship, then cultural critique is needed to expose it. Few political thinkers have done this as extensively as John Dewey, who focused repeatedly on the forms of power found in cultural beliefs and practices that enable or block the capacity for thought and action. Dewey viewed political institutions such as elections and parties as important but ultimately secondary in impor-tance to culture. "If it is true," he argued, "that the political and legal react to shape the other [cultural forms], it is even more true that political institutions are an effect, not a cause" of culture. The problem of democratic institutions "is tied up with the question of what kind of culture exists; with the necessity of free culture for free political institutions." Consequently, the struggle for democracy must be "maintained on as many fronts as culture has aspects: po-litical, economic, international, educational, scientific and artistic, religious."[12]

Dewey focused his attention in two interrelated areas: (1) the cultural con-ditions that would support the growth and development of capable demo-cratic citizens and (2) the cultural-communal conditions that would enable collective action to address common concerns and issues. In both cases, power—understood to mean capacity for critical thought and effective ac-tion—lay at the heart of his concerns. Dewey's critical examination of U.S. culture revealed many undemocratic forms of power. He criticized the hierar-chical, elitist, and inegalitarian relations taken for granted in political econ-omy and countered with a form of democratic socialism marked by workplace democracy and social control of economic forces. He criticized the mass me-dia for distorting, omitting, and manipulating information needed by democratic citizens and offered instead a vision of science and inquiry whose results were widely disseminated through a democratized media. He criticized the prevailing "museum conception" of art favored by elites and countered it with a democratic philosophy of art and aesthetics emphasizing the ability of common citizens to create and appreciate art.

Presaging Freire, Dewey criticized the prevailing "cistern" model of education in which the teacher fills the empty student vessels with knowledge, and he developed an alternative vision emphasizing the creation of problem-solving communities within the classroom and the assumption by students of responsibility for their own learning. Overall, he argued that U.S. culture offered its residents many opportunities to practice the arts of submission, obedience, and subjection and theorized an alternative culture that would nurture skills of critical thinking, initiative, assumption of responsibility, creativity, and a willingness to participate with others in the definition and resolution of shared problems. By offering opportunities to practice these skills in their everyday lives, this alternative culture would increase citizens' capacity. Embodied as habits, they would form an identity worthy of democratic citizenship:

> Government, business, art, religion, all social institutions have a meaning, a purpose. That purpose is to set free and to develop the capacities of human individuals without respect to race, sex, class or economic status. And this is all one with saying that the test of their value is the extent to which they educate every individual into the full stature of his possibility. Democracy has many meanings, but if it has a moral meaning, it is found in resolving that the supreme test of all political institutions and industrial arrangements shall be the contribution they make to the all-around growth of every member of society.[13]

Dewey's concern for democratizing power throughout culture is most evident in his critique of a capitalist political economy and its impact on all of culture. In *Individualism, Old and New* (1929–30), he attacked "the existing system of control of power" found in political economy. In his introduction to the book, he argued that, "anthropologically speaking, we are living in a money culture" whose "cult and rites dominate" and condition all aspects of culture and everyday life. This money culture separates individuals into two separate, unequal socioeconomic classes, with one suffering constant material insecurity. We take this economic inequality and insecurity for granted,

Dewey believed. We treat it as "an inevitable part of our social system." Its uncritical acceptance results in "complete economic determinism" and "drastic Darwinism," where economic forces determine the fate of individuals, liberty has lost all meaning, value is wholly material, and self worth is measured by success in a competition for financial gain. In a money culture, "our technique and technology are controlled by interest in private profit."

This emphasis on private profit extends to the production and distribution of knowledge, with the result that needed cultural criticism is deflected. An economic system oriented toward private rather than social gain dominates people's everyday lives and educates them in deeply undemocratic ways. The people who do the bulk of the work of production and distribution "have no share—imaginative, intellectual, emotional—in directing the activities in which they physically participate." Workers "execute plans which they do not form, and of whose meaning and intent they are ignorant." This produces "an undeniable limitation of opportunities, and minds are warped, frustrated, unnourished by their activities—the ultimate source of all constant nurture of the spirit." In short, the current economic system undermines genuine democratic character and capacity.

However, the problem is not simply economic. At its core, the problem is a "crisis in culture" in which people widely accept a way of life—exemplified most clearly in political economy but extending throughout culture—in which undemocratic forms of power dominate. And if the problem extends throughout culture, then solutions too must encompass all of culture.

Dewey wanted to make all social relationships educative of democratic character and capacity by allowing routine practice in the arts of democratic citizenship. In political economy, he argued for worker participation in the management of industry. In order to better make industry a force for democratic education, Dewey recommended "a system of cooperative control of industry," involving "a coordinating and directive council in which captains of industry and finance would meet with representatives of labor and public officials to plan the regulation of industrial activity." Each worker must share responsibly in the conception and execution of work—there can be "no stable and balanced development of mind and character" without it.[14]

Dewey asks us to become aware of the ways that cultural forms shape our identities and capacities, and of how we are created as active, capable citizens or passive subjects of domination. Democratic citizenship requires that we seize at least some control over power—including the fourth face of power—by creating cultural forms conducive to the creation of capable, active citizens rather than consumers, clients, and subjects.

POWER AND COLLECTIVE ACTION

According to political theorist Hannah Arendt (1906–1975), power "corresponds to the human ability not just to act but to act in concert."[15] Individuals working alone are unlikely to change the world. Solving public problems democratically requires that individual citizens join together to "act in concert." This section addresses three general ways that citizens can participate in collective political action that fall under the headings of deliberation, pragmatic problem solving, and confrontation. The three forms sometimes overlap in practice.

Deliberation

Aristotle (384–322 B.C.) valued deliberation both as an end in itself and for practical reasons. As an end in itself, deliberation represented for him participation in the good life of politics. Unlike most liberal thinkers, Aristotle offered a view of politics as positive, natural, and ennobling. We find this in the opening passages of his *Politics* (335–322 B.C.). "All associations aim at some good," he wrote, and the "most sovereign and inclusive association is the polis, as it is called, or the political association." He identified several different forms of association that he considered natural. These included the associations of male and female, who "must unite for the reproduction of the species"; of master and slave, or "a union of the naturally ruling element with the element which is naturally ruled, for the preservation of both"; of the household or family that the first two form together; and of the village formed from two or more households "for the satisfaction of something more than daily recurrent needs." Aristotle reserved his highest praise for the "final and perfect association" of the *polis*, the term that designates the primary form of political association in ancient Athens, the city-state. He called it "the completion of associations existing by nature . . . , the end or consummation to which those associations move." And since "man is by nature an animal intended to live in a polis," humans find and develop their full potential only in political association. The polis thus exists "for the sake of a good life."[16] Aristotle believed that participation in the political life of the polis itself constitutes the good life. Deliberation in the assembly and in the courts marked, for Aristotle, the most important form of political participation and thus the most direct experience of the good life of politics.

Aristotle's practical valuation of deliberation emerged from two points made in his analysis of different constitutional forms. First, according to Aristotle, a political association entails some level of sharing, and there are three alternatives for the extent of sharing: all citizens must have everything in common; citizens must have nothing in common; or citizens must have some, but not all, things in common. The second alternative is clearly impossible, according to Aristotle, since a polis requires at least some common elements, beginning with a common place of residence. The first alternative, that citizens share everything in common, is theoretically possible, Aristotle acknowledged. However, it is undesirable since it ignores a second point leading to the need for deliberation: the fact of diversity and social differentiation. A polis, he argued, contains not just "a *number* of men: it is also composed of different *kinds* of men," and it "necessarily requires a difference of capacities among its members, which enables them to serve as complements to one another." This social differentiation allows the polis to achieve self-sufficiency. The need for deliberation arises from the practical implications of social differentiation on the one hand and a need to find or create common political ground on the other. Through deliberation, diverse people find or create common ground for action.

When and where do citizens actually deliberate? We find Aristotle's answer in his discussion of the nature of citizenship. Aristotle defined a citizen as "a man who shares in the administration of justice and in the holding of office" and noted that this definition is "particularly and especially the citizen of a democracy."[17] Two of the most important forms of participation in office, he believed, were acting as judges in the popular courts, a role that required deliberation among citizens to arrive at a verdict, and participating actively in the deliberations of the popular assembly.

Although Aristotle preferred both monarchy and aristocracy to democracy, he nevertheless believed that democracy had its merits, which he articulated partially in terms of the value of deliberation among citizens. First, he argued that although separate individuals may not be talented or virtuous, taken together they may exceed the best among them in quality. "There is this to be said for the Many," argued Aristotle. "Each of them by himself may not be of a good quality; but when they all come together it is possible that they may surpass—collectively and as a body, although not individually—the quality of the few best." He compared this quality of deliberation to a feast to which many contribute and whose quality exceeds the feast provided at one person's expense. In just the same way, he argued, "when there are many who contribute to the process of deliberation, each can bring his share of goodness and moral prudence."

The obvious objection to this is that surely experts are better able to judge in many and perhaps most cases. Aristotle acknowledged this argument, but insisted that experts are not always the best judges. There are "a number of arts in which the creative artist is not the only, or even the best, judge."[18] In these cases, the art products can be understood and judged by nonexperts. Aristotle offered as examples the householder who can judge the quality of a home without necessarily understanding its construction, the pilot who can judge the quality of a rudder better than the shipwright, and the diner who knows better than the chef the quality of a feast. Aristotle clearly saw political matters as captured under this class of "arts." As this suggests, unlike Plato, Aristotle was not one to dismiss or disparage common people's capacity for judgment, nor more generally the views of common people in the form of public opinion. Aristotle retained a basic respect for general, public opinion. However, he agreed with Plato that public opinion needed to be scrutinized and sometimes corrected by philosophers.

Aristotle emphasized that common people's ability to judge requires that they actually gather for deliberation. The people as a whole are able to judge as well or better than experts specifically "when they meet together," he argued. Only in meeting together are citizens confronted with alternative viewpoints and forced to reconsider and rethink their own views. Ernest Barker, an editor and translator of the *Politics*, emphasizes this point:

> This qualification, "when they meet together," is a qualification which recurs [in Aristotle's *Politics*]. . . . The people at large have the merit of a good collective judgment not as a static mass, but when they are dynamic—in other words when they assemble, and when the process of debate begins.

Aristotle recommended compulsory attendance in the assembly, since "the results of deliberation are better when all deliberate together; when the populace is mixed with the notables and they, in their turn, with the populace." Through this mixing, diverse individuals must directly reckon with each other and with divergent viewpoints, not just to hear them but to take them into account in formulating their own opinions and views.

Aristotle also argued that a good citizen "must possess the knowledge and the capacity requisite for ruling as well as for being ruled, and the excellence of a citizen may be defined as consisting in 'a knowledge of rule over free men from both points of view.'"[19] In other words, a good citizen must be able to see different perspectives from an enlarged point of view. This makes it more possible to achieve an agreement that genuinely represents the common, general interest.

Two thinkers have figured prominently in a resurgence of interest in deliberative politics during the twentieth century. Like Aristotle, Hannah Arendt's conception of politics emphasized active citizen engagement and the importance of collective deliberation about public affairs. Arendt valued active citizenship both as an exercise of positive freedom and because it develops the capacity for judgment and enables collective action. Central to Arendt's thinking is the notion of a public sphere where deliberation and collective action occur. Citizens interact in public through speech, discussion, and debate to decide on matters of common concern. This public sphere depends on the existence of a common, shared world and the presence of multiple public spaces. Such a public space is created whenever and wherever citizens assemble politically to deliberate and act on shared goals. In addition to institutionalized deliberative spaces such as legislatures, examples might include coffeehouses, town halls, libraries, workers' councils, and other venues where citizens gather. In Arendt's formulation, citizens identify and debate public interests in these public spaces, while setting aside their private, self-interests.

Much of Arendt's discussion of deliberation echoes Aristotle's emphasis on the importance of being present together with others in order to listen, consider, and reconsider. Citizens must actually confront each other in a public space to examine issues from multiple perspectives, to adapt and modify their views, and to expand their thinking to account for others' views. According to Arendt, valid political opinions cannot be formed in private. They must be formed in public through debate, discussion, and disagreement. Like Aristotle, she insisted on the importance of gathering in public spaces so that citizens could see and hear each other, confront differences, and seek commonality through deliberation. This process would "purify" individual opinion:

> Opinions will rise wherever men communicate freely with one another and have the right to make their views public; but these views in their endless variety seem to stand also in need of purification and representation. . . . Even though opinions are formed by individuals and must remain, as it were, their property, no single individual . . . can ever be equal to the task of sifting opinions, of passing them through the sieve of an intelligence which will separate the arbitrary and the merely idiosyncratic, and thus purify them into public views.

According to Arendt, political thought is by definition "representative" in that it incorporates diverse and multiple views and perspectives. A political opinion is formed

> by considering a given issue from different viewpoints, by making present to my mind the standpoints of those who are absent; that is, I represent them. . . . The more people's standpoints I have present in my mind while I am pondering a given issue, and the better I can imagine how I would feel and think if I were in their place, the stronger will be my capacity for representative thinking and the more valid my final conclusions, my opinion.

Responsible political judgment requires this political engagement in public spaces. Political judgment "cannot function in strict isolation or solitude; it needs the presence of others 'in whose place' it must think, whose perspectives it must take into consideration, and without whom it never has the opportunity to operate at all. . . . Judgment, to be valid, depends on the presence of others."[20] Thinking from the standpoint of others requires a shared, public culture in which diverse perspectives thrive and can be publicly articulated. Arendt was skeptical of public opinion and political judgment during her time, since the public culture she envisioned largely did not exist, and she would likely be skeptical of public opinion and political judgment today. Alternative views are marginalized and often silenced in multiple ways including the concentration of media ownership, an electoral process that guarantees domination by two parties whose views often converge, and the difficulty for alternative views to gain a public hearing.

Like Arendt, Jürgen Habermas (1929–) has deeply influenced contemporary thinking about deliberation and public life. At the heart of Habermas's work is an attempt to identify an ideal public sphere in which undistorted communication among citizens can occur. Responding in part to the failure by Marxists and others to ground liberatory collective action on a revolutionary proletariat or other historical agent, he turned instead to communication itself as a potentially liberating vehicle. He poses this as an alternative to the growing dominance of state and market as determinants of human life. Habermas asks, what are the social conditions that would allow inclusive, rational, critical discussion and debate over public issues, where power and status are set aside in favor of good arguments? He is concerned therefore with both the quality of deliberation and the availability of inclusive public spaces for participation by common citizens. Like Arendt, he rues the decline and disappearance of a public sphere and the distortion of political communication in modern times.

In his *Structural Transformation of the Public Sphere* (1962), Habermas traced the development of a vital public sphere in the eighteenth and early nineteenth centuries, and its subsequent decline by the late nineteenth century. Its emergence and development were fueled in part by the growth of urban cultures, the development of print media, the extension of market economies, and the growth in long-distance communication and transportation networks that superseded local household economies and created public awareness and knowledge across old boundaries. This public sphere took shape in voluntary associations, coffeehouses, opera houses, meeting houses, theaters, lecture halls, public parks, and museums that fostered political debate, discussion, and rational discourse. Though many of these public spaces were "cultural" spaces, some were converted into sites for political discussion. At the same time, older bases for judging the validity of religion, traditional hierarchy, and social status gradually yielded to Enlightenment norms of logic and rationality.

The public spaces were marked by values and norms of inclusion, rational discourse, argument, and leveling of power. They made possible "a kind of social intercourse that, far from presupposing the equality of status, disregarded status altogether." Within them, rational argument served as the sole arbiter of any issue. Discussion within them "presupposed the problematization of areas that until then had not been questioned." Questions and issues formerly settled by fiat by church and state authorities were opened to critical debate and discussion. Within this public sphere, citizens were able to debate and challenge public authorities over the determination of rules governing daily life. Finally, the public spaces were inclusive, at least in principle. According to Habermas, "However exclusive the public might be in any given instance, it could never close itself off entirely and become consolidated as a clique; for it always understood and found itself immersed within a more inclusive public of . . . readers, listeners, and spectators [who] could avail themselves via the market of the objects that were subject to discussion."

According to Habermas, by the last decades of the nineteenth century, this public sphere had begun to decline under pressure from large corporations, a growing social-welfare state, and cultural industries of arts and entertainment, communications, and media that gradually turned citizens into consumers. Together, these developments undermined the voluntary, interactive associations that formed a foundation for a vital public sphere, and they also contributed to the splintering of the public into private special interests. Habermas described the result in terms that fairly characterize the situation today:

> The process of the politically relevant exercise and equilibration of power now takes place directly between the private bureaucracies, special-interest associations, parties, and public administration. The public as such is included only sporadically in this circuit of power, and even then it is brought in only to contribute its acclamation.

In place of active participation by citizens in rational discussion and critique of public issues and figures, passive consumption and apolitical private social life emerged and prevailed. As contemporary historian and political theorist Craig Calhoun (1950–) argues, the public sphere became an arena for advertising, where corporations hawk their products, politicians "stage displays for constituents," and special-interest groups publicize their positions "without making the topics to which those positions refer subjects of genuine public debate." More fundamentally, according to Calhoun,

> the public sphere becomes a setting for states and corporate actors to develop legitimacy not by responding appropriately to an independent and critical public but by seeking to instill in social actors motivations that conform to the needs of the overall system dominated by those states and corporate actors.

In *Structural Transformation of the Public Sphere*, Habermas offered as a solution to the perversion and decline of public life the reopening of market and state institutions to critical scrutiny and rational debate. He sought to recover the public sphere as a site for reasoned deliberation toward public consensus, and away from its increasingly dominant character as a site for public opinion distortion and manipulation. He wanted to bring public opinion "into play as a critical authority in connection with the normative mandate that the exercise of political and social power be subject to publicity" and to move away from public opinion as "the object to be molded in connection with a staged display of, and manipulative propagation of, publicity in the service of persons and institutions, consumer goods, and programs."

In his later work,[21] Habermas has sought a solution more directly in communication itself. He advocates a progressive rationalization of communication in which undistorted communication would replace power and money as social determinants. While *Structural Transformation* located the potential for democratic practical reason in a public sphere, his later theory of communicative action located it instead in universal, transhistorical communicative capacities. While the public sphere remained an important ideal in his work, it was relegated to the status of a *product* of communicative action rather than its basis.

Habermas's account has been influential both as critique and as a normative ideal. His empirical account of the growth and decline of a public sphere serves as a critical foothold for measuring today's gutted public sphere and the consequences for a democratic politics of the wholesale retreat by common citizens from public life and derationalization of public opinion and debate. His theorizing of a public realm of undistorted, uncoerced communication, free of power inequities and the dictates of market and state also draws attention to the consequences today of "public" communication marked predominately by sound bites, attack ads, image advertising, and media manipulation.

Aristotle, Arendt, and Habermas agree that democracy requires a vital public sphere in general and multiple public spaces in particular, where citizens can engage with each other. The specific form of engagement they emphasize—deliberation—constitutes the process through which citizens learn about each other and their diverse interests, learn to take others' views into account when forming political opinions, and discover or create common ground for action. All three view deliberation as a good in itself and also a pragmatic basis for citizen action.

When and where can common citizens deliberate today? Perhaps the most famous example of existing deliberative options is the New England town meeting, where local townspeople gather to discuss public matters that affect them. Despite its appeal to political theorists, however, the New England town meeting occurs relatively infrequently today compared to generations ago. Opportunities to debate and discuss issues of local public significance some- times exist at city council meetings, local planning board meetings, and other local municipal group meetings, if citizens are actually invited and their role is not limited simply to complaining. Other local initiatives such as a school levy campaign often integrate a series of meetings to solicit citizens' partici- pation and views. Local school Parent-Teacher Associations (PTAs) typically encourage participation by parents, and these sometimes allow multiple op- portunities for deliberation.

Elections *should* be opportunities for widespread deliberation. Some elec- tions fulfill this promise, but many do not. The electoral process introduces many political issues for debate and discussion in a variety of settings. Com- mon citizens often have an opportunity to attend campaign events, or organ- ize them themselves, to listen, question, and respond to candidates' proposals. Although the mainstream media tend to focus on "horse-race" issues such as who leads in the latest poll, offering weak analysis at best, they nevertheless disseminate some information about some issues. Actual debates between candidates are sometimes helpful in sharpening differences between candi- dates and allowing direct participation by citizens. On the other hand, the re- sult may be more rather than less confusion as candidates trade dubious statistics, exaggerated claims, and even outright lies. Local elections allow more direct interactive participation in meeting with candidates, posing ques- tions to them, and offering opportunities to challenge their answers and sug- gest others. As noted earlier, elections in the United States remain too tied to the two-party system, ensuring that the spectrum of ideas represented in a typical election remains relatively narrow. Adopting the reforms suggested by political theorists such as William Hudson—ending the power of special in- terests in choosing candidates, a system of public financing of elections, free media access for candidates, limits on campaign spending—would broaden this spectrum. Moving to a proportional system of representation would further broaden the spectrum of political voices included in the electoral process.

Talk radio draws millions of listeners and direct participants through the call-in feature. Talk radio programs also often feature guests invited to address public affairs. Conservatives notoriously dominate the talk radio scene. Locked from participation from these programs, progressives have responded by attempting, thus far with limited success, to create their own talk radio programs. To be of value as a forum for public deliberation, however, these programs must feature a genuine diversity of opinions with genuine dialogue. National Public Radio (NPR) approaches this ideal, though still falls short. Its featured programs such as the *Diane Rehm Show* and *Talk of the Nation* typically feature guests from conservative publications and organizations such as the *Wall Street Journal* and the American Enterprise Institute as well as the more liberal *New York Times* and the Economic Policy Institute. The moderate Brookings Institute frequently represents the "liberal" side. Although NPR's talk shows can be deemed balanced, in that they typically include both conservative and progressive voices, they nevertheless draw from a very narrow spectrum of political ideas. Truly alternative points of view drawn, for example, from third parties of both the left and right are rarely included.

Since the early 1990s, a civic journalism initiative has produced some fruitful possibilities for increasing the options and quality for public deliberation. The Wichita (Kansas) People Project, initiated in 1992 by the *Wichita Eagle*, invited citizens to join in public deliberation over local and regional problems. The newspaper collaborated with a local television station and a commercial radio station to offer a forum for citizens to share ideas about political issues and controversies and potential solutions to them. In a similar venture, Wisconsin Public Television joined in 1992 with Madison's *Wisconsin State Journal*, a CBS television affiliate, and Wisconsin Public Radio to form "We the People." This initiative offered public forums, coverage of particular issues, and sponsorship of citizen discussion groups aimed at developing a public sphere of deliberation in Wisconsin. The NPR Election Project featured collaboration among affiliates and local newspapers in five large cities designed to allow citizens to lead election coverage through surveys, discussions, and forums.

Citizen juries, proposed by James Fishkin and adopted in a variety of venues, offer another option for increasing direct citizen deliberation. Organizers assemble these whenever and wherever a diversity of citizens' views on various public affairs might usefully be solicited. The jury participants typically spend several hours discussing and debating the issues on the table. Participants have an opportunity to listen and learn from each other, as well as to present their own views. Sometimes, the jury deliberations, along with any conclusions or results, are publicized.

Some observers look with hope at the explosion of Internet options for disseminating information and offering multiple opportunities for direct engagement by common citizens. Like talk radio, these range from the good to the bad and the ugly. Certainly, citizens can now find a plethora of information about public affairs on the Internet. Much of its quality is good and credible, but much is not. Distinguishing between the two can often be difficult. Web logs, or blogs, tend to offer more rant than rational review of issues. Chat rooms allow for interaction among participants, but are difficult to filter and maintain.

Many campus student groups host forums for addressing political issues and other issues of concern to students. Each of these offers at least some opportunity for students to gather to listen and discuss. The issues can range from U.S. foreign policy and global warming to appropriate noise levels in dormitories and campus security. The important point is that they integrate different perspectives and offer students a chance to discuss, debate, and learn from each other.

Many other initiatives designed to increase public deliberation can be identified. One example is the National Issues Forum supported by the Kettering Foundation and the Public Agenda Foundation, integrating several thousand community-based groups as diverse as churches, literacy programs, community colleges, and prison study groups to explore competing perspectives on public issues. The Forum aimed at developing the capacity for public judgment. American Health Decisions, originating in Oregon and spreading to nineteen states by 1994, integrated citizens in discussions over options and priorities for health care. Central Oklahoma 2020, covering twenty cities and four counties, brought citizens together in a regional planning process. It included youth, elderly, elected officials, educators, business owners, immigrants, clergy, and others. The process aimed at developing strategies and action plans for regional development. The periodical *Utne Reader* during the

1990s fostered a "salon" movement by encouraging readers to gather informally in readers' homes to discuss contemporary issues.

Deliberation builds upon existing citizens' capacities for recognizing and responding to differences as well as similarities, for discussion and debate, for listening to diverse others, and for considering both public and private interests. Deliberation also increases and develops citizens' capacities in two ways. First, it allows citizens to hone their speaking and listening skills, their ability to recognize and respond appropriately to diversity, and their ability to consider the public interest as well as their private interests. It gives them practice in the arts of citizenship. Second, deliberation enables citizens to work out their differences and discover or create common ground for action. Without this common ground, effective action for problem solving is difficult or impossible. Deliberation thus offers one means of empowerment: it increases the capacity of citizens to engage in public life and work with others to identify common ground and solve shared problems.

Pragmatic Problem Solving

A second general kind of public engagement occurs in the form of pragmatic problem solving. John Dewey epitomized this form of politics. In *The Public and Its Problems* (1927), Dewey argued that under modern conditions of mass communication, rapidly developing technology, and increasing mobility, citizens were increasingly unable to organize to effectively address shared problems. As always the participatory democrat, he rejected any notions of elite management of public affairs or of simply turning responsibility for solutions over to government. Average citizens, he believed, must take responsibility for problem solving. From there he concentrated on the underlying social conditions that enable public problem solving.

In *The Public and Its Problems* he posed these primarily in terms of community. Citizens, he argued, must develop the commonalities of community: common awareness of each other as members of a public with common interests and common problems, and a common commitment to work together collaboratively to address them. He saw a key role for science and inquiry as tools for understanding public problems and creating solutions. Widespread communication of the results of inquiry would help develop community by broadening understanding of shared interests and shared problems. Dewey envisioned a participatory role for average citizens in local communities where they would work with others to identify shared interests and problems and would organize to address them. He also believed in the possibility of an extensive, national community that he called a "great community."

In Dewey's later works, he continued to concentrate on the social and cultural foundations that would support democratic participation in pragmatic problem solving. He sought a democratic culture that would nurture capable democratic citizens willing and able to assume responsibility for public affairs in general and problem solving in particular. These interests propelled him into consideration of art, education, social psychology, political economy, and philosophy to theorize the bases for democratic citizenship. He had surprisingly little to say about specific forms of political organizing in everyday life to solve problems.

If Dewey slighted theorizing everyday forms of public problem solving, contemporary political theorist Harry Boyte (1945–) has done much to fill in the blanks. Since the 1980s, Boyte has variously labeled his approach to pragmatic problem solving "commonwealth politics," "citizen politics," "pragmatic citizen politics," "common work," "practical citizenship," and "public work." Boyte views this form of political engagement as an alternative to the current status of citizens as "permanent outsiders" and "spectators" for whom elected officials and appointed bureaucrats do the work of solving public problems. Boyte's alternative emphasizes ongoing active participation by common citizens where "ordinary people feel themselves to be creators and subjects of history, not simply spectators and objects," and this provides "a key to democratic political renewal."

Central to securing citizen participation is acknowledging and building upon the "largely pragmatic, problem-solving motives that often move people in the public sphere, in both formal and informal contexts," especially as found in multiple voluntary traditions.[22] Some proponents of citizen engagement dismiss private and self-interests as illegitimate baggage in public affairs, but Boyte, while acknowledging the importance of public spiritedness, also insists on the legitimacy of private concerns and self-interests. In Boyte's formulation, this tie to legitimate self-interests links the everyday concerns of common citizens to public life. Rather than reject the private interests of common citizens, he argues, we should listen carefully in order to connect everyday life experiences to larger concerns. Conversely, the larger public problems that affect us all can be broken into smaller, manageable pieces that connect to the private lives of all citizens.

Highlighting his insistence on extensive and ongoing participation by common citizens, Boyte argues that public work is not simply work for the public or in the public, it is "also work of the public and by the public." Boyte's citizens take responsibility for identifying and addressing shared issues, concerns, and problems. Rather than simply complaining to government, citizens organize to do the work themselves. Even if government and business elites could solve our public problems without active citizen engagement, Boyte nevertheless rejects that option as undemocratic. We must emphasize process, not product, if we are serious about democracy. "When the emphasis is simply on the product," he argues, "then regardless how grand the creation or how noble the aspiration, democracy is not part of the equation."[23]

The primary outcome of participation in pragmatic problem solving is, hopefully, the successful resolution of shared problems. Boyte identifies additional outcomes, including especially the development of citizen capacities to recognize and address their shared concerns, the creation and discovery of new resources for problem solving, and institutionalizing the experience within communities. Boyte also views participation in civic republican terms as a good in itself in which the public world "carries resonances of positive freedom."[24] By participating in public work, citizens realize in practice their freedom as citizens.

Power is a central theme in Boyte's work and he articulates it partly in terms of developing the skills and aptitudes of common citizens. Boyte seeks to draw attention to "civic agency: the capacities, powers, and skills" needed by citizens to be responsible, accountable actors in public affairs. "Citizen politics," he argues, "is an art, requiring such abilities as good judgment, skillful use of power, critical thinking, imagination, and rhetoric." Effective problem solving also requires skills of negotiation, bargaining, and accountability and an ability to work with people with different backgrounds, interests, and approaches. Like other participatory democrats, Boyte believes that participation develops these capacities of citizenship. Through participation in public problem solving, people

> change. They discover in themselves and their traditions new resources, potentials, resonances. They repair capacities to work together for collective problem solving. They find out new political facts about the world. They build networks and seek contacts with other groups . . . to forge a more heterogeneous group

identity. And this whole process in turn helps to clarify basic power relations in society. In sum, people deepen the meaning of what they are doing, from understanding politics merely as a protest against threat to coming to see the need for a struggle for new conceptions of rights and participation and power. This kind of change is the identifying mark, specifically, of a democratic movement that seeks a transformation of power relations, not simply a return to past conditions or the replacement of one elite with another.

Boyte also addresses power in terms of issues of community control and self-determination. He views the commonwealth tradition as an alternative to the politics of both capitalism and socialism and says it shifts the main focus of politics from "the question of redistributive justice to the issue of who wields power over the fundamental structures of our common life." Commonwealth politics raises questions of power, who wields it over our common lives, and what instruments of power are in the hands of ordinary citizens. Boyte concludes that the "question of power is the basic problem of democracy" today.[25] He insists repeatedly that citizens must reclaim power that they have ceded to elected representatives and to dominant elites in governmental and corporate institutions.

Many of these themes converge in "Call for a New Citizenship," drafted in 1994 under the auspices of the American Civic Forum in conjunction with the University of Minnesota's Center for Democracy and Citizenship, directed by Harry Boyte, and the Walt Whitman Center at Rutgers University. The New Citizenship echoes some of the communitarian themes, including balancing rights and responsibilities, emphasizing active citizen engagement, the importance of voluntary associations, and returning responsibility for issues such as poverty and crime to families and communities. It diverges from the communitarian platform especially in its more focused attention to power. As in Boyte's other work, power is conceived both in terms of citizenship capacities, and the basic issues of control and self-determination.

The New Citizenship calls for the development of civic capacities, including skills of listening, compromise, and negotiation; respect for differences; ability to work with political opponents; and honesty about interests. It advocates a transfer of power from "central bureaucracies, public and private, to citizens and civic institutions." The New Citizenship "seeks the return of authority from unaccountable structures to the public and to community and civic associations, and the renewal of government and civic institutions alike as sites for public work." It also seeks renewal of the "citizen-politician," with common citizens taking responsibility for politics—for debating ends and means and for solving public problems. This would allow them to reclaim the power promised them in a democracy, while allowing the exercise of positive freedom and self-determination, and to "grasp the popular sovereignty that is the root of our democracy."

The New Citizenship also departs from the communitarian platform in its emphasis on difference and diversity. Although both documents include discussions of issues such as moral education, the New Citizenship pointedly dismisses any attempts to develop or impose moral consensus. It takes as a given the widespread differences of views and opinions on public matters. To solve problems, it says, "it will be necessary to engage diverse interests, points of view, and moral frameworks. Few problems lend themselves to the either/or, 'good versus evil' style of argument which dominates public discussions today." The New Citizenship views public life as

> an arena of exchange, discourse, conflict, mutual respect, and collaborative work. The point is not personal bonding or complete agreement but rather constructive, creative action on common problems. Many different moral frameworks and perspectives are appropriately at the table, with no one dominating.[26]

Boyte's work is informed by his empirical study of different community-based citizen groups that epitomize commonwealth politics. For example, the Industrial Areas Foundation is the oldest coalition of community organizations in the United States, with multiple affiliates in different cities based mainly in religious congregations, often in the nation's poorest areas. In San Antonio, Communities Organized for Public Service (COPS) organized to bring millions into its barrios for infrastructure improvement. East Brooklyn Churches created housing for 2,500 families in rundown areas of New York City. Baltimoreans United in Leadership Development (BUILD) organized school administrators, city officials, business leaders, and faith-based leaders to provide every high school graduate some economic support for college or a job opportunity. Shelby County Interfaith of Memphis organized fifty congregations, half black and half white, to create jobs and to provide adult education, housing, and crime prevention. The National Center for

Neighborhood Enterprise assists local community organizing efforts in various locations. At Cochran Gardens in St. Louis, tenants took control of a declining public housing project and redeveloped it. According to Boyte, the key to the success of these groups is that they develop "the civic and public leadership capacities of individuals, institutions, and communities."[27]

Other examples of pragmatic problem solving are as diverse and varied as are American neighborhoods and communities. Neighbors solve problems pragmatically when they establish crime watches, organize to participate in a local development planning process, or set up after-school programs for youth. Likewise, students engage in pragmatic problem solving when they organize to address hate crimes on campus, to increase the availability of recycling bins, or to establish later hours at the library. The efforts of these organizers sometimes find lasting institutional expression, but frequently do not. In the latter case, participants address a problem and then move on to other concerns. The main idea remains the same: ordinary citizens organize to do the work of politics themselves, without relying on elected officials or government bureaucrats to do it, though they may seek and secure assistance from government. They organize locally to address local, regional, national, and global problems. These organizing efforts are already occurring; advocates such as Boyte call for more, with wider participation.

Like deliberation, pragmatic problem solving both requires and develops citizens' capacities. To participate effectively in problem-solving efforts, citizens must bring certain abilities and aptitudes, especially the willingness to work with diverse others, to initiate organizing efforts, to assume responsibility for action, and to foster a collaborative effort. But these skills and aptitudes are developed in the process of working with others to solve problems. Problem solving, like deliberation, provides practice in the arts of citizenship. In a larger sense, pragmatic problem solving increases the capacity of average citizens to seize their right to popular sovereignty and to make decisions and act on them to determine the circumstances of their daily lives, with or without the assistance of elected officials and government programs.

Confrontation

A third general kind of political engagement typically pits one or more groups against one or more other groups, usually in a zero-sum struggle where one group's gain is another's loss. In contrast to the collaborative emphasis of pragmatic problem solving, political actors using this form often seek to wreck their opponents' agenda rather than engage constructively with it. This form is characterized by the language and practice of protest, opposition, militancy, insurgency, struggle, dissidence, and resistance. Political actors engaged in this form of political action typically seek to best one or more rivals in order to secure control and influence. Marginalized groups in particular, because of their outsider status, often turn to this form of political engagement. With little or no access to formal political arenas, they must open alternative political spaces and press their agendas aggressively. As Holloway Sparks describes it, this "dissident" politics involves "the practices of marginalized citizens who publicly contest prevailing arrangements of power by means of oppositional democratic practices that augment or replace institutionalized channels of democratic opposition when those channels are inadequate or unavailable."[28] Political action of this sort often occurs outside formal arenas of politics, suggesting that appreciating its value may require stretching the notion of a political, public sphere to encompass alternative political spaces ranging from dance halls to the Internet to city streets.

Karl Marx (1818–1883), one of the most famous and powerful advocates of this approach, wrote at the beginning of the *Communist Manifesto* that "the history of all hitherto existing society is the history of class struggles" pitting freeman and slave, patrician and plebeian, lord and serf, guild-master and journeyman, and most recently capitalist and proletarian against each other. These were conflicts between "oppressor and oppressed" who "stood in constant opposition to one another" and "carried on an uninterrupted, now hidden, now open fight" against each other. The confrontational, oppositional nature of politics as framed by Marx could hardly be more stark. The bourgeoisie has enlisted the support of the state to secure and cement its dominance. It engages in "naked, shameless, direct, brutal exploitation" of working people, turning them into commodities on a par with land and materials, imposing on working people "repulsive" work, low wages, and an increasing "burden of toil."[29] Thus framed, it is no wonder that Marx saw politics as a zero-sum struggle for power, for there could be no compromise, no accommodation with a capitalist class whose interests were so opposed to those of working people and whose very existence represented class oppression, exploitation, and domination.

Subsequent Marxists have continued to assert the ubiquity of class struggle as the defining feature of politics. The twentieth-century Italian Marxist Antonio Gramsci (1891–1937) has exerted considerable influence since the translation into English in 1971 of his *Selections from the Prison Notebooks.* Imprisoned on trumped-up charges during the 1930s by the Fascist regime in Italy, Gramsci committed his thinking to a series of notes smuggled from prison. As a Marxist and leader of the Italian Communist party, Gramsci remained faithful to the overarching framework of class struggle, and he theorized within that framework.

Like other Marxists, he saw politics as a ubiquitous struggle of labor against capital. Presumably, according to Marxist theory, the working class would realize its oppression by capitalists and would one day create or seize the opportunity to overthrow them. However, workers in Italy and elsewhere appeared instead to accept capitalist domination. In attempting to understand why, Gramsci developed the concept of hegemony. *Hegemony* can be defined as a relatively close fit between prevailing economic practices and the ideas, beliefs, and political practices that enable and legitimize them. Hegemony is expressed in the

> consent given by the great masses of the population to the general direction imposed on social life by the dominant fundamental group; this consent is "historically" caused by the prestige (and consequent confidence) which the dominant group enjoys because of its position and function in the world of production.[30]

It is a form of domination that takes the form of consent and persuasion as well as coercion, and the dominant class rules through intellectual and moral leadership as well as through force. Hegemony thus combines force, in the forms of state coercion, the military, the police, and the criminal justice system, with consent secured through the media, education, propaganda, universities, and the popular press.

Dominance cannot be won or maintained solely through coercion, Gramsci argued. Dominance that attains the character of common sense better ensures its own perpetuation. Integrating an appreciation for the third face of power, Gramsci argued that the working and peasant classes had been convinced of the legitimacy of their own oppression and that they adhered to beliefs counter to their own interests. They thus consented to their own oppression. Gramsci summarized the process of attaining consent as follows:

> [Ideologies] come into confrontation and conflict, until only one of them, or at least a single combination of them, tends to prevail, to gain the upper hand, to propagate itself throughout society—bringing about not only a unison of economic and political aims, but also intellectual and moral unity, posing all the questions around which the struggle rages . . . and thus creating the hegemony of a fundamental social group over a series of subordinate groups.[31]

Note that the hegemonic group is able to exercise and reinforce its hegemony in part by controlling the definition of basic questions. This allows it to exercise extensive control over public discussion and debate. Potential critics are marginalized in part by having their questions, concerns, and challenges driven from public consideration. One could say that, like Thrasymachus, Gramsci realized that the wealth and power of the strong enable them to legitimize their domination via control over public discussion and the manipulation of symbols.

The dominant class harnesses the power of the state to reinforce its positions. Gramsci defined the state broadly as "the entire complex of practical and theoretical activities with which the ruling class not only justifies and maintains its dominance, but manages to win the active consent of those over whom it rules." The ruling class, acting through the state, uses the schools, the court system, and "a multitude of other so-called private initiatives and activities . . . which form the apparatus of the political and cultural hegemony of the ruling classes" to maintain and reinforce its dominant position. It uses its dominant position to keep people apathetic and passive "by means of moralizing sermons, emotional stimuli, and messianic myths of an awaited golden age, in which all present contradictions and miseries will be automatically resolved and made well."[32] Hegemony is also won, exercised, and reinforced in part through the operation of the law, which the ruling class molds to meet its needs and interests.

What political options are available for nonhegemonic groups, which Gramsci called "subalterns"? In answering this question, Gramsci first distinguished between the class conflict found in periods of crisis and that of periods of relative stability. Periods of crisis in which the legitimacy and stability of existing forms of power are shaken present opportunities for "wars of movement" involving direct assault on state institutions in order to take control of them. However, history offers relatively few opportunities for this sort of direct assault on state institutions. In most industrialized countries, working-class consciousness is too undeveloped, and bourgeois control of the state too solidified, to attempt direct challenges for control of the state. Under these circumstances of bourgeois hegemony, Gramsci advocated a "war of position" to challenge the current forms of bourgeois power and to begin to develop revolutionary working-class consciousness. A war of position is a protracted struggle on many fronts, including everyday cultural arenas, in order to undermine the legitimacy of the existing social order. It is initially and fundamentally educative, with education aiming at developing the widespread "capacity for intellectual and practical creativity, and of autonomy of orientation and initiative."[33]

Crucial to a war of position, according to Gramsci, is the work of what he called "organic intellectuals." He believed that ordinary people were intellectuals in the sense that they could think critically about their lives and their situations in life. However, not all men and women play the role in society of intellectuals. The working class has its own intellectuals who express the aspirations and interests of the working class, who help people develop a critical awareness of their position and role, who give the working class "homogeneity and an awareness of its own function not only in the economic but also in the social and political fields," and who serve as "constructor, organizer, 'permanent persuader.'"[34] They help transform common sense, slowly and minutely. The work of hegemony and counterhegemony also is conducted by "political parties," a term that Gramsci understood broadly to mean the various groups and organizations throughout civil society that develop and unify class consciousness. Faced with the task of forming a collective consciousness and a collective will, political parties carry out this task on multiple fronts, including, once again, cultural fronts.

Since Gramsci framed politics wholly in confrontational terms, he never considered the option of engaging constructively with competing groups. Rather, he sought ways to overcome and supplant them. This included the moderate-left social democrats. Political action should be aimed, he believed, at exposing the injustices represented by bourgeois domination and the hegemony that legitimized it, and not at coming to terms with it in a positive accommodation and compromise. Gramsci also dismissed any notion of permanent accommodation with dominant bourgeois structures and institutions. They represented, by definition, oppression and injustice wielded over working people. The only political outcome he could embrace would require a complete victory of working class and peasant forces over bourgeois forces, rather than compromise or accommodation.

One kind of confrontational political engagement called civil disobedience deserves special attention. "Civil disobedience" means consciously and willfully breaking a law in order to make a political statement and to avoid becoming an accomplice to the injustice represented by the law. The American transcendentalist Henry David Thoreau (1817–1862) wrote one of the most famous justifications for civil disobedience. Published in 1849, Thoreau's essay "Civil Disobedience" later inspired such thinkers and activists as Mahatma Gandhi and Martin Luther King Jr. Although Thoreau wrote specifically to protest slavery and American aggression against Mexico, his work established general principles of civil disobedience that contemporaries continue to draw upon.

Echoing early liberal thinking, Thoreau first argued that government is, at best, "an expedient." As such, it enjoys no intrinsic legitimacy. The legitimacy or illegitimacy of a government depends instead on its actions. According to Thoreau, if the government is doing something that you believe is wrong, then you should withdraw your support. Thoreau withdrew his own support via tax resistance, refusing to pay his poll tax, for which he briefly landed in jail. If a law is patently unjust, Thoreau counseled, disobey it. He urged citizens to "break the law. Let your life be a counter friction to stop the machine" of government and the injustices it perpetrates. And if your actions result in jail time, so much the better since "under a government which imprisons any unjustly, the true place for a just man is also a prison."

Thoreau's argument relied partly on his critique of majority rule and voting as a mechanism for determining government behavior. Thoreau believed that the vote, however important it might be in a democracy, is but a "feeble" political act. "Even voting *for the right*," he argued, "*is doing* nothing for it. It is only expressing to men feebly your desire that it should prevail." He noted that the vote is fully consistent with injustice since the majority that wins an election may support unjust ends and means. Dissenters can either simply accede at that point to the majority, in which case they become accomplices to the injustice, or they can turn to civil disobedience. Civil disobedience has the added virtue of empowering minorities in a majority-rule regime. If the minority relies solely on the vote to make its case for political change, its efforts will prove fruitless. On the other hand, if members of the minority take direct action in the form of civil disobedience, their actions will have more of a direct impact. As Thoreau put it, "A minority is powerless while it conforms to the majority; it is not even a minority then; but it is irresistible when it clogs by its whole weight." If enough members of the minority clog the system, the system is forced to take account of it and potentially change.

How does one know when a law or policy is unjust? According to Thoreau, "The only obligation which I have a right to assume, is to do at any time what I think right." Nobody should ever "resign his conscience to the legislator."[35] In short, individual conscience precedes and supersedes the law. It provides the basis for determining the just or unjust character of laws and government action. Thoreau thus appears to have defined *injustice* as whatever an individual's conscience says it is. His prescription for citizens in the face of injustice is to break the law. This is probably untenable in practice, since for most laws there are at least some people who oppose them. Carried to their logical conclusion, Thoreau's prescriptions lead to anarchy, despite his caveat that he is not against government per se, only bad government. Yet, Thoreau's writing on civil disobedience offers a passionate and persuasive justification for civic activism aimed at overcoming injustice, using the tactic of civil disobedience when necessary. It is especially useful as a tactic for relatively marginalized individuals and groups who have too little access to, and control over, mainstream political institutions and processes. It draws attention to their concerns in a way that other forms of political activism might not.

As Thoreau argued, majorities can and unfortunately often do support injustice. This was the case during the 1950s and 1960s in the American South, where a majority of white citizens defended patently unjust Jim Crow policies perpetuating second-class status for African Americans. Martin Luther King Jr., writing more than a hundred years after Thoreau, defended civil disobedience as a strategy for change against charges by his fellow black clergy that his tactics were counterproductive in alienating potential allies and provoking violent backlash. Writing from jail in 1963, King addressed their pleas for patience and for waiting until the time was riper. "'Wait,'" King wrote, "has almost always meant 'Never.'" If left to a majority vote, he believed, change would never happen.

In defending civil disobedience, King distinguished between two kinds of laws: just and unjust. According to him, citizens have a moral responsibility to obey just laws and to disobey unjust laws. Anyone who disobeys an unjust law "must do it *openly, lovingly* . . . and with a willingness to accept the penalty." Such a person, King asserted, "is in reality expressing the very highest respect for law."

How do you tell the difference between a just and an unjust law? King gave two distinctly different answers. The first drew from his experience as a Christian and a preacher. "A just law," he argued, "is a man-made code that squares with the moral law or the law of God. An unjust law is a code that is out of harmony with the moral law." Although this first answer appeals to many, it also raises concerns for others. How can we know for certain "the law of God"? Different religious traditions offer different moral codes. Even within a particular religious tradition, well-meaning adherents disagree over basic interpretations and tenets. The many different Christian denominations agree on many points of interpretation and belief, but disagree on others.

Perhaps anticipating these concerns, King offered a second, secular way to distinguish between just and unjust laws. This secular approach has two parts. First, King argued that "an unjust law is a code that a numerical or power majority group compels a minority group to obey but does not make binding on itself," while "a just law is a code that a majority compels a minority to follow and that it is willing to follow itself." In other words, a just law is a law that applies equally to everyone. Second, "a law is unjust if it is inflicted on a minority that, as a result of being denied the right to vote, had no part in enacting or devising the law." By implication, a just law requires that minorities have equal rights of political participation, including the vote.

As Thoreau pointed out, a majority is fully capable of enacting unjust laws. Laws applied equally to all satisfy King's first stipulation but leave open the possibility that the laws are nevertheless unjust. This is precisely why civil disobedience is a valuable tool, as King and Thoreau both recognized. For King, in a context of injustice supported by a majority of the population, a minority could legitimately "present our very bodies as a means of laying our case before the conscience of the local and the national community." The minority could engage in civil disobedience "to dramatize the issue" so that "it can no longer be ignored." Like Thoreau, King saw civil disobedience as a valuable tool for minorities to draw attention to their concerns and to force the majority to take notice and perhaps change. Simply acceding to the majority's wishes only perpetuates the injustice.

What if this creates disorder and disrupts the peace? King's response was clear. He insisted that the needs of justice should take precedence over the need for political order. According to King:

> The Negro's great stumbling block in his stride toward freedom is not the White Citizen's Counciler or the Ku Klux Klanner, but the white moderate, who is more devoted to "order" than to justice; who prefers a negative peace which is the absence of tension to a positive peace which is the presence of justice.[36]

Civil disobedience remains a favored strategy of some groups, particularly those who feel that their concerns and efforts are marginalized. During the 1980s, various groups employed the tactic in opposition to the Reagan administration's policies in Central America. In the late twentieth and early twenty-first centuries, groups throughout the world employed civil disobedience against the World Trade Organization (WTO) and its representatives. Most notoriously in recent times, the tactic helped shut down WTO negotiations held in Seattle in the fall of 2000 and disrupted WTO negotiations held in other cities throughout the world.

As Martin Luther King Jr.'s fellow black clergy noted, civil disobedience can backfire. Much depends on how the media portray events. And since dominant elites with vested stakes in status quo policies own and control most major media, dissidents rarely receive favorable, or even neutral, coverage. The Seattle WTO protests received mostly negative coverage from the mainstream media. The protesters included union members, teachers, anarchists, environmentalists, grandmothers, children, and activists from all over the world, yet mainstream media coverage focused on topless vegan dykes, environmentalists dressed as sea turtles, and anarchists. Most of the commentators representing mainstream media scornfully dismissed the protestors as ignorant idealists or, worse, venal attention-seekers. This inevitably leaves the public with a one-sided jaundiced view of the groups using civil disobedience, and the groups employing the tactic see their ideas and concerns further marginalized.

Whether involving civil disobedience or not, contemporary social movements represent the most common form of confrontational political action today. Social movements are many and varied. They include the civil rights, antiglobalization, environmental, feminist, tenants' rights, labor, disability, peace, pro-life, white power, neo-Nazi, and fundamentalist Christian movements. Sidney Tarrow (1938–) defines social movements as people engaged in "contentious politics" who are "backed by dense social networks and galvanized by culturally resonant, action-oriented symbols" that lead to "sustained interaction with opponents."[37] In a social movement, individuals organize for collective action in pursuit of one or more goals, typically employing strategies of confrontation and opposition to entrenched interests and powers. A social movement may contain disparate individuals, more than one group or organization, and individuals who belong to no organization but who support the goals of the social movement. Movement organizations tend to be short lived, lack resources, and emerge from concerns for justice. They often pursue an "outside" strategy and seek "the broad-scale mobilization of citizens at the 'grass roots.'" Participants share in common "their situation within a broader movement, characterized by its social networks, its mobilizing symbols, and its systematic contention with those in power." Social movements seek to confront those who wield substantial power, by mobilizing disparate individuals, groups, and resources with relatively little power prior to mobilization.

People organize or join social movements for a variety of reasons. Typically, they are moved by passion for a cause, by a commitment to justice, by a sense that it is the right thing to do, and by felt need to contribute to change. Social movement activists typically employ an array of confrontational strategies, including demonstrations, marches, protests, sit-ins, and potentially civil disobedience.

Confrontational politics increases capacity by giving voice to people with few other options, publicizing or dramatizing an issue or cause, opening political spaces, mobilizing large numbers of people for action, and helping unify disparate individuals and groups for collective action. Its value is of particular importance to relatively marginalized groups who enjoy little access to public spaces and agendas, who find admittance to institutionalized political processes barred, and whose material resources do not allow the purchase of political power.

QUESTIONS, PROBLEMS, AND ACTIVITIES

1. Do you find the claim plausible that elites in the United States exercise the third face of power to distort average people's self-understandings and their perceptions of their interests? Can you give examples? Explain.
2. Robert Putnam identifies the television as the single most powerful force undermining social capital formation in modern times. Do you agree with him? Can the same arguments be applied to the computer? the automobile? Explain your answers.
3. Design a work of art that draws upon affective power to motivate political action on an issue that interests you.
4. Listen to a talk radio program, then evaluate it according to the criteria for deliberative politics developed by Aristotle, Arendt, and Habermas. What changes, if any, would need to be made? Do the same for one or more Internet blogs. Can you identify opportunities in your life for participating in deliberative politics?
5. Should civil disobedience always be nonviolent? Consider the Central American peasant who witnesses the murder of his family, and who has seen years of ongoing similar atrocities, all of them done in the name of the state and all unpunished. Should we tell him that nonviolence is the answer?
6. Identify a problem on campus, or in your neighborhood. Develop a strategy for addressing the problem that emphasizes active citizenship and that relies as little as possible on government or other established authorities.
7. Under what circumstances, if any, would you be willing to engage in civil disobedience?
8. Can you think of examples of "false consciousness" where people misunderstand or misperceive their own interests?
9. Which of the three kinds of political engagement most appeals to you? Which do you think is most effective at creating political change?

NOTES

1. Robert Putnam, "Democracy in America at the End of the Twentieth Century," in *Participation and Democracy: East and West*, ed. Dietrich Rueschemeyer, Marilyn Rueschemeyer, and Björn Wittrock (Armonk, NY: M. E. Sharpe, 1998), pp. 236, 256; Robert Putnam, *Bowling Alone: The Collapse and Revival of American Community* (New York: Simon & Schuster, 2000), pp. 402–14.

2. See, for example, Scott McLean, David Schultz, and Manfred Steger, eds., *Social Capital: Critical Perspectives on Community and "Bowling Alone"* (New York: New York University Press, 2002).

3. Martin Luther King Jr., "Letter from a Birmingham Jail," in *I Have a Dream: Writings and Speeches That Changed the World*, ed. James Washington (New York: HarperCollins, 1986), p. 93.

4. Jill Gregory, April Lewton, Mark Mattern, Stephanie Schmidt, and Diane Smith, "Body Politics with Feeling: The Power of the Clothesline Project," *New Political Science* 24, no. 3 (November 2002): pp. 434–48.

5. Plato *The Republic* 7:515–17.

6. Paolo Freire, *Pedagogy of the Oppressed* [1970], rev. ed., trans. Myra Bergman Ramos (New York: Continuum, 1990), pp. 33, 19, 31, 32, 49, 52.

7. Ibid., pp. 33, 20, 41.

8. Ibid., pp. 60, 67–69, 71; emphasis in original.

9. Lisa Disch, "'Please Sit Down, but Don't Make Yourself at Home': Arendtian 'Visiting' and the Prefigurative Politics of Consciousness-Raising," in *Hannah Arendt and the Meaning of Politics*, ed. Craig Calhoun and John McGowan (Minneapolis: University of Minnesota Press, 1997), p. 132; Anita Shreve, *Women Together, Women Alone* (New York: Viking Press, 1989), p. 6; Debra Michals, "From 'Consciousness Expansion' to 'Consciousness Raising': Feminism and the Countercultural Politics of the Self," in *Imagine Nation: The American Counterculture of the 1960s and '70s*, ed. Peter Braunstein and Michael William Doyle (New York: Routledge, 2002), p. 57.

10. Betty Friedan, *The Feminine Mystique* (New York: W. W. Norton, 1963), pp. 15, 43, 31.

11. Jo Freeman, *The Politics of Women's Liberation* (New York: David McKay, 1975), p. 118; bell hooks, *Feminism Is for Everybody* (Cambridge, MA: South End Press, 2000), p. 8.

12. John Dewey, *Freedom and Culture* [1939], in *John Dewey: The Later Works, 1925–1953*, vol. 13, ed. Jo Ann Boydston (Carbondale: Southern Illinois University Press, 1991), pp. 67, 72, 186.

13. John Dewey, *Reconstruction in Philosophy* [1920], in *John Dewey: The Middle Works, 1899–1924*, vol. 12, ed. Jo Ann Boydston (Carbondale: Southern Illinois University Press, 1988), p. 186.

14. John Dewey, *Individualism, Old and New* [1929–30], in Boydston, *John Dewey: The Later Works*, vol. 5 (1988), pp. 45–46, 55, 104, 98, 106.

15. Hannah Arendt, *On Violence* (New York: Harcourt, Brace, & World, 1969), p. 44.

16. Aristotle, *Politics* 1.1.1, 1.2.2, 1.2.2, 1.2.5, 1.2.8, 1.2.8, 1.2.9.

17. Aristotle, *Politics* 2.2.3, 3.1.6, 3.1.10; emphasis in original.

18. Aristotle, *Politics* 3.11.2, 3.11.2, 3.11.14.

19. Aristotle, *Politics* 3.11.14; Aristotle, *The Politics of Aristotle*, ed. and trans. Ernest Barker (335–322 B.C.; Oxford: Oxford University Press, 1946), p. 126, n. 1; Aristotle, *Politics* 4.14.12, 3.4.15.

20. Hannah Arendt, *On Revolution* (New York: Viking Press, 1965), pp. 229–30; Arendt, *Between Past and Future* (New York: Viking Press, 1968), pp. 241, 220–21.

21. Jürgen Habermas, *The Structural Transformation of the Public Sphere: An Inquiry into a Category of Bourgeois Society*, trans. Thomas Burger and Frederick Lawrence (1962; Cambridge, MA: MIT Press, 1989), pp. 36–37, 176, 236; Craig Calhoun, "Introduction," in *Habermas and the Public Sphere*, ed. Craig Calhoun (Cambridge, MA: MIT Press, 1992), p. 26. For Habermas's later work, see especially his *Theory of Communicative Action* (Boston: Beacon Press, 1984).

22. Harry Boyte, "The Pragmatic Ends of Popular Politics," in Calhoun, *Habermas and the Public Sphere*, pp. 341, 342, 346.

23. Harry Boyte and Nancy Kari, *Building America: The Democratic Promise of Public Work* (Philadelphia: Temple University Press, 1996), pp. 23, 21.

24. Harry Boyte, "Beyond Deliberation: Citizenship as Public Work," paper delivered at the Political Economy of the Good Society (PEGS) Conference, February 11–12, 1995, available at http://www.cpn.org/crm/contemporary/beyond.html.

25. Ibid.; Boyte, *CommonWealth: A Return to Citizen Politics* (New York: Free Press, 1989), pp. 12, 32, 13, 16.

26. American Civic Forum, "Civic Declaration: Call for a New Citizenship," December 9, 1994, available at http://www.cpn.org/crm/essays/declaration.html.

27. Ibid.

28. Holloway Sparks, "Dissident Citizenship: Democratic Theory, Political Courage, and Activist Women," in *Theorizing Feminism: Parallel Trends in the Humanities and Social Sciences*, ed. Anne C. Herrmann and Abigail J. Stewart, 2nd ed. (Boulder, CO: Westview Press, 2001), p. 444.

29. Karl Marx, *The Communist Manifesto*, ed. Frederic L. Bender (1848; New York: W. W. Norton, 1988), pp. 55, 58, 61.

30. Antonio Gramsci, *Selections from the Prison Notebooks*, ed. and trans. Quintin Hoare and Geoffrey Nowell Smith (1929–35; New York: International Publishers, 1971), p. 12.

31. Ibid., pp. 181–82.

32. Ibid., pp. 244, 258, 150.

33. Ibid., p. 29.

34. Ibid., pp. 5, 10.

35. Henry David Thoreau, "Civil Disobedience" [1849], in *"Walden" and "Civil Disobedience"* (New York: Airmont, 1965), pp. 235, 242–43, 239, 244, 236; emphasis in original.

36. King, "Letter from a Birmingham Jail," pp. 88–91, 86; emphasis in original. King was jailed for parading without a permit.

37. Sidney Tarrow, *Power in Movement: Social Movements and Contentious Politics* (Cambridge: Cambridge University Press, 1998), p. 2; Jack Walker Jr., *Mobilizing Interest Groups in America: Patrons, Professions, and Social Movements* (Ann Arbor: University of Michigan Press, 1991), p. 9; John Berg, ed., *Teamsters and Turtles: U.S. Progressive Political Movements in the 21st Century* (Lanham, MD: Rowman & Littlefield, 2003), p. 7.

Bibliography

Ackerman, Bruce. *Social Justice in the Liberal State*. New Haven: Yale University Press, 1980.

Adams, John. "Letter to Samuel Adams." 1790. In *The Political Writings of John Adams*, edited by George W. Carey. Washington, DC: Regnery, 2000.

Addams, Jane. *Democracy and Social Ethics*. New York: Macmillan, 1916.

———. *The Spirit of Youth and the City Streets*. 1909. In *The Social Thought of Jane Addams*, edited by Christopher Lasch. Indianapolis, IN: Bobbs-Merrill, 1965.

———. "The Subjective Necessity for Social Settlements." 1892. In *Jane Addams on Education*, edited by Ellen Condliffe Lagemann. New York: Teachers College Press, 1985.

"Adding It Up: The Price–Income Squeeze in Higher Education." *Change* 29, no. 3 (May–June 1997).

Alterman, Eric. *What Liberal Media? The Truth about Bias and the News*. New York: Basic Books, 2003.

Alvarez, Rodolfo, et al. "The Responsive Communitarian Platform: Rights and Responsibilities." *Responsive Community* 2, no. 1 (Winter 1991/92): 4–20.

American Civic Forum. "Civic Declaration: Call for a New Citizenship." December 9, 1994. Available at http://www.cpn.org/crm/essays/declaration.html.

Andrews, Marcellus. "Liberty *and* Equality *and* Diversity? Thoughts on Liberalism and Racial Inequality after Capitalism's Latest Triumph." In *Race, Liberalism, and Economics*, edited by David Colander, Robert Prasch, and Falguni Sheth. Ann Arbor: University of Michigan Press, 2004.

Anthony, Susan B. "Speech in Defense of Equal Suffrage." 1873. In Levy, *Political Thought in America*.

———. "Suffrage and the Working Woman." 1871. In *American Political Thinking: Readings from the Origins to the 21st Century*, compiled by Robert Isaak. Fort Worth: Harcourt Brace College Publishers, 1994.

Anzaldúa, Gloria. *Borderlands, La Frontera: The New Mestiza*. San Francisco: Aunt Lute Books, 1987.

———. "En Rapport/In Opposition: Cobrando Cuentas a Las Nuestras." In Anzaldúa, *Making Face, Making Soul*.

———. "Haciendo Caras, Una Entrada." In Anzaldúa, *Making Face, Making Soul*.

———. "La Conciencia de la Mestiza/Towards a New Consciousness." In Anzaldúa, *Making Face, Making Soul*.

———. "La Prieta." In Moraga and Anzaldúa, *This Bridge Called My Back*.

———, ed. *Making Face, Making Soul/Haciendo Caras: Creative and Critical Perspectives by Feminists of Color*. San Francisco: Aunt Lute Books, 1990.

Arendt, Hannah. *Between Past and Future*. New York: Viking Press, 1968.

———. *On Revolution*. New York: Viking Press, 1965.

———. *On Violence*. New York: Harcourt, Brace, & World, 1969.

Aristotle. *The Politics of Aristotle*. 335–322 B.C. Edited and translated by Ernest Barker. Oxford: Oxford University Press, 1946.

Arrow, Kenneth. "Distributive Justice and Desirable Ends of Economic Activity." In *Issues in Contemporary Microeconomics and Welfare*, edited by G. R. Feiwel. New York: Macmillan, 1985.

Augustine of Hippo. *City of God*. 426. Garden City, NY: Image Books, 1958.

Babbie, Earl. *What Is Society? Reflections on Freedom, Order, and Change*. Thousand Oaks, CA: Pine Forge Press, 1994.

Bachrach, Peter, and Morton Baratz. "Two Faces of Power." *American Political Science Review* 56 (1962): pp. 947–52.

Baier, Annette. "Trust and Antitrust." *Ethics* 96, no. 2 (January 1986): pp. 231–60.

Bellamy, Edward. *Looking Backward.* 1888. Reprint, New York: New American Library, 1960.

Benn, S. I., and W. L. Weinstein. "Being Free to Act and Being a Free Man." *Mind* 80 (1971): pp. 194–211.

Bentham, Jeremy. *Jeremy Bentham's Economic Writings.* Edited by W. Stark. New York: Burt Franklin, 1952–54.

———. *The Theory of Legislation.* 1802. Edited by C. K. Ogden. London: K. Paul, Trench, Trubner & Co., 1931.

Benton-Banai, Edward. *The Mishomis Book: The Voice of the Ojibway.* St. Paul, MN: Red School House, 1988.

Berg, John, ed. *Teamsters and Turtles: U.S. Progressive Political Movements in the 21st Century.* Lanham, MD: Rowman & Littlefield, 2003.

Berlin, Isaiah. *Two Concepts of Liberty.* Oxford: Clarendon Press, 1958.

Berti, Lapo. "Society and the Market: Remote and Less Remote Sources of a Present Issue." In Nudler and Lutz, *Economics, Culture and Society.*

Black Elk. *The Sacred Pipe.* Edited by J. E. Brown. New York: Penguin Press, 1971.

Blum, William. *Rogue State: A Guide to the World's Only Superpower.* Monroe, ME: Common Courage Press, 2000.

Boaz, David. *Libertarianism: A Primer.* New York: Free Press, 1997.

———, ed. *The Libertarian Reader: Classic and Contemporary Readings from Lao-Tzu to Milton Friedman.* New York: Free Press, 1997.

Boggs, Carl. *The End of Politics: Corporate Power and the Decline of the Public Sphere.* New York: Guilford Press, 2000.

Bowles, Samuel, and Herbert Gintis. "The Invisible Fist: Have Capitalism and Democracy Reached a Parting of the Ways?" *American Economic Review* 68, no. 2 (May 1978): pp. 358–63.

Boydston, Jo Ann, ed. *John Dewey: The Later Works, 1925–1953.* 17 vols. Carbondale: Southern Illinois University Press, 1981–90.

———. *John Dewey: The Middle Works, 1899–1924.* 15 vols. Carbondale: Southern Illinois University Press, 1976–83.

Boyte, Harry. "Beyond Deliberation: Citizenship as Public Work." Paper delivered at the Political Economy of the Good Society (PEGS) Conference, February 11–12, 1995. Available at http://www.cpn.org/crm/contemporary/beyond.html.

———. *CommonWealth: A Return to Citizen Politics*. New York: Free Press, 1989.

———. "The Pragmatic Ends of Popular Politics." In Calhoun, *Habermas and the Public Sphere*, pp. 340–55.

Boyte, Harry, and Nancy Kari. *Building America: The Democratic Promise of Public Work*. Philadelphia: Temple University Press, 1996.

Brownlee, W. Elliot. *Federal Taxation in America: A Short History*. Cambridge: Cambridge University Press, 1996.

Bryan, Samuel. "Letter of Centinel, No. 1." 1787. In *The Anti-Federalist*, edited by Herbert Storing. Chicago: University of Chicago Press, 1981.

Calhoun, Craig, ed. *Habermas and the Public Sphere*. Cambridge, MA: MIT Press, 1992.

Calhoun, John. "Speech on the Reception of Abolition Petitions." 1837. In *Union and Liberty: The Political Philosophy of John C. Calhoun*, edited by Ross M. Lence. Indianapolis: Liberty Fund, 1992.

Camus, Albert. *The Plague*. Translated by Stuart Gilbert. New York: Modern Library, 1948.

Carmichael, Stokely, and Charles Hamilton. *Black Power: The Politics of Liberation in America*. New York: Vintage Books, 1967.

Carnegie, Andrew. "Wealth." 1889. In *Gospel of Wealth, and Other Timely Essays*. Edited by Edward Kirkland. Cambridge, MA: Belknap Press of Harvard University Press, 1965.

Chenowith, Karin. "HBCUs [Historically Black Colleges and Universities] Tackle the Knotty Problem of Retention." *Black Issues in Higher Education* 15, no. 26 (February 18, 1999).

Chomsky, Noam. *Year 501: The Conquest Continues*. Boston: South End Press, 1993.

Cohen, G. A. *If You're an Egalitarian, How Come You're So Rich?* Cambridge: Harvard University Press, 2000.

Collins, Chuck. "Aid to Dependent Corporations." In *Current Economic Issues*, edited by Marc Breslow, Abby Scher, and the Dollars and Sense Collective, 4th ed. Cambridge, MA: Economic Affairs Bureau, 1999.

Collins, Chuck, and John Miller. "Tax Reform Follies." In *Current Economic Issues*, edited by Marc Breslow, John Miller, Jim Phillips, and the Dollars and Sense Collective. 5th ed. Somerville, MA: Economic Affairs Bureau, 2000.

Collins, Chuck, and Felice Yeskel. *Economic Apartheid in America: A Primer on Economic Inequality and Insecurity.* New York: New Press, 2000.

Connolly, William. *The Terms of Political Discourse.* 2nd ed. Princeton: Princeton University Press, 1983.

Constant, Benjamin. "The Liberty of the Ancients Compared with That of the Moderns." 1816. In Boaz, *Libertarian Reader.*

Cox, Craig. *Storefront Revolution: Food Co-ops and the Counterculture.* New Brunswick, NJ: Rutgers University Press, 1994.

Current, Richard, T. Harry Williams, and Frank Freidel. *American History: A Survey.* 3rd ed. New York: Knopf, 1971.

Daes, Erica-Irene A. *Freedom of the Individual under Law.* New York: United Nations, 1990.

Dahl, Robert. "The Concept of Power." 1957. In *Political Power: A Reader in Theory and Research*, edited by Roderick Bell, David M. Edwards, and R. Harrison Wagner. New York: Free Press, 1969.

———. *How Democratic Is the American Constitution?* 2nd ed. New Haven: Yale University Press, 2003.

———. *A Preface to Economic Democracy.* Berkeley: University of California Press, 1985.

Davis, Angela. "Political Prisoners, Prisons, and Black Liberation." 1971. In *The Angela Y. Davis Reader*, edited by Joy James. Oxford: Blackwell, 1998.

———. "Race and Criminalization: Black Americans and the Punishment Industry." 1997. In *The Angela Y. Davis Reader*, edited by Joy James. Oxford: Blackwell, 1998.

———. *Women, Culture, and Politics.* New York: Vintage Books, 1990.

Deloria, Vine. *The Metaphysics of Modern Existence.* San Francisco: Harper & Row, 1979.

Dervarics, Charles, and Ronald Roach. "Fortifying the Federal Presence in Retention." *Black Issues in Higher Education* 17, no. 3 (March 30, 2000).

Dewey, John. "The Crucial Role of Intelligence." 1935. In Boydston, *John Dewey: The Later Works*, vol. 11.

———. *Democracy and Education*. 1916. In Boydston, *John Dewey: The Middle Works*, vol. 9.

———. "Democracy and Education in the World of Today." 1938. In Boydston, *John Dewey: The Later Works*, vol. 13.

———. *Ethics*. 1908. In Boydston, *John Dewey: The Middle Works*, vol. 5.

———. *Freedom and Culture*. 1939. In Boydston, *John Dewey: The Later Works*, vol. 13.

———. *Individualism, Old and New*. 1929–30. In Boydston, *John Dewey: The Later Works*, vol. 5.

———. *Liberalism and Social Action*. 1935. In Boydston, *John Dewey: The Later Works*, vol. 11.

———. "Liberty and Social Control." 1935. In Boydston, *John Dewey: The Later Works*, vol. 11.

———. *The Public and Its Problems*. 1927. In Boydston, *John Dewey: The Later Works*, vol. 2.

———. *Reconstruction in Philosophy*. 1920. In Boydston, *John Dewey: The Middle Works*, vol. 12.

———. "The Social Significance of Academic Freedom." 1936. In Boydston, *John Dewey: The Later Works*, vol. 11.

Digeser, Peter. "The Fourth Face of Power." *Journal of Politics* 54, no. 4 (November 1992): pp. 977–1007.

Disch, Lisa. "'Please Sit Down, but Don't Make Yourself at Home': Arendtian 'Visiting' and the Prefigurative Politics of Consciousness-Raising." In *Hannah Arendt and the Meaning of Politics*, edited by Craig Calhoun and John McGowan. Minneapolis: University of Minnesota Press, 1997.

Douglass, Frederick. *Narrative of the Life of Frederick Douglass*. 1845. In *Early African-American Classics*, edited by Anthony Appiah. New York: Bantam Books, 1990.

Du Bois, W. E .B. *The Souls of Black Folk.* 1903. Reprint, New York: Vintage Books, 1990.

Etzioni, Amitai. *The Spirit of Community: Rights, Responsibilities, and the Communitarian Agenda.* New York: Crown Publishers, 1993.

Fallows, James. "The Business Motive." *American Prospect* (July 2004).

Fitzhugh, George. *Cannibals All! or, Slaves without Masters.* 1857. Edited by C. Vann Woodward. Cambridge, MA: Belknap Press of Harvard University Press, 1960.

Foster, Phillips. *The World Food Problem: Tackling the Causes of Undernutrition in the Third World.* Boulder, CO: Lynne Rienner, 1992.

Foucault, Michel. *The History of Sexuality.* 3 vols. New York: Vintage Books, 1978–1990.

Fowler, Robert Booth, and Jeffrey Orenstein. *An Introduction to Political Theory.* New York: HarperCollins, 1993.

Freeman, Jo. *The Politics of Women's Liberation.* New York: David McKay, 1975.

Freire, Paolo. *Pedagogy of the Oppressed.* 1970. Rev. ed. Translated by Myra Bergman Ramos. New York: Continuum, 1990.

Friedan, Betty. *The Feminine Mystique.* New York: W. W. Norton, 1963.

Friedman, Milton. *Capitalism and Freedom.* Chicago: University of Chicago Press, 1962.

Galbraith, John Kenneth. *The Affluent Society.* Boston: Houghton-Mifflin, 1958.

Gaventa, John. *Power and Powerlessness: Quiescence and Rebellion in an Appalachian Valley.* Urbana: University of Illinois Press, 1980.

Gilder, George. *Wealth and Poverty.* New York: Basic Books, 1981.

Gilligan, Carol. *In a Different Voice: Psychological Theory and Women's Development.* Cambridge: Harvard University Press, 1982.

Gilman, Charlotte Perkins. *His Religion and Hers: A Study of the Faith of Our Fathers and the Work of Our Mothers.* 1923. Reprint, Walnut Creek, CA: Alta Mira Press, 2003.

——— . *Women and Economics: A Study of the Economic Relation between Men and Women as a Factor in Social Evolution.* 1898. Reprint, Mineola, NY: Dover Publications, 1998.

———. "The Yellow Wall-Paper." 1890. In *The Yellow Wall-Paper, and Selected Stories of Charlotte Perkins Gilman*, edited by Denise Knight, 39–53. Newark: University of Delaware Press, 1994.

Gould, Carol. "Feminism and Democratic Community Revisited." In *Democratic Community*, edited by John W. Chapman and Ian Shapiro. New York: New York University Press, 1993.

Gramsci, Antonio. *Selections from the Prison Notebooks.* 1929–35. Edited and translated by Quintin Hoare and Geoffrey Nowell Smith. New York: International Publishers, 1971.

Green, T. H. *The Political Theory of T. H. Green: Selected Writings.* Edited by John Rodman. New York: Appleton-Century-Crofts, 1964.

Greenberg, Edward. *Workplace Democracy: The Political Effects of Participation.* Ithaca, NY: Cornell University Press, 1986.

Greenberg, Edward, and Benjamin Page. *The Struggle for Democracy.* 3rd ed. New York: Longman, 1997.

Gregory, Jill, April Lewton, Mark Mattern, Stephanie Schmidt, and Diane Smith. "Body Politics with Feeling: The Power of the Clothesline Project." *New Political Science* 24, no. 3 (November 2002): pp. 434–48.

Grimké, Angelina. "Human Rights Not Founded on Sex." 1837. In Levy, *Political Thought in America.*

Grossman, Lawrence. "Lessons of the *Sixty Minutes* Cave-In." *Columbia Journalism Review* (January/February 1996).

Habermas, Jürgen. *The Structural Transformation of the Public Sphere: An Inquiry into a Category of Bourgeois Society.* 1962. Translated by Thomas Burger and Frederick Lawrence. Cambridge, MA: MIT Press, 1989.

———. *Theory of Communicative Action.* Boston: Beacon Press, 1984.

Hamill, Susan Pace. "An Argument for Tax Reform Based on Judeo-Christian Ethics." *Alabama Law Review* 54 (Fall 2002): 1–112.

Hamilton, Alexander, James Madison, and John Jay. *The Federalist Papers.* Toronto: Bantam Books, 1982.

Harrington, James. *The Commonwealth of Oceana.* 1656. In *The Political Works of James Harrington*, edited by J. G. A. Pocock. Cambridge: Cambridge University Press, 1977.

Hayek, F. A. *The Mirage of Social Justice*. Vol. 2 of *Law, Legislation, and Liberty*. Chicago: University of Chicago Press, 1976.

Heintz, James, and Nancy Folbre. *The Ultimate Field Guide to the U.S. Economy*. New York: New Press, 2000.

Held, David. *Democracy and the Global Order: From the Modern State to Cosmopolitan Governance*. Stanford: Stanford University Press, 1995.

———. *Models of Democracy*. Stanford: Stanford University Press, 1987.

Held, Virginia. "The Meshing of Care and Justice." *Hypatia* 10, no. 2 (Spring 1995).

Herman, Edward, and Noam Chomsky. *Manufacturing Consent: The Political Economy of the Mass Media*. New York: Pantheon, 1988.

Herrnstein, Richard J., and Charles Murray. *The Bell Curve*. New York: Free Press, 1994.

Hobbes, Thomas. *Leviathan*. 1651. New York: Penguin Books, 1985.

Hobhouse, L. T. *Liberalism*. New York: Henry Holt, 1911.

Hobson, J. A. *Economics and Ethics: A Study in Social Values*. Boston: D. C. Heath, 1929.

———. *The Social Problem*. London: Nisbet, 1901.

———. *Work and Wealth: A Human Valuation*. 1914. Reprint, New York: Augustus M. Kelley, 1968.

Hofstadter, Richard. *The American Political Tradition and the Men Who Made It*. New York: A. A. Knopf, 1948. Reprint, New York: Vintage Books, 1989.

hooks, bell. *Feminism Is for Everybody*. Cambridge, MA: South End Press, 2000.

Hoover, Herbert. "Campaign Speech, New York City, October 31, 1932." In Herbert Hoover, *Campaign Speeches of 1932*. Garden City, NY: Doubleday, 1933.

Hudson, William. *American Democracy in Peril: Seven Challenges to America's Future*. 3rd ed. New York: Chatham House, 2001.

Huffington, Arianna. "Blog Heaven." *American Prospect* (July 2004).

Huq, A. M. "Welfare Criteria in Gandhian Economics." In *Essays in Gandhian Economics*, edited by Romesh Diwan and Mark Lutz. New Delhi: Gandhi Peace Foundation, 1985.

Jacobs, Harriet. *Incidents in the Life of a Slave Girl: Written by Herself.* 1845. In *Early African-American Classics,* edited by Anthony Appiah. New York: Bantam Books, 1990.

Jefferson, Thomas. "Letter to James Madison [1785]." In *The Life and Selected Writings of Thomas Jefferson,* edited by Adrienne Koch and William Peden. New York: Random House, 1944.

——— . "Letter to James Madison [October 28, 1785]." In *Basic Writings of Thomas Jefferson,* edited by Philip Foner. New York: Willey Book Company, 1944.

——— . "Letter to James Madison [1787]." In *The Life and Selected Writings of Thomas Jefferson,* edited by Adrienne Koch and William Peden. New York: Random House, 1944.

——— . "Letter to John Bannister, Jr. [October 15, 1785]." In *Basic Writings of Thomas Jefferson,* edited by Philip Foner. New York: Willey Book Company, 1944.

——— . "Letter to Samuel Kercheval." 1816. In *Basic Writings of Thomas Jefferson,* edited by Philip Foner. New York: Willey Book Company, 1944. Abridged version also available in *The Life and Selected Writings of Thomas Jefferson,* edited by Adrienne Koch and William Peden. New York: Random House, 1944.

John Paul II. *Centesimus Annus* (On the 100th anniversary [of Pope Leo XIII's *Rerum Novarum*]). *Origins* 21, no. 1 (May 16, 1991).

——— . *Laborem Exercens* (On human work). *Origins* 11, no. 15 (September 24, 1981).

——— . *Sollicitudo Rei Socialis* (Encyclical on social concerns). *Origins* 17, no. 38 (March 3, 1988).

Kane, Hal. "Growing Fish in Fields." *World Watch* (September/October 1993): 20–27.

Kant, Immanuel. *The Moral Law.* 1785. Trans. and ed. H. J. Paton. 3rd ed. London: Hutchinson, 1956.

Kelly, Marjorie. *The Divine Right of Capital: Dethroning the Corporate Aristocracy.* San Francisco: Berrett-Koehler, 2001.

King, Martin Luther, Jr. "Letter from a Birmingham Jail." In *I Have a Dream: Writings and Speeches That Changed the World,* edited by James Washington. New York: HarperCollins, 1986.

Kristol, Irving. *Two Cheers for Capitalism.* New York: Basic Books, 1978.

Lairson, Thomas, and David Skidmore. *International Political Economy: The Struggle for Power and Wealth.* Fort Worth: Holt, Rinehart and Winston, 1993.

Lenin, V. I. *Imperialism: The Highest Stage of Capitalism.* 1916. Rev. trans., New York: International Publishers, 1939.

Levy, Michael, ed. *Political Thought in America: An Anthology.* 2nd ed. Chicago: Dorsey Press, 1988.

Lincoln, Abraham. "Speech in Springfield, Illinois, June 26, 1857." In *Abraham Lincoln: Complete Works, Comprising His Speeches, Letters, State Papers, and Miscellaneous Writings,* edited by John Nicolay and John Hay. New York: Century Co., 1902.

Lister, Ruth. *Citizenship: Feminist Perspectives.* 2nd ed. Washington Square, NY: New York University Press, 2003.

Locke, John. *The Second Treatise on Civil Government.* 1690. Buffalo, NY: Prometheus Books, 1986.

Long, Dianne. "Women and Development." In Weatherby et al., *The Other World,* pp. 91–107.

Loury, Glenn C. "The Role of Normative Values in Rescuing the Urban Ghetto." In *Building a Community of Citizens: Civil Society in the 21st Century,* edited by Don E. Eberly. Lanham, MD: Commonwealth Foundation, 1994.

Lukes, Steven. *Individualism.* Oxford: Basil Blackwell, 1973.

———. *Power: A Radical View.* New York: Macmillan, 1974.

Luther, Martin. *Martin Luther: Selections from His Writings.* Edited by John Dillenberger. Garden City, NY: Anchor Books, 1961.

Lutz, Mark. "The Reforming of Economics: Retrospect and Prospect." In Nudler and Lutz, *Economics, Culture and Society,* pp. 85–142.

MacCallum, Gerald. "Negative and Positive Freedom." *Philosophical Review* 76 (1967): pp. 312–34.

Machiavelli, Niccolò. *"The Prince" and "The Discourses."* 1513–17. New York: Random House, 1950.

Macpherson, C. B. *The Life and Times of Liberal Democracy.* Oxford: Oxford University Press, 1977.

Madison, James. "Federalist No. 10." 1787. In Hamilton, Madison, and Jay, *The Federalist Papers.*

——— . "Federalist No. 39." 1788. In Hamilton, Madison, and Jay, *The Federalist Papers.*

——— . "Federalist No. 51." 1788. In Hamilton, Madison, and Jay, *The Federalist Papers.*

——— . "Federalist No. 57." 1788. In Hamilton, Madison, and Jay, *The Federalist Papers.*

Mansbridge, Jane. *Beyond Adversary Democracy.* Chicago: University of Chicago Press, 1980.

——— . "Feminism and Democratic Community." In *Democratic Community,* edited by John Chapman and Ian Shapiro. New York: New York University Press, 1993.

Margalit, Avishai. *The Decent Society.* Cambridge: Harvard University Press, 1996.

Marx, Karl. *Capital,* vol. 1. 1867. Moscow: Progress Publishers, 1954.

——— . *The Communist Manifesto.* 1848. Edited by Frederic L. Bender. New York: W. W. Norton, 1988.

——— . *A Critique of the Gotha Programme.* 1875. In *Karl Marx and Frederick Engels: Selected Works,* vol. 3. Moscow: Progress Publishers, 1970.

——— . *Economic and Philosophical Manuscripts of 1844.* 1844. New York: International Publishers, 1964. Also in *Karl Marx: Early Writings.* Translated and edited by T. B. Bottomore. New York: McGraw-Hill, 1963.

McChesney, Robert. "Waging the Media Battle." *American Prospect* (July 2004).

McGinn, Anne Platt. "Blue Revolution: The Promises and Pitfalls of Fish Farming." *World Watch* (March/April 1998): 10–19.

McLean, Scott, David Schultz, and Manfred Steger, eds. *Social Capital: Critical Perspectives on Community and "Bowling Alone."* New York: New York University Press, 2002.

Michael, Marie. "The 'Other America' Revisited: The War on Poverty—Gains and Losses." In *Current Economic Issues,* edited by Phineas Baxandall, Tami Friedman, Thad Williamson, and the Dollars and Sense Collective. 6th ed. Cambridge, MA: Economic Affairs Bureau, 2001.

Michals, Debra. "From 'Consciousness Expansion' to 'Consciousness Raising':
Feminism and the Countercultural Politics of the Self." In *Imagine Nation: The
American Counterculture of the 1960s and '70s*, edited by Peter Braunstein and
Michael William Doyle. New York: Routledge, 2002.

Mill, James. "On the Ballot," *Westminster Review* (July 1830).

Mill, John Stuart. *On Liberty*. 1859. In *Mill: A Norton Critical Edition*. Edited by Alan
Ryan. New York: W. W. Norton, 1997.

———. *Principles of Political Economy with Some of Their Applications to Social
Philosophy*. 1884. Fairfield, NJ: Augustus M. Kelley, 1987.

———. *Representative Government*. 1860. New York: Liberal Arts Press, 1958.

Mishel, Lawrence, Jared Bernstein, and Sylvia Allegretto. *The State of Working
America, 2004–2005*. Ithaca, NY: Cornell University Press, 2005.

Mishel, Lawrence, Jared Bernstein, and Heather Boushey. *The State of Working
America, 2002–2003*. Ithaca, NY: Cornell University Press, 2003.

Mishel, Lawrence, Jared Bernstein, and John Schmitt. *The State of Working America,
2000–2001*. Ithaca, NY: Cornell University Press, 2001.

Mitchell, Lawrence. *Stacked Deck*. Philadelphia: Temple University Press, 1998.

Moraga, Cherríe. "La Güerra." In Moraga and Anzaldúa, *This Bridge Called My Back*.

Moraga, Cherríe, and Gloria Anzaldúa. *This Bridge Called My Back: Writings by
Radical Women of Color*. New York: Kitchen Table/Women of Color Press, 1981.

Mouffe, Chantal. "Feminism, Citizenship and Radical Democratic Politics." In
Feminists Theorize the Political, edited by Judith Butler and Joan Scott, pp. 369–84.
New York: Routledge, 1992.

National Environmental Education Advancement Project. "Crafting Your Messages
with Soundbites." *EE and the Media Gazette*, June 29, 2004,
http://www.uwsp.edu/cnr/neeap/media/crafting.htm.

Neihardt, John, ed., *Black Elk Speaks*. Lincoln: University of Nebraska Press, 1961.

Nozick, Robert. *Anarchy, State, and Utopia*. New York: Basic Books, 1974.

Nudler, Oscar, and Mark Lutz, eds. *Economics, Culture and Society—Alternative
Approaches: Dissenting Views from Economic Orthodoxy*. New York: Apex Press,
1996.

Orwell, George. *1984*. New York: Penguin Books, 1949.

Pateman, Carol. *Participation and Democratic Theory*. Cambridge: Cambridge University Press, 1970.

Paterson, Thomas, and J. Garry Clifford. *America Ascendant: U.S. Foreign Relations since 1939*. Lexington, MA: D. C. Heath, 1995.

Peet, Richard. *Theories of Development*. New York: Guilford Press, 1999.

Phillips, Kevin. *The Politics of Rich and Poor*. New York: HarperCollins, 1990.

Plato. *The Republic*. 375 B.C. New York: Penguin Books, 1987.

Pohlmann, Marcus. *Black Politics in Conservative America*. 2nd ed. New York: Addison Wesley Longman, 1999.

Polanyi, Karl. *Dahomey and the Slave Trade*. Seattle: University of Washington Press, 1966.

——— . *The Great Transformation*. New York: Farrar & Rinehart, 1944.

——— . *The Livelihood of Man*. New York: Academic Press, 1977.

Putnam, Robert. *Bowling Alone: The Collapse and Revival of American Community*. New York: Simon & Schuster, 2000.

——— . "Democracy in America at the End of the Twentieth Century." In *Participation and Democracy: East and West*, edited by Dietrich Rueschemeyer, Marilyn Rueschemeyer, and Björn Wittrock, pp. 233–65. Armonk, NY: M. E. Sharpe, 1998.

Pye, Lucian W. "The State and the Individual: An Overview Interpretation." In *The Individual and the State in China*, edited by Brian Hook, pp. 16–42. Oxford: Clarendon Press, 1996.

Rand, Ayn. *The Fountainhead*. Indianapolis: Bobbs-Merrill, 1943. Reprint, New York: Penguin Books, 1952.

Rawls, John. "Justice as Fairness." *Philosophical Review* 67 (1958): 164–94.

——— . *Political Liberalism*. New York: Columbia University Press, 1993.

——— . *A Theory of Justice*. Cambridge, MA: Belknap Press of Harvard University Press, 1971.

——— . "A Well-Ordered Society." In *In Defense of Human Dignity*, edited by Robert Kraynak and Glenn Tinder. Notre Dame, IN: University of Notre Dame Press, 2003.

Redelmeier, Donald, and Robert Tibshirani. "Association between Cellular-Telephone Calls and Motor Vehicle Collisions." *New England Journal of Medicine* (1997): 453–58.

Ritter, Alan, and Julia Conaway Bondanella, eds. *Rousseau's Political Writings.* Translated by Julia Conaway Bondanella. New York: W. W. Norton, 1988.

Rorty, Richard. *The Consequences of Pragmatism.* Minneapolis: University of Minnesota Press, 1982.

——— . *Philosophy and the Mirror of Nature.* Princeton: Princeton University Press, 1979.

Rousseau, Jean-Jacques. *Discourse on Inequality.* 1755. In Ritter and Bondanella, *Rousseau's Political Writings.*

——— . *Discourse on Political Economy.* 1755. In Ritter and Bondanella, *Rousseau's Political Writings.*

——— . *Émile.* 1762. Translated by Barbara Foxley. London: Everyman, 1911.

——— . *Julie, ou la Nouvelle Héloïse.* 1761. Paris: Hachette, 1925.

——— . *The Social Contract.* 1762. In Ritter and Bondanella, *Rousseau's Political Writings.*

Rowden, Rick. "A World of Debt." *American Prospect* 12, no. 12 (July 2, 2001): 29–32.

Ruskin, John. "Letters on Political Economy." In *Arrows of the Chace*, vol. 2. Boston: Colonial Press, 1880.

——— . *Unto This Last.* 1864. New York: John Wiley & Son, 1988.

Sachs, Wolfgang. *The Development Dictionary.* London: Zed Books, 1992.

——— . *Planet Dialectics: Explorations in Environment and Development.* New York: Zed Books, 1999.

Said, Edward. *Orientalism.* New York: Vintage Books, 1978.

Schor, Juliet B. *The Overspent American.* New York: Basic Books, 1998.

————. *The Overworked American.* New York: Basic Books, 1991.

Schumacher, E. F. *Small Is Beautiful.* New York: Harper & Row, 1973.

Schumpeter, Joseph. *Capitalism, Socialism, and Democracy.* 1942. Reprint, New York: Harper & Row, 1950.

Seline, Anita M. "The Shift away from Need-Blind: Colleges Have Started Their Version of 'Wallet Biopsies.'" *Black Issues in Higher Education* 13, no. 13 (August 22, 1996), p. 38.

Sen, Amartya. *On Economic Inequality.* Oxford: Clarendon Press, 1997.

Shklar, Judith. "Jean-Jacques Rousseau and Equality." In Ritter and Bondanella, *Rousseau's Political Writings.*

Shreve, Anita. *Women Together, Women Alone.* New York: Viking Press, 1989.

Sismondi, J.-C.-L. Simonde de. *New Principles of Political Economy: Of Wealth in Its Relation to Population.* 1826. 2nd ed. New Brunswick, NJ: Transaction Publishers, 1994.

Slater, Courtenay M., and Cornelia J. Strawser, eds. *Business Statistics of the United States.* 5th ed. Lanham, MD: Bernan Press, 1999.

Smith, Adam. *The Theory of Moral Sentiments.* 1759. Edited by D. D. Raphael and A. L. Macfie. Oxford: Clarendon Press, 1976.

————. *The Wealth of Nations.* 1776. New York: Random House, 1937.

Smith, Michael. *Portraits of Empire: Unmasking Imperial Illusions from the "American Century" to the "War on Terror."* Monroe, ME: Common Courage Press, 2003.

Solomon, Robert, and Mark Murphy, eds. *What Is Justice?* 2nd ed. Oxford: Oxford University Press, 2000.

Sparks, Holloway. "Dissident Citizenship: Democratic Theory, Political Courage, and Activist Women." In *Theorizing Feminism: Parallel Trends in the Humanities and Social Sciences,* edited by Anne C. Herrmann and Abigail J. Stewart, 2nd ed. Boulder, CO: Westview Press, 2001.

Squires, Gregory. *Capital and Communities in Black and White: The Intersections of Race, Class, and Uneven Development.* New York: State University of New York Press, 1994.

Stanton, Elizabeth Cady. "Address Delivered at Seneca Falls." 1848. In *The Elizabeth Cady Stanton–Susan B. Anthony Reader: Correspondence, Writings, Speeches*, edited by Ellen Carol DuBois. Boston: Northeastern University Press, 1981.

Steinem, Gloria. *Moving beyond Words*. New York: Simon & Schuster, 1994.

Stoesz, David, Charles Guzzetta, and Mark Lusk. *International Development*. Needham Heights, MA: Allyn & Bacon, 1999.

Tarrow, Sidney. *Power in Movement: Social Movements and Contentious Politics*. Cambridge: Cambridge University Press, 1998.

Tawney, Richard. *The Acquisitive Society*. New York: Harcourt, Brace, 1920.

Thoreau, Henry David. "Civil Disobedience." 1849. In *"Walden" and "Civil Disobedience."* New York: Airmont, 1965.

Thucydides. *History of the Peloponnesian War*. 411 B.C. New York: Random House, 1982.

Tocqueville, Alexis de. *Democracy in America*. 1840. New York: Random House, 1981.

Tronto, Joan. *Moral Boundaries*. New York: Routledge, 1993.

U.S. Conference of Catholic Bishops. "Statement on Capital Punishment." November 1980. Available at http://www.usccb.org/sdwp/national/criminal/death/uscc80.htm.

———. "Statement on Political Responsibility for 1996." *Origins* 25, no. 22 (November 16, 1995).

Veblen, Thorstein. *The Theory of the Leisure Class*. New York: Modern Library, 1934.

Walker, Jack, Jr. *Mobilizing Interest Groups in America: Patrons, Professions, and Social Movements*. Ann Arbor: University of Michigan Press, 1991.

Walzer, Michael. *The Company of Critics: Social Criticism and Political Commitment in the Twentieth Century*. New York: Basic Books, 1988.

Ward, Barbara. *The Home of Man*. New York: W. W. Norton, 1976.

Wartenberg, Thomas. *The Forms of Power: From Domination to Transformation*. Philadelphia: Temple University Press, 1990.

Weatherby, Joseph, Emmit Evans Jr., Reginald Gooden, Dianne Long, and Ira Reed. *The Other World: Issues and Politics of the Developing World.* 5th ed. New York: Addison Wesley Longman, 2003.

Winthrop, John. "A Little Speech on Liberty." 1645. In Levy, *Political Thought in America.*

——— . "A Modell of Christian Charity." 1630. In Levy, *Political Thought in America.*

Wittkopf, Eugene, Charles Kegley, and James Scott. *American Foreign Policy.* 6th ed. Belmont, CA: Thomson-Wadsworth, 2003.

Young, Iris Marion. "The Ideal of Community and the Politics of Difference." In *Feminism/Postmodernism*, edited by Linda Nicholson. London: Routledge, 1990.

Zinn, Howard. *A People's History of the United States, 1492–Present.* New York: HarperCollins, 1980.

Index

About the Author

❜

Mark Mattern is associate professor of political science at Baldwin Wallace College in Berea, Ohio. He is the author of *Acting in Concert: Music, Community, and Political Action* and articles on art, public life, and political action. He received his Master of Public Affairs (1990) and Ph.D. in political science (1994) at the University of Minnesota. Mattern's current teaching and research interests include political theory, political economy, and the politics of art. He invites readers to email him at mmattern@bw.edu with suggestions for improving this book.

Breinigsville, PA USA
12 October 2010
247228BV00004B/1/P